eACCESS TO JUSTICE

eACCESS TO JUSTICE

EDITED BY

Karim Benyekhlef, Jane Bailey, Jacquelyn Burkell,
and Fabien Gélinas

University of Ottawa Press
2016

uOttawa

The University of Ottawa Press gratefully acknowledges the support extended to its publishing list by Canadian Heritage through the Canada Book Fund, by the Canada Council for the Arts, by the Federation for the Humanities and Social Sciences through the Awards to Scholarly Publications Program and by the University of Ottawa.
Copy editing: Interscript
Proofreading: Robbie McCaw
Typesetting: Interscript
Cover design: Édiscript enr. and Elizabeth Schwaiger. With thanks to the Cyberjustice Laboratory at the University of Montreal for permission to use the logo.

Library and Archives Canada Cataloguing in Publication

eAccess to justice / edited by Karim Benyekhlef, Jane Bailey, Jacquelyn Burkell, and Fabien Gélinas.

(Law, technology and media)
Includes bibliographical references.
Issued in print and electronic formats.
ISBN 978-0-7766-2429-7 (paperback).--ISBN 978-0-7766-2430-3 (pdf).--
ISBN 978-0-7766-2431-0 (epub).--ISBN 978-0-7766-2432-7 (mobi)

1. Justice, Administration of--Automation. 2. Court administration--Automation. 3. Conduct of court proceedings--Technological innovations. I. Burkell, Jacquelyn, author, editor II. Gélinas, Fabien, 1966-, author, editor III. Benyekhlef, Karim, 1962-, editor IV. Bailey, Jane, 1965-, author, editor V. Series: Law, technology and media

K2100.E22 2016   347.00285   C2016-906247-3
                                            C2016-906248-1

Printed in Canada

Table of Contents

Acknowledgements

The publication of this book was made possible by the Social Sciences and Humanities Research Council of Canada's (SSHRC) support of *Re-thinking Processual Law: Towards Cyberjustice*, a 7-year research initiative (2011–2018) funded through the *Major Collaborative Research Initiatives* (MCRI) program. The MCRI program's objective was to support cutting-edge research with potential for intellectual breakthrough that addresses broad and critical issues of intellectual, social, economic, and cultural significance. Thanks to this important funding, the *Towards Cyberjustice* project has initiated numerous knowledge mobilization activities, including this book and the international, intersectoral, and interdisciplinary conference that preceded it. Aspects of the publication also benefited from the support of the Fonds de recherche du Québec Société et Culture through a cluster grant to the Regroupement stratégique Droit, changements et gouvernance and a team grant to the McGill Private Justice and the Rule of Law Research Group.

Introduction

Karim Benyekhlef

The significant expansion of digital technologies over recent years has rendered them ubiquitous. They have been integrated into numerous domains throughout society, and the justice sector is no exception. This incorporation of modern technologies into the justice system has led to the emergence of a new and innovative field referred to as cyberjustice. This term encompasses both the integration of information and communication technologies into judicial and extrajudicial dispute resolution processes and the digital networking of all stakeholders involved in judicial cases. Conceived in this manner, the primary aim of cyberjustice is to use modern technologies to aid in the administration of justice such as to allow for the conceptualization of a more efficient method of achieving justice for litigants, thus ultimately reducing the abounding access to justice issues with which the legal system is plagued.

In this light, we will begin by (1) presenting the *Towards Cyberjustice* project, which was created in the hopes of achieving this very purpose and upon which this book is based. We will then proceed by (2) outlining the main research perspectives that underlie the research conducted in association with this project. Finally, we will conclude by (3) offering insight on what lies ahead in terms of the development of cyberjustice.

Towards Cyberjustice: A Multidisciplinary Research Project

In an effort to advance toward achieving this goal, the Cyberjustice Laboratory, supported by a multidisciplinary group of 36 international researchers and funded by the Social Sciences and Humanities Research Council, launched a 7-year research project in 2011: *Towards Cyberjustice*.[1] The project's main hypothesis was that information and communication technologies could significantly contribute to improving traditional legal processes as well as entirely modifying the conventional structure of trials. In this light, the research conducted was aimed at identifying and developing concrete solutions that could optimize traditional legal processes and ultimately enhance the administration of justice as a whole, such that efficiency would be increased, costs and delays would be reduced, and mechanisms would be simplified.

While many attempts have been made toward achieving this goal throughout the legal world, as will be discussed in more detail below, the project's novelty and success lies in two unique factors. To begin with, it conducts socio-legal studies regarding both the impacts of technology on law and the identification of rituals and practices that hinder the networking of the justice system. Additionally, through techno-legal studies funded mainly by the *Canadian Foundation for Innovation*, it simultaneously develops open-source software solutions that are adapted to judicial and extrajudicial contexts and can be tailored to the varying needs of each individual justice system. This cross-fertilization of socio-legal and techno-legal studies not only allows for the development of technological tools tailored to the justice system, but also makes it possible to substantially re-examine the judicial process in a manner that is primarily designed to improve access to justice.

These various studies that emerged from the *Towards Cyberjustice* project were conducted by an elaborate team of international researchers from twenty universities worldwide, separated into three working groups, each of which was dedicated to examining a differing and particular aspect of the research in question. The first working group, whose research will be discussed in further detail in the first part of this collection, considered (a) the digitalization of justice and its interaction with the values inherent in the justice system. The second working group, whose aim was to identify (b) the limits of digitalization, will be examined in the second part of the collection through an in-depth analysis of both courtroom interactions and self-empowerment. Finally, the third working group was dedicated to (c) identifying new procedural models, which will be considered in detail in the third and final part of the collection.

Digitalization of Justice

The objective of the first working group was to identify the manner in which the digitalization of justice can increase the efficiency of the legal system and facilitate access to judicial processes. The main hypothesis and departure point was therefore that access to justice could be improved by implementing concrete technological tools such as electronic filing, electronic case-management systems as well as the management of a paperless system, and finally, technological courtroom management, which includes the use of videoconferencing for remote testimony.

In this vein, and as discussed in more depth in the first two chapters of the first part, penned by Renaud Beauchard and Giampiero Lupo, respectively, the various technologies used for cyberjustice purposes throughout several jurisdictions worldwide, as well as the manner in which they are used by all the stakeholders involved, were researched and reported. By making an inventory of the cyberjustice initiatives that had already been conducted by other actors in the legal world, it was possible for this working group to assess the impact that technology has had on both trials and interactions between parties. By placing a heavy focus on the conditions under which technology was introduced into these justice systems, this in turn made it possible to develop technological solutions that were perfectly tailored to the needs of the legal system. These solutions were further improved upon by consulting with all the stakeholders involved. By providing these individuals with an active role in the technological modernization of the justice system, it was possible to ensure that the technologies developed for their benefit truly target their needs, such that they will ultimately use them. Essentially, therein lies the key: technologies allowing for the digitalization of justice already exist in abundance, but it is their adoption by the relevant stakeholders that has remained elusive.

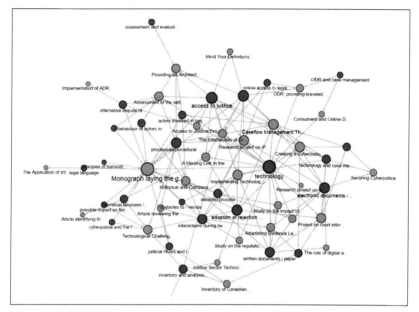

Figure 1: Network map connecting keywords to cyberjustice projects.

Source: http://mapping.cyberjustice.ca.

The ultimate adoption of said technologies by the stakeholders involved, however, is not the only concept upon which the digitalization of justice may be conceived. As Jane Bailey so eloquently puts it in her introduction to the first part of this collection, "technological innovation in the justice sector should not simply be technology for technology's sake. Instead, it is essential to understand how a technology may facilitate or affect the fundamental values underlying the justice system, values that are essential to access to justice as well." To this effect, two such values, namely the right to information about court proceedings and the right to privacy, are therefore examined by Graham Reynolds and Nicolas Vermeys, respectively, in the final two chapters of the first part. As such, the first component of this collection and the research conducted by the first working group provide a very well-rounded view, not only of all that is involved in the digitalization of court proceedings, but also as regards the consideration that must be paid to crucial fundamental rights when attempting to make such a significant transition.

Limits of Digitalization

The second working group focused on identifying the constraints and limits that may prevent the digitalization of justice, such as the traditions, practices and rituals of the judiciary. Beginning as early as the late 1990s, numerous large-scale digitalization of justice initiatives have been launched. Unfortunately, however, these attempts have often failed[2] as a result of their top-down approach, involving a complete overhaul of the system through the implementation of modern technologies characterized by high initial investments in technology and excessive ambition.

What has led to the lack of success of such initiatives is the level of complexity of the newly developed systems,[3] which the main stakeholders are often not willing to learn in a timely fashion and demonstrate an outright resistance to adopt.[4] Research has illustrated that this opposition tends to stem from psychological, social, cultural and political factors, representing the main limits to the modernization and computerization of justice. The second working group therefore recognized that it was only by studying and understanding the impact of these various elements on the stakeholders, through their interpersonal interactions within the hearing room, that it would be possible to surpass the barriers with which the digitalization of justice has been confronted and ultimately offer technological solutions regarding the legal system that would truly respond to the needs of all the stakeholders involved.

In this vein, the second working group adopted an innovative approach through which they worked in close collaboration with both state actors and professional organizations, such as ministries of justice and bar associations, in order to re-think the judicial process in a manner that would welcome the integration of information technologies while ultimately improving access to justice. By involving the different stakeholders and partners from the very beginning of the process, and by requesting their active participation at every step of technological implementation, it was possible to ensure that their needs were both adequately assessed and met in the most optimal of manners.

The adoption of this approach not only anchored the development process in the needs of all the stakeholders in question, but their involvement at every step of the way has also served to empower litigants such that they will exhibit less resistance to technological changes in the judicial process, and will ultimately welcome legal reforms. This perspective is examined at length in the second part of the collection, entitled Courtroom Interactions and Self-Empowerment, by "prob[ing] the reality and consequences of implementing technologies in the court system, discussing in the process a wide range of court technologies including online court information systems, e-filing, videoconferences, and technologies for evidence presentation and review." In her introduction to this second part, however, Jacquelyn Burkell outlines a single and important message that is echoed by each of the chapters it contains, namely, that care must be taken when attempting to improve both the legal system and access to justice as "[w]e cannot assume that there is a necessary and necessarily positive relationship between court technologies and access to justice: instead, we should proceed with cautious rather than unbridled optimism to ensure that technologies are implemented in such a way as to achieve the positive outcomes that we envision."

This often entails constant involvement from the stakeholders in the legal system, as discussed above, and demonstrated by Justice Horowitz in his chapter, which recounts his own experiences with the digitalization of the justice system. In a similar vein, Sherry MacLennan's chapter addresses the implementation of British Columbia's online legal information system and the manner in which collaboration with stakeholders led to an empowerment of the litigants in question. The following chapter, by Amy Salyzyn, takes a different and refreshing perspective on empowerment. Essentially, rather than discussing the manner in which technology should be incorporated into the judiciary in such a manner so as to empower the stakeholders involved, she outlines how the inevitability of the adoption of courtroom technologies imposes an ethical responsibility on the actors in the justice system to comprehend the technologies, as well as their impact, so that they may better represent their clients. The final chapter of this part, presented by David Tait and Meredith Rossner, further elaborates on the need to understand the manner in which technology impacts the administration of justice by presenting the results of a study regarding the manner in which the use of tablets for evidence presentation affects jury deliberation and, ultimately, the fairness of trials.

As is evidenced by the diversity of subjects examined in the second part of this collection, the second working group has identified and studied numerous limitations to the digitalization of justice and attempted to overcome them through constant collaboration with all the stakeholders involved, including those individuals that the legal system is meant to benefit. In so doing, they have adapted their scientific work based on feedback from partners such that they can offer a more targeted support and ultimately induce change in the legal system, in the hope of simultaneously improving access to justice.

New Procedural Models

The third working group's objective was to rethink judicial and extrajudicial practices by developing new procedural models based on the integration of information and communications technologies, all the while ensuring that this profound change will properly respect fundamental rights and freedoms. This working group's journey toward effecting change through technology in the legal system is illustrated in the third part of the collection, which provides a more exhaustive examination of "the adoption of new technology [in such a manner] that would lead us to achieving cost- and time-effective justice delivery, the course that would lead us to the Holy Grail of access to justice." From this perspective, the chapters of both Xandra Kramer and Katia Balbino de Carvalho Ferreira discuss the ability to improve access to justice through the implementation of technology by examining the specific experiences of the European and Brazilian judicial systems, respectively.

However, in order to trigger the technological change that would lead to better access to justice, the third working group had to first observe "the practices, norms, and assumptions of justice delivery [which] proved more resistant to change than most had anticipated." This aspect is therefore analyzed in more depth in the contributions of Pierre Noreau and Daniel Weinstock, with Noreau "[inviting] us to reflect upon the broader and deeper reasons for resistance to change in highly institutionalized settings" and Weinstock discussing the tension between opposing values that often make them difficult to balance and create obstacles to effecting change in the justice sector. In contradistinction to these chapters, however, the contribution of Clément Camion reminds us of the possible negative consequences of rendering justice *too* accessible, and in so doing provides further insight into the requisite balance that must be ensured when adopting new procedural models.

The third part of this collection therefore presents a comprehensive view of the deep reflection that had to be conducted by the third working group, a reflection which led them to recognize that in order for cyberjustice to have its desired effects not only must the rules of evidence and procedure be reformed to allow for digitalization, but a new work culture in the judiciary must be implemented. By working from this stance, research in the cyberjustice arena supported a successful implementing of concrete change in Quebec's legal system, as embodied by the new *Code of Civil Procedure*,[5] which encourages the use of technology whenever possible:

> In applying this Code, *appropriate technological means that are available to both the parties and the court should be used whenever possible*, taking into account the technological environment in place to support the business of the courts.
> *The court, even on its own initiative, may use such means or order that such means be used by the parties, including for case management purposes*; if it considers it necessary, the court may also, despite an agreement between the parties, require a person to appear in person at a hearing, a conference or an examination.[6] (Emphasis added)

This modification represents a truly important shift in judicial mentality and is a definite step forward toward rethinking procedural law and correspondingly improving access to justice. In an effort to give full effect to these new procedural changes, the third working group ultimately took it upon themselves to suggest ways of improving access to justice, namely by re-structuring the judiciary through the use of online dispute resolution. Their research in this respect has emerged as an entirely new concentration of study and now essentially constitutes one of the main research perspectives of the Cyberjustice Laboratory, as will be discussed in further detail in the next section.

Main Research Perspectives

In order to truly appreciate the complexities of the research performed by the *Towards Cyberjustice* team, as presented in the three parts of this collection, it is crucial to keep in mind the perspectives that underlie their work. As has been mentioned on several occasions throughout this introduction, (a) improving access to justice has become a main focal point of each of the working groups of the *Towards Cyberjustice* project. In an attempt to identify new and technologically enhanced procedural models that could achieve this purpose, the third working group suggested (b) re-structuring the judiciary through the use of online dispute resolution, which ultimately emerged as a new concentration of study for the Cyberjustice Laboratory. Both of these perspectives will be discussed in further detail heretofore.

Improving Access to Justice

Access to justice is an issue that has long been plaguing court systems. According to recent figures, only 17% of Quebecers believe that all can afford to go to court,[7] whereas a mere 18% are of the opinion that the deadlines associated with the courts are reasonable.[8] In Canada, the situation is similar, where " approximately 65% of the population is uncertain about what rights are available, do not know how to handle legal problems, is afraid, thinks that nothing can be done, or thinks that it will cost too much money or take too much time."[9] What is further striking about these numbers is that they do not solely encompass individuals with fewer resources, but rather also include educated individuals who possess the means to afford a lawyer but prefer to resort to self-representation.

In light of this worrying reality, improving access to justice has become a central preoccupation in the legal world. With new advances in technology, however, it quickly became apparent that new technologies could be of assistance in solving this problem. As such, and as is evident throughout the chapters of this book, the use of technology with the specific aim of improving access to justice has become a common thread and guiding principle of cyberjustice research.

In this light, the *Towards Cyberjustice* project researched several aspects of the legal system that could affect access to justice and which the use of modern technologies may remedy. As discussed in further detail above, project researchers analyzed legal rituals as well as evidentiary and procedural rules in an effort to entirely rethink the legal process such that it would more successfully welcome new technological solutions that would decrease both costs and delays, and thus ultimately improve access to justice.

Improving access to justice by reducing the costs and delays of procedures through the use of technology is not, however, the sole focus of this research. Indeed, cyberjustice research aimed toward improving access to justice has significantly contributed to promoting the idea that independence and security of the justice system can happily coexist with both openness and a new collaborative culture within the judicial system. In effect, this general idea maintains that using information technology to improve access to justice requires that justice be redefined as a "space of open interactions." The ultimate goal is essentially to change the social ties and dynamics between the various actors of the legal field, such that this will eventually trigger a democratization of the justice system as a whole and ultimately increase access to justice by improving litigants' overall impression of the justice system as well as their sense of empowerment, as examined in further detail in Part II of this book.

One of the significant ideas that emerged from approaching the issue of cyberjustice through the lens of access to justice was to understand and adapt legal rituals to promote the amicable settlement of disputes, mainly so as to ease congestion of the court system. In this respect, it was believed that by enhancing the willingness of parties to participate in remote exchanges, as well as by increasing accessibility in terms of costs and availability, the promotion of out-of-court amicable settlements through the use of modern technologies would increase access to justice while simultaneously reducing costs and delays within the justice system. This ultimately led to a new angle of research for the Cyberjustice Laboratory, revolving mainly around online dispute resolution and alternative dispute resolution, as will be discussed further in the next section.

Online Dispute Resolution and Alternative Dispute Resolution
One of the most noteworthy recent research directions taken in the field of cyberjustice has revolved around the idea that disputes can be settled outside the courthouse through alternative dispute resolutions, whose focus on collaboration and participation can often be a better option for litigants as they may benefit from proceedings that are less adversarial in nature. This represents a significant shift in mentality toward a participatory justice perspective that will necessarily involve establishing a new work culture within the justice system. Essentially, advocating for alternative dispute resolution and a stronger role for the extra-judiciary in an effort to bring litigants closer to the justice system will require redefining the roles of all the main actors involved and the dynamics of their relationships. This

need to redefine elements that have been part of the fabric of the legal system for so long can cause hesitations and expectations on the part of legal professionals, which must be thoroughly addressed if a system of alternative dispute resolutions is to be properly implemented.

With these considerations in mind, as well as the ultimate goal of increasing access to justice, the Cyberjustice Laboratory has been examining the idea of re-structuring the judiciary through the use of a branch of alternative dispute resolution, known as online dispute resolution (ODR) in an attempt to reduce caseloads. ODR refers to the use of alternative dispute resolution (negotiation, mediation, arbitration) generally conducted by a neutral third party but in a dematerialized context.[10] The specific angle of research adopted in this respect was the use of online mediation to settle low-intensity disputes, such as consumer disputes or small claims, which originated on the Internet.[11]

This particular approach to the use of ODR brought to the fore the growing interest of the private technology sector in this form of dispute resolution, which is constantly privatizing ODR mechanisms and associated software development. Essentially, this move on the part of the technology sector demonstrates that cyberspace is well adapted to being regulated by norms developed by non-state stakeholders.[12]

At the same time, however, this phenomenon raises questions regarding the foundations of the justice system. Are we comfortable with the idea of having an entire sector of dispute resolution controlled by the private sector without any oversight from the public sector? Perhaps the best option lies in having privately developed solutions but with the final decision being supervised by the judiciary? Or perhaps it might still be better to simply have a publicly developed and managed ODR mechanism?

While all these questions may seem to suggest that a choice need be made between dispute resolution regulated by the private sector as opposed to having it regulated by the public sector, this is not necessarily the case. Essentially, having ODR mechanisms that are managed by the private sector does not inevitably exclude the state's contribution. Instead the state may seem of the utmost importance in ensuring the real deployment of the principle of ODR, without necessarily needing to control the process itself. In this light, successful implementation of ODR as a means of increasing access to justice was deemed to depend on state action.

With this in mind, there were three possible situations that needed to be studied.[13] To begin with, an ODR system could be developed to meet the needs of businesses engaging in B2B (business to business) commerce, which would thus involve mediation and arbitration of disputes between two companies. A long tradition dating back to the Middle Ages (*lex mercatoria*) recognizes that merchants have the capacity to resolve their disputes among themselves, without state intervention. In this case, the development and operation of an ODR system would depend on the players themselves. In such cases, the state's role is minimal.[14]

Another possible situation that needed to be studied is reminiscent of the dispute resolution process imposed by eBay, the leading online auction site. This case entails the purchase and sale of products by both consumers and merchants, requiring that any dispute-resolution system adopted would have to address the needs of both C2C (consumer to consumer) and B2C (business to consumer) commerce as well as B2B commerce. The case of eBay, however, involves a closed community that buys and sells products and services (well-defined actions) and that has developed its own rules of operation:[15] to buy or sell on eBay, the user has no choice but to obey the rules.[16] As such, this case does not require the intervention of the state with respect to processing disputes or operating their ODR system.

The third and final situation that needed to be examined was that of an ODR system for the general public. This would therefore not involve any specific group of individuals, such as merchants, or a closed community in which compliance with the rules is a membership requirement. Rather, this would involve both domestic and foreign users who use the Internet in their everyday lives. Although research regarding this form of ODR began with a focus on settling low-intensity disputes that originated on the Internet, as research progressed it quickly became apparent that online mediation was just as suited to resolving similar disputes that arise in the physical world as well.

With this enlarged scope of the application of ODR to regular citizens, it was then necessary to reflect upon the manner in which to implement such a system successfully. To this effect, it was questioned as to whether state intervention might be necessary to achieve this goal. Indeed, who other than the state[17] possesses the financial power required to back such a system (from design to implementation and operation) while simultaneously ensuring the level of consumer protection required for the maintenance of public order throughout both the European Union and Quebec? When viewed from this angle, it becomes clear that enabling the introduction of ODR mechanisms for managing and resolving small claims becomes the responsibility of the state.[18]

What is consistent throughout all of the situations described above is that ODR systems are necessary when norms for the regulation of electronic commerce are being developed. It is rather the state's involvement in the system that will vary depending on the situation. That having been said, it is crucial to note that Quebec's new *Code of Civil Procedure*, which came into force in January 2016, places a strong emphasis on the use of private dispute resolution processes.[19] If the past is any indication of the future, this new development may very well enhance the capacity of private actors to conceptualize, develop, and eventually export new norms in the continuously growing field of online consumer dispute resolution.[20]

A New Way Forward

The domain of cyberjustice is constantly evolving and holds much that is promising for the years ahead. To provide a glimpse into what the future of cyberjustice holds, we will (a) discuss which developments might be expected that will further empower litigants, and (b) outline recently emerging research in the domain of computational law as it pertains to cyberjustice.

Empowering Litigants

The phenomenon of self-representation is slowly becoming a structural element of judicial practice. As previously mentioned, Canada is faced with access to justice problems resulting from the significant delays and complexities inherent in judicial procedures and accentuated by the considerable costs associated with the process.[21] According to a recent report of the Action Committee on Access to Justice in Civil and Family Matters, up to 50% of litigants are aiming to represent themselves, without any consultation with a lawyer.[22] The reasons that motivate these litigants to act without legal representation when dealing with the court system are varied and are not necessarily due to a lack of financial resources,[23] but may be due to their lack of trust in the justice system.[24]

Whatever the reasons may be, however, the future of access to justice research will necessarily include a component that revolves around the empowerment of litigants, as addressed in the second part of this book. Future research in cyberjustice will thus be aimed toward achieving this purpose and will essentially be based on a reflection surrounding both judicial representation and the expectations of the users of the judicial system. In this light, while it is important to develop solutions for improving access to justice that are not solely limited to socio-economic criteria, it will also prove crucial to provide self-represented litigants with the proper tools to educate and guide them throughout their experiences with the justice system.

Additionally, it will be essential to evaluate any interrelation between the low level of confidence exhibited by litigants in justice systems as opposed to their views on other social transformations, such as the use of digital technologies in their everyday lives. This initial reflection will then need to be deepened so as to examine which new expectations will emerge for self-represented litigants as a result of the incorporation of technology into the justice system, expectations which will largely be shaped by the daily experiences of these individuals as well as their dialogical interactions with technological devices.[25]

Essentially, with the growing number of technological tools that are being used by public institutions to interact with citizens so as to give the fullest effect to the principle of direct democracy, the manner in which these tools are offered will have to properly address citizens' needs. This is especially so if the goal of the implementation of such tools is to be achieved, which is to allow citizens the independence[26] to develop their own strategies and standards of interactions with technologies (such as to skim through certain pages or choose to focus more on certain pieces of information that were deemed irrelevant by search engines, etc.). The use of technology to provide citizens with services in the justice sector can likewise be used to ensure a similar level of user autonomy and will, it is hoped, also improve access to justice and thus change the public perception of the justice system.

It is at this juncture that new non-judicial forms of dispute resolution, such as ODR, will come into play. These dispute resolution mechanisms can be combined with technological tools to provide citizens with renewed interactions that answer their needs, and ultimately empower them within the justice system by providing them with a sense of ownership and control over the system while also respecting the needs and values of the individuals that it affects. In this respect, future research with respect to the empowerment of litigants will likely revolve around the fundamental role that this appropriation will take toward the empowerment of individuals, inasmuch as it would change the nature and impetus of their interactions with the justice system.

Computational Law

In recent years, a new field of research emerged that attracted the attention of cyberjustice scholars: computational law and artificial intelligence. Essentially, what is intriguing about this field is the plethora of possibilities that artificial intelligence and algorithms might provide toward helping stakeholders in the decision-making process as well as in the field of legal research. Even at its infancy, it is clear that the use of artificial intelligence in the legal field will likely trigger transformations that will allow for a faster, less costly and more predictable judicial process,[27] while also enabling its use as a tool for public administrative services. In this vein, by associating artificial intelligence with computational law, it may be possible to improve legal and administrative services by providing tools that can fully adapt to each litigant and offer individuals targeted legal advice based on their level of digital education, the specific context of their legal research, and their specific needs.

While the benefits presented by the use of algorithms and artificial intelligence in computational law may be significant, this form of technology raises some ethical questions with regards to fundamental rights that will need to be addressed should it be properly integrated into the legal system. We are essentially at a point "at which the law and technology can be said to collide as there are a vast array of implications which arise as technology is threatening to cross the divide from being a passive tool to taking an active part in legal deliberations."[28] The implications of using such technologies, which are mostly of an ethical nature, will therefore need to be thoroughly examined in order to assess the risks of using artificial intelligence for the administration of justice.

In light of this new direction of research in the domain of cyberjustice, the Cyberjustice Laboratory's scientific program remains closely linked to technical advances aimed at facilitating *networking between the various stakeholders within the justice system.* Since 2010, the convergence of increased Internet access, the maturing of web technologies that allow for greater communication and wider exchange of data between Internet applications, as well as a wider usage of smart devices (computers, phones, tablets, etc.) have provided new motives for accessing justice and its administration. This new reality has therefore been harnessed by the research performed by the Cyberjustice Laboratory in several of its projects undertaken to date.

Research Projects Undertaken to Date:
- Research on amicable conflict settlement (online negotiation, mediation, or arbitration)
- Research on the digital administration of justice (electronic registry, e-filing, digital serving of decisions, etc.)
- Research on digital audiences (electronic presentation of evidence, remote testimony, etc.)

Cloud Computing: The advent of cloud computing represents a significant increase in the capacity to store, process, and communicate data at a decreased cost. While this may greatly benefit the administration of justice, whose costs with respect to information management are not inconsiderable, turning to the cloud is not without risks. For example, judicial data hosted in or transiting through the cloud may be difficult to control and protect, a concern which has already been expressed by the Supreme Court of Canada[29] in its refusal to allow Shared Services Canada to manage its computer services on the basis that doing so would jeopardize the court's judicial and administrative independence. On the contrary, American federal tribunals did not hesitate to adopt cloud-computing solutions so as to improve the management of their court records, but they did so by obtaining their own private system, called PACER. These misgivings, which are shared by a large part of the judicial community, have the potential to slow down or even stop the successful adoption of judicial cloud computing. As a result, it is important to further study the manner in which cloud computing can benefit our legal system, a task which the Cyberjustice Laboratory's team has taken upon itself.

Research Projects Undertaken to Date:
- Research on the usage of cloud computing in the justice system

- Research on best practices in cloud computing while adhering to the relevant legal framework and the justice system's basic principles.

Artificial Intelligence: The age of "big data," defined by the massive creation of computer data, brings to the fore new opportunities for scientific research, technological development, service providing, and product manufacturing. Provided we can make sense of those large data sets, it will be possible to design new, more-or-less autonomous decision-making tools. Using the combined power of automatic machine learning and operation research (meaning the science of optimizing the decision-making process), the first practical applications for artificial intelligence in the field of natural language or image analysis are preambles to those transformations which might occur in the fields of law and justice. Should we come to master those tools and obtain a sufficient quantity of exploitable data, meaning data labelled in a way that can be analyzed by a machine, legal and judicial sciences may have to thoroughly readjust their modes of operation. This phenomenon is currently being analyzed by (1) the computational law division, which is studying digital tools to aid in legal decision-making. Ultimately, this research could bring about (2) the concept of computational justice, which examines the creation of autonomous, automated decision-making tools for the justice system.

1. Research on Computational Law

Tools designed to help in the legal decision-making process have existed for several years. They consist mainly of algorithms that have been developed with the ability to reproduce some elements of legal reasoning. Although it remains difficult to ascribe mathematical logic to the process, significant progress has been made in various areas, such as the analysis of natural language, which helps improve interactions between man and machine, the refinement of expert systems that aid in the decision-making process, and the gathering of data. However, these advances remain in the field of so-called Soft AI for the time being. At this point, the Laboratory's research projects will concentrate on their possible applications to help in the decision-making process for the community of legal experts and the various users of legal services, and will be created using legal data that is already available and exploitable (such as through data compiled by various legal information institutes like CanLII). In their wake, and

in order to set the scene for an advanced phase of research on automated learning, also called Deep Learning, researchers at the
Laboratory will develop a methodology to collect and label legal data
(including court records, evidence, etc.) so as to eventually make
them easier to gather in order to improve our legal system.

Planned Research Projects:
- Research on the development of expert systems to help in
  legal decisions based on analyzing and processing problem
  descriptions prepared in natural language:
  ○ Accessing legal information
  ○ Selecting a competent instance
  ○ Preparing legal documents
- Research on the development of predictive systems to help
  in legal decision-making:
  ○ Predicting the prospects of success of a legal action
  ○ Suggesting negotiated solutions
  ○ Evaluating evidence acceptability
  ○ Evaluating damages
- Research on labelling methods for legal data in preparation
  of their future gathering in order to render them useful for
  the development of legal and judicial sciences:
  ○ Methodology for gathering judicial data
  ○ Methodology for labelling judicial data

2. Research on Computational Justice

Should they be able to model judicial reasoning in whole or in part
and to automate the decision-making process for some court judgments, new developments in the field of computational law might
come to fruition. Before then, inasmuch as it may be accessible or
desirable, there is a short-term possibility to automate the decision-
making process in some well-defined instances (social benefits,
opposition to certain rules, homologation of mediation agreements,
homologation of proceedings agreement, etc.). The following is a
short list of the planned research projects in this sector:

Planned Research Projects:
- Research on the development of automated decision-making
  processes:
  ○ Opposition to various social benefits (unemployment
    insurance, etc.)

- ○ Opposition to various infractions and rules
- ○ Homologation of a mediation agreement
- ○ Homologation of a proceedings agreement

Projects conducted so far by the research program *Towards Cyberjustice* and future projects have the ability to transform our understanding of the judicial process. We must however be wary of any techno-utopianism. The objective is to pursue opportunities and at the same time be aware of the limits of technology. Justice demands at least that.

Notes

1   "The Project – Rethinking Processual Law: Towards Cyberjustice," online: Laboratoire de cyberjustice <www.cyberjustice.ca/en/projets/vers-la-cyberjustice/>.

2   See, e.g., the *Integrated Justice Project*. This project was launched in 1996 by the Ministry of the Attorney General and the Ministry of Public Safety and Security of Ontario. "The objective of the Project was to improve the information flow in the justice system by streamlining existing processes and replacing older computer systems and paper-based information exchanges with new, compatible systems and technologies." Office of the Provincial Auditor of Ontario, "Integrated Justice Project," 2003 Annual Report, at 283, online: <www.auditor.on.ca/en/content/annualreports/arreports/en01/303en01.pdf>.

3   Karim Benyekhlef and Nicolas Vermeys, "Best Practices in the Field of Cyberjustice," in *Seminar on Recent Trends and Good Practices in the Application of Electronic Technology to Judicial Processes (E-Justice)*, ed. Carlos Gregorio, Mexico, April 2011.

4   Ibid.

5   *Code of Civil Procedure*, CQLR c C-25.01 [NCCP].

6   Ibid. at art 26.

7   Catherine Dubé, "Les Québécois font de plus en plus confiance aux tribunaux," *L'Actualité*, December 8, 2014, online: <www.lactualite.com/societe/tribunaux-le-besoin-de-croire/>.

8   Ibid.

9   Trevor Farrow, "What is Access to Justice?," *Osgoode Hall Law Journal* 51:3 (2014):957 at 964; see also Ab Currie, *The Legal Problems of Everyday Life: The Nature, Extent and Consequences of Justiciable Problems Experienced by Canadians* (Ottawa: Department of Justice Canada, 2007) at 55–56 and generally 55–67, 88.

10   Mohamed S. Abdel Wahab, Ethan Katsch and Daniel Rainey, eds., *Online Dispute Resolution: Theory and Practice: A Treatise on Technology and Dispute Resolution* (The Hague: Eleven International Publishing, 2012).

11   Nicolas Vermeys and Karim Benyekhlef, "ODR and the Courts," in *Online Dispute Resolution: Theory And Practice: A Treatise On Technology And Dispute Resolution,* ed. Mohamed S Abdel Wahab, Ethan Katsh and Daniel Rainey (The Hague: Eleven International Publishing, 2012) at 295.

12   Karim Benyekhlef, "La résolution en ligne des différends de consommation: un récit autour (et un exemple) du droit postmoderne," in *L'accès des consommateurs à la justice,* ed. Pierre-Claude Lafond (Cowansville: Yvon Blais, 2010) at 89.

13   Ibid.

14   Ibid.

15   See "eBay.ca User Agreement," online: <pages.ebay.ca/help/policies/user-agreement.html>.

16   Benyekhlef, *supra* note 11 at 89.

17   Surely we can look at the state, but we are well aware of the territorial limitations of its action. It is therefore worth considering *ad hoc* associations of states, as well as organizations of states, such as the European Union. In 2013 the European Union adopted a regulation on ODR for consumer disputes which entails setting up an ODR platform to resolve such disputes online. This ODR platform was launched in February 2016. See Regulation (EU) No 524/2013 of the European Parliament and of the Council of 21 May 2013 on ODR for consumer disputes, amending Regulation (EC) No 2006/2004 and Directive 2009/22/EC (Regulation on consumer ODR), online: <eur-lex.europa.eu/legal-content/EN/TXT/PDF/?uri=CELEX:32013R0524&from=FR>.

18   In 2010, Working Group III of the United Nations Commission on International Trade Law began drafting a set of non-binding procedural rules governing ODR for cross-border electronic commerce transactions. Once finalized, such rules could be used as reference frameworks for states wishing to regulate ODR mechanisms. For more information on these draft procedural rules, see the United Nations Commission on International Trade Law's webpage: <www.uncitral.org/uncitral/en/commission/working_groups/3Online_Dispute_Resolution.html>.

19   For example, sections 1 to 7 of this new *Code of Civil Procedure, supra* note 4, deal exclusively with "principles of procedure applicable to private dispute prevention and resolution processes," whereas section 26 states: "In applying this Code, appropriate technological means that are available to both the parties and the court should be used whenever possible."

20   Benyekhlef, *supra* note 11 at 89.

21 Action Committee on Access to Justice in Civil and Family Matters, *Access to Civil and Family Justice: A Roadmap for Change*, October 2013, online: <www.cfcj-fcjc.org/action-committee>.

22 Ibid. at 4.

23 See in this regard, the work of Trevor Farrow, including this text: Trever Farrow et al., *Addressing the Needs of SRLs in the Canadian Justice System* (White paper prepared for the Association of Canadian Court Administrators) (Toronto: Canadian Court Administrators, 2012).

24 Charlotte Fraser, "Public Confidence in the Canadian Criminal Justice System: A Review of the Evidence" (Report presented at the Sixth National Symposium on Criminal Justice, Ottawa, January 2014) [unpublished].

25 Francis Jauréguerry and Serge Proulx, *Usages et enjeux des technologies de communication* (Toulouse: Èrès, 2011).

26 Ibid.

27 Isolde De Villiers, "Instant Justice, Cyber Style – "Artificially Intelligent" Judges: the Law," *Without Prejudice* 7–9 (2007) at 12.

28 Ben Jarvis, "Artificial Intelligence and the Resolution of Disputes: Where the Law and Technology Collide" (Honours Thesis, University of Technology, Sydney, 2005) at 2.

29 Supreme Court of Canada, press release, January 7, 2016, online: <scc-csc.lexum.com/scc-csc/news/en/item/5132/index.do>.

PART I

JUSTICE VALUES AND DIGITALIZATION

Fundamental Values in a Technologized Age of Efficiency

Jane Bailey

In the twentieth century it is usually taken for granted that the only reliable sources for improving the human condition stem from new machines, techniques, and chemicals.... [Yet] as we "make things work" what kind of world are we making?

Langdon Winner[1]

The immense faith that Western societies have placed in technology's capacity to improve the human condition and the equation of technological change with progress are also, at least rhetorically, evident with respect to justice systems. The chapters in this section step back from rhetorical approaches that simplistically equate the introduction of technology with the improvement of justice systems. In particular, they demonstrate the complexities involved in the relationship between technological innovation and access to justice, and call for analyses of the world we are making that move beyond quantitative analyses of efficiency. They urge us to recognize that much more than efficiency is required of justice systems in democratic societies and support a more critical approach to technological innovation in the justice sector. As Vermeys aptly puts it in his chapter, the question should not be "what do we have to gain or lose" from any given technology, but rather "how best to use the technology in a way that corresponds to our fundamental legal principles."

In other words, technological innovation in the justice sector should not simply be technology for technology's sake. Instead, it is essential to understand how a technology may facilitate or affect the fundamental values underlying the justice system, values that are essential to access to justice as well. Without in any way dismissing the capacity of technology to improve justice systems and access to those systems, the authors in this section put us on a path where fundamental values such as privacy, equality, transparency, and others no longer take a backseat to efficiency or to an uncritical and automatic equation of technology with progress or access to justice.

Beauchard's chapter frames the critical discussion of technology that runs throughout this section by focusing on cyberjustice initiatives in the context of international development. While his analysis is specific to that development agenda, it highlights a number of universal lessons with respect to the implementation of technology in the justice sector. Beauchard demonstrates the ways in which technology in the form of computerized case management and justice showrooms can and have been used to create visibility and media attention designed to stimulate faith in courts in emerging economies, rather than addressing the issues of relevance to the people who live there. In addition to employing mega models that have been shown to fail in other jurisdictions, the cyberjustice initiatives he discusses prioritize efficiency and "Taylorized justice" without addressing other fundamental justice values, such as procedural compliance, decisions in accordance with law, and the inviolability of basic rights. Further, he notes that the technology-worshipping vision that has tended to predominate in the context of cyberjustice initiatives associated with international development has led to a celebration of technology in and of itself and a constant postponement of measuring whether the technology has actually been effective. Where cyberjustice initiatives have been evaluated, assessment has tended to focus on efficiency alone, effectively ignoring justice values such as the availability of law common to all parties and the inviolability of basic rights that are key to "creating the conditions of trust required for economic development."

Lupo's chapter directly addresses the importance of evaluating cyberjustice initiatives. He shows how existing evaluation models that draw on information-systems literature focus on efficiency measures that leave out fundamental values that are essential to ensuring that justice systems contribute meaningfully to a well-functioning democracy. While Lupo accepts that efficiency and efficacy criteria such as system quality, information quality, user satisfaction, and organizational benefits are important aspects of evaluating cyber-justice systems, he proposes a model that also incorporates evaluation of such systems' impacts on six key justice values. By seeking to evaluate cyberjustice systems' impacts on independence, account-ability, impartiality, equal access, transparency, privacy, and legal validity, Lupo's proposed model would address a key concern identi-fied by Beauchard. This model of evaluation would augment evalu-ation of a system's efficiency with an analysis of its impacts on the kinds of fundamental values essential to creating conditions of trust in and access to justice systems.

The last two chapters in this section transition from more gen-eral concerns around cyberjustice initiatives and fundamental justice values to examine in depth the sometimes conflicting effects that online access to court records and information can have for the foun-dational justice values of transparency and privacy.

Reynolds' chapter grounds the right to access information about court proceedings in the Canadian *Charter*'s guarantee of freedom of expression, which includes a right to access information. While noting that traditional forms of media have been recognized as essential to Canadians' access to information about court proceed-ings, Reynolds argues that digital connectivity now makes it possible for Canadians to access court information without the need for an intermediary. Working from this foundation, he asserts that courts ought to take all reasonable steps to make court information acces-sible online in order to enhance Canadians' right to freedom of expression. After documenting some of the ways in which Canadian courts have begun to make information available online, as well as examples of restrictions Canadian courts have placed on use of tech-nology in courtrooms, Reynolds suggests that courts ought to continue with initiatives that facilitate digitized access to informa-tion. He recognizes, however, that countervailing concerns around privacy and security will have to be balanced against expressive rights in order to ensure that cyberjustice initiatives of this sort remain faithful to the full range of fundamental justice values at play.

Vermeys' chapter explores in depth the implications of the countervailing privacy considerations arising from online access to court records. While recognizing that the transparency and expres-sive values emphasized in Reynolds' chapter have traditionally prevailed over countervailing privacy concerns in the context of court records and information, Vermeys notes that even in the pre-internet context, the open-court principle gave way in some instances to other values of "superordinate importance." Vermeys advances a compelling case for taking privacy even more seriously in an era of online access, pointing out that inconveniences that once ensured most people would not access physical court records have been eroded by the ease with which records can be accessed online. He suggests that this erosion of practical obscurity that worked informally to protect sensitive information in court documents from widespread disclosure necessitates recognition of privacy as a value of superordinate importance that merits some restrictions on electronic access to court records and information, especially in light of widespread corporate data-mining practices. Ultimately, Vermeys and Reynolds are *ad idem* with respect to harnessing the expressive and transparency advantages to be gained from online access to court records and information. The solution, Vermeys suggests, is not to avoid the technology that can facilitate the key justice value of transparency. Instead, he proposes potential technological and legal mechanisms that would minimize improper access to and use of sensitive data (especially by data miners), without sacrificing the aspects of online accessibility that meaningfully facilitate justice-system transparency.

In the final analysis, the chapters in this section are consistent with Winner's advice in the epigraph to this introduction. While Beauchard, Lupo, Reynolds, and Vermeys accept that cyberjustice initiatives and technology more generally *can* facilitate improvements in the human condition, they call for careful and critical consideration of the impact of technological artefacts on a range of fundamental justice values that are key to ensuring and improving access to justice.

Notes

1   Langdon Winner, *The Whale and the Reactor: A Search for Limits in an Age of High Technology* (Chicago: The University of Chicago Press, 1986) at 5 and 17.

CHAPTER I

Cyberjustice and International Development: Reducing the Gap Between Promises and Accomplishments

Renaud Beauchard

Ever since President Truman's famous Point Four Program, the gap between the promises and the achievements of official development assistance (ODA) has obsessed what is customarily known as the "development community" and its observers. This can be seen from the repeated conferences and declarations on assistance effectiveness (the Monterrey Summit, Paris Declaration on Aid Effectiveness, Accra Accords, Busan Forum, etc.) and the critical literature on development assistance, such as the works by Dambisa Moyo and William Easterly.[1] However, it is probable that no one has expressed this questioning better than Gilbert Rist in his non-hagiographic history of development:

> How could it have been thought necessary and urgent to do everything to speed up the process of "development," ostensibly favouring the prosperity of countries in both North and South? After all, for centuries no one – or virtually no one – took it into their head to relieve the misery of others by structural measures, especially when they lived in different continents. What is the origin of this collective task which, though constantly criticized for its lack of success, appears to be justified beyond all dispute? What sense can we make of the numerous debates which, for nearly fifty years, have offered a solution to the problems that majority destitution poses in the face of minority opulence? How

> are we to explain this whole phenomenon, which mobilizes not
> only the hopes of millions but also sizeable financial resources,
> while appearing to recede like the horizon just as you think you
> are approaching it?[2]

Indeed, as Rist shows, the situation is a little like that of the first Christians, who were expecting the Kingdom and got the Church instead: ODA policy consists in continual renewal of discourse and tools to maintain the belief in salvation/development despite constant postponement of achievement of the "developmentalist" ideal.

An analysis of the gap between the promises and the achievements of development assistance, no matter what the sector, therefore has to take some distance from the idea that the "development community" has of itself, and this requires trying to understand the mentality and bureaucratic behaviour that guide its action.

One of the characteristic features of this mentality is what we can describe as the superego of modernization. The theory of modernization, according to which development, owing to a unilinear conception of history, is driven by impersonal forces—urbanization, literacy, mass communications, and development of the media—has been instrumental in the genesis of development assistance. However, although modernization has been rejected as a source of inspiration owing to its Western ethnocentrism, it nonetheless constitutes a superego of development built on a foundation of conceptually attractive images.

The injunctions of this superego are particularly important in the relationship of the development community with technological innovation and reform of institutions, including those of justice. The belief of the "development community" in impersonal forces dictating the fate of communities without human contributions makes it receptive to a technology-worshipping vision, leading to celebration of technology in itself and to modelling visions of institutions on a conception of "information machines." In the relationship to justice institutions, this superego leads those institutions to focus on effective services so as to send signals that give investors a reassuring image of transaction security.

However, it becomes clear that justice, in particular, is an area where the reforms guided by the superego of the development industry collide with symbolic images of the institution/virtue of justice that are fully anchored in reality and shared by ordinary people. It is based on this distortion between the real need for justice institutions and the illusory benefits of development assistance that the present article will try to analyse the missed opportunities in the meeting of development, justice, and digital technology.

Modernization: the Development Superego

In order to illustrate the illusory nature of development, we have to point out that there is not even a shared definition of the term itself. On this, Gilbert Rist rightly observed that psychologists speaking of development of intelligence, mathematicians speaking about developing an equation, and photographers talking about developing film share the same definition of the word "development." However, this definition is different from the one that can be used to signify the level of economic prosperity in North America and Europe,[3] a process of growth with its primary source in society,[4] or a goal to expand the range of choices offered to the population, which makes it possible to render development more democratic and more participatory.[5]

As Rist explains it, "[t]he principal defect of most pseudo-definitions of "development" is that they are generally based upon the way in which one person (or set of persons) pictures the ideal conditions of social existence." Rist characterizes this as a system of Western thought.[6] Nonetheless, he adds the following caveat:

> Yet "development" does exist, in a way, through the actions that it legitimates, through the institutions it keeps alive and the signs testifying to its presence. How could it be denied that there are developed and developing countries, development projects, development co-operation ministers, a United Nations Development Programme, an International Bank for Reconstruction and Development (better known as the World Bank), institutes for development studies, NGOs responsible for furthering development, and many other institutions and activities with the same stated aim. In the name of this fetishistic term – which is also a portmanteau or "plastic" word – schools and clinics are built, exports encouraged, wells dug, roads laid, children vaccinated, funds collected, plans established, national budgets revised, reports drafted, experts hired, strategies concocted, the international community mobilized, dams constructed, forests exploited, deserts reforested, high-yield plants invented, trade liberalized,

technology imported, factories opened, wage-jobs multiplied, spy satellites launched. When all is said and done, every human activity can be undertaken in the name of "development."[7]

Thus, the effort to find a definition does not seem to overcome the tension between a "subjective feeling of fulfilment varying from individual to individual" and "a series of operations for which there is no *a priori* proof that they really contribute to the stated objective."[8]

In order to remedy this indeterminacy, Rist applies Durkheimian methodology consisting, on one hand, in including the totality of the phenomena under consideration and, on the other, looking only at external features, which leads to classifying, from a sociological point of view, one set of countries as "developed" while others are labelled "developing" based on practices that are clear to all.[9] Rejecting quantitative comparison (number of schools and roads, size of currency reserves, per capita calorie intake, computers and cell phones, etc.) Rist suggests a definition that makes it possible to describe the mechanisms of social change characteristic of development:

> "Development" consists of a set of practices, sometimes appearing to conflict with one another, which require – for the reproduction of society – the general transformation and destruction of the natural environment and of social relations. Its aim is to increase the production of commodities (goods and services) geared, by way of exchange, to effective demand.[10]

Rist's work is especially laudable in that he has managed to capture the superego of development impregnated by the theory of modernization, the crucial primary inspiration of the development community, the importance of which can never be emphasized enough.

Greatly inspired by the work of Walt Rostow, whose seminal book, *The Stages of Economic Growth: A Non-Communist Manifesto*, tried to identify the constant features of modernization of societies, the theory of modernization is about social change that presumes a universal, linear evolution of the development process. According to Rostow, every country experiences in the course of its development a certain number of identical stages in going from the traditional society, characterized by an essentially agricultural, low-productivity economy, to the society of mass consumption, which meets the basic needs of the population and has a major service sector. According to this theory, developing countries are perceived as "backward" in relation to developed countries, which are portrayed as models because, having entered the era of mass consumption, they have reached the ultimate stage of development.

However, probably the most important aspect of the theory of modernization is less Rostow's thesis, presented at the time as an "anti-communist manifesto," than its sociological component, inspired in particular by Talcott Parsons and Alex Inkeles. It has been summarized in the following way by Christopher Lasch, based on a reading of Inkeles:

> Once information about the modern world had begun to circulate among newly urbanized populations, it was impossible to deny the masses a place in the sun. "Exposure to modernizing influences," as Alex Inkeles put it, generated an irresistible demand for the better things of life. It led to an "openness to new experience," "increasing independence from the authority of traditional figures like parents and priests," a "belief in the efficacy of science and medicine," "ambition for oneself and one's children," and a strong interest in politics—the whole "syndrome of modernity."[11]

The "development community" has taken distance from modernization theory, an American conceptual weapon during the Cold War, considered too marked by Western ethnocentrism. It has been replaced by a series of reformulations (dependency theory, social autonomy or self-reliance, the New International Economic Order (NIEO), the vital-needs approach, structural adjustment, human development, and the struggle against poverty), but it has remained in a way the superego of development. To assess this, let us look at the following passage from the book by Hilton Root, *Dynamics among Nations*:

> Modernization theory has had a deterministic influence on contemporary understanding of global development, both within the academy and among the policy community. Its influence is so widespread that it is even difficult to refer to modernization as a theory; its visceral intensity in the framing of US development policy has been a matter of faith under democratic and republican administrations. Under Bill Clinton, modernization theory led US policy makers to believe that open trade and rising

incomes would bring democracy to China and Russia. Under George W. Bush, it led to the belief that a democratic transition would spontaneously follow the eradication of dictatorship in Iraq and helped gain bipartisan support for the invasion. Bush's secretary of state, Condoleezza Rice, espoused confidence that a rising middle class in China would assume its "universal" role and demand democratic rights of representation and a free media. The grip of modernization theory on policies of international relations did not change when the Democrats won the 2008 election. President Barack Obama links open economies, open societies, and open governments, just as his predecessor did. All administrations since Jimmy Carter's have asserted that human progress has a single trajectory: it may start with the economy, but it must ultimately end with democracy.[12]

In short, in the development community, modernization is what remains when everything else has been forgotten, except that this "visceral intensity" continues to infuse the imagination of the "development community" with a set of impressionistic visual images of modernization, including of the relationship to technology, especially of the information society, which is an essential component.

In this respect, modernization's impact on development brings to mind Raymond Ruyer's analyses concerning the construction of a magical vision of society by the effects of technology in technological societies that have become unaware of technology. Analysing the effect of the media in particular, Ruyer says:

> It [media technology] has, through an apparent paradox, fostered the reign of the image or pseudo-idea based on an image of a very sensorial form of aesthetics with very little intellectual content. We photograph and film, seeking effects that are "superficial" by definition: it is not a question of a scientific film. Cinema is the specialty not of technicians, but of young aesthetes, fascinated by cultural or political revolution. Ingenious reproduction processes end up putting sensational photos in the hands of the public, and those photos act like hallucinatory drugs. The reign of technology does not result in a magical vision of nature, but indeed in a magical vision of society, or in an impressionistic vision, in other words, a very superficial vision of certain social "effects," in a state of unawareness of any infrastructure.

The (cerebral) consciousness of a living being is also superficial in relation to the infra-consciousness of organic machines.
However, it does not claim to constantly intervene in the life of
the body in accordance with its own ideas. As we know, when
it does intervene it creates neuroses and psychosomatic problems. Superficial consciousness of social life, combined with
ignorance of technological means, leads to analogous, ideo-
functional social problems. Superficial awareness does not
renounce the claim to know what it ignores. It compensates in
a single stroke for all its ignorance with pseudo-decoding,
pseudo-explanatory ideologies. Lovers of "socially committed"
films are no better informed about social mechanisms and crucial economic and government issues than they are about chemi-
cal optics. They are competent only with respect to the aesthetic
of images in the director's *final* cut. Yet they nonetheless aim to
remake all of society in reverse, in other words, based on what
can be learned from the final cut or aesthetic of images, and its
impressionistic manipulation.

The scientific technology of the media thus ends up having
fostered less the propagation of ideologies than their creation,
the creation of ideologies that are increasingly superficial, based
on aesthetic images.[13]

Like Ruyer's film buff, development-agency workers and consultants
are trying to remake a distant society in reverse, beginning with
what can be learned from the final system with which they are sur-
rounded, in other words, based on a representation of a superficial
aesthetic of what constitutes development informed by the superego
of modernization.

In the field of law and justice, since the superego of modernization requires that the social transformation has to be orchestrated to
generate growth and development toward mass consumption, this
produces a penchant for transaction security guaranteed by a deployment of technological innovation.

Given this penchant, the encounter of the development community, justice institutions, and information technologies is thus
structured essentially around the tastes, customs, and aesthetics of
the international investor. Moreover, that investor shares the same
features with those who work for international financial institutions
and their international consultants because they have all done the

same studies, often worked for the same bodies, spent time in the same business-class lounges in major international airports, and stayed in the same hotels, where the price is the same as that of the hotels in major Western cities.

It is thus not surprising that, in courthouses, hospitals, schools, and police stations, development entrepreneurs want to find, as in their hotel rooms in Luanda and Kuala Lumpur, the same external signs of modernization as at home, and sometimes better, since they are involved and, in order to keep their jobs, have to justify expenditures that produce measurable, and consequentially visible, development. Indeed, what could be better in the imagination of a justice-reform consultant than an entirely computerized postmodern courthouse that smashes the case-processing speed records of richer countries and is peopled by smiling stakeholders, confirming in opinion polls all their trust in the justice institutions and expressing their gratitude to the generous donors? In short, the equivalent, in the field of dispute resolution, of a four- or five-star hotel; in other words, a place that might just as well be located in Kansas City as in Jakarta or Bangui.

However, since development-assistance budgets, as impressive as they may be in absolute terms, unfortunately remain essentially well below the goal of 1% of GDP repeatedly promised by Western leaders, choices have to be made. For development consultants and officials, if it is not possible to have a high-tech crystal-palace courtroom managed in an orderly way according to Toyota "lean justice services" principles by alumni of McKinsey or the Boston Consulting Group, the next best solution is thus "showroom justice" equipped with external signs of technology. This may be embodied by a commercial arbitration and mediation centre, or by a state-of-the-art commercial tribunal created to provide international investors with the aesthetics of transaction security, while having the advantage of giving governments the peace of mind delivered by the Dantesque show of civil and criminal justice for the local people.

A variation leads to funding for computerized case-management systems, the massive, costly nature of which calls to mind the spirit of telematics inspired in France by the Minc/Nora report on the "computerization of society."[14] Like telematics, centralized, "massificating" computerization supported by development through case-management systems is sure to be a failed combination of digital technologies and justice, for which microprojects will be able to compensate only along the margins.

From Ideal to Achievement: The Reality of Cyberjustice Programs Funded by Development Assistance

In *L'Empire et les nouveaux barbares* (The Empire and the New Barbarians), published in 1991, Jean-Christophe Rufin provided a subtle analysis of the fundamentals of public development assistance based on quantitative assessment of the economy. Here is what he said about low-income countries, which were called at the time "the least developed countries" (LDCs):

> Today, the purpose of cooperation in the poorest countries is no longer development. It remains outside of political-economic processes and intervenes on two levels: the first, right on the bottom, is the microproject that tries, despite everything, to meet the country's needs and help the people. Apolitical, those running the microproject refuse to look higher and further. They act locally and in the present, coping with corruption. The other level, right at the top, is macroeconomic assistance, the form of aid that funds government programs either a priori (cooperation) or a posteriori, by cancelling or regularly re-arranging debt. [...] Cooperation is limited to introducing wealth so that the predatory mechanism operates without breaking down. In a way, it does this from both ends: at the local microproject level and at the overall government level.[15]

Let us illustrate these remarks as they pertain to cyberjustice using the case of Ivory Coast.

In October 2012, the Abidjan Commercial Court opened its doors in Ivory Coast. It had received financial support from both the World Bank and the government of Ivory Coast. After "decades of criticism from business people concerning the failures of the Ivory Coast justice system," its goal was "to reassure national and foreign economic players."[16]

In order to do things properly, the World Bank did not stint on means and funded a computerized management system inaugurated in the presence of the president of Ivory Coast in July 2014. Its purpose was to improve the court's efficiency while fostering transparency.[17]

At the same time, Ivory Coast's "technological and financial partners," among which figure in particular European Union and French and American cooperation agencies, were rushing to the bedsides of the common-law courts to fund their information systems based on a pilot project for developing business applications for criminal and civil-justice systems at the court of Yopougon.[18] The French cooperation project, implemented under a debt-reduction and development contract for which an agreement concerning payment of the second installment has just been signed, allocates €190 million to the justice sector over 20 years. A substantial portion of the money is to be used for computerizing the justice system.

To complete the picture, we need to consider the situation regarding preventive detention, considered one of the major problems affecting developing countries in particular.[19] Before Ivory Coast's 2010–2011 post-electoral crisis, the NGO Prisoners Without Borders (PWB) had developed, with very little funding, software that made it possible to enter the data on each prisoner on a simple computer supplied to detention centres so as to ensure rules of procedure were followed and to clearly and immediately identify all those whose term of preventive detention had come to an end. Every two weeks, a representative of the NGO collected the data using a USB key and took it to the public prosecutor and the investigating judge, if applicable. The program was reinstated by PWB with funding from the European Union after the post-electoral crisis in the form of a limited prison computerization project specifically targeting preventive detention.

This is a perfect illustration of what Rufin said about the vast ODA bureaucracies' strategic interest in communication concerning microprojects:

> Microprojects are on a human scale according to a formulation shared by Bernard Holzer, Chair of the *Comité contre la Faim et le développement*, and Plato, the Greek philosopher. The modesty of the action pleases everybody. Private organizations, with limited means, are rightly considered the inventors of microprojects. They are proud to have been joined in the field. Major international institutions see microprojects as remedies for dilution of their work, which causes their action to dissipate given the size and inertia of their bureaucratic mechanisms. The mountain gives birth to a mouse, but it is a visible mouse.[20]

Ivory Coast is far from the worst case since it has a strong economic fabric with the most commercial litigation in the region, along with better trained, more numerous technicians than in neighbouring countries.

However, donors tend to replicate the same sort of operation everywhere. For example, the World Bank is also funding the creation of a commercial court in Cotonou, Benin, even though there are no more than 500 commercial cases under the jurisdiction of the Court of First Instance of Cotonou.

Similarly, for more than ten years, Benin has been enjoying the assistance of technology teams funded by various sources, including the European Union and the Millennium Challenge Corporation.[21] However, here is the 2013 assessment by the program director and the forecast for the Ministry of Justice provided at a workshop on prediagnosis of computerizing the justice system:

> Thirteen years after the Estates General of Justice, and ten years after adoption of the PIRSJJ (*Programme Intégré de Renforcement des Systèmes Juridiques et Judiciaires* – comprehensive program to strengthen the legal and judicial systems), the anticipated direct and indirect effects of computerization on the efficiency, effectiveness and quality of services for users have not been achieved. Computerization of the system remains limited to implementation of business applications of which the jurisdictions make little use. It has not been possible to ensure interconnection of jurisdictions in a reliable, sustainable manner. Internet access is in the best cases at low speed and not universal. The intranet and electronic messaging have never really functioned. Networking and computerization of the Ministry of Justice, the public prosecutor's office, officers of the court, and stakeholders are non-existent.[22]

In comparison with Ivory Coast, the problem of preventive detention is even worse in Benin, where 74.9% of prisoners are estimated to be in preventive detention and cases of such detention can last up to 17 years.[23] Moreover, the conditions in which prisoners are kept are deplorable, with a very low number of guards per prisoner (6 for 397 in one Benin prison), not to mention the over-population in some institutions.[24] Prisoners Without Borders also operates in Benin, but is not undertaking any ICT projects there.

Moving away from microprojects, the instrumentality and communications uses of which we have highlighted, let us look at two of the most costly types of intervention: commercial-justice showrooms and computerized case-management systems.

There is at least one rational, eminently challengeable and cynical foundation for building "justice showrooms": to improve rankings in scales such as Doing Business in order to send signals to foreign investors.[25] This is all the more irresistible when funding agencies are willing to allocate resources to such reforms for the purpose of improving the business environment.

However, it is more difficult to justify the attractiveness of a major justice computerization project based on business-management systems when we know the tendency for such projects to fail in developed countries.

According to a 2012 McKinsey study, half of information and communications technology projects with budgets over $15 million spend 45% more than the estimated budget, 7% are late (33% in the case of application projects), and systems deliver 56% fewer functionalities than anticipated.[26] In 17% of cases, computer projects turn out so poorly that they end up endangering the undertaking's survival.

The number of projects that have turned out to be complete fiascos can no longer be counted. For example, there was the *Système intégré d'information de justice* (SIIJ) in the province of Québec, which was abandoned after an estimated CAN$75 million had been wasted, and the integrated justice system management project in California, whose estimated cost upon its design in 2004 was $260 million, but whose budget was revised in 2010 to $1.9 billion, according to the Auditor General of California.[27] Moreover, the system would have been obsolete as soon as it was implemented if it had not been abandoned in 2012, after having cost the jurisdictions and the Administrative Office of the Courts over $400 million.[28] This is not to mention the Cassiopée saga in France, with its over 40-month delay, the goal of which had been for no sector of the French government service to be spared the idiosyncrasies of a telematic computerization of society, flowing straight out of the imagination of the Inspector of Finances' office. We will also avoid thinking about the Phénix soap opera in Belgium, which was a grand-scale computerization program for the Belgian justice system launched in 2001 but abandoned in 2007, after spending three years in death throes and forcing the Belgian government to take legal action for an estimated €28 million in damages from the provider, Unisys.

As the above examples show, major justice computerization projects are especially perilous, even in OECD countries, because they require time, money, and good project governance, as well as steadfast support from the government, which is responsible for making and implementing a number of decisions crucial to the undertaking's success (internal and external development of chains of implementation, choices in terms of networks and related interconnections, choices of technology and application systems, computer stock renewal planning, governance structures in charge of developing and enforcing justice information system policy, amendment of legal infrastructure to integrate the use of Information and communications technology (ICT), etc.).

The main problem with major projects is that they are often seen by an organization as an opportunity to solve problems that the project is relatively poorly equipped to deal with, or that the project makes even more complex. For example, a body that is experiencing organization problems with respect to filing cases and documents certainly has fundamental organization problems. A transition to a "global virtual computerized infrastructure for work stations, servers, storage and establishment of a 'private cloud'"[29] requires much more complex organizational capacities for planning and management—and much greater means—than those required to file cases in a manner that makes it possible to extract what is necessary when needed.

Sometimes the rush to insert complex technology into institutional creations that are difficult to sell can endanger the creation of the institution, as was pointed out by *Financial Times* columnist Gary Silverman concerning the disastrous launch of the Affordable Health Care Act in the United States:

> The problem with Obamacare is that its creators couldn't resist putting the whole kit and caboodle online. It wasn't good enough to just do good; they had to do it with the latest bells and whistles.... The irony is that this tendency to opt for the highest tech solution to a problem is one reason we needed to reform the healthcare in the first place. We all know we spend too much on expensive drugs and invasive procedures – and pay too little attention to traditional remedies that might work just as well.[30]

Latin America, the site of the first experiments with justice computerization projects funded by development assistance, is, in this respect, according to available information, far from having achieved tangible results, as Linn Hammergren notes:

> Latin American courts also have a considerable amount of automation, some of them having invested substantial time and

national funds in introducing it. However, most of this automation has not been used to create improved databases, but rather for word processing of ordinary documents, e-filing and creation of "e-files" which are really only a collection of the traditional documents now scanned and uploaded, retrieval of information on case status by internet, and automated catalogues of archive holdings and/or bar-coding of files and documents. All of this is helpful, but represents bits and pieces of a reform, and in the absence of good data on case flow, it is not even possible to evaluate the impacts. In Brazil, even after nearly twenty years of automation, and the introduction of some state-of-the-art ICT, performance data and statistics remain rudimentary, limited to disposition rates calculated by comparing dispositions with filings for each year, and most courts either do not have or do not use the capacity to do finer analysis. While courts there and in most other countries speak of a goal of reducing delays, they rarely can calculate current average disposition times or the incidence of factors contributing to them. The stock of pending cases is frequently a black hole – no one knows how many cases are included, of what they are composed, how old they are or what tends to get left behind. The automated registries created by many court systems are composed largely of text entries making analysis difficult if not impossible. Cases going from one instance to another rarely retain the same case number making it difficult to track them. All of these omissions represent the most basic elements of any good case management system, but few countries seem prepared to adopt them or see any reason to do so. Instead there appears to be a blind faith in the power of more ICT to fix systemic problems, something which experience suggests is unlikely to happen, and which the very absence of data makes impossible to verify.[31]

Despite the known dangers, the development community's preference for major projects and justice showrooms stems from the objective-based management that characterizes development assistance, the result of which is that visibility and, let us not forget, frequency of spending, are sought more than utility. As William Easterly notes, objective-based management in the development industry produces the consequence that, when goals are defined ahead of time, development programs pursue some of them (those entailing long-term benefits for the communities concerned at low cost) weakly, while concentrating resources on those producing the least benefits at a high cost (the ones on which a lot can be spent in a short time and concerning which we can communicate results in the short term, in other words, activities transformed into proven results by tracking-assessment magicians wearing the hats of communication specialists).[32]

For funding bodies, major projects have the advantage of attracting attention when they are announced and ensuring strong media coverage of the expected benefits. They make it possible to give a visible impression of modernization and at the same time pave the way for programs with deep disbursements. Since they are supposedly apolitical, costly, complicated to implement, and thus mobilize major amounts of local and foreign expertise, computerized management systems are perfect for development project designers. All of this leads to overinvestment in what Barry Walsh has called the myths of cyberjustice projects.[33] These myths go from interconnection of tribunals through integrated systems[34] to e-filing as a means of accelerating procedures,[35] and indeed entirely computerized tribunals, which is the justice-system version of the paperless office.[36] These overinvestments are made to the detriment of what is really useful for rendering justice (e.g., compliance with procedures; decisions rendered in accordance with the law; knowledge of flows, case congestion and processing times per type of case; access to legislation and case law; etc.).

In contrast, it seems that no project has seriously considered allowing use of mobile phones for linking stakeholders and justice institutions in countries where postal systems are non-existent and people are difficult to reach by means traditionally used in legal systems in developed countries.[37]

The Limits of the Focus on Effectiveness Dictated by Modernization

Can funding of justice showrooms and/or tribunals equipped with computerized case-management systems be the foundation for policy designed to legitimize justice institutions in emerging countries?

We have to wonder about this given what can already be observed in developed countries, where it would be somewhat of a stretch to say that the creation of exceptional non-territorial justice for financial players and multinationals and the use of technology in public justice services have helped to strengthen the legitimacy of justice institutions.

In fact, ICT have been used instead by stakeholders to avoid the legal system at all cost and to evade the transaction expenses associated with justice professionals when resolving low-value legal problems and disputes.[38]

It is a different matter in developing countries, where low-value problems such as those addressed by way of online dispute resolution platforms are only peripheral and generally better resolved by community pressure than by law.[39] In contrast, issues that hardly ever go to court in developed countries, such as cases involving civil status, tend to absolutely require recourse to the justice system owing to the weakness of the government services in charge. This makes solutions complex, long, and essentially iniquitous.[40] Problems of relatively small importance in developed countries tend to become human tragedies, such as prison sentences for very minor offences[41] and police involvement in debt collection that puts the debtor in custody despite the fact that debtors' prisons have long been abolished.

When we look at these problems, we have to be suspicious of what the concentration of ODA means in computerized case management projects and justice showrooms for foreign investors.

In addition, justice, to a greater extent than other institutions, has had its own symbolic imagery since time immemorial. It is anchored in reality, which explains why the phony reforms by the development industry fail on the whole: their symbolic anchoring among the people is insufficient.

For example, if we refer to Dickens' description in *Bleak House* of a case set at the time of the first Industrial Revolution in England, we can only be skeptical about the belief of the development community that court networks operating according to the precepts of Taylor's "scientific management" and producing decisions in record times will effect the desired social transformation by creating the conditions of trust required for economic development.

> Jarndyce and Jarndyce drones on. This scarecrow of a suit has, in course of time, become so complicated that no man alive knows what it means. The parties to it understand it least, but it has been observed that no two Chancery lawyers can talk about it for five minutes without coming to a total disagreement as to

all the premises. Innumerable children have been born into the cause; innumerable young people have married into it; innumerable old people have died out of it. Scores of persons have deliriously found themselves made parties in Jarndyce and Jarndyce without knowing how or why; whole families have inherited legendary hatreds with the suit. The little plaintiff or defendant who was promised a new rocking-horse when Jarndyce and Jarndyce should be settled has grown up, possessed himself of a real horse, and trotted away into the other world. Fair wards of court have faded into mothers and grandmothers; a long procession of Chancellors has come in and gone out; the legion of bills in the suit have been transformed into mere bills of mortality; there are not three Jarndyces left upon the earth perhaps since old Tom Jarndyce in despair blew his brains out at a coffeehouse in Chancery Lane; but Jarndyce and Jarndyce still drags its dreary length before the court, perennially hopeless.

Jarndyce and Jarndyce has passed into a joke. That is the only good that has ever come of it. It has been death to many, but it is a joke in the profession. Every master in Chancery has had a reference out of it. Every Chancellor was "in it," for somebody or other, when he was counsel at the bar. Good things have been said about it by blue-nosed, bulbous-shoed old benchers in select port-wine committee after dinner in hall. Articled clerks have been in the habit of fleshing their legal wit upon it. The last Lord Chancellor handled it neatly, when, correcting Mr. Blowers, the eminent silk gown who said that such a thing might happen when the sky rained potatoes, he observed, "or when we get through Jarndyce and Jarndyce, Mr. Blowers"—a pleasantry that particularly tickled the maces, bags, and purses.[42]

Dickens' description of *Jarndyce v Jarndyce* at the time when England was indisputably the world's leading economic power and the great modern nation in Europe suffices to put to rest the idea that economic development depends on Taylorized justice. It illustrates the great confusion that bogs down the "development community" when it reduces the problems of justice institutions in developing countries to their effectiveness, when in reality what it needed is to make them common.

The point is in no way to maintain a kind of nostalgia for a form of justice resembling the Dantesque descriptions of Dickens or Balzac or to claim that justice rendered with greater speed is an objective that should not be pursued, but rather to point out that making institutions legitimate initially requires something other than effectiveness alone. Paraphrasing Antoine Garapon, we can say that as soon as justice has settled on effective delivery, it ceases being a common point of reference.[43] He says that a symbolic institution "is precisely one that introduces a rupture in space and time, and suspends reaction to take time for reflection." Justice institutions cannot claim to foster trust if they compromise on "the authority of speech over automation [...] the transcendence of discussion, the domination of law common to all parties, the inviolability of basic rights." These principles are poles apart from development economists' obsession with modelling, and it is clear that they are not the guiding forces behind the justice reforms funded out of ODA coffers.

Justice-reform experts' conceptually attractive image of irenic justice with surgical precision and clockwork timing is contrasted with a completely different image in the allegory by Giotto in the Arena Chapel in Padua, which made Proust think of "a Justice whose grayish and meanly regular face was the very same which, in Combray, characterized certain pretty, pious, and unfeeling bourgeois ladies I saw at Mass, some of whom had long since been enrolled in the reserve militia of Injustice."[44] According to Proust,

> the startling strangeness, the special beauty of these frescoes was due to the large place which the symbol occupied in them, and the fact that it was represented, not as a symbol, since the thought symbolized was not expressed, but as real, as actually experienced or physically handled, gave something more literal and more precise to the meaning of the work, something more concrete and more striking to the lesson it taught.[45]

The idea that justice institutions fixating on mere efficiency could be the foundation for mechanisms of social transformation through growth contradicts the symbolic reality expressed by Giotto. Certainly, the allegory of the virtue of justice evokes security, but as Judith Shklar points out, justice offers no commandments respecting social engineering. Shklar notes that in the allegory, there is nothing implying public or private wealth, or people actively engaged in political debates or cooperative projects.[46]

Insisting that the purpose of justice is universal and abstract, Shklar instead shifts attention to the contrary of impassible, distant justice: the vice of injustice, represented by Giotto on the opposite side of the fresco in the Arena Chapel by the features of a cruel, shifty bureaucrat, who is not however fleeing his function. According to Shklar, reducing passive injustice, in other words, political injustice resulting from public inaction, is much more the purview of the inventiveness of politics, so repugnant to development ideologues, than of Taylorized justice. By engaging in a politics of avoidance of the true problems of legitimacy facing justice institutions, by setting up justice showrooms for foreign investors, and by injecting millions into projects to computerize court case-management systems, has not the development community condemned itself to remaining in the same "reserve militia of Injustice" as the young ladies of Combray?

Notes

1   Dambisa Moyo, *L'aide fatale, les ravages d'une aide inutile et solutions pour l'Afrique* (Paris: JC Lattès, 2009); William Easterly, *The White Man's Burden: Why the West's Efforts to Aid the Rest Have Done So Much Ill and So Little Good* (London: Penguin Books, 2007); William Easterly, *Tyranny of Experts, Economists, Dictators and the Forgotten Rights of the Poor* (New York: Basic Books, 2014).

2   Gilbert Rist, *The History of Development from Western Origins to Global Faith,* translated by Patrick Camiller (London: Zed Books, 2009), at 1.

3   *Le Petit Robert,* 1987, *sub verbo* "development."

4   South Commission, *The Challenge to the South: The Report of the South Commission* (Oxford: Oxford University Press, 1990) at 10–11.

5   United Nations Development Programme, *World Human Development Report 1991* (Oxford: Oxford University Press, 1991) at 1.

6   Rist, *supra* note 2.

7   Ibid. at 10–11.

8   Ibid. at 11.

9   Ibid. at 12. [Translator's note: I could not access page 12, so I have paraphrased the quote. I have intentionally used words that are a little different from the French in the hope that my translation will be different from the official translation.]

10   Ibid. at 13.

11   Christopher Lasch, *The True and Only Heaven: Progress and its Critics* (New York: W. W. Norton & Company, 1991) at 189.

12   Hilton L Root, *Dynamics Among Nations* (Cambridge, MA: MIT Press, 2013) at 35. We could also refer to the following passage from Christopher Lasch, *supra* note 11 at 194: "The concept of modernization no longer dominates the study of economic development in the non-Western world; but the conceptually seductive images with which it is associated still color the West's view of its own history. It was the transformation of Western society by the industrial revolution that first gave rise to the concepts of tradition and modernity, and the habit of charting our course by these familiar landmarks lingers on. Critics have again and again exposed the inadequacies of the modernization model, even for an understanding of the West. It still stands, however—a deserted mansion, its paint peeling, its windows broken, its chimneys falling down, its sills rotting; a house fit only for spectral habitation but also occupied, from time to time, by squatters, transients, and fugitives."

13   Raymond Ruyer, *Les nuisances idéologiques* (Paris: Calmann-Lévy, 1972) at 234–35 [passage translated by author].

14   Alain Minc and Simon Nora, *L'informatisation de la société: Rapport à M le Président de la République* (Paris: Seuil, 1978) [passage translated by author].

15   Jean-Christophe Rufin, *L'Empire et les nouveaux barbares* (Paris: JC Lattès, 1991) at 125–27 [passage translated by author].

16   "Tribunal de commerce d'Abidjan, une juridiction qui redonne confiance," *Abidnan.net*, February 25, 2014, online: <news.abidjan. net/h/490104.html> [passage translated by author].

17   Mireille Kouakou, "Le Tribunal de Commerce d'Abidjan adopte la technologie pour plus de transparence," *RTI*, online: <www.rti.ci/ actualite-8825-le-tribunal-de-commerce-d-abidjan-adopte-la-technologie-pour-plus-de-transparence.html>.

18   See Agence Française de Développement, "Request for Proposal" (25 September 2013), online: <afd.dgmarket.com/tenders/np-notice. do?noticeId=9309670>.

19   Open Society Initiative, "Presumption of Guilt, the Global Overuse of Pretrial Detention, OSI" (September 2014), online: <www. opensocietyfoundations.org/publications/presumption-guilt-global-overuse-pretrial-detention>.

20   Rufin, *supra* note 15 at 123–24 [passage translated by author].

21   Benin's business applications were initially experimented with in a few jurisdictions before being used throughout the justice network. Then, following a new call for tenders and a change in the technical assistance provider, the second team recommended abandoning the system and developing a new one, which is in the pilot project phase.

22   "Pré-diagnostic de l'informatisation du MJLDH: pour instaurer une justice de qualité, crédible et accessible au justiciable," La Nouvelle

Tribune, April 5, 2013, online: <www.lanouvelletribune.info/index.php/societe/vie-societale/14091-pre-diagnostic-de-l-informatisation-du-mjldh-pour-instaurer-une-justice-de-qualite-credible-et-accessible-au-justiciable> [passage translated by author].

23 OSI, *supra* note 10 at 26.

24 Ibid. at 66.

25 In reality, everyone knows very well that security in an environment such as that of Benin depends more on good relations with the government and that recourse to a formal dispute resolution system is virtually impossible aside from commercial arbitration abroad or through an investment arbitration centre.

26 Michael Bloch, Sven Blumberg and Jürgen Laartz, "Delivering Large-Scale IT Projects on Time, on Budget and on Value," *McKinsey Quarterly* (2012), online: <www.mckinsey.com/business-functions/business-technology/our-insights/delivering-large-scale-it-projects-on-time-on-budget-and-on-value#o>.

27 California State Auditor, *"Administrative Office of the Courts, The Statewide Case Management Project Faces Significant Challenges Due to Poor Project Management,"* Report of the Auditor General of the State of California, Report 2010-102, February 2011, online: <www.bsa.ca.gov/pdfs/reports/2010-102.pdf>.

28 Ibid.

29 According to the wording in a digital court project announced in Morocco, *Le Matin*, online: <www.lematin.ma/journal/-/194036.html> [passage translated by author].

30 Gary Silverman, "Obamacare Woes Need a Paper Cure," *FT*, October 17, 2013, online: <www.ft.com/cms/s/0/f5963b14-35c8-11e3-952b-00144feab7de.html#axzz45doDOgBK>.

31 Linn Hammergren, "Judicial Governance and the Use of ICT," online: <www.iijusticia.org/docs/Linn.pdf>.

32 Easterly, *supra* note 1 at 255.

33 Barry Walsh, "E-Justice Projects – Distinguishing Myths from Realities," online: <www.iijusticia.org/docs/Barry.pdf>.

34 Regarding the above, Walsh notes that California, where all the courts had developed their own individual business management computer systems, ended up with 130 different types of software and 70 independent operating systems for a justice network of 58 counties and 2,100 judges. Moreover, between 1999 and 2009, the California justice systems managed to process 99% of the 10 million cases per year within 24 months and 86% of criminal cases within 12 months. However, the centralizing, massification ambition of the government's senior justice officers lead to a program that was abandoned after having spent more than $300 million. Ibid. at 2.

35   A number of projects focus on e-filing, which saves only a very small amount of time and requires heavy, costly solutions, as Barry Walsh explains. While such systems make it possible for stakeholders to avoid travel and to save small amounts of money, the benefits of e-filing systems are concentrated exclusively at the point when a claim is lodged or a request filed, and in no way concern the speed with which cases are processed. Ibid. at 3.

36   Many projects aim to make all files virtual (e-files), put case status online and use bar codes for files and documents. However, according to Walsh, digitalizing legal documents would essentially result in duplication, not substitution and digitalization, which is a heavy process and does not eliminate inaccuracies or ensure files are complete. Moreover, it requires equipping not only courthouses but also lawyers, and providing stakeholders with broad access to the same technologies. This condition is difficult to meet in low-income countries. Finally, digitalization of proceedings makes the service vulnerable to equipment breakdowns and power failures, which are especially frequent in developing countries. Ibid. at 10–11.

37   For example, on a radio show, Lionel Zinsou, a French-Benin businessman, said that in the year 2000 it was forecast that 100,000 people in Benin would have a mobile phone by 2014. Currently five million Beninese have such a device. See Lionel Zinsou, "Le développement économique de l'Afrique," podcast audio, July 6, 2014, online: <www.franceculture.fr/emission-l-esprit-public-le-developpement-economique-de-l-afrique-avec-lionel-zinsou-2014-07-06>.

38   Finding a model contract on a site like legalzoom without going through a lawyer, resolving a consumer dispute using the dispute resolution system of E-bay or Amazon; however, there are few applications aside from dispute resolution platforms for online transactions.

39   On this, see R. Beauchard, "La résolution en ligne des litiges, gage d'une justice de proximité en Afrique?," *Notes de l'IHEJ*, Institut des Hautes Études sur la Justice, June 2, 2013, online: <www.ihej.org/la-resolution-en-ligne-des-litiges-gage-dune-justice-de-proximite-en-afrique/>. Problems related to distance sales are only marginal and disputes are more often between members of a given community, which often regulates relations more effectively than the justice system, which is feared by all.

40   In many developing countries, especially in Africa, the registry of civil status is poorly kept, or inexistent. This opens the way to many abuses and problems for citizens, and recourse to state justice to solve problems is not uncommon. Here again worship of technology leads to an all-or-nothing choice: a computerized registry with biometric applications or nothing at all.

41   It is not unusual, in a country like Benin, to see a prosecutor call for a prison sentence for low-value theft (a box of soap, two chickens, etc.). In fact, such offenders are relatively lucky because more often than not, suspects fall into a hellish spiral leading from custody to provisional detention to oblivion and, finally, to the realization that detention has exceeded the maximum duration authorized without trial or compensation.

42   Charles Dickens, *Bleak House* (London: Phiz, serialized 1852–53).

43   Antoine Garapon, *La raison du moindre État* (Paris: Odile Jacob, 2010) at 79 [passage translated by author].

44   Marcel Proust, *Swann's Way: In Search of Lost Time*, translated by Lydia Davis (New York: Penguin Classics, 2002).

45   Ibid.

46   Judith N Shklar, *Faces of Injustice* (New Haven: Yale University Press, 1990) at 103 [Translator's note: I do not have access to the original English text, so I have removed the quotation marks and paraphrased it].

CHAPTER II

Evaluating e-Justice: The Design of an Assessment Framework for e-Justice Systems

Giampiero Lupo

Introduction

The studies on e-justice, that is Information Systems (IS) developed in justice systems, scarcely focus on the topic of their evaluation. Some scholars, such as Contini and Lanzara, and Kallinikos,[1] advocate adopting a set of design principles (such as system modularization) to ensure quality performance of e-justice systems (EJS).[2] However, measuring systems' performance has thus far been overlooked. Scholars have missed measuring a dependent variable because there is no evaluative framework through which to analyze EJS. Bernoider and Koch made some attempts at evaluating e-justice.[3] They analyze two Austrian e-justice systems (the Legal Information System (LIS) and the *Elektronischer Rechtsverkehr* (ERV), an e-filing system). These scholars evaluated the two systems' performance using the DeLone and McLean model.[4] However, the model was not designed specifically for e-justice evaluation, and so it does not consider that e-justice evaluation also needs to take into account the fact that justice systems in a democratic society should support specific values, such as equal access, transparency, respect of privacy, and impartiality. Therefore, IS used in the justice sector should also support these values. E-justice evaluation should be based on a model that integrates IS evaluation methodology with variables that measure the capacity of e-justice systems to support judicial values. In this respect, the DeLone and McLean model by itself is not entirely appropriate for grasping the complexity of e-justice assessment because its focus on efficacy as a measure of IS performance is too limited for the e-justice context.

The above arguments reflect the tenets of the Public Value School[5] and its criticism of the efficacy-oriented strategies of New Public Management[6] (NPM).[7] The Public Value School criticizes the NPM approach, stating that the evaluation of public-sector reforms should consider their effects on private economic exchanges and efficacy, as well as their support of collective preferences and values.[8] On these grounds, the evaluation paradigms of public reforms elaborated in the context of the Public Value School integrate managerial strategies of assessment, which focus on efficiency, with strategies of assessment that focus on public-values support.[9]

On this basis, this study proposes the design of an e-justice assessment framework that integrates efficacy-oriented variables with variables that focus on the judicial values that e-justice should support. In so doing, it fills a gap in the literature that, as anticipated, only focuses on efficacy-oriented variables when assessing e-justice systems.

The first part of the study introduces the main methodologies used for IS assessment that are a part of the IS and e-government approaches (see Measuring IS Performances below) and explores the DeLone and McLean model, which is the basis for the e-justice assessment framework. The second part discusses judicial values that justice systems and e-justice systems should support. Each value is analyzed based on the literature and is transposed to the e-justice context (see Justice Systems Values and e-Justice, page 57).

In the final part, the paper addresses the assessment framework, integrating the DeLone and McLean model variables with a set of variables that operationalize e-justice's capacity to support judicial values (see A New Framework for e-Justice Evaluation, page 61). Here, I introduce each variable's relative indicators and proposed operationalization. The methodology consists in both quantitative and qualitative methods of analysis.

Measuring IS Performances

With the aim of designing an e-justice assessment framework, I explored the main contributions on assessment in the IS literature.[10]

Additionally, the study also deals with the e-government school[11] and its approach to evaluation.

The literature on IS evaluation proposes different models[12] for system assessment.[13] These models focus on several aspects of IS performance. Some authors deal mainly with *system quality*, which refers to the efficient functioning of the IS, its flexibility, reliability, and ease of use.[14] Others take into account *use ratio* and *user satisfaction* as reliable measures of IS performance.[15] Moreover, other contributions focused on *information quality*, which regards the quality, accuracy, timeliness, and reliability of information that the system conveys.[16]

In 1993, DeLone and McLean proposed to integrate the different IS evaluation approaches into a unique, multidimensional model that combined the variables on which previous studies focused separately. The DeLone and McLean model of 1993, and their revised 2003 model, became one of the "most popular" tools for IS evaluation.[17]

The e-government literature also deals with IS evaluation, with a special focus on systems developed in public institutions. Several e-government assessment frameworks address different aspects of e-government evaluation. On this basis, they can be divided into hard and soft approaches.[18] The "hard" frameworks[19] usually assess tangible risks and benefits and focus on variables such as return on investment, cost/benefit, payback period, and benchmarking (the evaluation of performances against best practices). The "soft" frameworks usually assess intangible risks and benefits, with a focus on the organizational, social, political, or cultural impact of the system,[20] and comprise citizen-centric approaches (impact of digitalization on the quality of service delivered to citizens), trust in e-government systems and citizens' technological acceptance.[21] The analysis of the e-government approaches acknowledged that they mainly assess a single aspect regarding the evaluation of IS that is included as a dimension in the DeLone and McLean model: net benefits (see page 57). However, as the IS literature acknowledges, many other aspects should be taken into account when evaluating information systems. The capacity of the DeLone and McLean model to grasp several aspects of IS performance inspired me to use the same variables to assess the "efficacy-oriented" performance of an e-justice system.

The DeLone and McLean Model and Successive Amendments

DeLone and McLean developed their evaluative framework in 1992. The model's design was based on the multidimensional and interdependent nature of IS performance. Their methodology consisted of reviewing a large number of studies that dealt with IS evaluation. The scholars classified several models and measures of IS performance by relying on the contributions of Mason's (1978) information-influence theory and on Shannon and Weaver's (1949) communication theory. Following these two approaches, DeLone and McLean (1992: 61) acknowledged that IS assessment can focus on three levels: first, the *technical level,* which refers to the quality and efficiency of the system; second, the *semantic level,* which refers to the IS capacity for delivering the right information; and third, the *effectiveness level,* which refers to the IS influence on its users. These levels represent stages of information flow: production, communication, and, finally, effects on recipients.

At each level, the DeLone and McLean model examines different aspects of IS performance. At the technical level, the focus is on *system quality* and on the *quality of the information* provided. At the semantic level, the model focuses on *usage* and *user satisfaction* in relation to the system. At the effectiveness level, the model deals with the impact of IS on *individual activity* and *organizational functioning.*[22] These variables derive from the DeLone and McLean analysis of previous IS assessment frameworks.

The result is a multidimensional model using six variables[23] that measure IS performance: (1) System Quality, (2) Information Quality, (3) System Use, (4) User Satisfaction, (5) Individual Impact, and (6) Organizational Benefits. The six dimensions of the DeLone and Mclean model will be included in the e-justice evaluation framework and therefore described later when presenting the framework's variables.

In 2003, DeLone and McLean redesigned the framework by reviewing more than a hundred articles, "including all the articles in *Information Systems Research, Journal of Management Information Systems,* and *MIS Quarterly*" that applied the model since 1993.[24] The objective of this update was to verify the hypothesized interdependencies between the model's dimensions (by analyzing the empirical studies that focused on the dimensions' relationships), and to reduce the possibility of replicating the same measure, thus enhancing the overall parsimony of the evaluation framework. The two authors proposed to include *individual benefit* and *organizational benefit* dimensions in a unique component, called *net benefits,* that takes into account the effects of IS introduction at both the individual and the organizational level. *Net benefits* indicate the balance between the positive and the negative impacts of the introduction of an information system for the organization and for individuals.

Moreover, taking into account the fact that information systems are not only information providers but also usually deliver some kind of service, the authors also included *service quality* among the variables that relate to the effectiveness level of the model. Scholars have operationalized *service quality* by focusing on the reliability of the service provided, or on the courtesy of personnel (with a focus on staff that interacts with the system and provides a service to external users).[25] Given that e-justice systems cannot be considered as stand-alone technological artefacts but have to be seen as assemblages of technology, procedures, and individual and organizational functions and activities,[26] *service quality* has to be included as a dimension in my model.

The starting point for the design of an e-justice assessment framework is DeLone and McLean's 2003 redesigned model. Each dimension was investigated to evaluate its adaptation to the e-justice context. The six dimensions were translated into variables that measure the efficacy-oriented performance of an e-justice system. This consisted of selecting the most widely used indicators for each dimension/variable (therefore, those on which some consensus exists in the literature), adapting them to the e-justice context, and adding new indicators where necessary and opportune.

Justice Systems Values and e-Justice

As mentioned, in order to integrate the DeLone and McLean model and to adapt it to the e-justice context, this study considers typical values that justice systems should uphold. The analysis of the literature on the topic of fundamental justice values resulted in the identification of seven values to be taken into account for the design of an e-justice evaluation framework: (1) Independence, (2) Accountability, (3) Impartiality, (4) Equal Access, (5) Transparency, (6) Privacy, and (7) Legal Validity.

The first value mentioned is *judicial independence*. Many scholars address judicial independence and its relationship with other values, such as the accountability and impartiality of judges.[27] The concept mainly refers to the insulation of courts and judges from outside pressures, in particular from the executive and legislative branches.[28]

As a result, judges should be protected from unjustified dismissal, transfer, and non-renewal of office.[29]

The framework described here takes *independence* into account. The evaluation should assess whether an e-justice system negatively affects judicial and court independence. The independence variable relates to evaluating specific types of systems and, in particular, case-management systems and electronic legal work desk, which support judges' day-to-day activities.

One example of an EJS that may affect judicial and court independence relates to systems that automate the allocation of cases, such as personnel-and-resource management systems.[30] The mechanism of case allocation should guarantee that a case is not entrusted to judges "who have or appear to have an interest in the case, or who may appear prejudiced."[31] A potential incorrect functioning of the systems used to automate the mechanisms of case allocation may affect judicial and court independence.

A second example relates to e-justice systems that support judges' sentencing operations. Judges often decide routine cases supported by sentencing guidelines.[32] Software for sentencing guidelines[33] may affect judges' capacity to decide cases independently since only selected guidelines are stored in the database and the retrieval functionalities may malfunction.

Another issue related to this topic is the externalization of functions, activities, and software design to private companies (outsourcing). Outsourcing activities related to implementing and maintaining ICT is widespread,[34] and involving external actors may hinder the independent functioning of an e-justice system. Where exclusive relationships between private suppliers and the ministry of justice are established, the dependency on external actors should be greater. In this case, evaluating e-justice independence may focus on the types of contracts between public institutions and the private company (if they are exclusive/bilateral, or if they favour competition between companies in order to select the best service at the best price), and on the reliability of the company involved.

The second value, *accountability*, refers to the mechanism by which courts and judicial activities are assessed in terms of respecting rule-of-law values and efficiency.[35] More specifically, accountability means that judges should be responsible for their conduct before the public and before legal and political institutions that counterbalance judicial power.[36] Judges' and courts' actions have to be accountable in terms of legal validity, equality, and impartiality.[37] The spread of NPM ideas since the 1990s, and the justice-systems reforms that they brought about, contributed to extend the concept of accountability to the monitoring of judicial institutions' efficacy (managerial accountability).[38] The mechanisms that guarantee judicial accountability may consist of formal processes, such as annual court report publication, judicial appointment scrutiny and appealable judgments. Civil society, specifically the media, can also guarantee judicial accountability by reporting on trials.[39] Due to the potential conflict between accountability and judicial independence, the relationship between the two values is broadly debated.[40]

The evaluation of e-justice systems in terms of accountability should focus on two main aspects: first, the system's capacity to improve judicial and court accountability; and second, the evaluation of the EJS's own "accountability" level. The former aspect refers to the possibility that e-justice systems can provide information on court and judicial activities. EJS can provide information on court and judicial efficiency, and on whether sentences comply with norms. EJS can monitor and store information on cases filed and on the average time to process a case, through systems such as case-management systems, electronic legal work desk, court records, and electronic data.

The evaluation framework should also consider EJS accountability and whether they should be limited by control mechanisms and procedures with which they must comply. For instance, an accountable service will likely undergo periodic checks and controls by the institution that hosts it (internal) and by external governmental bodies (such as the ministry of justice).

A third value quoted in the literature and related to independence is *impartiality*.[41] Impartiality refers to the absence of prejudice, preconceived ideas, or outside pressures on the judicial decision-making process.[42] Impartiality also refers to a specific case at hand, which narrows the scope from the more general value of independence. It means that the judge is not biased in favour of either party.[43]

Impartiality should be taken into account when evaluating particular types of EJS that support judges' adjudication of cases and that may affect their impartiality. I refer in particular to electronic work desk[44] systems that enable the retrieval of case law and give the judge access to laws that are related to the case.[45]

Equal access to the justice system is another fundamental value in liberal democratic countries, highlighted by international organizations such as the Council of Europe and the United Nations.[46] According to this principle, justice systems should not prevent access to justice on the basis of gender, sexual orientation, geographic location, socioeconomic status, religion, right of representation, or disabilities, for example.[47] Access to courts is a right enshrined in the European Convention on Human Rights (Article 6, ECHR).[48] Moreover, Article 8 of the Universal Declaration of Human Rights states that "Everyone has the right to an effective remedy by the competent national tribunals for acts violating the fundamental rights granted him by the constitution or by law."

Similarly, equal access is also important for e-justice systems. In this context, some users could be marginalized because of their level of technological literacy. The assessment of e-justice systems should take into consideration whether the system is accessible to those that have limited technological literacy. Another issue related to equal access is the capacity of e-justice systems to reduce the costs of the service for users in comparison with paper-based procedures.

Transparency concerns disseminating information on justice procedures, rights, and norms to the parties and the public.[49] Transparency also encompasses the accessibility of information on norms and procedure, which may be limited due to complex legal jargon.[50] Information can be disseminated through several channels, such as public hearings, the media, reports, use of information, and communication technologies.

E-justice systems are powerful tools that may affect transparency. Those systems dedicated to external users, provide information on procedures, norms, and rights. Additionally, transparency refers to access to information that users need in order to use the digital procedure. For example, digital procedures and the procedural rules that govern them should be clearly explained and known by users.

Transparency is directly linked to the next value analyzed in this section: privacy. The two values refer to divergent preferences and are sometimes in contrast.

Privacy refers to the protection of citizens' personal information when they are involved in civil or criminal cases. Privacy breaches are caused by identity theft, risk to personal safety, re-victimization, distress, and fraud. For Sherman,[51] access to judicial information should be balanced with the protection of personal rights.[52]

Privacy issues in EJS are important and may conflict with transparency. There are many opportunities for information systems to analyze data from different databases, including sensitive personal data of a judicial nature. For instance, on the one hand, an internet-based e-justice system used for communication between users and the IS, or between different IS, improves the accessibility of the system and probably its transparency. On the other hand, it may give rise to security problems and privacy breaches (for a more in-depth analysis of this aspect, see Hanseth and Lyytinen[53]).

The last value taken into account is *legal validity*, which refers to the fact that the activities of courts, lawyers, and judges must conform to norms and procedures. All judicial operations, from the allocation of cases to civil and criminal trials, must comply with valid law.[54] Moreover, judges should adjudicate cases and apply written laws to the matters over which they have jurisdiction.[55] Adherence to laws and procedure is fundamental to the stability of a liberal democracy,[56] and it is the basis for the legal system's public legitimacy.

Regarding e-justice evaluation, the means by which procedural digitalization binds user operation and facilitates the respect of norms should be taken into account. Technology may be ingrained in users' courses of action.[57] In the case of e-justice systems, it may imbue actions such that they adhere to norms. For instance, e-filing systems that support legal validity should not allow access for users who falsify their identity (security of the accounting system). The evaluation of EJS's legal validity should also include the perceived consistency between the designed digital procedure and formal procedural rules. It should consider whether users perceive the system as legally valid. If they do not view it as valid, this may negatively affect the service, reduce its dissemination among users, or raise the possibility that the legality of judicial data exchanged through the system is not recognized.

In the next sections, I expand on the e-justice assessment framework. The framework includes values that are conceptualized and adapted to the e-justice context, and it is operationalized through qualitative and quantitative methods of analysis.

A New Framework for e-Justice Evaluation

The e-justice evaluative framework proposed here includes a set of variables that focus on efficacy and a set of variables that assess the system's capacity to support judicial values. In their paper, DeLone and McLean introduced numerous indicators for efficacy-oriented variables utilized by scholars. In order to enable the measurability of our indicators, and to design a parsimonious model, I listed a set of indicators selected from the literature for each efficacy-oriented variable on the basis of two parameters: first, the availability of data, and second, the consensus among scholars on the use of the indicator. Additionally, my e-justice evaluative framework includes a set of variables related to justice values. In the following pages, I suggest a set of indicators that can be used to operationalize variables related to justice system values. These were designed on the basis of the literature introduced in the previous part.

My e-justice evaluative framework includes eleven components: (1) System Quality, (2) Transparency of Information, (3) Service Quality, (4) Use, (5) Organizational and Individual Benefit, (6) Independence, (7) Accountability, (8) Impartiality, (9) Equal Access, (10) Privacy, and (11) Legal Validity.

In the following pages, I deal with the operationalization of efficacy-oriented variables (see below) and "judicial values" variables (see page 78). Each section describes framework variables and proposes a set of indicators. It is worth repeating that the framework described in the following section is a generic model for e-justice evaluation. Its application needs to be adapted to the specific EJS under review. Hence, the sections that follow describe how to adapt the model to specific systems by indicating, for each type[58] of EJS, which variable and associated indicators should be included in the analysis.

The methodology for measuring variables and relative indicators is mixed. It consists of a users' survey and quantitative and qualitative analyses.

Variables, Indicators and Measures: The Efficacy-Oriented Variables

The EJS assessment framework includes six efficacy-oriented variables derived from the 2003 DeLone and McLean model: (1) System quality, (2) Transparency of information, (3) Service quality, (4) Use, (5) User satisfaction, and (6) Net benefit.

System Quality deals with effective system functionality, reliability, and accessibility. It could be operationalized with a focus on six indicators: (1) Accessibility, (2) Flexibility, (3) Reliability, (4) Response Time, (5) Usefulness, and (6) Interoperability (the operationalization of each system quality indicator are listed in Table 1). These can be used to analyze any type of system (from case-management systems to videoconferencing).

Accessibility refers to the simplicity of system use. Users' technological literacy may interfere with this variable. In order to overcome this barrier, the evaluator has to consider users' technological literacy when measuring accessibility. The indicator may be operationalized through a user survey that asks respondents to evaluate, on a scale of 0 to 7, the ease of use of the system or the ease of learning to use the system. Finally, respondents may be asked how many times they encountered technical issues when using the system (question A.1.3 in Table 1).

Flexibility refers to how the system adapts to new circumstances, conditions, and demands. This can be evaluated through a qualitative analysis (participatory observation). The qualitative analysis should assess the system's capacity to be adapted to new circumstances, conditions, and use-case domains (see the e-Barreau case in France, created for first-instance courts and then transferred to the courts of appeal[59]). The evaluator should also take into account whether the software supporting the system is open source. If so, the system should be more adaptable to new demands. Accordingly, I suggest operationalizing this indicator with three qualitative research questions (see Table 1). The evaluator should assign a 0 to 7 score for each question listed in Table 1 (indicators A.2.1, A.2.2, and A.2.3). The assessment may consist in summing up the scores and calculating the average value of flexibility on a 0 to 7 scale.

Reliability refers to its capacity to consistently perform required functions on demand and without failures.[60] Reliability can be measured with questionnaires administered to users and technicians. The questionnaire may ask about a number of technical issues that arise during operations, while the survey may ask how often the system has failed to run (see Table 1, questions A.3.1, A.3.2, and A.3.3).

Timeliness refers to the length of time a system takes to respond to instructions or to complete a task. This can be measured using a user survey question and a quantitative analysis of the system. The user survey may ask respondents to provide the average time to complete the digital procedure and to complete the paper-based procedure. The evaluator then calculates the ratio of time necessary to complete operations to the time required to do so following the paper-based procedure. Moreover, the evaluator may count the number of operations eliminated with the digitalization of the paper-based procedure.

Usefulness of the system refers to both its problem-solving capabilities and how useful it is to various actors. Usefulness may be operationalized through a user survey asking respondents how useful they consider the system to be in carrying out specific juridical operations (see question A.5.1 in Table 1). Moreover, the indicator's measurement can be integrated through a quantitative analysis that focuses on the number of operations that can be carried out through the system and on the number of its functionalities (question A.5.2). Also, the number of diverse user typologies (citizens, court staff, judges) can be used as a "usefulness" measure (question A.5.3).

Table 1: A – System Quality

Indicator	Authors Who Used the Indicator	Operational-ization	Method of Measurement	EJS (to which measurement is applicable)
A.1 – Accessibility	Bailey and Pearson (1983), Srinivasan (1985), Elezadi-Amoli and Earhoomand 1996, Goodhue (1995), Seddon and Kiew (1994), Teo and Wong (1998), Wixom and Watson (2001).	**A.1.1** Ease of use per operation (0–7 scale). **A.1.2** Ease of learning (0–7 scale). **A.1.3** Technical issues arising during operations.	User survey	Case Management Systems Electronic Legal Work Desk Court Record Electronic Data Interchange Video and Audio Conferencing
A.2 – Flexibility	Bailey and Pearson (1983), Mahmood (1987), Elezadi-Amoli and Earhoomand (1996), Goodhue (1995), Seddon and Kiew (1994), Teo and Wong (1998), Wixom and Watson (2001).	**A.2.1** Capacity of the information system to change or to adjust in response to new conditions. **A.2.2** Capacity of the information system to adapt to different use case domain.	Qualitative analysis Participatory observation	

Table 1: (Continued)

Indicator	Authors Who Used the Indicator	Operational-ization	Method of Measurement	EJS (to which measurement is applicable)
		A.2.3 Use of open-source software. Evaluator should assign a 0 to 7 value to each question and finally calculate the average value of flexibility (0 no flexibility – 7 maximum flexibility).		
A.3 – Reliability	Belardo, Karwan, and Wallace (1982); Srinivasan (1985).	**A.3.1** Technical issues arise during operations (0–7 scale). **A.3.2** System up and running whenever user wants. **A.3.3** Number of breakdowns/failure of the system registered in one month.	Technicians' user survey	
A.4 – Timeliness	Bailey and Pearson (1983), Belardo, Karwan, and Wallace (1982), Conklin, Gotterer, and Rickman (1982), Srinivasan (1985).	**A.4.1** Ratio of time to complete operations to time to complete operation with paper based procedure. For each single task.	User survey	
		A.4.2 Number of operations eliminated with digitalization of standard procedure.	Quantitative analysis	

Table 1: (Continued)

Indicator	Authors Who Used the Indicator	Operational-ization	Method of Measurement	EJS (to which measurement is applicable)
A.5 – Usefulness	Franz and Robey (1986), Goslar (1986), Hiltz and Turoff (1981).	**A.5.1** Usefulness in problem solving (0–7 scale).	User survey	
		A.5.2 Number of operations/ functions. **A.5.3** Number of diverse typologies of users.	Quantitative analysis	
A.6 – Interoper-ability	Sherman (2013)	**A.6.1** Non-redundancy of data inputted (dichotomous).	User survey	
		A.6.2 Functional connection with other systems (how many operations can be pursued – cumulative of entire infrastructure).	Quantitative analysis	

Note: System-quality variable operationalization, plus authors who used the relative indicators. Each question that operationalizes an indicator is marked with a reference code (e.g., A.1.1) that indicates the referring variable (A), the indicator (1), and the measurement (1).

Interoperability regards the capacity of the e-justice system to connect with other IS. Evaluating interoperability may focus on the non-redundant operations requested by the system for users (for instance if users' data are imputed only once and reused in each system's operations; user survey question, A.6.1). Moreover, the evaluation should count the number of operations that can be pursued by the entire infrastructure constituted by the system being analyzed, and by the other systems potentially connected to it.

The *transparency of information* variable refers to the information the e-justice system provides. In particular, it refers to information about system functioning, the procedural norms regulating the system, and the availability of documents that provide this information.

This variable is adapted from DeLone and McLean's variable "Information Quality," which refers to the quality of information that the system provides. Transparency may be measured by four indicators: (1) information completeness, (2) information reliability, (3) information timeliness, and (4) information accessibility (the operationalization and consequential method of measurement for each indicator of information transparency are listed in Table 2). These indicators may be used for any type of EJS.

Completeness of information may be measured by asking users whether the information provided for using the system is complete[61] or incomplete.[62] The evaluation may be integrated with a quantitative analysis that checks the number of FAQs (frequently asked questions) covered. A qualitative analysis should assess the completeness of the explanatory documents using a 0 to 7 scale (measure B.1.4 in Table 2).

Reliability of information can be measured by asking users if the information provided by the system is correct (B.2.1). Additionally, a qualitative analysis may verify if the information provided on the digital procedure corresponds to the actual functioning of the system (the evaluator may use a 0 to 2 scale: where "0" means no correspondence; "1" some mistakes are present; and "2" correspondence of information; see Table 2).

Table 2: B – Transparency of Information

Indicator	Authors Who Used the Indicator	Operational-ization	Method of Measurement	EJS (to which measurement is applicable)
B.1 – Completeness	Bailey and Pearson (1983), King and Epstein (1983), Miller and Doyle (1987), Etezadi-Amoli, Farhoomand (1996), Seddon and Kiev (1994), Teo and Wond, (1998).	**B.1.1** Completeness of the information provided to use the system (0–7 scale). **B.1.2** Information missing.	User survey	Case Management Systems Electronic Legal Work Desk Court Record Electronic Data Interchange Video and Audio Conferencing

Table 2: (Continued)

Indicator	Authors Who Used the Indicator	Operational-ization	Method of Measurement	EJS (to which measurement is applicable)
		B.1.3 Presence of FAQs (number of FAQs covered).	Quantitative analysis	
		B.1.4 Completeness of explanatory documents. Result placed in a 0–7 scale (0: incomplete; 7 complete).	Qualitative analysis Participatory observation	
B.2 – Reliability	Bailey and Pearson (1983), King and Epstein (1983), Miller and Doyle (1987), Srinivasan (1985).	B.2.1 Correctness of information provided (0–7 scale).	User survey	
		B.2.2 Correspondence of information with actual functioning. Evaluator uses a 0–2 scale (0, no correspondence; 1, some mistakes are present; 2, correspondent).	Qualitative analysis Participatory observation	
B.3 – Timeliness of Information	Bailey and Pearson (1983), King and Epstein (1983), Miller and Doyle (1987). Etezadi-Amoli, Farhoomand (1996), Seddon and Kiev (1994), Teo and Wond, (1998).	B.3.1 Information rapidly updated. Evaluator uses a 0–2 scale (0, never updated; 1, rarely updated (from once per year to more than once per year); 2, constantly updated (more than once per year).	Qualitative analysis Participatory observation	

Table 2: (Continued)

Indicator	Authors Who Used the Indicator	Operational- ization	Method of Measurement	EJS (to which measurement is applicable)
B.4 – *Accessibility of Information*	Srinivasan (1985), King and Epstein (1983).	**B.4.1** Comprehensi- bility of infor- mation (0–7 scale). **B.4.2** Difficulties in using the sys- tem due to incomprehensi- ble information (0–7 scale).	User Survey	
		B.4.3 Number of help desk inter- ventions. **B.4.4** Number of norms that discipline the system.	Quantitative analysis	

Note: Transparency-of-information indicators operationalization, plus authors who used the indicators. Each question that operationalizes an indicator is marked with a reference code (e.g., B.1.1) that indicates the referring variable (B), the indicator (1), and the measurement (1).

The timeliness of the information may be assessed by verifying if the information on the system is updated regularly or if it is out-dated[63] (see Table 2 for methods of measurement).

Finally, *accessibility of information* may be measured through survey questions that ask the user if the information provided is understandable and if they encountered difficulties using the system due to incomprehensible information. A quantitative analysis may focus on checking the number of help-desk interventions in a given time span. Finally, the assessment may count the procedural norms that frame the system,[64] since having a lower number of norms facili-tates EJS accessibility.

Service quality refers to the quality and reliability of the service provided. Service quality may be operationalized through three indicators: (1) reliability of service, (2) competent personnel, and (3) overall service quality (see Table 3). These indicators, and their relative sub-indicators, should be taken into account in evaluating all types of EJS, with the exception of systems that are not supported by back-office operations.

Assessing *reliability of service* may consist in asking users if the service associated with the EJS has been provided in time and on demand (referring, for instance, to the involvement of a help desk; see questions C.1.1 and C.1.2 in Table 3). A qualitative analysis may integrate this information by checking the availability of online support, a telephone help desk, or front offices for user assistance. The evaluator may count the number of support services that are available.

Competent personnel may be operationalized through four user survey questions that ask if the user considers the help-desk staff (or the personnel that interacts with the IS in order to provide its services) kind, experienced, competent, and available (questions C.2.1, C.2.2, C.2.3, and C.2.4 in Table 3).

Overall service quality may be evaluated with a user survey question that asks users if they are satisfied with the service provided by the help desk/online support, positioning the answer on a 0 to 7 Likert scale.

Table 3: C – Service Quality

Indicator	Authors Who Used the Indicator	Operational-ization	Method of Measurement	EJS (to which measurement is applicable)
C.1 – *Reliability of Service*	Leyland, Watson and Kavan (1995), Kettinger and Lee (1995), DeLone and McLean (2003).	C.1.1 Service provided in time (0–7 scale). C.1.2 Service provided on demand (0–7 scale).	User survey	Case Management Systems Electronic Legal Work Desk
		C.1.3 Presence of online support, help desk, front office. Calculate number of supports.	Quantitative analysis Participatory observation	Court Record Electronic Data Interchange Video and Audio Conferencing
C.2 – *Competent Personnel*	Leyland, Watson and Kavan (1995), Kettinger and Lee (1995), DeLone and McLean (2003).	C.2.1 Help desk staff kind (0–7 scale). C.2.2 Help desk available (0–7 scale).	Users survey	

Table 3: (Continued)

Indicator	Authors Who Used the Indicator	Operational-ization	Method of Measurement	EJS (to which measurement is applicable)
		C.2.3 Help desk capable (0–7 scale). **C.2.4** Help desk experienced (0–7 scale).		
C.3 – *Overall Service Quality*	Leyland, Watson and Kavan (1995), Kettinger and Lee (1995), DeLone and McLean (2003).	**C.3.1** General rate of the service provided by help desk/ online support (0–7 scale).	Users survey	

Note: Service-quality indicators operationalization, plus authors who used the indicators. Each question that operationalizes an indicator is marked with a reference code (e.g., C.1.1) that indicates the referring variable (C), the indicator (1), and the measurement (1).

Use and *User satisfaction* (see Table 4) are two of the most widely used indicators of IS performance. For this reason, they are also used as proxies of performance in several studies.[65] As we will see, the indicator of use cannot be applied to all types of systems.

Use can be measured through quantitative analysis focusing on the number of accesses to the IS or by calculating the ratio of the percentage of system use to the use of the traditional procedure. This can only be included in the system assessment if system use is optional. Therefore, the indicator should be omitted when analyzing court-to-court systems such as case-management systems, the use of which is compulsory. *User satisfaction* can be evaluated by asking users to rate their satisfaction with the EJS. User satisfaction level may also be assessed in comparison to the paper-based procedure. In both cases, respondents may position their answer on a 0 to 7 scale (where "0" indicates no satisfaction and "7" maximum satisfaction; see Table 4).

Organizational and individual benefits refers to the impact IS has when it is introduced into individual and organizational performances.

Table 4: D – Use and User Satisfaction

Indicator	Authors Who Used the Indicator	Operational-ization	Method of Measurement	EJS (to which measurement is applicable)
D.1 – Use	Authors quoted in DeLone and McLean (1992, p. 70) and DeLone and McLean (2002, p. 16).	**D.1.1** Number of access to the IS. **D.1.2** Ratio of percentage of use to the use of the paper-based procedure.	Quantitative analysis	Electronic Legal Work Desk Court Record Electronic Data Interchange *(only when use is facultative)*
D.3 – User Satisfaction	Authors quoted in DeLone and McLean (1992, p. 70) and DeLone and McLean (2002, p. 16).	**D.3.1** Satisfaction for IS (0–7 scale). **D.3.2** Satisfaction in comparison with paper-based procedure (0–7 scale).	User survey	Case Management Systems. Electronic Legal Work Desk Court Record Electronic Data Interchange Video and Audio Conferencing.

Note: Use and user-satisfaction indicators operationalization, plus authors who used the indicators. Each question that operationalizes an indicator is marked with a reference code (e.g., D.1.1) that indicates the referring variable (D), the indicator (1), and the measurement (1).

Individual benefits may refer to a change in individual productivity or in the way new IS impact operations performance. In order to evaluate individual benefit, I suggest focusing on three indicators: (1) time to complete the procedure, (2) efficiency of information flow, and (3) cost savings (for the user). As Table 5 shows, some of these indicators can be used only for the evaluation of specific typologies of EJS. In particular, "cost savings for users" refers only to those systems dedicated to external users that have to pay a fee to receive a service, as is the case for the electronic data interchange (and in particular for e-filing systems).[66]

Time to complete the procedure refers to time-saving benefits that the digitalization of procedure may entail. A user survey can measure this indicator by evaluating how much time it takes for the user to complete the digital procedure and how much to complete the relative paper-based procedure. Then the evaluator should calculate the ratio of time needed to complete the digital procedure to the time needed to complete the paper-based procedure (question E.1.1 in Table 5). Videoconferencing systems may be excluded from this measurement as they and the paper-based procedure are not comparable.

For court-to-court systems, such as case-management systems, this indicator can be measured through quantitative analysis. The analysis can, for example, calculate the ratio of the number of procedures completed in one week to the number of comparable paper-based procedures completed in one week, by one clerk.

An operationalization of the *time to complete the procedure* indicator may be applied to videoconferencing systems. A quantitative analysis may calculate the average amount of time saved by avoiding witness travel thanks to the use of the system (question E.1.3 in Table 5).

Efficiency of information flow refers to improving user capacity to retrieve information (on the procedure, on users' rights, and on the information stored into the database) by digitalizing the paper-based procedure. A user survey can assess whether respondents think the EJS has improved their capacity to retrieve information. Respondents can use a 0 to 7 scale, where "0" represents no improvement and "7" indicates maximum improvement (question E.2.1 in Table 5). Video-conferencing systems may be excluded from measurement because it is not possible to compare them with a paper-based procedure.

Table 5: E – Individual Benefit

Indicator	Authors Who Used the Indicator	Operational-ization	Method of Measurement	EJS (to which measurement is applicable)
E.1 – *Time to Complete the Procedure*	Bembasat and Dexter (1985), DeBrabander and Thiers (1984), Luzi and Mackenzie (1982), Etezadi-Amoli and Farhoomand (1996), Seddon and Kiew (1994), Teo and Wong (1998), Wixon and Watson (2001).	E.1.1 Ratio of time to complete the entire procedure to time to complete the paper-based procedure.	User survey	Case Management Systems Electronic Legal Work Desk Court Record Electronic Data Interchange

Table 5: (Continued)

Indicator	Authors Who Used the Indicator	Operational-ization	Method of Measurement	EJS (to which measurement is applicable)
		E.1.2 (Only for court-to-court systems) Ratio number of procedures completed in one week/ number of paper-based procedure completed in one week by one clerk.	Quantitative analysis	Case Management Systems Electronic Legal Work Desk Court Record
		E.1.3 Average amount of time saved by avoiding the transportation of a witness thanks to the use of the system.	Quantitative analysis	Video and Audio Conferencing
E.2 – *Efficiency of Information Flow*	Watson and Driver (1983)	E.2.1 Improvement of users' capacity to retrieve infor-mation (on the procedure, on users' rights, and on the information stored into the database), (0–7 scale).	User survey	Case Management Systems Electronic Legal Work Desk Court Record Electronic Data Interchange
E.3 – *Cost Savings (for the user)*	Etezadi-Amoli and Farhoomand (1996), Seddon and Kiew (1994), Teo and Wong (1998), Wixon and Watson (2001).	E.3.1 Costs saved in comparison to standard procedure (reduced court fees).	Quantitative analysis	Electronic Legal Work Desk

Note: Individual-benefits indicators operationalization plus authors who used the indicators. Each question that operationalizes an indicator is marked with a reference code (e.g., E.1.1) that indicates the referring variable (E), the indicator (1), and the measurement (1).

Quantitative analysis can assess *cost savings* by checking users' cost savings in comparison to standard procedure (for instance through reduced court fees). This indicator applies to EJS used by external users, such as citizens or lawyers (e.g., court-to-user systems such as the electronic data interchange). In a court-to-court system analysis this indicator can be omitted, because users are court staff and do not pay for using the system. In this case, cost savings may be calculated only at the organizational level and in the cluster of organizational benefits.

As far as *organizational benefits* are concerned, four indicators may be considered: (1) cost-benefit ratio, (2) time reduction, (3) organizational efficiency, and (4) trust (these indicators' operationalizations and relative methods of measurement are listed in Table 6).

The objective of the *cost-benefit ratio* is to calculate cost savings for the organization when an IS is introduced. A quantitative analysis can measure system cost savings by calculating the ratio of the costs associated with the development of the system to the cost reduction due to the introduction of the system. For videoconferencing systems, the indicator can be measured by focusing on cost reduction for the justice institution (in terms of personnel and fuel; question F.1.2 in Table 6) because witnesses no longer need to travel.

The operationalization of *operation reduction* may consist in focusing, through a quantitative analysis, on the reduction of the operations needed to complete a procedure with the introduction of the IS compared to the paper-based procedure.

Organizational efficiency refers to the benefits for the organization in terms of efficiency derived from the introduction of the IS. This indicator may be calculated for evaluating court-to-court systems or court-to-users systems, with a focus on their back-office operations. For instance, when analyzing an e-filing system, the evaluator should focus on the improvement of the efficiency of the court staff associated with the introduction of the system. This indicator can be evaluated by calculating the office's improved capacity to manage routine operations with the introduction of the IS, in a specific time period and in comparison with the paper-based procedure. Specifically, the evaluator may calculate the ratio of the number of routine operations that can be performed by the office in a given time span with the help of IS to the number of operations completed in the same time span before the introduction of the application.

Trust refers to citizens' confidence in the justice system, and the legitimacy that the system can consequently claim. For instance, the use of an e-justice system that improves the efficacy of the judiciary and contributes to improving citizens' trust in the courts and their activities has to be considered as an organizational benefit. On the basis of the above argument, this indicator should be included in the analysis only when evaluating court-to-users systems such as electronic data interchange systems (in this case, users may be citizens or lawyers, depending on the access that the EJS provides). A user survey can assess trust by asking respondents whether they trust the court in which the digital procedure has been implemented, and whether they trust the digital procedure itself.

Table 6: F – Organizational Benefit

Indicator	Authors Who Used the Indicator	Operational-ization	Method of Measurement	EJS (to which measurement is applicable)
F.1 – Cost-Benefit Ratio	Lincoln (1986), Miller and Doyle (1987), Millman and Hartwick (1987), DeLone and McLean (2003).	**F.1.1** Cost-benefit Ratio: ratio of the development costs to the cost reduction due to the introduction of the system.	Quantitative analysis	Case Management Systems Electronic Legal Work Desk Court Record Electronic Data Interchange
		F.1.2 (Only for videoconferencing systems) Ratio of system's development costs to reduction of costs due to the avoidance of witnesses transportation (costs in terms of personnel and fuel).	Quantitative analysis	Video and Audio Conferencing

Table 6: (Continued)

Indicator	Authors Who Used the Indicator	Operationalization	Method of Measurement	EJS (to which measurement is applicable)
F.2 – *Operation Reduction*	Lincoln (1986), Millman and Hartwick (1987), DeLone and McLean (2003).	**F.2.1** Reduction of operations to complete a procedure.	Quantitative analysis	Case Management Systems Electronic Legal Work Desk Court Record Electronic Data Interchange
F.3 – *Organizational Efficiency*	Lincoln (1986), Millman and Hartwick (1987), DeLone and McLean (2003).	**F.3.1** Ratio of the number of routine operations that can be finalized by the office in a time span with the help of the IS to the average number of operations finalized in the same time span before the introduction of the application.	Quantitative analysis	Case Management Systems Electronic Legal Work Desk Court Record Electronic Data Interchange
F.4 – *Trust* – *Legitimacy*	Contini and Mohr (2011), Sherman, (2013).	**F.4.1** Trust in the court in which the service is provided. **F.4.2** Trust in the EJS.	User survey	Electronic Data Interchange

Note: Organizational-benefits indicators operationalization, plus authors who used the indicators. Each question that operationalizes an indicator is marked with a reference code (e.g., F.1.1) that indicates the referring variable (F), the indicator (1), and the measurement (1).

Variables, Indicators and Measures: The Variables Related to e-Justice Values

Aside from efficacy-oriented indicators adapted to the e-justice context, our evaluative framework focuses on a set of variables that

assess EJS capacity to support judicial values. The framework
focuses on the "e-justice values" that I introduced in Justice Systems
Values and e-Justice, above: (1) Independence, (2) Accountability,
(3) Impartiality, (4) Equal Access, (5) Transparency, (6) Privacy, and
(7) Legal Validity.[67] The operationalization of each of these variables
is based on the judicial values' conceptualization described in the
second part (see page 82). The methodology suggested is mixed and
consists of both qualitative and quantitative analysis of user surveys
(see Table 7). Following the method I used for the efficacy-oriented
variables, I will specify how indicators may be operationalized on
the basis of the type of system that is being analyzed. This allows
the assessment framework to be adapted to evaluating specific
types of EJS.

Independence refers to the influence of the EJS on both judicial
and court independence and on the independent functioning of the
e-justice system, free from external influences of private actors.
Qualitative and quantitative indicators and surveys administered to
judges and court staff can be used to assess independence.

When assessing systems that support judicial activities, such
as EJS that automate the allocation of cases and the storing and
retrieving of sentencing guidelines, or personnel-and-resource management systems, the evaluator may address the following survey
questions to a representative sample of judges. The evaluator may
ask the judges whether they think that the EJS has affected their
independence (question G.1 in Table 7). Moreover, the assessment
may include the judges' involvement in the design and implementation of the system on a numbered scale.[68]

For systems that automate the allocation of cases, it may be
important to check the number of accepted requests for disqualifying
a judge (where provided for by law; see Fabri and Langbroed, 2007)
during a specific time span.

A number of indicators should be taken into account regarding
how outsourced, external actors affect the independence of courts.
First, the type of contract must be evaluated in order to determine
whether it was exclusive or whether it encouraged competition
among several companies, thus fostering independence from a single
company. The evaluator may use a dichotomous score, assigning a
value of "0" for exclusive contracts and "1" where a periodical com-
petitive tender guarantees competition among several companies for
the management of the system. Second, the duration of the outsourcing

contract can be evaluated. A long time span reduces the opportunities for other companies to compete for involvement in the project. The evaluator may use a 0 to 5 scale where longer contract durations are associated with lower numbers, given that longer time spans mean greater dependence of the system on a single private actor.[69]

In order to evaluate independence, a survey should be administered to the staff who interact with the system and who provide back-office support. The survey may ask, first, whether the staff trusts the company selected for designing/managing the e-justice system (0–7 scale); second, how many issues arose in a specific time span due to the outsourcing to an external company (0–7); and third, how many times during a specific time span the system was unavailable due to maintenance and due to the company that manages the system (see Table 7, measure G.8).

As mentioned in the third and final part, *accountability* refers to two concepts: the influence EJS has on judicial and court accountability on the one hand, and the mechanisms and channels available to ensure that e-justice complies with procedural norms on the other.

A qualitative investigation can assess the influence EJS has on judicial and court accountability. It can look at how EJS stores and provides information on the number of cases filed, on the average time to process a case, on the number of hours in session, or on the number of sentences annulled by an appellate court. The evaluator may check if systems such as case-management systems, electronic legal work desk, court record, and electronic data interchange provide the possibility to store and retrieve the above-mentioned information (question H.1 in Table 7). Moreover, the analysis may check if information is used for statistical purposes, if it is published, and if the information is used as a basis for resource management (see question H.2 in Table 7).

A qualitative analysis may focus on three additional aspects: whether the system is monitored by internal staff; whether it is monitored by external governmental actors (e.g., a ministry of justice); and lastly, a survey assessment of the number of channels users can access to deal with issues, such as a help desk or online support that receive users' complaints, as well as the "quality" of these services (question H.6 in Table 7).

Impartiality refers to the absence of prejudice, preconceived ideas, or outside pressures on judges that may influence their decision-making (see page 84).[70] EJS that support adjudication may affect judicial impartiality. Some electronic work desk[71] systems enable the retrieval of case law and access to laws that are related to the case analyzed by the judge. A survey addressed to judges using EJS may assess impartiality (see Table 7). It can ask judges to compare the system with more traditional and paper-based methods of case-law consultation, in particular in regards to how complete the database is compared to paper records.[72] Secondly, it may ask judges whether the case-law retrieval system is reliable.[73] A third question may request judges' opinions on whether the use of the system may affect their impartiality (0–7 scale).

A quantitative analysis can assess impartiality by comparing the number of cases stored in the digital database and in paper records (see Table 7). It may also look at the number of appeals that reverse rulings applying case law in one year.

Equal access refers to access to justice, without any kind of discrimination, including based on technological literacy. This value refers to external access, for instance of citizens and lawyers, and therefore the evaluation focuses on e-justice systems that have "court-to-users" functionalities. I refer in particular to e-filing systems. A qualitative analysis may assess whether the system allows for reverting to the traditional paper-based procedure at any stage of the process, so that parties with limited technological literacy are not disadvantaged (question J.1 in Table 7). Moreover, the evaluation may verify whether the system includes different kinds of supports for users with limited technological knowledge (such as courses, online support, or face-to-face support). In this case, the evaluation may ask users who found the system difficult to use, or users with poor technological skills, whether they obtained online or face-to-face support, and how satisfied they were with the support they received (question J.2 in Table 7).

Finally, a qualitative analysis (participatory observation) may assess *equal access* by focusing on socio-economic discrimination. This will demonstrate whether the system is accessible to lay users[74] and assign a dichotomous score of "0" when only lawyers use the system or when the percentage of lawyers that use the system is greater than the percentage of lay users, or "1" when the percentage of lay users exceeds the percentage of lawyers.[75]

Privacy refers to the protection of personal information filed or stored in an e-justice system. Qualitative/quantitative research questions and a technicians' survey can measure "privacy." The evaluation may assess the presence of infrastructure firewalls that limit unwanted access from external users (the evaluator may count the number of firewalls that protect the system). The assessment may also cover the presence of encryption methods (question K.2 in Table 7). The third required assessment item is whether unnecessary personal data are requested by the system (question K.3 in Table 7). Finally, a survey administered to the staff that run the system should ask how many privacy breaches the system experienced in a particular time span.

Legal validity refers to EJS's capacity to improve compliance with norms by both actors (citizens, lawyers, and judges) and the digital procedure. Digital procedure that binds user operations and facilitates compliance should be accounted for (see page 84) in an assessment of EJS's legal validity. A qualitative analysis may assess this by checking how many filed claims are rejected by the court for procedural errors within a given time frame. Perceived consistency between the designed digital procedure and formal procedural rules is another aspect of legal-validity assessment. A qualitative indicator and user surveys can assess this aspect. The analysis here refers primarily to court-to-users systems and involves external users such as citizens and lawyers. The qualitative analysis should assess whether digital procedure is regulated by formal norms. In particular, it may check the number of procedural issues presented by parties that question the legal validity of the digital procedure in a particular time span (question L.2 in Table 7). In addition, the evaluation may focus on a user survey question that asks interviewees to indicate if they deem digital procedure valid from a legal point of view (question L.3).

Conclusion: Final Remarks and Future Developments

The new evaluative framework presented distinguishes between efficacy-oriented variables and variables related to e-justice values. Even though this distinction is useful for facilitating the description of each variable and its relative indicators, I support the application of the entire framework for the assessment of e-justice. The entire set of variables helps provide a complete picture of e-justice systems performance, in regards to both efficacy and other judicial values.

The framework design can serve as the basis for future research stemming from this study. In particular, the framework should be applied to the assessment of a set of e-justice systems. Empirical analysis is important in order to test whether the model is applicable to different contexts and whether results gathered through the framework are comparable. Moreover, empirical analysis may make it possible to investigate the relationship between the model's variables. In a future study, I will recommend the application of the framework to the assessment of national and transnational cases.

Table 7: Variables Related to E-Justice Values

Variable	Operationalization	Method of Measurement	EJS (to which measurement is applicable)
G. – *Independence*	G.1 Independence affected with the introduction of the system (0–3 scale).	Judge survey	Systems for the allocation of cases
	G.2 Involvement of judges in the design and implementation of the system (0–2 scale).	Qualitative analysis Participatory observation	Management and personnel systems Automation of sentencing guidelines
	G.3 Number of requests of judges' rejection accepted in one year.	Quantitative analysis	Systems for the allocation of cases
	G.4 Typology of contract for outsourcing: exclusive, not exclusive (dichotomous). G.5 Duration of contract (0–5 scale).	Qualitative analysis Participatory observation	Case Management Systems Electronic Legal Work Desk
	G.6 Trust in the company selected for designing/ managing the e-justice system, in one year. G.7 Issues that arise due to the outsourcing to external company (0–7 scale). G.8 System unavailable for maintenance, due to the company that manages the system, in one year.	Staff survey	Court Record Electronic Data Interchange Video and Audio Conferencing

Table 7: (Continued)

Variable	Operationalization	Method of measurement	EJS (to which measurement is applicable)
H. – Accountability	**H.1** Information provided by the system. Count the scores, "0" no information, "1" information are provided for each item: H.1.1 Information on the number of case filed. H.1.2 Average time to process a case. H.1.3 Number of hours in session. H.1.4 Number of sentences annulled by an appellate court. **H.2** Information use. Count the scores, "0" no - "1" yes for each item: H.2.1 Information for statistical purposes. H.2.2 Information on court efficiency published. H.2.3 Information as basis for resource management.	Qualitative analysis Participatory observation	Case Management Systems Electronic Legal Work Desk Court Record Electronic Data Interchange
	H.3 System periodically checked by internal staff (0–2 scale). **H.4** System periodically checked by external govern-mental actors (e.g., ministry of justice; 0-2 scale). **H.5** Number of channels through which users may express issues.	Qualitative analysis Participatory observation	Case Management Systems Electronic Legal Work Desk Court Record Electronic Data Interchange Video and Audio Conferencing.
	H.6 Satisfaction for the service for receiving users' complaints and issues (help desk online or face-to-face; 0–7 scale).	User survey	

Table 7: (Continued)

Variable	Operationalization	Method of measurement	EJS (to which measurement is applicable)
I. – *Impartiality*	**I.1** Completeness of the database in comparison with the paper records (0–3 scale). **I.2** Reliability of the system for case-law retrieval (0–2 scale). **I.3** System affect impartiality (0–7 scale).	Judge survey	Case-law database and retrieval
	I.4 Ratio of case-law recorded on the digital database to case-law in paper records. **I.5** Number of appeals that reject the reference to case-law in one year.	Quantitative analysis	
J. – *Equality of Access*	**J.1** Possibility to switch to paper based procedure at any stage of the procedure (score 0–3).	Qualitative analysis Participatory observation	Electronic Data Interchange
	J.2 Satisfaction for support to users with scarce technological literacy (0–7 scale).	User survey	
	J.3 No necessity to involve and pay a lawyer (higher percentage of lay users comparatively to lawyers) (score 0–1). Or alternatively, possibility to have access to legal aid (score 0–1).	Qualitative analysis Participatory observation	
K. – *Privacy*	**K.1** Use of firewalls (Count). **K.2** Use of updated encryption methods (Dichotomous). **K.3** System that asks only personal data necessary for the procedure (0–2 scale).	Qualitative/ Quantitative analysis Participatory observation	Case Management Systems Electronic Legal Work Desk
	K.4 Number of privacy breaches in one year.	Technician survey	Court Record Electronic Data Interchange
L. – *Legal Validity*	**L.1** Claims filed rejected by the court for procedural errors in one year. **L.2** Number of procedural exceptions presented by parts in one year.	Qualitative analysis	Electronic Data Interchange

Table 7: (Continued)

Variable	Operationalization	Method of measurement	EJS (to which measurement is applicable)
	L.3 Legal validity of the digital procedure. Score: "0" completely invalid, "1" partially valid, "2" completely valid.	User survey	

Note: Operationalization of variables related to e-justice values. Each indicator is marked with a reference code (e.g., G.1) that indicates the referring variable (G) and the indicator (1).

Notes

1   Francesco Contini and Giovan Francesco Lanzara, eds., *The Circulation of Agency in e-Justice: Interoperability and Infrastructures for Europe Trans-Border Judicial Proceedings* (Dordrecht: Springer, 2013); Jannis Kallinikos, "Institutional Complexities and Functional Simplification: The Case of Money Claims Online: ICT and Innovation in the Public Sector," in *European Studies in the Making of e-Government*, ed. Francesco Contini and Giovan Francesco Lanzara, (Basingstoke, UK: Palgrave Macmillan, 2009).

2   In this paper, I will refer to e-justice systems instead of e-justice services or applications. The term "e-justice system" derives from the adaptation of Information System to the justice context. Therefore, I prefer to focus on "systems" instead of "applications" because of their assemblage nature, and their characterization by the interaction of applications, offices, organizations, and people. By the same token, the paper will refer principally to Information Systems (IS), instead of Information and Communication Technology (ICT). While IS refers to the combination of human and technological agency, ICT refers to the integration of computers, software, hardware, telecommunications (telephone lines and wireless signals), storage, and audio-visual systems that allow for accessing, storing, transmitting, and manipulating information (Silverstone, 1991).

3   Edward Bernoider and S. Koch, "Aligning ICT and Legal Framework in Austria's e-Bureaucracy, from Mainframe to the Internet," in *ICT and Innovation in the Public Sector: European Studies in the Making of e-Government*, ed. Francesco Contini and Giovan Francesco Lanzara, (New York: Palgrave Macmillan, 2009).

4   William H DeLone and Ephraim R McLean, "Information Systems Success: The Quest for the Dependent Variable," *Information Systems Research* 3:1 (1992) at 60 [DeLone and McLean, "Information Systems

Success"]; William H DeLone and Ephraim R McLean, "The DeLone and McLean Model of Information Systems Success: A Ten-Year Update," *Journal of Management Information System* 19:4 (2003) at 9 [DeLone and McLean, "Ten-Year Update"].

5   John Alford and Janine O'Flynn, "Making Sense of Public Value: Concepts, Critics and Emergent Meanings," *International Journal of Public Administration* 32 (2009) at 171; John Benington, "From Private Choice to Public Value?," in *Public Value: Theory and Practice*, ed. John Benington and Mark H Moore (Basingstoke: Palgrave Macmillan, 2011) at 31; Antonio Cordella and Carla M Bonina, "A Public Value Perspective for ICT Enabled Public Sector Reforms: A Theoretical Reflection," *Government Information Quarterly* 29 (2012) at 512; Mark H Moore, *Creating Public Value: Strategic Management in Government* (Cambridge, MA: Harvard University Press, 1995); Gerry Stoker, "Public Value Management: A New Narrative for Networked Governance?," *American Review of Public Administration* 36:1 (2006) at 41.

6   Richard Batley and George Larbi, *The Changing Role of Government: The Reform of Public Services in Developing Countries* (Basingstoke, New York: Palgrave Macmillan, 2004); Wendy L Currie and Matthew Guah, "Conflicting Institutional Logics: A National Program for IT in the Organizational Field of Healthcare," *Journal of Information Technology* 22:3 (2007) at 235; Gernod Gruening, "Origins and Theoretical Basis of New Public Management," *International Public Management Journal* 4:1 (2001) at 1; Lawrence E Lynn, Jr, "The NPM as an International Phenomenon: A Skeptical View," in *Advances in International Comparative Public Management*, ed. Lawrence R Jones, Kuno Schedler and Stephen W Wade, (Greenwich, CT: Jai Press, 1997); David Osborne and Ted Gaebler, *Reinventing Government: How the Entrepreneurial Spirit is Transforming the Public Sector* (Reading, MA: Addison-Wesley, 1992).

7   The NPM approach influenced the justice sector as well, and brought about reforms in some justice systems regarding the evaluation of courts and judges with a focus on performances and on reached objectives. See Francesco Contini and Richard Mohr, "Reassembling the Legal: The Wonders of Modern Science in Court-Related Proceedings" Griffith Law Review 20:4 (2011) at 994 [Contini and Mohr, "Reassembling the Legal"]; Hellmut Wollmann, *Evaluation in Public Sector Reforms: Concepts and Practices in International Perspective* (Cheltenham: Edward Elgar, 2003).

8   Moore, *supra* note 5; Cordella and Bonina, *supra* note 5.

9   Anthony M Cresswell, G Brian Burke and Theresa A Pardo, *Advancing Return on Investment Analysis for Government IT: A Public Value Framework* (Albany, NY: Center for Technology in Government, 2006); Richard Heeks, "Benchmarking eGovernment: Improving the National and International Measurement," iGovernment Working Paper No 18 (2006);

Iain Kearns, *Public Value and e-Government* (London: Institute for Public Policy Research, 2004).

10   James E Bailey and Sammy W Pearson, "Development of a Tool for Measuring and Analyzing Computer User Satisfaction," *Management Science* 29:5 (1983) at 530; Paul H Cheney, Robert I Mann and Donald L Amoroso, "Organizational Factors Affecting the Success of End User Computing," *Journal of Management Information Systems* 3 (1986) at 65; DeLone and McLean, "Information Systems Success," *supra* note 4; DeLone and McLean, "Ten-Year Update," *supra* note 4; Peter Seddon and Min-Yen Kiew, "A Partial Test and Development of the DeLone and McLean model of IS Success," in *Proceedings of the International Conference on Information Systems,* ed. Janice I DeGross, Sid L Huff and Malcom C Munro, (Atlanta, GA: Association for Information Systems, 1994) at 99; Dale Young and John Benamati, "Differences in Public Web Sites: The Current State of Large U.S. Firms," *Journal of Electronic Commerce Research* 1:3 (2000) at 94.

11   Sarmad Alshawi, Ali Alahmary and Hamid Alalwany, "E-Government Evaluation Factors: Citizen's Perspective," in *Proceedings of European and Mediterranean Conference on Information Systems 2007 (EMCIS2007)* (Valencia, Spain: Polytechnic University of Valencia, 2007); Amihai Glazer, Vesa Kanniainen and Esko Niskanen, "Bequests, Control Rights, and Cost-Benefit Analysis," *European Journal of Political Economy* 19 (2002) at 71; Charles Kaylor, Randy Deshazo and David Van Eck, "Gauging e-Government: A Report on Implementing Services among American Cities," *Government Information Quarterly* 18 (2001) at 293.

12   Bailey and Pearson, *supra* note 10; Cheney, Mann and Amoroso, *supra* note 10; DeLone and McLean, "Information Systems Success," *supra* note 4)

13   Among the IS assessment frameworks, one worth mentioning is derived from the User Requirements Notation (URN). The URN is a modelling language whose objective is supporting the "elicitation, analysis, specification, and validation of requirements" (Daniel Amyot and Gunter Mussbacher, "User Requirements Notation: The First Ten Years, the Next Ten Years," *Journal of Software* 6:5 (2011):747 at 747). The modelling exposes, in a graphical way, requirement scenarios and goals and how these satisfy stakeholders' needs (Gao, 2010). Therefore, it can be used for performance evaluation by comparing architecture goals and results of the implementation for stakeholders. See Gunter Mussbacher, Daniel Amyot, João Araújo and Ana Moreira, "Modeling Software Product Lines with AoURN," in *Proceedings of the 2008 AOSD Workshop on Early Aspects* (New York: ACM, 2008). In this study, I did not take the modelling into consideration for e-justice evaluation, for two reasons. First, because it is a very technical tool for the assessment of only a specific aspect of IS: the architecture requirements. Second, because the

focus on the comparison between goals and results is already covered by one dimension of the DeLone and McLean model (the net benefits) which appears to be more complete and more easily applied to the e-justice context.

14   Charles H Kriebel and Artur Raviv, "An Economics Approach to Modeling the Productivity of Computer Systems," *Management Science* 26:3 (1980) at 297; Scott Hamilton and Norman L Chervany, "Evaluating Information System Effectiveness. Part I. Comparing Evaluation Approaches," *MIS Quarterly* 5:3 (1981) at 55; Seddon and Kiew, *supra* note 10.

15   Michael J Ginzberg, "Finding an Adequate Measure of OR/MS Effectiveness," *Interfaces* 8:4 (1978) at 59; Henry C Lucas, Jr, "A Descriptive Model of Information Systems in the Context of the Organization," in *Proceedings of the Wharton Conference on Research on Computers in Organizations,* ed. Howard Lee Morgan, (New York: Association for Computing Machinery, 1973) at 27; Ashraf Shirani, Milam Aiken and Brian Reithel, "A Model of User Information Satisfaction," *Data Base* 25 (1994) at 17; Young and Benamati, *supra* note 10.

16   Niv Ahituv, "A Systematic Approach Toward Assessing the Value of an Information System," *MIS Quarterly* 4:4 (1980) at 61; Charles A Gallagher, "Perceptions of the Value of a Management Information System," *Academy of Management Journal* 17:1 (1974) at 46; Malcolm C Munro and Gordon B Davis, "Determining Management Information Needs: A Comparison of Methods," *MIS Quarterly* 1:2 (1977) at 55.

17   DeLone and McLean, "Ten-Year Update," *supra* note 4; Alemayehu Molla and Paul S Licker, "E-commerce Systems Success: An Attempt to Extend and Respecify the DeLone and McLean Model of IS success," *Journal of Electronic Commerce* 2:4 (2001) at 131; Bernoider and Koch, *supra* note 3.

18   Alshawi, Alahmary and Alalwany, *supra* note 11.

19   Glazer, Kanniainen and Niskanen, *supra* note 11; Kaylor, Deshazo and Van Eck, *supra* note 11; Neil Seitz, *Capital Budgeting and Long Term Financing Decision* (Hindsdale, IL: Dyden Press, 1989); Koji Shinjo and Xingyuan Zhang, "Productivity Analysis of IT Capital Stock: The U.S.A.–Japan Comparison," *Journal of Japanese International Economies* 17:1 (2003) at 81.

20   Kristin R Eschenfelder and Clark A Miller, "The Openness of Government Websites: Toward a Socio-Technical Government Website Evaluation Toolkit" (Paper delivered at the MacArthur Foundation/ALA Office of Information Technology Policy Internet Credibility and the User Symposium, Seattle, WA, 11 April 2005) [unpublished]; Efraim Turban, Ephraim McLean and James Wetherbe, *Information Technology for Management: Making Connections for Strategic Advantage* (New York: John Wiley & Sons Inc, 2001); Lili Wang, Stuart Bretschneider and Jon Gant,

"Evaluating Web-Based E-Government Services with a Citizen-Centric Approach," in *Proceedings of 38th Annual Hawaii International Conference on Systems Sciences* (Washington, DC: IEEE Computer Society, 2005).

21 Lemuria Carter and France Bélanger, "Citizen Adoption of Electronic Government Initiatives," *Info Systems J* 15 (2005) at 5; Paul Legris, John Ingham and Pierre Collerette, "Why Do People Use Information Technology? A Critical Review of the Technology Acceptance Model," *Association for Information Systems* 40:3 (2003) at 191.

22 DeLone and McLean, "Information Systems Success", *supra* note 4.

23 DeLone and McLean utilized the term "dimension" when referring to the variables of their framework. However, when dimensions are operationalized, it is better to refer to them as variables. They in fact are operationalized attributes of an IS and their value varies across the variable domain (Babbie, 2009). For the sake of the argument and in order to introduce the DeLone and McLean model, only in this section the terms "dimension" and "variable" will be used as synonyms, both referring to model's variables. In the successive sections, I will utilize the word "variables."

24 DeLone and McLean, "Ten-Year Update," *supra* note 4 at 10.

25 DeLone and McLean, "Ten-Year Update," *supra* note 4; Leyland F Pitt, Richard T and C Bruce Kavan, "Service Quality: A Measure of Information Systems Effectiveness," *MIS Quarterly* 19:2 (1995) at 173; William J Kettinger, and Choong C Lee, "Perceived Service Quality and User Satisfaction with the Information Services Function," *Decision Sciences* 25:5–6 (1995) at 737.

26 Giovan Francesco Lanzara, "Building Digital Institutions: ICT and the Rise of Assemblages in Government," in *ICT and Innovation in the Public Sector: European Studies in the Making of e-Government*, ed. Francesco Contini and Giovan Francesco Lanzara, (New York: Palgrave Macmillan, 2009) at 9.

27 See above; Francesco Contini and Richard Mohr, "Reconciling Independence and Accountability in Judicial Systems," *Utrecht Law Review* 3:2 (2007) at 26; James W Douglas and Roger Hartley, "The Politics of Court Budgeting in the States: Is Judicial Independence Threatened by the Budgetary Process?," *Public Administration Review* 63:4 (2003) at 441; Giuseppe Di Federico, "Judicial Independence in Italy," in *Judicial Independence in Transition*, ed. Anja Seibert-Fohr (Berlin: Springer, 2012) at 357; Martin L Friedland, "A Place Apart: Judicial Independence and Accountability in Canada: A Report Prepared for the Canada Judicial Council" (Ottawa, Canadian Judicial Council, 1995); Carlo Guarnieri and Patrizia Pederzoli, *The Power of Judges* (New York: Oxford University Press, 2002); Peter H Russell and David M O'Brien, eds., *Judicial*

Independence in the Age of Democracy, Critical Perspectives from Around the World (Charlottesville, VA: University of Virginia Press, 2001); Andrew Le Sueur, "Developing Mechanisms for Judicial Accountability in the UK," *Legal Studies* 24:1–2 (2004) at 73.

28 Jo Sherman, "Court Information Management Policy Framework to Accommodate the Digital Environment" (Discussion paper prepared for the Canadian Judicial Council, 2013), online: <www.cjc-ccm.gc.ca/cmslib/general/AJC/Policy%20Framework%20to%20Accommodate%20the%20Digital%20Environment%202013-03.pdf>; European Network of Councils for the Judiciary, "ENCJ Working Group: Judicial Ethics Report 2009-2010,", online: <www.encj.eu> [ENCJ].

29 Le Sueur, *supra* note 27.

30 Marco Fabri and Francesco Contini, eds., *Justice and Technology in Europe: How ICT Is Changing the Judicial Business* (Alphen aan Den Rijn: Kluwer Law International, 2001).

31 Marco Fabri and Philip M Langbroek, "Is there a Right Judge for each Case? A Caomparative Study of Case Assignment in Six European Countries," *European Journal of Legal Studies* 1:2 (2007):292 at 292.

32 Andrew Ashworth and Julian V Roberts, eds., *Sentencing Guidelines: Exploring the English Model* (New York: Oxford University Press, 2013).

33 See for instance the Nostra, IVS, and Bos project developed in the Netherlands (Aernout Schmidt, "Re-Engineering Independence and Control: ICT in the Dutch Judicial System," in *Justice and Technology in Europe: How ICT Is Changing the Judicial Business*, ed. Marco Fabri and Francesco Contini [Alphen aan Den Rijn: Kluwer Law International, 2001]).

34 Bill Vassiliadis et al., "From Application Service Provision to Service-Oriented Computing: A Study of the IT Outsourcing Evolution," *Telematics and Informatics* 23:4 (2006) at 271.

35 Contini and Mohr, "Reassembling the Legal," *supra* note 7.

36 Bruno Latour, *La fabrique du droit. Une ethnographie du Conseil d'État* (Paris: La Découverte, 2002); Herbert A Simon, Donald W Smithburg and Victor A Thomson, *Public Administration* (New York: Knopf, 1961).

37 Richard Mohr, "Identity Crisis: Judgment and the Hollow Legal Subject," *Law Text Culture* 11 (2007) at 106.

38 Contini and Mohr, "Reassembling the Legal," *supra* note 7.

39 Le Sueur, *supra* note 27.

40 For some scholars, accountability and independence cannot coexist (Cooke, 1992), while other authors support the compatibility between the two values. The latter group believes that accountability is a means to the end of guaranteeing judges' impartiality and independence (Contini and Mohr, "Reassembling the Legal," *supra* note 7; Di Federico, *supra* note 27; Guarnieri and Pederzoli, *supra* note 27; Le Sueur, *supra* note 27). For a detailed bibliography on the relationship between

independence and accountability, see Amy B Atchinson, Lawrence Tobe Liebert and Denise K Russell, "Judicial Independence and Judicial Accountability: a Selected Bibliography," *Southern California Law Review* 72:3 (1999) at 723.

41   Atchinson, Liebert and Russell, *supra* note 40; Stephen B Burbank and Barry Friedman, eds., *Judicial Independence at the Crossroads: An Interdisciplinary Approach* (New York: Sage Publishers, 2002); Ronald Dworkin, *Taking Rights Seriously* (Oxford: Oxford University Press, 1978); Le Sueur, *supra* note 27; Stefan Trechsel, *Human Rights in Criminal Proceedings* (New York: Oxford University Press, 2006); David Weissbrodt, *The Right to a Fair Trial: Article 8, 10, and 11 of the Universal Declaration of Human Rights* (Alphen aan Den Rijn: Kluwer Law International, 2001); ENCJ, *supra* note 28.

42   ENCJ, *supra* note 28.

43   Trechsel, *supra* note 41.

44   Fabri and Contini, *supra* note 30.

45   In some software, such as the Italian SICC (Sistema Informatico del Contenzioso Civile, or Information System for Civil Cases), judges can search previous sentences in a database, using keywords. Other legal information systems, such as the Austrian LIS (Legal Information System), allow judges to retrieve national and international laws from a database. In both cases, the functioning of such support systems affects the decision of a judge, and therefore his or her impartiality.

46   Mauro Cappelletti, *Access to Justice* (Milan: Giuffrè, 1978); Rebecca Sandefur, "Access to Justice: Classical Approaches and New Directions," in *Access to Justice: Sociology of Crime, Law, and Deviance*, ed. Rebecca L Sandefur, Volume 12 (Bingley, UK: Emerald/JAI Press, 2009); Sherman, *supra* note 28; ENCJ, *supra* note 28.

47   Deborah L Rhode, *Access to Justice* (New York: Oxford University Press, 2004); Joseph L Staats, Shaun Bowler and Johnathan Hiskey, "Measuring Judicial Performance in Latin America," *Latin American Politics & Society* 47:4 (2005) at 77; William C Prillaman, *The Judiciary and Democratic Decay in Latin America: Declining Confidence in the Rule of Law* (Westport: Praege, 2000).

48   In the determination of an individual's civil rights and obligations or of any criminal charge against that person, everyone is entitled to a fair and public hearing within a reasonable time by an independent and impartial tribunal established by law (Article 6, ECHR).

49   Andrew Sanders, "Core Values, the Magistracy, and the Auld Report," *Journal of Law and Society* 29:2 (2002) at 324; A Wallace, "Overview of Public Access and Privacy Issues" (Paper delivered at Queensland University of Technology Conference, 6 November 2003) [unpublished].

50   Sherman, *supra* note 28.

51 Ibid.

52 Some liberal democracies include privacy as a constitutional right. The US Supreme Court has conferred constitutional status on some aspects of privacy (William M Beaney, "The Constitutional Right to Privacy in the Supreme Court," *Supreme Court Review* [1962] at 212).

53 Ole Hanseth and Kalle Lyytinen, "Design Theory for Dynamic Complexity in Information Infrastructures: The Case of Building Internet," *Journal of Information Technology* 25:1 (2010) at 1.

54 Hans Kelsen, *Pure Theory of Law: Reine Rechtslehre* (Berkeley: University of California Press, 1967).

55 Contini and Mohr, "Reassembling the Legal," *supra* note 7 at 12.

56 Staats, Bowler and Hiskey, *supra* note 47.

57 Kallinikos, *supra* note 1 at 175.

58 As anticipated, in this study, I relied on the list of different typologies of e-justice systems made by Fabri and Contini (*supra* note 30 at 21–23). The authors distinguish between 1. Case Management Systems, 2. Electronic Legal Work Desk, 3. Court Record, 4. Electronic Data Interchange, and 5. Video and Audio Conferencing.

59 Marco Velicogna, Antoine Errera and Stéphane Derlange, "E-Justice in France: The e-Barreau Experience," *Utrecht Law Review* 7:1 (2011) at 163.

60 Salvatore Belardo, Kirk R Karwan and William Alan Wallace, "DSS Component Design Through Field Experimentation: An Application to Emergency Management," in *Proceedings of the Third International Conference on Information Systems*, December 1982 (Chicago: Society for Management Information Systems, 1982) at 93; Ananth Srinivasan, "Alternative Measures of System Effectiveness: Associations and Implications," *MIS* Quarterly 9:3 (1985) at 243.

61 The question may ask to place the answer on a 0 to 7 scale where "0" is incomplete and "7" complete.

62 Number of information missing.

63 Recent studies demonstrate that the information on national justice systems and procedural norms provided by the European e-justice portal has not been updated (Marco Mellone, "Legal Interoperability in Europe: An Assessment of the European Payment Order and the European Small Claims Procedure," in *The Circulation of Agency in e-Justice: Interoperability and Infrastructures for Europe Trans-Border Judicial Proceedings*, ed. Francesco Contini and Giovan Francesco Lanzara [Dordrecht: Springer, 2013] at 245; Contini and Lanzara, *supra* note 1). The European e-Justice portal provides information on EU justice systems and it allows to access to a set of European e-justice services.

64 The over regulation, the slow change in legislation, and the rules that hinder the smooth functioning of e-justice are examples of the low

accessibility of information that characterized the development of the Italian TOL (Trial On Line, the Italian e-filing system) and hindered its diffusion in the Italian civil justice. See Marco Fabri, "E-justice in Finland and in Italy: Enabling versus Constraining Models," in *ICT and Innovation in the Public Sector: European Studies in the Making of e-Government,* ed. Francesco Contini and Giovan Francesco Lanzara (New York: Palgrave Macmillan, 2009) at 115; Davide Carnevali and Andrea Resca, "Pushing at the Edge of Maximum Manageable Complexity: The Case of 'Trial Online' in Italy," in *The Circulation of Agency in e-Justice: Interoperability and Infrastructures for Europe Trans-Border Judicial Proceedings,* ed. Francesco Contini and Giovan Francesco Lanzara, (Dordrecht: Springer, 2013); Giampiero Lupo, "Design Principles for e-Justice: a Comparative Assessment of Four European e-Justice Services" (Paper delivered at the Law and Society Conference, Boston, June 2013) [unpublished].

65 For a review, see DeLone and McLean, "Ten-Year Update," *supra* note 4 at 16–17.

66 E-filing systems such as Money Claim Online (MCOL; Kallinikos, *supra* note 1) and the Italian Trial Online (TOL; Carnevali and Resca, *supra* note 64) allow citizens and lawyers to file documents and claims to a court through a computer-based interface.

67 The transparency value, described as an e-justice value in the section on Justice Systems Values and e-Justice, has been included between the efficacy-oriented variables as an integration of the DeLone and McLean model and in substitution of the information-quality variable.

68 With "0" meaning the system has been imposed upon the judges without their involvement; "1" meaning judges have been partially involved into the design stage; and "2" meaning judges have been involved both in the design and the implementation stage.

69 For instance the scores assigned may be "0": more than five-year contract; "1": five-year contract; "2": from three- to four-year contract; "3": from two- to three-year contract; "4": from one- to two-year contract; and "5": less than a one-year contract.

70 Atchinson, Liebert and Russell, *supra* note 40; Burbank and Friedman, *supra* note 41; Dworkin, *supra* note 41; Le Sueur, *supra* note 27; Trechsel, *supra* note 41; Weissbrodt, *supra* note 41; ENCJ, *supra* note 28.

71 Fabri and Contini, *supra* note 30.

72 Utilizing a 0-3 scale, where "0" is for very incomplete; "1" partially complete; "2" more than partially complete; "3" very complete.

73 Utilizing a 0–3 scale, "0" the system is completely unreliable; "1" I experienced some mistakes in retrieving information; "2" the system is reliable.

74   An e-justice service that allows the access to users that cannot afford a lawyer (as it happens in Money Claim Online, MCOL, in England and Wales), scores better in terms of equal access.

75   In addition to this measure, and in the cases of EJS that only allow lawyers to use them (and that therefore scored "0" in the previous measure), the evaluation may check if the digital procedure foresees forms of legal aid that allow the less wealthy to access the system through a lawyer (score "0" where this opportunity is missing and "1" where legal aid is available).

CHAPTER III

The Role of Courts in Assisting Individuals in Realizing Their s. 2(b) Right to Information about Court Proceedings

Graham Reynolds

Introduction

Individuals are entitled, under s. 2(b) of the *Canadian Charter of Rights and Freedoms,* to information about court proceedings (including information about court documents).[1] One way of obtaining this information is through visits to courthouses, where individuals may attend trials and consult court documents, among other information-gathering activities. However, not all individuals are able to attend court in person, in which case they are dependent on information about court proceedings being made available in alternative ways in order to fully realize this aspect of their s. 2(b) right.

The news media play an important role in ensuring that individuals unable to attend court in person have access to information about court proceedings. Noting how difficult it is for many individuals to attend court in person, Cory J, in *Edmonton Journal v Alberta (Attorney General) (Edmonton Journal),* a 1989 decision of the Supreme Court of Canada (SCC), went so far as to write that "[p]ractically speaking, [information about court proceedings] can only be obtained from the newspapers or other media" (emphasis added).[2] In a speech delivered on January 31, 2012, at Carleton University, Chief Justice McLachlin also referred to *Edmonton Journal* in noting that "[o]nly through the efforts of the press can the vast majority be informed of proceedings before the courts and their judgments" (emphasis added).[3]

In 1989, the year in which the SCC's judgment in *Edmonton Journal* was handed down, the media may have been the only party with the ability to disseminate court information quickly and efficiently to the public. Technological developments since this date, however, including the development of the World Wide Web, the rise of social networking sites such as Facebook and Twitter, and the wide availability of internet access, have significantly enhanced the ability of parties other than the media to disseminate court information broadly, quickly, accurately, and efficiently. As a result of these technological developments, the media are no longer the only party capable of conveying information about court proceedings to the public.

In this paper, I will challenge the idea that the media are the only party capable of assisting individuals unable to attend court in person to fully realize their s. 2(b) right to information about court proceedings. Technological developments have enabled a number of other parties, including members of the public and courts themselves, to play this role as well. I will also argue that as "guardians of the Constitution and of individuals' rights under it,"[4] Canadian courts in particular ought to take all reasonable steps to assist individuals in fully realizing their s. 2(b) right to information about court proceedings, both by providing individuals with online access to information about court proceedings (directly and by partnering with third parties), and by implementing policies on the use of electronic devices in courts that minimize restrictions on the ability of individuals and news media to disseminate information about court proceedings to the public.

This is not to say, however, that courts should make all information about court proceedings available online; that limitations should never be imposed on the use, by the media or members of the public, of electronic devices in courtrooms; or that there should be no subsequent limitations on the ability of the media or members of the public to disseminate court information. As noted by Abella J in *AB v Bragg Communications Inc* (*AB v Bragg*), citing Dickson J's judgment in *Attorney General of Nova Scotia v MacIntyre*, "there are cases in which the protection of social values must prevail over openness."[5] This includes cases such as *AB v Bragg,* in which a girl's "privacy from the relentlessly intrusive humiliation of sexualized online bullying" was held to be a value that warranted restricting the dissemination of information about court proceedings and the application of the open-court principle.[6]

This paper will proceed as follows. I will begin by establishing that individuals are entitled, under s. 2(b) of the *Charter,* to information about court proceedings (see below). I will also demonstrate how this aspect of an individual's s. 2(b) right to freedom of expression is linked to, but separate from, the open-court principle. Next, I will discuss the technological developments that have enhanced the ability of parties other than the media (such as courts themselves and members of the public) to disseminate court information quickly and efficiently to the public (see page 100). In the part that follows, I will describe how Canadian courts have used these technological developments to provide a significant degree of court information to the public, either directly or in partnership with other parties. I will then describe the electronic-device policies enacted by Canadian courts. At the same time as Canadian courts have made additional information about court proceedings available online, a number of courts have also enacted policies regarding the use of electronic devices in courtrooms that—at least in some cases—have significantly limited the extent to which both media and members of the public can disseminate court information. Finally, I will discuss the types of limitations that might be imposed on court information made available online and on the use of electronic devices in courts, in order to protect countervailing constitutional rights and values such as privacy (see page 108).

Individuals Are Entitled, under s. 2(b) of the *Charter,* to Information about Court Proceedings

The Canadian *Charter of Rights and Freedoms,* which came into force in 1982, guarantees, in s. 2(b), the right to freedom of expression.[7] This right protects both individuals' ability to express themselves and to receive expression.[8] Furthermore, in certain contexts, s. 2(b) gives individuals the right to access information held by the government. Information to which individuals are entitled under s. 2(b) includes information about court proceedings (including "the nature of the evidence that was called, the arguments presented, and the comments made by the trial judge") as well as "information pertaining to court documents."[9]

In *Canadian Broadcasting Corp v New Brunswick (Attorney General)*, La Forest J linked the s. 2(b) right to information about court proceedings to the open-court principle.[10] As La Forest J noted:

> Openness permits public access to information about the courts, which in turn permits the public to discuss and put forward opinions and criticisms of court practices and proceedings. While the freedom to express ideas and opinions about the operation of the courts is clearly within the ambit of the freedom guaranteed by s. 2(b), so too is the right of members of the public to obtain information about the courts in the first place.[11]

Thus, access to court information is protected under s. 2(b), as noted by McLachlin CJ and Abella J in their reasons for judgment in *Ontario (Public Safety and Security) v Criminal Lawyers' Association,* on the basis that it is "necessary for the meaningful exercise of free expression on matters of public or political interest."[12]

Technological Changes Have Allowed Parties Other than News Media to Disseminate or Otherwise Make Available Large Amounts of Information about Court Proceedings

In order to assist individuals in exercising their s. 2(b) right to information about court proceedings, courts have opened their doors to the public, allowing individuals to attend court proceedings, review court documents, and otherwise be present in court facilities. However, as Cory J wrote in his reasons for judgment in *Edmonton Journal*, "[i]t is exceedingly difficult for many, if not most, people to attend a court trial. Neither working couples nor mothers or fathers house-bound with young children, would find it possible to attend court."[13]

One way for members of the public unable to attend court in person to obtain information about court proceedings is through the news media. The production capabilities possessed by the news media (including the services of reporters responsible for covering court proceedings or justice issues), and the distribution networks to which the news media have access, can and have been used to disseminate information quickly and accurately to the public at large, ensuring that the public has timely and regular access both to information about court proceedings and to commentary about such proceedings.

As noted above, in *Edmonton Journal,* Cory J wrote that "[p]ractically speaking, [information about court proceedings] can *only* be obtained from the newspapers or other media" (emphasis added).[14] At least in part, however, this statement was rooted in the technological context of the period in which it was written. As I will discuss below, since *Edmonton Journal* was handed down, technological developments—including the development of the World Wide Web, the emergence and popularity of social networking websites such as Twitter and Facebook, the rapid increase in the number of individuals with access to the Internet, the greater speed with which individuals can access information on the Internet, and the development of smartphones—have broadened the range of parties capable of communicating large amounts of information (including information about court proceedings) to the public in a quick, accurate, and efficient manner, as well as the ways through which this information can be disseminated.

World Wide Web

1989—the year in which *Edmonton Journal* was handed down—was a landmark year in the evolution of digital communications. Specifically, in 1989, Tim Berners-Lee, at that time a researcher at the European Organization for Nuclear Research (CERN), wrote and circulated a proposal to create a system that he called the "World Wide Web."[15] Released outside CERN for the first time in 1991, the World Wide Web has enabled a wide range of parties to make information (including court information) available through the internet to the public through the creation of websites.[16] It has been estimated that as of April 2015, there were approximately 932 million websites.[17]

Social Networking Sites

Social networking sites are another vehicle through which parties may make information (including information about court proceedings) available to the public. Johnny Ryan describes sixdegrees.com, established in 1997 by Andrew Weinreich, as "the first social network."[18] Ryan writes that this network "allowed users to build a personal network of their friends by entering the e-mail addresses of people they knew."[19] Three of the most popular social networks in existence in 2015 are Facebook, Twitter, and YouTube. One function of each of these social networks is to provide a platform for the sharing of information. Facebook writes on its website that as of December 31, 2014, it had 1.39 billion monthly active users;[20] Twitter writes that 500 million tweets are sent each day;[21] and YouTube states that "300 hours of video are uploaded to YouTube every minute."[22]

Rates of Internet Connectivity and Internet Speed

Another factor that has impacted the ability of the public to obtain information made available online is the degree to which the public has access to the internet. A 2012 study by Statistics Canada indicated that 83% of individuals in Canada have access to the internet at home.[23] Furthermore, this study showed that out of the households with internet access in 2012, 97% had a high-speed connection.[24] Internet access is also available in many public spaces (including certain courthouse libraries).[25] While not everyone has internet access (the 2012 study, for instance, noted that "[a]bout 20% of households reported having no [home internet] access because of the cost of the service or equipment"[26]), the wide availability of internet access both in households and in public spaces has meant that a significant percentage of Canada's population can access information about court proceedings made available online.

Handheld Devices through Which Information about Court Proceedings Can Be Transmitted and Received

A study released by Catalyst Canada & Group M Next indicated that in 2015 68% of Canadians owned a smartphone.[27] The prevalence of handheld devices with internet connectivity has meant that individuals can both obtain and disseminate information (including information about court proceedings) in or from a much greater range of spaces.

Canadian Courts Have Used Technological Developments to Expand the Range of Information about Court Proceedings Available to the Public

As described above, technological developments have given a broad range of parties the ability to disseminate information quickly and efficiently to the public. In a number of ways, as will be discussed in more detail below, Canadian courts have used these technological developments to disseminate information about court proceedings to the public. First, all Canadian courts operate websites on which they make available specific court information. Second, some Canadian courts convey information directly to individuals through email notifications. Third, Canadian courts work with third parties to disseminate court information on third-party websites such as CanLII and Lexum. Fourth, some Canadian courts use social networking sites such as Twitter and Facebook to disseminate information about court proceedings to the public.

Canadian Courts Make Information about Court Proceedings Available on Their Websites

In each province and territory, courts operate websites that provide information about provincial courts, superior courts, and courts of appeal (among other courts and tribunals).[28] As well, websites have been created by the Supreme Court of Canada (SCC), the Federal Court, the Federal Court of Appeal, the Tax Court of Canada, and the Court Martial Appeal Court of Canada, among other courts.[29]

Canadian courts make available, on their websites, a wide range of information about court proceedings. The exact range of information made available varies depending on the court in question. For instance, many courts make hearing lists available online, providing individuals with basic information about upcoming court cases.[30] While the SCC is the only Canadian court to make factums available online,[31] several Canadian courts make court-record information available online.[32] In addition, a number of courts make a subset of their judgments available through their websites.[33] Although no Canadian courts make audio of their proceedings available online, one court—the SCC—webcasts its proceedings live on its website[34] and makes the archives thereof available online.[35] Certain other Canadian courts are engaged (or have engaged) in pilot projects regarding the webcasting of court proceedings.[36]

Canadian Courts Convey Information to Individuals Through Email and Other Notifications

In addition to making information available on websites, some courts have created electronic bulletins, mailing lists, or subscription services which they use to provide court information to individuals. The Federal Court, for instance, notes that

> [b]y sending a blank message…with the words "media subscription" in the subject line, anyone may register to be sent Federal Court Bulletins. The bulletins provide notice of Court decisions for which these is special media interest, as well as other Court news such as judicial appointments or retirements.[37]

Additionally, a number of courts (including the Federal Court) offer the opportunity to individuals to subscribe to Rich Site Summary (RSS) feeds as a way to receive notifications about decisions handed down and announcements made.[38]

Canadian Courts Work with Third Parties to Make Information about Court Proceedings Accessible Online

In addition to making information about court proceedings available on their websites, some Canadian courts work with third parties to provide online access to information relating to court proceedings. The SCC, for instance, partners with Lexum to make its judgments available online.[39] Similarly, judgments rendered by the Courts of Québec are freely available online from the *Société québécoise d'information juridique* (SOQUIJ).[40] A number of courts indicate on their websites that their judgments are available through CanLII.[41] Court judgments can also be accessed by the public for a fee through subscription-based services like Westlaw Canada and LexisNexis Quicklaw.[42]

Canadian Courts Use Social Media Tools to Disseminate Information about Court Proceedings

Several Canadian courts use Twitter to disseminate information about court proceedings. For instance, the Nova Scotia Courts have several Twitter accounts: (@CourtsNS_NSSC ["Get decisions of the Nova Scotia Supreme Court and Supreme Court Family Division"]; @CourtsNS_News ["Keep up on news from the Courts of Nova Scotia"]; and @CourtsNS_NSCA ["Get decisions of the Nova Scotia Court of Appeal"]); the Manitoba Courts have a Twitter account, (@MBCourts ["This account will provide notification of Manitoba court news, such as judicial appointments, notices and practice directions and website initiatives"]); and the Court of Québec has two Twitter accounts: (@cour_du_quebec and @CQ_info_avocats).[43] Lexum tweets information about recently released SCC decisions at @Lexum_inc.[44]

Very few Canadian courts use Facebook and YouTube as mechanisms through which to disseminate information about court proceedings. Only the Supreme Court of Canada appears to have an official Facebook page.[45] As well, the only Canadian court to have a YouTube channel appears to be the Saskatchewan Law Courts.[46]

Courts Have Restricted the Extent to Which Individuals Can Disseminate Information Using Electronic Devices in Courtrooms

As described above, Canadian courts have used technological opportunities to disseminate a significant amount of information about court proceedings to the public. However, while doing so, they have also enacted policies restricting the extent to which media and individuals can use electronic devices to disseminate information about court proceedings to the public. In enacting these policies, courts have limited the extent to which both individuals and the news media can assist individuals to fully realize their s. 2(b) right to freedom of expression.

Generally speaking, policies enacted by Canadian courts regarding the use of electronic devices in courts both indicate who may use electronic devices in courts while courts are in session and set out the range of uses that are either permitted or prohibited. The types of electronic device policies enacted by Canadian courts can be situated on a spectrum from most permissive to least permissive (or, said differently, from least restrictive to most restrictive).[47] In this section, I will describe three categories of policies on this spectrum: policies that can be characterized as permissive; policies under which some types of uses are prohibited and others permitted; and policies that can be characterized as restrictive.[48]

Permissive Policies

The most permissive policies enacted by Canadian courts with respect to the use of electronic devices in courtrooms permit a wide range of individuals—including but not limited to members of the media and members of the public—to receive and transmit text on a range of electronic devices while in courtrooms and while court is in session, provided the devices are used discreetly and do not disrupt court proceedings. The most permissive policies also permit audio recording for a range of uses. Even the most permissive policies enacted by Canadian courts, however, do not permit video recording without prior permission, or voice communication while in courtrooms.

The most permissive policy adopted by Canadian courts with respect to the use of electronic devices in courtrooms is that of the SCC.[49] The SCC's policy indicates that "[t]he use of laptops and handheld devices such as Blackberries and cell phones is permitted, as long as the sound is turned off."[50] The SCC "provides [both] power outlets at the media seats as well as free wireless access."[51] In addition, the SCC is unique amongst Canadian courts in permitting the use of audio recorders in the courtroom by both media and the public without requiring prior permission from the presiding judicial officer.[52]

The policy on the use of electronic devices in courtrooms enacted by the Ontario Court of Justice (OCJ) also permits the use, by all individuals, "of electronic communication devices in silent or vibrate mode."[53] A number of types of uses, however, are explicitly prohibited under this policy, including the taking of photos and videos.[54] Audio recording is permitted for a range of individuals (namely counsel, licensed paralegals, court staff, members of the media and litigants) for note-taking purposes.[55] This policy expressly indicates that "[m]embers of the public are also permitted to make audio recordings for note-taking purposes…if the express permission of the presiding judicial officer is first obtained."[56]

A third example of a permissive policy is the policy enacted by the Courts of Nova Scotia that applies in the Court of Appeal, Supreme Court, Supreme Court Family Division, Provincial Court, Domestic Violence Court, Drug Court, Small Claims Court, Probate Court, and Bankruptcy Court.[57] This policy, referred to specifically as the "permissive" version of the electronic devices policy, can be contrasted with the "restrictive" version of this policy (discussed below), which applies in the Youth Court, Mental Health Court, and Family Court.[58]

Under the Courts of Nova Scotia's permissive policy, "the transmission of text information about court proceedings from inside a courtroom while court is in session, for publication and by any means (including Twitter, Texting, E-mail, etc.), *is allowed* unless the presiding Judge orders otherwise" (emphasis in original).[59] Under this policy, members of the media may also make audio recordings of court proceedings in order to "augment their note-taking."[60]

The Federal Courts have also enacted permissive policies for the use of electronic devices in courtrooms. The Federal Court's policy document indicates that "[f]or the purpose of note-taking or electronic communication, [electronic devices]…are generally permitted in court provided they do not cause any disturbance to the proceedings. This applies to members of the media, counsel and members of the public."[61] The Federal Court permits audio recordings to be made by accredited media for note verification purposes.[62] Similarly, the Federal Court of Appeal's policy document indicates that "[t]he use of electronic devices in the courtroom is permitted, provided the devices are used in 'silent' or 'vibration' mode so as not to affect the decorum, the good order and the course of the proceedings."[63]

Lastly, under the Policy on Use of Electronic Devices in Courtrooms in use in the Courts of British Columbia (another policy that, at least with respect to the use of electronic devices in the British Columbia Court of Appeal, can be characterized as permissive), it is noted that in Court of Appeal courtrooms, "any person may use an electronic device to transmit or receive text in a discreet manner that does not interfere with the proceedings."[64]

Policies that Permit the Use of Electronic Devices by Some Categories of Individuals While Restricting Use by Members of the Public

A number of policies enacted by Canadian courts permit the use of electronic devices in courtrooms by certain individuals or categories of individuals (for instance, media), while at the same time prohibiting their use by members of the public. Some of these policies are framed as total prohibitions on the use of electronic devices in courts, with certain categories of users (not including members of the public) exempted from this prohibition. Other policies explicitly prohibit the use of electronic devices in courtrooms by members of the public while permitting their use by others.

1. Total Prohibitions, With Certain Categories of Users Exempted (None Being Members of the Public)

One policy framed as a total prohibition on the use of electronic devices in courtrooms, with certain categories of users exempted from this prohibition, is that of the Court of Queen's Bench of Alberta.[65] This policy states that "[a]ll devices must be turned off in courtrooms."[66] However, both counsel and "members of the media who have signed an undertaking with the Court" are "exempted from this restriction."[67] A second policy consistent with this category is that of the Manitoba courts, which sets out that "[o]nly members of the legal profession and eligible media may use electronic devices to transmit and receive data during a court proceeding or hearing before a court."[68] A third policy consistent with this category is the New Brunswick Courts' policy document, which states that "[t]ext shall not be transmitted."[69] An exception is made, under the New Brunswick Courts' policy document, for journalists, who are permitted to "use electronic devices to capture notes and transmit text."[70]

The Saskatchewan Law Courts' Twitter protocol

> allows media who have been accredited by the Court Services Division of the Ministry of Justice to activate and use in silent mode, a mobile phone, small laptop or similar piece of equipment to perform live text-based communications from court, unless the presiding judge gives instructions otherwise.[71]

More broadly, however, in the Saskatchewan Law Courts, "all [electronic and wireless] devices must be turned off in courtrooms."[72] Several categories of users are exempted. Specifically, "[l]egal counsel and those members of the media who have been accredited … may keep their devices turned on in silent mode and use them to receive and transmit information, provided they are not disruptive to court proceedings."[73] Media may also make audio recordings "for purposes of accuracy."[74]

Under the Policy on Use of Electronic Devices in Courtrooms in use in the British Columbia courts, "[e]xcept as permitted under this policy, the use of electronic devices in courtrooms to transmit and receive text is prohibited."[75] In courtrooms of the Supreme Court and the Provincial Court, both accredited media and lawyers who are members of the Law Society of British Columbia "may use electronic devices to transmit and receive text in a discreet manner that does not interfere with the proceedings."[76] In all British Columbia courts, audio recordings are only able to be made by accredited media, and only for "verifying…notes."[77]

Lastly, under the policy implemented by the Supreme Court of Yukon, "[w]ith the exception of counsel and accredited media, no real-time communication is permitted from any courtroom in which proceedings are taking place."[78] This policy document explicitly states that "counsel and accredited media are permitted to use devices…inside the courtroom for the purposes of making notes and/or transmitting digital information about the proceedings, including tweeting and blogging."[79]

2. *Certain Categories of Users Permitted to Use Electronic Devices; Members of the Public Expressly Prohibited From Use*

One policy that explicitly prohibits the use of electronic devices in courtrooms by members of the public, while permitting their use by others, is that of the Court of Appeal of Alberta, which states that "[m]embers of the public are not permitted to use electronic devices in the courtroom. Electronic devices possessed by members of the public must be turned off and kept out of sight."[80] However, lawyers and members of the media are—with certain exceptions—"permitted to use electronic devices in the courtroom."[81]

A second policy consistent with this category is the policy enacted by the Courts of Prince Edward Island, which states that "[m]embers of the public are not permitted to use electronic devices in the courtroom, unless the presiding judge orders otherwise."[82] Authorized Persons, however (defined by the court as "mean[ing] only members of the Bar, law clerks, law students, law enforcement officers, self-represented litigants, and members of the media"), "may use an Electronic Device in silent mode and in a discreet and unobtrusive manner in the Court."[83] For greater clarity, this policy states that "[a]n Authorized Person may use an Electronic Device to transmit information from the courtroom to a publicly accessible medium (e.g., via Twitter, Facebook, or live blog)."[84] Authorized persons are also permitted to make audio recordings for the purpose of note-taking.[85]

A third policy consistent with this category is that of the Ontario Superior Court of Justice.[86] Under this policy, "[m]embers of the public are *not permitted* to use electronic devices in the courtroom unless the presiding judge orders otherwise" (emphasis in original).[87] By contrast, under this policy

> the use of electronic devices in silent mode and in a discreet and unobtrusive manner is *permitted* in the courtroom by counsel, paralegals licensed by the Law Society of Upper Canada, law students and law clerks assisting counsel during the proceeding, self-represented parties, and media or journalists [emphasis in original].[88]

Only counsel, self-represented parties, media, and journalists are allowed to make audio recordings, and only for note-taking purposes.[89]

A fourth policy consistent with this category is that of the Nunavut Court of Justice.[90] Under this policy, media can "use live text-based communication technology to send copy to their employers from the courthouse and courtrooms."[91] By contrast, "[t]he use of live text-based communications by members of the public in the courthouse or courtrooms is prohibited without special leave."[92]

3. Restrictive Policies

The most restrictive policies adopted by Canadian courts prohibit—without exception—all persons from using electronic devices, in courtrooms, to transmit or receive text. One example of a restrictive policy is that enacted by the Courts of Nova Scotia for application in the Youth Court, Mental Health Court, and Family Court. Under this policy, "the transmission of text information about court proceedings from inside a courtroom while court is in session, for publication and by any means …, *is not allowed* without the permission of the presiding Judge" (emphasis in original).[93]

The policy enacted by the Northwest Territories Courts also falls within this range of the spectrum.[94] This policy notes that "[t]he use of [electronic] devices…is prohibited" for the general public.[95] Furthermore, although lawyers, justice professionals, and members of the media may use electronic devices in the courtroom, they must "turn [] off or otherwise disable []…[t]he device's transmitting and receiving features."[96] This policy specifically notes that "[e]mails and texts are not to be sent or received; [t]here is no electronic broadcasting in any manner whatsoever from the courtroom; audio output is turned off or otherwise disabled (silent mode is on)."[97] As well, no photographs are to be taken, nor audio or videos recorded.[98]

The policy enacted by the Courts of Québec, as well, can be situated on the restrictive end of the spectrum.[99] This policy provides that "[w]itnesses and members of the public must always turn off their electronic devices within a courtroom and keep them turned off."[100] This policy also provides that "[i]t is prohibited at all times …to send or communicate text messages, observations, information, notes, photographs or audio or visual recordings from within a courtroom to outside a courtroom."[101]

Cases in Which the Protection of Other Social Values Must Prevail over the s. 2(b) Right to Information about Court Proceedings

I am not arguing that courts should make all information about court proceedings available online, or that limitations should never be imposed on the use, by members of the public, of electronic devices in courtrooms. Rather, I am arguing that given that individuals are entitled to information about court proceedings as an aspect of their s. 2(b) right to freedom of expression, the starting point with respect to both information made available by courts online and the policies put in place by courts with respect to the use, by media and members of the public, of electronic devices in courtrooms, should be openness. This starting point is consistent with recent statements of the SCC concerning the "critical importance of the open court principle"[102] as well as with the approach taken by the SCC to the s. 2(b) analysis more broadly.[103]

However, as is the case with any other aspect of the s. 2(b) right to freedom of expression—or any *Charter* right more broadly—it is entirely appropriate for courts or legislatures to impose reasonable limitations on the exercise of this right in order to protect other countervailing constitutional rights and values. In an address entitled "The Relationship Between the Courts and the Media," McLachlin CJ noted that "[c]oncerns of privacy, security and court process may …justify limits on *how* the media go about gathering and transmitting information about judicial proceedings" (emphasis in original).[104] Similarly, such concerns may justify limits, imposed by courts, on how members of the public might go about gathering and transmitting such information; on how courts themselves go about transmitting information relating to judicial proceedings; and on what types of information are collected and disseminated, and by whom.

Commentators have suggested a number of ways in which the collection and dissemination of court information should be limited in order to take into consideration other countervailing constitutional rights and social values. Nicolas Vermeys, for instance, suggests that concerns about the impact of eAccess to court records on privacy, a "social value of superordinate importance,"[105] could be addressed in part by the use of technological means to limit access to or the use of court information (Vermeys, Chapter 4 of this volume).

Vermeys suggests that "[i]n the case of eAccess, Code [or eAccess software] can be used to control access to a document, by means of a restricted view technique, such as blanking. It could also be used to set constraints on consultation periods, to block aggregation tools, or to simply limit research functions within certain types of documents" (Vermeys, Chapter 4 of this volume).

Karen Eltis has also written about the need to guard against "unrestrained disclosure" of court information, which she argues can "disturbingly chill access to the courts."[106] Eltis argues that one important step is to "clearly define" both the values of privacy and access.[107] As she put it:

> If privacy is more broadly understood as deriving from human dignity then it can be viewed as a facilitator rather than detractor of accessibility and comport with the court's various duties (to foster transparency and to protect litigants and control its documents). In other words, judges would presumably be more inclined to use their discretion to protect litigants' (and other participants') privacy if doing so would not be regarded as sacrificing openness or transparency but rather as a facilitator of access and enabler of court control over its records.[108]

A complete discussion of the ways in which the collection, dissemination, and use of court information should be limited in order to take into consideration other countervailing constitutional rights and social values such as privacy is beyond the scope of this paper.[109] Such a discussion, however, plays an integral part in any attempt to implement the principles and core ideas discussed in this paper (for instance the reconsideration, by Canadian courts, of their policies regarding the use of electronic devices in courtrooms).

Conclusion

For many years, the press was one of, if not the only, entity capable of disseminating information about court proceedings quickly and efficiently to the public. As a result, it played, and was recognized by Cory J in *Edmonton Journal* as playing, a "fundamentally important" role in assisting individuals unable to attend court in person to realize their s. 2(b) right to information about court proceedings.[110]

In this paper, I have argued that it is no longer the case that the news media are the only entities capable of assisting individuals in fully realizing their s. 2(b) right to information about court proceedings. As outlined above, technological developments have significantly enhanced the ability of parties other than the news media—including members of the public and courts themselves—to disseminate information about court proceedings to the public.

I have also argued that empowered by these technological developments, Canadian courts in particular—as "guardians of the

Constitution and of individuals' rights under it"[111]—can and should play a central role in assisting individuals in fully realizing their s. 2(b) right to information about court proceedings. Canadian courts can do so both by providing individuals with information about court proceedings (directly and by partnering with third parties), and by implementing policies on the use of electronic devices in courts that minimize restrictions on the ability of individuals and news media to disseminate information about court proceedings to the public.

I have argued that the starting point with respect to both of these sets of policies should be openness. As is the case with the application of the s. 2(b) right to freedom of expression in other contexts, however, it is appropriate to impose reasonable limits on the collection, use, and dissemination of court information in order to protect countervailing constitutional rights and values, such as privacy, security, courtroom management, and fairness in the administration of justice.[112]

As described above, while some courts, such as the SCC, the Federal Courts, the Courts of British Columbia, the Courts of Nova Scotia, and the Manitoba Courts, have provided online access to a wide range of court information, other courts have not followed suit to the same degree. As well, although certain Canadian courts such as the SCC, the Federal Courts, the Ontario Court of Justice, the Courts of Nova Scotia and the Courts of British Columbia have adopted policies with respect to the use of electronic devices in courts that can be char-acterized—at least in certain ways—as permissive, other courts have adopted more restrictive policies.

In reconsidering their policies relating to the collection, use, and dissemination of court information, courts will need to make a series of decisions with respect to the types of information that should be made available online by courts, the ways through which this informa-tion should be made available, and the reasonable restrictions that might be applied both to the types of information made available by courts and the use of electronic devices in courtrooms. While each court could consider these questions independently, they could also be considered in the context of a national conversation.[113] Such an initia-tive—for instance, one that is led or facilitated by the Canadian Judicial Council—could result in the creation of best-practice guidelines that could be adopted by courts across the country. As well, to the extent that certain courts are not taking steps to make information available due to a lack of resources, a nation-wide discussion could lead to cost-sharing or resource-sharing solutions being proposed and adopted.

Ultimately, the responsibility to provide individuals with access to information about court proceedings need not and must not be borne by news media alone. Rather, it is through the joint efforts of the press, the courts, and members of the public that individuals unable to attend court in person will fully realize their s. 2(b) right to access information about court proceedings. Courts, in particular, play an integral role in this process. In addition to setting their own policies with respect to the types and extent of court information made available online, courts also set policies that have a significant impact on the ability of both media and members of the public to disseminate information about court proceedings (for instance, policies with respect to the use of electronic devices in courts). Courts should draft these policies with an eye to the "fundamentally important" role that they play in assisting individuals in fully realizing their s. 2(b) right to information about court proceedings, as well as with an eye to all relevant countervailing constitutional rights and values.[114]

Notes

1   *Canadian Charter of Rights and Freedoms, Part I of the Constitution Act, 1982,* being Schedule B to the Canada Act 1982 (UK), 1982, c. 11. See *Edmonton Journal v Alberta (Attorney General)* [1989] 2 SCR 1326 at paras 10–11, 64 DLR (4th) 577 [*Edmonton Journal*].

2   *Edmonton Journal, supra* note 1 at para 10. In 2011, in *Canadian Broadcasting Corp v. Canada (Attorney General) (CBC),* Deschamps J, who delivered the judgment of the Court, echoed Cory Js remarks, writing that without the presence of journalists in courthouses, "the public's ability to understand our justice system would depend on the tiny minority of the population who attend hearings." *Canadian Broadcasting Corp v Canada (Attorney General)* 2011 SCC 2 at para 45, [2011] 1 SCR 19 [*CBC*]).

3   Chief Justice Beverley McLachlin, "The Relationship Between the Courts and the Media (Address at Carleton University)" (31 January 2012) *Supreme Court of Canada,* online: <http://www.scc-csc.gc.ca/court-cour/judges-juges/spe-dis/bm-2012-01-31-eng.aspx>.

4   *Hunter v Southam Inc,* [1984] 2 SCR 145 at 169, 11 DLR (4th) 641.

5   *Attorney General of Nova Scotia v MacIntyre* [1982] 1 SCR 175 at 186–87, 132 DLR (3d) 385, cited in *AB v Bragg Communications Inc,* 2012 SCC 46 at para 13, [2012] 2 SCR 567 [*AB v Bragg*].

6   *AB v Bragg, supra* note 5 at para 14. McLachlin, *supra* note 3 (other types of concerns that might warrant limiting the dissemination of court information include "security and court process").

7   *Charter,* supra note 1 at s 2(b).
8   As noted by the Court in *Ford v Québec (Attorney General)*, the s. 2(b) right to freedom of expression protects "listeners as well as speakers" (*Ford v Quebec (Attorney General)* [1988] 2 SCR 712 at para 58, 54 DLR (4th) 577).
9   *Edmonton Journal, supra* note 1 at paras 10–11.
10 *Canadian Broadcasting Corp v New Brunswick (Attorney General); Re R. v. Carson,* [1996] 3 SCR 480, 182 NBR (2d) 81.
11 Ibid. at para 23.
12 *Ontario (Public Safety and Security) v Criminal Lawyers' Association* 2010 SCC 23 at para 36, [2010] 1 SCR 815.
13 *Edmonton Journal, supra* note 1 at para 10.
14 *Edmonton Journal, supra* note 1 at para 10.
15 Tim Berners-Lee, *Weaving the Web* (New York: Harper Collins, 1999) at 21–23.
16 Neither the internet nor the World Wide Web were discussed by the SCC until many years after they had been introduced. The first SCC case to reference the internet, for instance, was *United Food and Commercial Workers, Local 1518 (UFCW) v Kmart Canada Ltd,* a 1999 decision. In this decision, Cory J, who delivered the judgment of the Court, referenced "Internet mailing" as a mechanism through which people could be persuaded not to buy something. Similarly, the SCC's first reference to the World Wide Web is in a 2004 decision (Society of Composers, Authors and Music Publishers of Canada v Canadian Association of Internet Providers, 2004 SCC 45, [2004] 2 SCR 427).
17 Internet Live Stats, "Total Number of Websites," online: <http://www.internetlivestats.com/total-number-of-websites/>.
18 Johnny Ryan, *A History of the Internet and the Digital Future* (London: Reaktion Books, 2010) at 149.
19 Ibid.
20 Facebook, "Company Info," online: <newsroom.fb.com/company-info/>.
21 Twitter, "Company," online: <https://about.twitter.com/company>.
22 YouTube, "Statistics," online: <https://www.youtube.com/yt/press/statistics.html>.
23 Statistics Canada, *Canadian Internet Use Survey, 2012* at 1, online: <www.statcan.gc.ca/daily-quotidien/131126/dq131126d-eng.htm>.
24 Ibid. at 2.
25 See e.g., Courthouse Libraries BC, "Vancouver Branch," online: <www.courthouselibrary.ca/about/libraries/vancouver.aspx?LIbid=faad9cb1-86c2-4929-a515-11910eb4b30d>.
26 Statistics Canada, *supra* note 23 at 2.
27 Brett Langlois, "With Growth Comes Changes: The Evolving Canadian Mobile Landscape," *Catalyst Canada,* online: <catalyst.ca/2015-canadian-smartphone-market/>.

28   See, for instance, Court of Appeal of British Columbia (1 January 2009), online: <www.courts.gov.bc.ca/Court_of_Appeal/>; Supreme Court of British Columbia (1 January 2009), online: <www.courts.gov.bc.ca/supreme_court/>; Provincial Court of British Columbia, online: <www.provincialcourt.bc.ca/>; Court of Appeal of Alberta, online: <https://albertacourts.ca/court-of-appeal>; Court of Queen's Bench of Alberta, online: <https://albertacourts.ca/court-of-queens-bench>; Provincial Court of Alberta, online: <https://albertacourts.ca/provincial-court>; Saskatchewan Law Courts, online: <www.sasklawcourts.ca/>; Manitoba Court of Appeal (28 February 2014), online: <www.manitobacourts.mb.ca/court-of-appeal/>; Manitoba Court of Queen's Bench (24 November 2014), online: <http://www.manitobacourts.mb.ca/court-of-queens-bench/> accessed May 1, 2015; Manitoba Provincial Court (March 13, 2014), online: <www.manitobacourts.mb.ca/provincial-court/>; Court of Appeal for Ontario, online: <www.ontariocourts.ca/coa/en/>; Ontario Superior Court of Justice, online: <www.ontariocourts.ca/scj/>; Court of Appeal of Quebec, online: <courdappelduquebec.ca/en/>; Superior Court of Québec, online: <www.tribunaux.qc.ca/mjq_en/c-superieure/index-cs.html>; Court of Québec, online: <www.tribunaux.qc.ca/mjq_en/c-quebec/index-cq.html>; Nova Scotia Court of Appeal, online: <www.courts.ns.ca/Appeal_Court/NSCA_home.htm>; Nova Scotia Provincial Court, online: <www.courts.ns.ca/Provincial_Court/NSPC_home.htm>; New Brunswick Court of Appeal, online: <https://www.gnb.ca/cour/03COA1/index-e.asp>; New Brunswick Court of Queen's Bench, online: <https://www.gnb.ca/cour/04CQB/index-e.asp>; New Brunswick Provincial Court, online: <https://www.gnb.ca/cour/06PCNB/index-e.asp>; Supreme Court of Newfoundland and Labrador (Court of Appeal), online: <www.court.nl.ca/supreme/appeal/index.html>; Supreme Court of Newfoundland and Labrador (General Division), online: <www.court.nl.ca/supreme/general/index.html>; Provincial Court of Newfoundland and Labrador, online: <http://www.court.nl.ca/provincial/>; Court of Appeal of Prince Edward Island, online: <www.courts.pe.ca/appeal/>; Supreme Court of Prince Edward Island, online: <www.courts.pe.ca/supreme/>; Provincial Court of Prince Edward Island, online: <www.courts.pe.ca/index.php?number=1051070>; Court of Appeal for the Northwest Territories, online: <https://www.nwtcourts.ca/Courts/ca.htm>; Supreme Court of the Northwest Territories, online: <https://www.nwtcourts.ca/Courts/sc.htm>; Territorial Court of the Northwest Territories, online: <https://www.nwtcourts.ca/Courts/tc.htm>; Court of Appeal for Yukon, online <www.yukoncourts.ca/courts/appeal.html>; Supreme Court of Yukon, online: <www.yukoncourts.ca/courts/supreme.html>; Territorial Court of Yukon, online: <www.yukoncourts.ca/courts/territorial.html>; Nunavut Court of Justice (June 2, 2011), online: <www.nucj.ca/welcome.htm>.

29 See Supreme Court of Canada (8 April 2015), online: <www.scc-csc.gc.ca/
home-accueil/index-eng.aspx>; Federal Court of Canada (2 November
2013), online: <cas-ncr-ntero3.cas-satj.gc.ca/portal/page/portal/fc_cf_en/
Index>; Federal Court of Appeal (14 June 2013), online: <cas-ncr-ntero3.
cas-satj.gc.ca/portal/page/portal/fca-caf_eng>; Tax Court of Canada (10
June 2014), online: <cas-ncr-ntero3.cas-satj.gc.ca/portal/page/portal/tcc-
cci_Eng/Index>; and Court Martial Appeal Court of Canada (13 February
2015), online: <www.cmac-cacm.ca/index-eng.shtml>.

30 See, for instance, Supreme Court of Canada, "Scheduled Hearings,"
online: <www.scc-csc.gc.ca/case-dossier/info/hear-aud-eng.aspx>;
Federal Court of Canada, "Hearing Lists," online: <cas-ncr-ntero3.cas-
satj.gc.ca/portal/page/portal/fc_cf_en/Hearing_Lists>; Federal Court of
Appeal, "Hearing Schedule," online: <cas-ncr-ntero3.cas-satj.gc.ca/
portal/page/portal/fca-caf_eng/hearings-auditions_eng>; Tax Court of
Canada, "Hearing Schedule," online: <cas-ncr-ntero3.cas-satj.gc.ca/
tcc_hearings/hearings_schedule_e.php>; Court Martial Appeal Court
of Canada, "Hearing List," online: <www.cmac-cacm.ca/business/
hearing_list-eng.shtml>; Court of Appeal for British Columbia, "Hearing
List," online: <www.courts.gov.bc.ca/court_of_appeal/hearing_
list/>; Court of Appeal of Alberta, "Hearing Lists," online: <https://
albertacourts.ca/court-of-appeal/sittings-hearing-lists-locations/current-
hearing-lists>; Manitoba Court of Appeal, "Scheduled Appeal Hearings,"
online: <www.manitobacourts.mb.ca/court-of-appeal/location-and-
hours/court-schedule/>; Court of Appeal for Ontario, "Case List," online:
<www.ontariocourts.ca/coa/en/caselist/>; Court of Appeal of Quebec,
"Rolls," online: <courdappelduquebec.ca/en/rolls/>; The Courts of Nova
Scotia, "Dockets of the Courts," online: <www.courts.ns.ca/General_
Content/dockets_on_line.htm>; Supreme Court of Newfoundland and
Labrador (Court of Appeal), "Sitting Schedule," online: <www.court.
nl.ca/supreme/appeal/schedule.html>; Prince Edward Island Court of
Appeal, "Court Schedule," online: <www.gov.pe.ca/courts/supreme/
schedule/index.php3>; Northwest Territories Courts, "Court Schedule,"
online: <https://www.nwtcourts.ca/Schedule/schedule.htm>.

31 See, for instance, Supreme Court of Canada, "SCC Case Information –
Factums on Appeal – 35918," online: <www.scc-csc.gc.ca/case-dossier/
info/af-ma-eng.aspx?cas=35918>.

32 See, for instance, Supreme Court of Canada, "SCC Case Information –
Search," online: <www.scc-csc.gc.ca/case-dossier/info/search-recherche-
eng.aspx>; Federal Courts, "Proceedings Queries," online:
<cas-ncr-ntero3.cas-satj.gc.ca/IndexingQueries/infp_queries_e.php>;
Manitoba Courts, "QB Court Registry," online: <www.jus.gov.mb.ca>. In
British Columbia, court record information is available online on British
Columbia Ministry of Justice, "Court Services Online," online: <https://

justice.gov.bc.ca/cso/index.do>. There is a link to Court Services Online on the Courts of British Columbia homepage (www.courts.gov.bc.ca).

33 See, for instance, Courts of British Columbia, "Search Judgments," online: <www.courts.gov.bc.ca/search_judgments.aspx?court=0>; Manitoba Courts, "Recent Judgments," online: <www.manitobacourts. mb.ca/court-of-appeal/recent-judgments/>; Court of Appeal for Ontario, "Decisions of the Court," online: <www.ontariocourts.ca/decisions_ index/en/>; Federal Court of Canada, "Decisions of the Federal Court," online: <decisions.fct-cf.gc.ca/fc-cf/en/nav.do>; Court of Appeal of New Brunswick, "Decisions," online: <www.gnb.ca/cour/03COA1/ decisions-e.asp>; Courts of Nova Scotia, "Decisions of the Courts of Nova Scotia," online: <www.courts.ns.ca/Decisions_Of_Courts/ decisions_recent.htm>; Yukon Courts, "Territorial Court Judgments," online: <www.yukoncourts.ca/courts/territorial/judgments.html>; Government of the Northwest Territories, "Judgment Database Search," online: <https://www.nwtcourts.ca/dbtw-wpd/nwtjqbe.shtml>.

34 Supreme Court of Canada, "Webcasts by Session," online: <www.scc-csc. gc.ca/case-dossier/info/webcasts-webdiffusions-eng.aspx>.

35 Ibid.

36 See Courts of British Columbia, "British Columbia Court of Appeal Webcast Pilot Project," online: <www.courts.gov.bc.ca/Court_of_Appeal/ webcast/Webcast.html>; Manitoba Courts, "Information for Media," online: <www.manitobacourts.mb.ca/information-for-media/#initiative>; Courts of Nova Scotia, "Live Webcasts," online: <www.courts.ns.ca/ Webcasts/webcasts_live.htm>; Ontario Ministry of the Attorney General, "Webcasting of Court Proceedings Begins Today" (7 September 2007), online: <www.attorneygeneral.jus.gov.on.ca/english/news/2007/20070907-cam-nr.asp>.

37 Federal Court of Canada, "Policy on Public and Media Access" (20 August 2013), online: <cas-ncr-nter03.cas-satj.gc.ca/portal/page/portal/ fc_cf_en/MediaPolicy>; see also Alberta Courts, "Court of Appeal: Manage My Subscriptions," online: <https://albertacourts.ca/court-of-appeal/manage-my-subscriptions>.

38 See, for instance, the Ontario Courts (http://www.ontariocourts.ca/coa/ en/rss/) and the Courts of British Columbia (http://www.courts.gov. bc.ca/rss.xml).

39 Supreme Court of Canada, "Judgments of the Supreme Court of Canada" (20 April 2015), online: <scc-csc.lexum.com/scc-csc/en/nav.do>.

40 SOQUIJ, "Services aux citoyens," online: <soquij.qc.ca/>.

41 CanLII, online: <https://www.canlii.org/en/>; see e.g., Alberta Courts, "Judgments," online: <https://albertacourts.ca/resolution-and-court-administration-serv/judgments>; Courts of Saskatchewan, "Decisions," online: <www.sasklawcourts.ca/index.php/home/decisions>; Courts of

Prince Edward Island, "Court Decisions," online: <www.courts.pe.ca/supreme/index.php?number=1050808&lang=E>; Supreme Court of Newfoundland and Labrador, "Decisions of the Court of Appeals," online: <www.court.nl.ca/supreme/appeal/decisions.html>; Nunavut Court of Justice, "Decisions of the Nunavut Court of Justice," online: <www.nucj.ca/decisions.htm>.

42   Westlaw Canada, "Westlaw Canada Sign-On," online: <canada.westlaw.com/signon/default.wl?vr=2.0&fn=_top&rs=WLWCRSW15.04&bhcp=1>; LexisNexis, "LexisNexis Quicklaw Sign In," online: <https://www.lexisnexis.com/ca/legal/>.

43   Twitter, "Nova Scotia Courts (@CourtsNS_NSSC)," online: <https://twitter.com/courtsns_nssc>; Twitter, "Nova Scotia Courts (@CourtsNS_News)," online: <https://twitter.com/courtsns_news>; Twitter, "Nova Scotia Courts (@CourtsNS_NSCA)," online: <https://twitter.com/courtsns_nsca>; Twitter, "Manitoba Courts (@MBCourts)," online: <https://twitter.com/mbcourts>; Twitter, "Cour du Québec (@cour_du_quebec)," online: <https://twitter.com/cour_du_quebec>; Twitter, "CQ info aux avocats (@CQ_info_avocats)," online: <https://twitter.com/cq_info_avocats>.

44   Twitter, "Lexum (@Lexum_inc)," online: <https://twitter.com/lexum_inc>.

45   Supreme Court of Canada, "Supreme Court of Canada," online: *Facebook* <https://www.facebook.com/supremecourtofcanada?fref=ts>.

46   Saskatchewan Law Courts, "Saskatchewan Law Courts – YouTube," online: *YouTube* <https://www.youtube.com/channel/UC192QXfF7WP3ktJvIIB3O4g/feed>.

47   The terms "restrictive" and "permissive" are drawn from the electronic-device policy enacted by the Nova Scotia Courts (Courts of Nova Scotia, "The Use of Electronic Devices in Courthouses" (15 May 2014), online: <www.courts.ns.ca/Media_Information/electronic_devices_policy.htm>.

48   For a comprehensive summary of Canadian court policies relating to the use of electronic devices in courtrooms, see IntellAction Working Groups (Canadian Centre for Court Technology), "Policies on Live Text Based Communications" (June 2013), online: <http://wiki.modern-courts.ca/images/5/57/Policies_on_Live_Text_Based_Communications.pdf>.

49   Supreme Court of Canada, "Access to the Court" (2 February 2009), online: <www.scc-csc.gc.ca/news-nouv/media/acc-eng.aspx>.

50   Ibid.

51   Ibid.

52   Ibid.

53   Ontario Court of Justice, "Protocol Regarding the Use of Electronic Communication Devices in Court Proceedings" (1 March 2013), online: <www.ontariocourts.ca/ocj/legal-professionals/practice-directions/electronic-devices/>.

54 Ibid.
55 Ibid.
56 Ibid.
57 Courts of Scotia, *supra* note 47.
58 Ibid.
59 Ibid.
60 Courts of Nova Scotia, "Policy Re: Use of Electronic Devices" (21 May 2014), online: <www.courts.ns.ca/Media_Information/media_docs/NS_Courts_permissive_devices_twitter_policy_14-05-15.pdf>.
61 Federal Court of Canada, "Policy on Public and Media Access," *supra* note 37.
62 Ibid.
63 Federal Court of Appeal, "Guidelines on Public and Media" (17 July 2014), online: <cas-ncr-nter03.cas-satj.gc.ca/portal/page/portal/fca-caf_eng/media_eng>.
64 Courts of British Columbia, "Policy on Use of Electronic Devices in Courtrooms" (6 October 2014), online: <www.courts.gov.bc.ca/supreme_court/media/PDF/Policy%20on%20Use%20of%20Electronic%20Devices%20in%20Courtrooms%20-%20FINAL.pdf>.
65 Court of Queen's Bench of Alberta, "Electronic and Wireless Devices Policy" (January 2012), online: <https://albertacourts.ca/docs/default-source/Court-of-Queen's-Bench/electronic_policy_final.pdf?sfvrsn=0>.
66 Ibid.
67 Ibid.
68 Manitoba Courts, "Electronic Devices Policy" (20 November 2013), online: <www.manitobacourts.mb.ca/news/electronic-device-policy/>.
69 New Brunswick Courts, "Directive Respecting Electronic Devices in the Courtroom" (29 June 2012), online: <www.gnb.ca/cour/03COA1/pdf/ProtocolDirective/002-Protocol.pdf>.
70 Ibid.
71 Saskatchewan Law Courts, "Twitter and Other Text-Based Forms of Media Communication from Saskatchewan Courtrooms Protocol," online: <www.sasklawcourts.ca/images/documents/Resources/Twitter_from_courtrooms_protocol.pdf>.
72 Ibid.
73 Ibid.
74 Ibid.
75 Courts of British Columbia, "Policy on Use of Electronic Devices in Courtrooms," *supra* note 64.
76 Ibid.
77 Ibid.

78 Supreme Court of Yukon, "Practice Direction #60, Use of Recording Devices and Electronic Equipment During Court Proceedings" (7 May 2013), online: <www.yukoncourts.ca/pdf/pd_60_use_of_recording_devices_and_electronic_equipment_during_court_proceedings..pdf>.

79 Ibid.

80 Court of Appeal of Alberta, "Policy on the Use of Electronic Devices in Courtrooms" (28 October 2013), online: <https://albertacourts.ca/docs/default-source/Court-of-Appeal/notice_to_profession_electronic_devices_in_courtrooms.pdf?sfvrsn=2>.

81 Ibid.

82 Courts of Prince Edward Island, "Use of Electronic Devices" (12 March 2014), online: <www.courts.pe.ca/supreme/index.php?number=1050788&lang=E>.

83 Ibid.

84 Ibid.

85 Ibid.

86 Ontario Superior Court of Justice, "Consolidated Provincial Practice Direction" (11 April 2014), online: <www.ontariocourts.ca/scj/practice/practice-directions/provincial/#D_Electronic_Devices_in_the_Courtroom>.

87 Ibid. at s 96.

88 Ibid. at s 97.

89 Ibid.

90 Nunavut Court of Justice, "Media Use of Technology in the Courtroom and Courthouse" online: <www.nucj.ca/rules/Media_TechnologyUse_CourtroomsA.pdf>.

91 Ibid.

92 Ibid.

93 Courts of Nova Scotia, "The Use of Electronic Devices in Courthouses," *supra* note 47.

94 Northwest Territories Courts, "Use of Electronic Devices in the Courtroom" (23 July 2012), online: <www.nwtcourts.ca/directives/PDTCa.pdf>.

95 Ibid.

96 Ibid.

97 Ibid.

98 Ibid.

99 Courts of Québec, "Guidelines Concerning the Use of Technological Devices in Courtrooms" (3 May 2013), online: <www.tribunaux.qc.ca/mjq_en/c-quebec/Communiques/Guidelines_TechnologicalDevices_CourtRooms.pdf>.

100 Ibid.

101 Ibid.

102 *AB v Bragg, supra* note 5 at para 13.

103 See e.g., *Irwin Toy Ltd v Quebec (Attorney General)* [1989] 1 SCR 927, 58 DLR (4th) 577.

104 McLachlin, *supra* note 3.

105 Citing to *MacIntyre, supra* note 5 at para 14 and *AB v Bragg, supra* note 5 at para 13.

106 Karen Eltis, "The Judicial System in the Digital Age: Revisiting the Relationship between Privacy and Accessibility in the Cyber Context," *McGill Law Journal* 56 (2011):289 at para 20.

107 Ibid. at para 20.

108 Ibid. at para 56.

109 For works that address this issue, see Vermeys, Chapter 4 of this volume; Eltis, *supra* note 106; Amanda Conley et al., "Sustaining Privacy and Open Justice in the Transition to Online Court Records: A Multidisciplinary Inquiry," *Maryland Law Review* 71 (2012) at 772; Jane Bailey, "'Sexualized Online Bullying' Through an Equality Lens: Missed Opportunity in AB v. Bragg?," *McGill Law Journal* 59:3 (2014) at 709; Timothy Bottomer, "Dagenais 2.0: Technology and its Impact on the Dagenais Test," *UBC L Rev* 45 (2012) at 1.

110 *Edmonton Journal, supra* note 1 at 10.

111 *Hunter, supra,* note 4 at 169.

112 As noted in the Nunavut Court of Justice's policy on use of technology in the courtroom, "[t]he use of live text-based technology inside a courtroom has the potential to interfere with the administration of justice. In the context of a criminal trial, live text-based communication or audio recording technology from inside a courtroom can be used to inform or coach potential witnesses about developments in the trial or evidence heard from other witnesses. This type of communication can circumvent a Court's exclusion order and influence the testimony to be given by subsequent witnesses. Justice may suffer as a result. Information posted from the courtroom on, for example, Twitter or Facebook about evidence ruled inadmissible by a Court may also adversely influence a jury. In a civil or family law context, simultaneous reporting from the courtroom may create additional pressure on witnesses by distracting or worrying them" (Nunavut Court of Justice, "Media Use of Technology in the Courtroom and Courthouse", *supra* note 90). See also McLachlin, *supra* note 3, where McLachlin CJ writes both that "sometimes the pressing concerns of privacy or security trump openness" and that "[c]oncerns of privacy, security and court process may also justify limits on *how* the media go about gathering and transmitting information about judicial proceedings" (emphasis in original).

113 One example of such an initiative is the National Guidelines Regarding the Use of Electronic Devices in Court Proceedings, developed by a Canadian Center for Court Technology (CCCT) working group and

released in December 2012 (Canadian Centre for Court Technology, "National Guidelines Regarding the Use of Electronic Communication Devices in Court Proceedings" (17 December 2012), online: <wiki. modern-courts.ca/images/9/96/Use_of_Electronic_Communication_ Devices_in_Court_Proceedings.pdf>. As well, in the Federal Court of Canada's Policy on Public and Media Access, it is noted that "[t]he Court is committed to ongoing consultation about this policy with representatives of the media, the bar and others, and to making adjustments in its application with experience" (Federal Court of Canada, "Policy on Public and Media Access," *supra* note 37).

114 *Edmonton Journal, supra* note 1 at 10.

CHAPTER IV

Privacy v. Transparency: How Remote Access to Court Records Forces Us to Re-examine Our Fundamental Values[1]

Nicolas Vermeys

Introduction

In February of 2010, the Victoria *Times Columnist* published a special report on the lack of uniformity regarding public access to court documents in British Columbia.[2] According to the report, British Columbia's courts would, at that time, "routinely and wrongly deny access to information that should be available to the public." In order to resolve this and other issues,[3] British Columbia has since moved toward eAccess to court records with the launch of B.C. Court Services Online, a service that "provides electronic searches of court files, online access to daily court lists and e-filing capacity."[4] Generally speaking, remote access or "eAccess" to court records implies that those interested in studying the contents of a court file, primarily the judge and litigators, no longer need to travel to the courthouse to do so, nor do they need to make multiple photocopies of the relevant documents to serve a copy to the court and/or opposing council. In fact, in British Columbia, as in other jurisdictions,[5] eAccess to court records is seen as an efficient way to guarantee that the procedures put into place are the same no matter who is behind the computer monitor. Such a practice also limits arbitrary access to procedures due to the clerk's personal understanding of policies or lack of experience. Thus, eAccess is seen both as a way to democratize access to court records, and to facilitate it—both strong arguments in favour of implementing such a solution.[6]

Furthermore, and notwithstanding these obvious efficiency arguments, eAccess to court records is also seen as a way to increase access to justice in a broader sense. In fact, as explained in a 2013 report prepared by the Action Committee on Access to Justice in Civil and Family Matters:

> The technology in all courts and tribunals must be modernized to a level that reflects the electronic needs, abilities and expectations of a modern society. Interactive court forms should be widely accessible. Scheduling, e-filing and docket management should all be simplified and made easily accessible and all court and tribunal documents must be accessible electronically (both on site and remotely).[7]

Although few would argue against better access to justice, eAccess to court records also raises the question of how much access is too much. Of course, the answer to that question really depends on what court records actually include. If the information contained therein is, as both federal[8] and provincial[9] legislators seem to suggest, purely public data, one could argue that there is no such thing as "too much access."[10] However, if court records are repositories of confidential information,[11] it could be argued that even limited access is unwarranted. Therefore, before going any further, one must define what the expression "court records" actually encompasses.

As defined by the Canadian Judicial Council's Judges Technology Advisory Committee in its 2005 *Model Policy for Access to Court Records in Canada*, court records can be defined as files that "include any information or document that is collected, received, stored, maintained or archived by a court in connection with its judicial proceedings."[12] Said court records can therefore include the following elements, among others:

- Case files;
- Dockets;
- Minute books;
- Calendars of hearings;
- Case indexes;
- Registers of actions; and
- Records of the proceedings in any form.[13]

As can be gleaned from this enumeration, court records will therefore often contain private, sometimes very sensitive data. Although this is particularly true of trial courts where records will often contain evidence, the same could be said regarding factums or other legal briefs submitted to appellate courts, although the risks are usually less important for higher courts since the documents they receive mainly address points of law and can therefore be edited to limit the use of sensitive private data and other personal information.[14] Notwithstanding this possibility, the fact remains that enhancing access to court records—primarily at a trial-court level—also means further eroding the privacy rights of parties, witnesses, and other stakeholders in the legal process, which could also have a direct impact on these individuals' willingness to take part in said process.

Of course, the competing values that are privacy and the transparency of court proceedings (which requires better access to court records) have always been at odds. Therefore, by increasing access to court proceedings, eAccess is seen by some as a threat to the somewhat fragile equilibrium that has existed between privacy and transparency by favouring the latter at the expense of the former.[15] This paper aims to examine this issue by (i) studying how eAccess can destabilise this careful equilibrium and, more importantly, (ii) what can be done to re-establish a balance while still taking advantage of this technological solution.

Privacy and Transparency of Court Proceedings: When Technology Destabilizes a Historically Complex but Feasible Equilibrium

As explained by the Supreme Court in *Lac d'Amiante du Québec Ltée v 2858-0702 Québec Inc*,[16] the perpetual tug-of-war between one's right to privacy under the *Privacy Act*[17] or other similar pieces of legislation[18] and the constitutional principle of transparency of court proceedings will usually end with transparency winning out.[19] As the court explains:

> Of course, the right to confidentiality will end if the adverse party decides to actually use the evidence or information obtained on discovery, when that party chooses to use all or part of it in his or her own case. The legislative intent that information

be communicated in a civil trial will then prevail, to ensure that the system is transparent. On the other hand, at the examination on discovery stage, concern for transparency is not an issue because the examination is not a sitting of the courts. It is therefore legitimate in that case to give greater weight to the privacy interest, by imposing the obligation of confidentiality on information that is disclosed.[20]

That being said, and as demonstrated in the previous quote, the fact that transparency will usually take precedence is not an immutable concept, as there are instances where privacy will win out over transparency.[21] Therefore, eAccess to court records cannot simply be adopted because transparency usually prevails if it does not allow for those cases where privacy is seen as the superseding value:

> The justice system has the dual responsibility of being open to the public and protecting personal privacy. Its technology should be designed and used to meet both responsibilities.
>
> Technology use may create or magnify conflict between values of openness and personal privacy. In such circumstances, decision makers must engage in a careful balancing process, considering both values and their underlying purposes, and should maximize beneficial effects while minimizing detrimental effects.[22]

How should decision makers undertake this balancing process? By trying to identify the underlying principles that command the accessibility of court records. Transparency, in itself, has no value. It is merely a means to an end: that courts be open. Furthermore, actual transparency has never truly existed in our system since access to court records requires knowledge of their contents and the time and energy to actually consult a given file. These hurdles often create a practical obscurity that ensures the relative confidentiality of private data. Therefore, with eAccess accentuating transparency while eliminating practical obscurity, technology is not simply allowing for more transparency; it is redefining how transparency is to be understood.

The Open Court Principle as an Argument for eAccess to Court Records

As stated above, the transparency of court proceedings is simply a means to an end. That end, as explained by the Supreme Court in

Edmonton Journal v Alberta (Attorney General),[23] is to allow "public scrutiny of the courts."[24] This, in turn, cannot be done unless court proceedings and, consequently, court records[25] are "open and accessible to the public and to the media."[26]

This notion of free access, commonly referred to as the "open court principle,"[27] is, as the Supreme Court puts it, intrinsically linked to our fundamental "freedom of thought, belief, opinion and expression, including freedom of the press and other media of communication," as guaranteed by section 2(b) of the *Canadian Charter of Rights and Freedoms*:[28]

> The principle of open courts is inextricably tied to the rights guaranteed by s. 2(b). Openness permits public access to information about the courts, which in turn permits the public to discuss and put forward opinions and criticisms of court practices and proceedings. While the freedom to express ideas and opinions about the operation of the courts is clearly within the ambit of the freedom guaranteed by s. 2(b), so too is the right of members of the public to obtain information about the courts in the first place.[29]

As explained by Dickson J in *Attorney General of Nova Scotia v MacIntyre*,[30] this very important notion is the underlying reason why transparency supersedes privacy when dealing with court proceedings:

> Many times it has been urged that the 'privacy' of litigants requires that the public be excluded from court proceedings. It is now well established, however, that covertness is the exception and openness the rule. Public confidence in the integrity of the court system and understanding of the administration of justice are thereby fostered. As a general rule the sensibilities of the individuals involved are no basis for exclusion of the public from judicial proceedings. The following comments of Laurence J. in *R. v. Wright*, 8 T.R. 293, are apposite and were cited with approval by Duff J. in *Gazette Printing Co. v. Shallow* (1909), 41 S.C.R. 339 at p. 359:
>
>> Though the publication of such proceedings may be to the disadvantage of the particular individual concerned, yet it is of vast importance to the public that the proceedings of courts

of justice should be universally known. The general advantage to the country in having these proceedings made public more than counterbalances the inconveniences to the private persons whose conduct may be the subject of such proceedings.[31]

As to how this same principle is to be applied to court records, Dickson J adds:

Undoubtedly every court has a supervisory and protecting power over its own records. Access can be denied when the ends of justice would be subverted by disclosure or the judicial documents might be used for an improper purpose. The presumption, however, is in favour of public access and the burden of contrary proof lies upon the person who would deny the exercise of the right.[32]

As it relates to eAccess to court records, the most important part of the previous statement is that "the ends of justice would be subverted by disclosure or the judicial documents might be used for an improper purpose." As we will now see, the fact that court documents might be used for an improper purpose is the true fear of those who oppose eAccess[33] since it goes far beyond the open court principle to facilitate access for "bail bondsmen, bank employees, title search companies, the real estate community, journalists and apartment managers to work more efficiently and dodge a trip to the courthouse,"[34] therefore basically ignoring the fact that "[w]hen litigants participate in the justice system, they do not waive their right to privacy."[35]

The Rise and Fall of Practical Obscurity as a Means to Ensure Privacy in a Public System

As stated above, there can be no doubt that eAccess is an effective tool in addressing access to justice issues by providing efficient and timely access for judges, parties, and litigators to court records. At the same time, however, eAccess offers these same advantages to others, including members of the general public and even commercial entities that might have a financial interest in the information contained in court files. This raises the question of *who* the open court principle is actually benefitting, since it improves access not only for those involved in a case, as well as members of the public and the press who wish to "comment on the courts as an essential aspect of our democratic society,"[36] but also for any curious third party who wishes to view the information for reasons unrelated to "public scrutiny of the courts."[37] From a privacy standpoint, this is the aspect of eAccess that is somewhat worrisome. After all, if anyone can view the content of a court record or file, they could mine the personal data found therein and use it in a manner that is contrary to a party's privacy expectations, which, although circumscribed, remain valid.[38]

That being said, eAccess is, in some ways, simply the continuation of prior practice. It has long been agreed, as we have previously demonstrated, that "[t]here is a strong presumption in favour of public access to court records,"[39] and that said presumption "should be displaced only with the greatest reluctance and only because of considerations of very significant importance such as the protection of the innocent."[40]

However, because of practical obscurity (the idea that, although public, data remains difficult to access),[41] the public aspect of court documents and, most importantly, the private information they contain, has remained more theoretical than factual.[42] Access is limited because, with paper records, "[p]eople would have to drive to a courthouse to see them."[43] Therefore, although in theory anyone *could* go to the courthouse to look through boxes of evidence to access this information, in practice, few make the effort.[44] In other words, although court records are public, and therefore courts do not typically need to protect the personal data they contain under privacy legislation such as the *Personal Information Protection and Electronic Documents Act*[45] (PIPEDA) or the *Privacy Act*,[46] the practical challenges associated with accessing these records have, in effect, helped to ensure the confidentiality of the private data provided by litigants.[47] However, as explained by Tom Wright, the former Information and Privacy Commissioner of Ontario, back in 1996,

> [i]n a world of electronic information, "practical obscurity" is no longer sufficient protection for publicly available personal information since in reality, it no longer exists. Indeed, the availability of information electronically creates an urgent need to address the overriding question – just how much is someone else entitled to know about you?[48]

Although this quote might seem outdated, its teachings remain relevant since little has been done to truly address this issue in the past two decades. In fact, some provinces, such as Quebec, have yet to adopt a policy regarding access to court records[49] even though, as mentioned earlier, the Canadian Judicial Council proposed a model policy back in 2005.[50] In other words, it remains as true today as it was in 1996 that, when court records constitute electronic documents,[51] the barriers to access are rendered almost inconsequential.[52] As a result, "nosy neighbours," "possible predators," and the like[53] can quickly and easily access the personal data contained in court documents, often from the comfort of their own homes. But intrusive individuals, although a cause for concern in some cases, do not necessarily represent as important a risk as one might think.[54] A more valid source of worry, however, is that private organizations such as data brokers, insurance companies, and banks could mine court records[55] as they do websites that publish legal decisions[56] for private data they could not otherwise obtain legally under PIPEDA or provincial privacy legislation. In other words, since eAccess makes court records "publicly available" in a way that was previously unimaginable, and since section 7 of PIPEDA allows for "an organization [to] collect personal information without the knowledge or consent of the individual" when the said information is "publicly available" and specified by the regulations,[57] unrestricted eAccess can become a legal loophole enabling the gathering of private data from a second-hand source without an individual's consent, something that is technically forbidden by clause 4.3 of Schedule 1 of PIPEDA.[58] Obviously, in many cases, it will be difficult for these organizations to establish that the personal data they collected "relate[s] directly to the purpose for which the information appears in the record or document,"[59] which is necessary in order to use, access, or share this data according to PIPEDA and its regulations,[60] as was pointed out by the Privacy Commissioner of Canada in a 2012 finding.[61]

However, it could be argued that such a finding is not sufficient to limit abuse since data mining is difficult to monitor and current punitive measures are considered by many to be ineffective.[62] Once again, this problem already exists in a paper-based court records system, but practical obscurity makes it less intrusive since these organizations do not have the resources to comb through boxes of court records for every individual encounter. They do, however, have the resources to click "find" in a search engine and wait a few nanoseconds to get the data they would otherwise do without.[63]

The risks associated with these practices that, in many ways, stem from the erosion of practical obscurity, have already arisen and been well documented in other areas such as intellectual-property registries,[64] assessment rolls,[65] and case-law database websites.[66] For example, regarding the latter, where court decisions were once published in books that were only available in law libraries and law firms, websites such as CanLII[67] now publish these same decisions online. These freely accessible sites therefore provide the aforementioned organizations with access to information that would otherwise be considered private, sometimes with disastrous results for individuals' privacy rights.

For example, in its *PIPEDA Report of Findings #2015-002*,[68] the Privacy Commissioner of Canada drew attention to the dealings of Globe24h, a Romanian company that mines case-law websites and republishes the decisions they contain under the guise of making "law accessible for free on the internet."[69] However, where CanLII "prohibits external search engines from indexing the text and case name of decisions published on its website"[70] to protect the privacy rights of parties, Globe24h.com is fully referenced in no less than twenty search engines, including Google.[71] Globe24h's business practices have led to at least one claim of violation of privacy against the Canadian court system and its agents, more specifically, against Quebec's *Société québécoise d'information juridique* (SOQUIJ).[72]

As per the *Act Respecting the Société québécoise d'information juridique*,[73] SOQUIJ is a self-funded government agency tasked with "the processing of legal data, in order to improve the quality of such information and to make it more accessible to the general public."[74] As a part of this mission, SOQUIJ makes court decisions available on its website,[75] as well as to third-party legal-research sites such as CanLII, QuickLaw, and Westlaw.[76] In the aforementioned case, a prior decision involving the plaintiff and containing some of his private information[77] was copied off one of these sites and republished on Globe24h.com, making it available through Google. Although SOQUIJ only did what both its constituting act and the Quebec Court of Appeals require it to do (i.e., grant access to the decision) as the official processor of legal data in Quebec, it was sued for not redacting the plaintiff's personal data (something it started doing five years after the fact),[78] therefore making it possible for Globe24h to publish said data online. Although the case was ultimately thrown out for failure to appear, it does emphasize the problems associated with online access to court documents.

To limit the damages linked to this newfound access, judges have changed the way they write their decisions so as to leave out any unnecessary information that could impact a litigant's (or third party's) privacy rights, and some editors such as SOQUIJ have chosen to redact sensitive data that do not affect the reader's understanding of a given decision.[79] Certain jurisdictions have gone even further and chosen to anonymize decisions to protect these rights.[80] Regrettably, there does not seem to be an equally satisfactory solution to protect privacy with regard to eAccess to motions, evidence, and other documents that have been filed with the court since editing or redacting these documents would affect their integrity, thereby rendering them unusable (for motions or other pleadings) or inadmissible (for evidence).[81] Furthermore, as previously stated, PIPEDA—as it is currently drafted—seems ill equipped to seriously curb commercial data mining of electronic court documents.

Does this mean that eAccess should not be allowed since it facilitates the improper use of court documents, therefore destabilizing the careful equilibrium between privacy and transparency? This would, in our view, equate with throwing out the proverbial baby with the bath water. If the fear is use of court documents for improper purposes, the answer is not to abandon eAccess but, rather, to limit its use.

eAccess to Court Records: Re-establishing a Proper Balance between Privacy and the Open Court Principle

In the first part of this paper, we established that the courts have stated on numerous occasions that public access to court records takes precedence over a litigant's right to privacy, therefore somewhat legitimizing the increased access afforded by eAccess. However, we also underlined the fact that eAccess not only ensures that the open court principle is respected; it also allows for third parties to exploit judicial data in ways that go far beyond what said principle aimed at allowing, therefore making all forms of private data contained in court records available for corporate means or unscrupulous spying.[82]

So how can the judiciary and/or a given department of justice allow for the legitimate use of eAccess, therefore reinforcing the open court principle, while curtailing abusive behaviour that leads to the use of court documents for improper purposes? We believe the answer lies in re-evaluating how we perceive privacy within a digital environment in order to qualify it as a "social value of superordinate importance," while finding new ways to deter illegitimate uses of court data through technological means that could have similar effects to those of practical obscurity.

Re-evaluating "Social Value of Superordinate Importance"

In order to discriminate as to which types of individuals can have access to court records, the first question is to establish whether such discrimination is even possible. As we stated earlier, the Supreme Court seems to be unequivocal in its belief that privacy rights should not impede access to court records:

> While the social interest in protecting privacy is long standing, its importance has only recently been recognized by Canadian courts. *Privacy does not appear to have been a significant factor in the earlier cases* which established the strong presumption in favour of open courts. *That approach has generally continued to this day* [...][83] (Emphasis added)

The day in question was March 29, 1996, a time when the Internet had about 77 million active users,[84] and when download speeds were of around 28,000 bits per second.[85] That context is quite different from today's, as reflected in current statistics (over 3 billion users[86] and downloading speeds of 26 megabytes per second[87]). In fact, most rulings made by the Supreme Court on this issue[88]—the same rulings that are used by proponents of untethered eAccess—predate the internet and the dematerialization of data: innovations that have made it easy for individuals and corporations to collect massive amounts of private information while mining public documents.[89] In this sense, court records accessible through eAccess could quickly become another repository of big data to be exploited by third parties,[90] something that was unfathomable in 1996.

In light of this technological evolution (some would say "revolution"), should unrestricted eAccess to court records be allowed to ensure that the rule of public accessibility is respected, or should it be limited due to the private nature of the requested contents? According to Dickson J in *AG of Nova Scotia v MacIntyre*: "[t]he rule should be one of public accessibility, to be departed from only if necessary to protect [...] *'social values of superordinate importance'*"[91] (emphasis added), such as protection of the innocent. The question therefore becomes that of establishing if, considering the current technological context, the protection of private data has become a "social value of superordinate importance." To put things differently, we need to identify what the expectation of privacy of Canadian citizens is and should be with regard to their private information once said information is filed with the courts and made available electronically to third parties. Thankfully, although no Canadian studies on this issue have been published,[92] anecdotal evidence does seem to support the position that "the transition to electronic records requires that the whole question of what personal information truly belongs on the public record needs to be rethought."[93] Here is an illustration:

> Earlier this year the City of Victoria made assessment information available on its internet web site. This lasted for one day at which time the mayor shut down the web site. Why? The public complained in large numbers that they didn't like the fact that anyone connected to the internet could have such ready access to assessment information. Yet the exact information has been and remains available on paper at city hall.
>
> I believe this example amply demonstrates that the public feels that it does make a difference when information which has been publicly available in a paper-only world becomes available electronically.
>
> In my opinion, in order for government organizations to determine what personal information should be publicly available electronically, a new test is needed – what I have heard described as putting the information to the "Internet Challenge". This test would involve an assessment of how the public would respond if the information was available on the internet where quite literally anyone in the world would have access to it. If the sense was that the public would respond negatively, the personal information should not be made publicly available in identifiable form in an electronic format.[94]

Although this "Internet Challenge" seems to fly in the face of the open court principle, there is precedent that makes it possible to qualify privacy as a social value of superordinate importance, therefore giving credence to such a litmus test:

> Privacy is recognized in Canadian constitutional jurisprudence as implicating liberty and security interests. In *Dyment*, the court

stated that privacy is worthy of constitutional protection because it is "grounded in man's physical and moral autonomy," is "essential for the well-being of the individual," and is "at the heart of liberty in a modern state."[95]

These are strong arguments in favour of considering privacy as a social value of superordinate importance which, when considered against the backdrop of technological innovations and data mining, make it difficult to claim that eAccess should be completely untethered, therefore justifying the implementation of ways to limit eAccess through technological means. A parallel could also be drawn with the recently recognized "right to be forgotten" under European law. In *Google Spain SL, Google Inc v Agencia Española de Protección de Datos (AEPD), Mario Costeja González*,[96] the Court of Justice of the European Union established that information should not be made available online if it "appears [...] to be inadequate, irrelevant or no longer relevant, or excessive in relation to the purposes of the processing at issue."[97] Since the purpose in the case of eAccess to court records is the aforementioned need for there to be "public scrutiny of the courts,"[98] it could be said that eAccess to certain court documents containing private data is excessive,[99] therefore justifying the application of technical measures such as those imposed on Google and other browsers (i.e., dereferencing certain types of documents).

Finding New Means to Ensure "Practical Obscurity"
The default reaction to the manner in which we should go about restricting eAccess to court records seems to be that we should allow only judges and officers of the court[100] to access information at a distance, while having all other individuals travel to a courthouse or other controlled location to consult a dedicated terminal, therefore ensuring that practical obscurity remains with regards to those who would consult court records for improper purposes. This solution, however, seems unsatisfactory for three reasons.

First, it creates an unfair advantage for litigants who are represented by an attorney, therefore going against the "equality of arms" principle that is considered by some to be a pillar regarding access to justice.[101] Even if the application of said principle within the Canadian legal system is cause for debate,[102] the fact remains that it seems unjust for the courts themselves to allow one party unencumbered access to court records, while limiting access to the opposing party.[103]

Second, practical obscurity also promotes uneven access for third parties. As Marc-Aurèle Racicot puts it, "Only those individuals or organizations with unlimited time or resources, could easily and rightfully access any locations to gather the data to build information banks for their own purposes. If practical obscurity was an integral privacy safeguard, it was a very poor one, and also very discriminatory."[104]

Third, limiting eAccess to onsite consultations doesn't really take advantage of all that the technology has to offer and, therefore, requires an important financial investment[105] with very little return where access to justice is concerned since, as described earlier, even those who have a legitimate reason to consult court records will be deterred by consultation schedules and travel costs.

Consequently, instead of limiting offsite access, limiting functionalities seems like a more appropriate manner of addressing the situation. This can be done through (1) technological means, or even (2) through the use of intellectual-property legislation.

1. Privacy Through Limited Search Functions and Other Technological Means
The obvious starting point in controlling eAccess is identifying which documents or, rather, which information should be made accessible. As one author puts it:

> The adjudicatory facts upon which a court relies to dispose of a case or controversy according to the rule of law need never include the specific, arbitrarily assigned street address of a person's home, the precise series of numerals composing his or her telephone number, or the exact digits of his or her Social Security number. That a person has a Social Security number may be relevant to the just and rational disposition of a case, but the specific number will not be. That a person resides along a particular street or next to one of the parties may be relevant, but the exact house number will not be. Similarly, the general education that an individual might be expected to acquire from the perusal of court records does not include committing to memory the street addresses of fellow citizens, their Social Security numbers, or their bank accounts. Accordingly, such information should be omitted from publicly accessible court records and documents, irrespective of their form or the public's method of accessing them.[106]

Second, it becomes important to assess what access entails. Does it simply grant a right to view, or does it also grant a right to copy, publish, broadcast, and such. Regarding this latter possibility, it seems that access should not encompass the right to broadcast, at least not during the trial: "No case has come to my attention in which a Canadian appellate court has ruled that a media applicant is to have unfettered access to an exhibit of this nature for copying purposes so that it may broadcast the evidence during an ongoing jury trial."[107]

Furthermore, in criminal matters, access should always be weighed against the accused's right to a fair trial: "In this particular case, dissemination to the public and public access to this material in videotaped format can only serve to sensationalize the evidence with the real possibility of an adverse impact on the accused's fair trial rights."[108]

The previous quote also elicits another interesting question: does access have to be given to the original version of a document (e.g., a video recording), or is access to a transcript sufficient to meet the "strong presumption in favour of public access to court records"?[109] According to one decision, a transcript would be sufficient when the dissemination of footage could be prejudicial to the accused:

> Having acknowledged that discretion, I caution myself that publication of court exhibits in pictorial form must not disrupt the proper and orderly discharge of this trial. Furthermore, the accused's right to a fair trial and the legitimate privacy rights of any witness or even non-witness must be protected from undue sensationalism. After all, written words tend to be more rational and less evocative than pictures or film. Pictures and film often evoke immediate visceral response whereas words generally require reflection and assessment. The public seeing the pictures or film lacks the calm serenity of a courtroom and the limiting instruction the trial judge gives the jury as to the use to be made of the pictorial exhibit.[110]

Of course, the previous examples all pertain to access *during* the proceedings, but what of the accessibility of these same documents *after* the trial is over? Should access be allowed to ensure that the open court principle is respected, or disallowed because of the sensational nature of the requested contents? Actually, if it is agreed that the documents made available to the public after the proceedings do not need to be originals[111] or, rather, documents resulting from the transfer of an original document,[112] and that certain types of private data are not deemed necessary to allow for "public scrutiny of the courts,"[113] then there is a way to allow eAccess while protecting personal information through the use of what Lawrence Lessig refers to as "Code,"[114] that is, the architecture of the internet or, in the case at hand, eAccess software. As one author puts it, Code "determines which people can access which digital objects…. How such programming regulates human interactions…depends on the choices made."[115]

In the case of eAccess, Code can be used to control access to a document "by means of a restricted view technique"[116] such as blanking.[117] It could also be used to set constraints on consultation periods, to block aggregation tools,[118] or to simply limit research functions within certain types of documents.[119] After all, as pointed out by some authors, access is only truly a problem when files and documents are searchable:

> Online, documents are not only easier to access – they are easier to find. Access to paper records typically requires that one first identify the case number (or name) and the courthouse. Paper records can be cross-indexed according to a (small) number of identifiers (e.g., case number and case name), thus providing alternate means of access. It is not possible, however, to index paper documents "on the fly" according to different criteria, nor is it possible to index paper documents according to specific aspects of content. Electronic documents, however, can be identified virtually instantaneously according to any number of criteria, and documents can be identified on the basis of content as well as "header" or traditional identifying information and specific case files could be identified on the basis of partial information that does not include the traditional identifiers of case name and/or case number.[120]

That being said, not only *can* Code be used to curb such extensive research functions,[121] it should. For example, in Quebec, section 24 of *An Act to Establish a Legal Framework for Information Technology*[122] states that

> The use of extensive search functions in a technology-based document containing personal information which is made public

for a specific purpose must be restricted to that purpose. The person responsible for access to the document must see to it that appropriate technological means are in place to achieve that end. The person may also set conditions for the use of such search functions, in accordance with the criteria determined under paragraph 2 of section 69.[123]

Therefore, through the use of Code, it is possible to provide public access to court records without having to answer the question "who is the public?"[124] Of course, the public will not have access to all the information contained in a court file, but it will have access to all pertinent information to "comment on the courts as an essential aspect of our democratic society."[125]

This will obviously require judges to enact rules as to which information will be made available through eAccess so that clerks can classify said information properly[126] (something that should be relatively quick if the eAccess software is programmed using a legally driven approach such as the one developed by the Cyberjustice Laboratory[127]), but, as section 49 of the Quebec *Code of Civil Procedure*[128] states, this remains within a judge's purview:

> The courts and judges, both in first instance and in appeal, have all the powers necessary to exercise their jurisdiction.
>
> They may, at any time and in all matters, even on their own initiative, grant injunctions or issue orders *to safeguard the parties' rights for the period and subject to the conditions they determine.* As well, they may make such orders as are appropriate to deal with situations for which no solution is provided by law. (Emphasis added)

2. Privacy Through Intellectual Property Rights

To close out this section, we would like to mention a less-travelled route than the "Code" argument that could become a hurdle to eAccess: intellectual property rights. As is well established, court records will almost certainly contain copyrighted materials.[129] Therefore, parties could theoretically object to their being accessible online through the use of copyright laws,[130] even if the true purpose of such an objection is the protection of their privacy or of that of a third party.

Granted, copyright laws were never designed to uphold privacy rights, and there are exceptions within the *Copyright Act*[131] as interpreted by the courts[132] that allow for copyrighted material to be made public when incorporated in court records, but these exceptions do not necessarily cover eAccess. As quoted in *Vallance v Gourlay-Vallance*,[133] "government should not be in the business of publishing public documents [...] government is simply required to make such documents available."[134] However, by allowing for eAccess to court documents, courts are not simply making copyright material available, they are effectively communicating them to the public by telecommunication, a right that is reserved to the copyright holder under section 3(1)(f) or the *Copyright Act*. As one author puts it, courts "have effectively moved from repositories of documents to active publishers."[135]

Obviously, a party suing the courts for copyright violation seems like a far-fetched idea, but it does raise a further argument to deter third parties from gathering data through court records. For example, Rule 2.504 of the 2015 California Rules of Court[136] states that

> The court must give notice of the following information to members of the public accessing its records electronically, in any manner it deems appropriate: [...]
>
> (2) That copyright and other proprietary rights may apply to information in a case file, absent an express grant of additional rights by the holder of the copyright or other proprietary right. This notice must advise the public that:
>
>   (A) Use of such information in a case file is permissible only to the extent permitted by law or court order; and
>
>   (B) Any use inconsistent with proprietary rights is prohibited.

Such a warning might be sufficient to deter certain members of the public and, when joined with the proper technological barriers, may yet make eAccess both efficient and protective of copyright and, indirectly, privacy rights.

Furthermore, since section 29 of the *Copyright Act* allows for "[f]air dealing for the purpose of research, private study, [and] education", and since "Lawyers carrying on the business of law for profit are conducting research within the meaning of s. 29 of the Copyright *Act*,"[137] individuals who seek to consult such documents to prepare their own cases could do so without fear of litigation.[138] The same principle would logically apply to members of the public and the press who wish to "comment on the courts as an essential aspect of our democratic society,"[139] as section 29.2 of the *Copyright Act* extends the fair dealing exception to news reporting. It should finally be applicable to those who would require access for the purpose of insuring "public scrutiny of the courts,"[140] which would logically fall under the exception of "[f]air dealing for the purpose of criticism or review" as per section 29.1 of the Act. However, mining these documents to gather marketable data would most likely fall outside the fair dealing exception, as one could gather from *Waldman v Thomson Reuters Corporation*,[141] where a class action suit was filed against the publisher for copying "court documents that have been authored by lawyers and reproduces them on an electronic data base and search and retrieval service known as 'Litigator.'"[142] Although the reach of a settlement in the case has ultimately prevented us from obtaining a clear decision as to whether or not lawyers have a copyright in court documents,[143] the class action authorization did, at the very least, hint at such a possibility.

Conclusion

To conclude, even if one agrees that better access to justice should remain the light that guides all decisions as to how our legal system is to evolve, there is no certainty that such a goal can be reached through facilitated eAccess to court records. As is often restated, technology is not neutral[144] and, therefore, eAccess software will generate both positive and negative externalities. On the one hand, it will make the legal system more transparent, but on the other, it might very well discourage potential litigants from addressing the courts for fear of exposing their lives to the public.[145] Therefore, eAccess could, if not properly curtailed, have the pernicious effect of discouraging individuals from seeking justice or, rather, to forgo the judicial system in favour of more private dispute resolution mechanisms such as arbitration.[146]

Keeping this in mind, before allowing eAccess to court records, the question, as with any other cyberjustice innovation, should not be "what do we have to gain or lose from the process?"—the answer to both questions seems obvious—but rather how to best use the technology in a way that corresponds to our fundamental legal principles.[147] Limiting the use of extensive search functions might be a way to reach this end, as could restraining access to certain types of data through advanced algorithms. However, one thing is certain: trying to recreate practical obscurity in an online environment is both counterproductive and hopeless. As the Information and Privacy Commissioner for British Columbia put it, "[t]he ease of paper-to-electronic transformation suggests that the practical obscurity that is often considered to be a feature of paper records is less meaningful than many observers have contended."[148] In other words, practical obscurity is dead. Consequently, rather than trying to revive it, we must find new ways of reaching the same ends: protecting privacy while allowing for transparency. In some ways, technology is actually better suited to doing this than paper documents since "controlling access to a document by means of a restricted view technique," while impossible with paper documents, is not only feasible in an online environment, it is also the law in many jurisdictions when dealing with private or otherwise confidential information.[149]

Notes

1   This paper was made possible by a grant from the Social Sciences and Humanities Research Council of Canada.
2   The report, which used to be available at: http://www.timescolonist. com/news/Special+Report+Access+denied+open+court+system/2520905/ story.html, is no longer accessible online.
3   Although not directly linked to this particular issue, "[t]he ministry's motivation to move online stems partially from a problem familiar to many employers: the impending mass retirement of baby boomers is expected to leave a big hole in its workforce." See Robert Todd, "The New Frontier" (7 September 2010), online: *Canadian Lawyer* <www. canadianlawyermag.com/2092/The-new-frontier.html>.
4   Action Committee on Access to Justice in Civil and Family Matters, "Access to Civil & Family Justice – A Roadmap for Change" (2013) at 35, online: *Canadian Forum on Civil Justice* <www.cfcj-fcjc.org/sites/default/ files/docs/2013/AC_Report_English_Final.pdf>.
5   This is the case, for example, in many U.S. state and federal courts. See Rebecca Hulse, "E-Filing and Privacy," *SUM Crim Just,* 24 (2009) at 14.
6   For more on the benefits of eAccess, see Gregory M Silverman, "Rise of the Machines: Justice Information Systems and the Question of Public Access to Court Records Over the Internet," *Wash L Rev* 79 (2004):175 at 179.
7   Action Committee on Access to Justice in Civil and Family Matters, *supra* note 4 at 16–17.

8   This seems to be the case as neither the *Personal Information Protection and Electronic Documents Act* (SC 2000, c 5) [PIPEDA], nor the *Privacy Act* (RSC 1985, c P-21) apply to court records. See David Loukidelis, "Privacy and Openness in Administrative Tribunal Decisions," *Can J Admin L & Prac* 22 (2009) at 75.

9   See e.g., *An Act respecting Access to Documents Held by Public Bodies and the Protection of Personal Information*, CQLR c A-2.1, section 3; and *Freedom of Information and Protection of Privacy Act*, RSA 2000, c F-25, section 4(1) a. See also *Alberta (Attorney General of) v Krushell*, 2003 ABQB 252 at para 26, [2003] 7 WWR 174: "There has long been a process whereby people can go to the courthouse and obtain access to court records, subject to orders of the court saying: these records will be sealed, and you can't get at them. That's primarily what we were after there. There's already a process in place for access to court records, and because of the importance of openness of the courts the provisions of privacy have been set aside for a higher social policy of allowing people to see what's going on in the court system. So that's the reason they're excluded, primarily."

10   For such a proposition, see Marc-Aurèle Racicot, "The Open Court Principle and the Internet: Transparency of the Judicial Process Promoted by the Use of Technology and a Solution for a Reasoned Access to Court Records," *R du B* 66 (2006) at 333.

11   Although the concept of "confidential information" is not defined by the Canadian legislator, we use the expression to regroup all data that the parties or the law considers private, secret or otherwise protected. See Nicolas Vermeys, Julie M Gauthier and Sarit Mizrahi, "Étude sur les incidences juridiques de l'utilisation de l'infonuagique par le gouvernement du Québec", a study prepared for the Conseil du trésor du Québec, 2014.

12   Judges Technology Advisory Committee - Canadian Judicial Council, "Model Policy for Access to Court Records in Canada" (2005), online: <http://www.cjc-ccm.gc.ca/cmslib/general/news_pub_techissues_AccessPolicy_2005_en.pdf>. As the model policy goes on to state: "This definition does not include other records that might be maintained by court staff, but that are not connected with court proceedings, such as license and public land records. It does not include any information that merely pertains to management and administration of the court, such as judicial training programs, scheduling of judges and trials and statistics of judicial activity. Neither does it include any personal note, memorandum, draft and similar document or information that is prepared and used by judges, court officials and other court personnel."

13   Ibid.

14   This could explain why the Supreme Court's decision to make factums available online hasn't caused an uproar in the privacy community. See Supreme Court of Canada, "Policy for Access to Supreme Court of Canada Court Records" (2015), online: <http://www.scc-csc.ca/case-dossier/rec-doc/pol-eng.aspx>.

15   See e.g., Karen Eltis, "The Judicial System in the Digital Age: Revisiting the Relationship between Privacy and Accessibility in the Cyber Context," *McGill LJ* 56:2 (2011) at 289. See also Beverley McLachlin, "Courts, Transparency and Public Confidence – To the Better Administration of Justice," *Deakin Law Review* 8:1 (2003) at 1; and Catherine Piché, "Justice Wide Open: Transparency of the Judicial Process in Modern Technological Courtrooms," in *Transparency, A Governance Principle,* ed. Dominique Custos, (Brussels: Bruylant, 2014) at 225. For the opposing view, see Racicot, *supra* note 10.

16   *Lac d'Amiante du Québec Ltée v 2858-0702 Québec Inc,* 2001 SCC 51, [2001] 2 SCR 743 [*Lac d'Amiante*].

17   *Privacy Act, supra* note 8.

18   See e.g., *An Act respecting Access to Documents Held by Public Bodies and the Protection of Personal Information, supra* note 9.

19   "Discussion Paper Prepared on Behalf of the Judges Technology Advisory Committee for the Canadian Judicial Council on Open Courts, Electronic Access to Court Records, and Privacy," online: <http://www.cjc-ccm.gc.ca/cmslib/general/news_pub_techissues_OpenCourts_20030904_en.pdf> [discussion paper] ("[...] the right of the public to open courts is an important constitutional rule, that the right of an individual to privacy is a fundamental value, and that the right to open courts generally outweighs the right to privacy").

20   *Lac d'Amiante, supra* note 16 at para 70.

21   *Attorney General of Nova Scotia v MacIntyre* [1982] 1 SCR 175 at para 14, 132 DLR (3d) 385 [*MacIntyre*].

22   Washington Courts, "Washington State Access to Justice Technology Principles" (2004), online: <https://www.courts.wa.gov/court_rules/?fa=court_rules.display&group=am&set=ATJ&ruleid=amatjo2principles>.

23   *Edmonton Journal v Alberta (Attorney General),* [1989] 2 SCR 1326 at paras 10-11, 64 DLR (4th) 577 [*Edmonton Journal*].

24   Ibid.

25   Ibid: "It is equally important for the press to be able to report upon and for the citizen to receive information pertaining to court documents. It was put in this way by Anne Elizabeth Cohen in her article "Access to Pretrial Documents Under the First Amendment," *Colum L Rev* 84 (1984):1813 at 1827: Access to pretrial documents furthers the same societal needs served by open trials and pretrial civil and criminal proceedings. Court officials can be better evaluated when their actions are seen by informed, rather than merely curious, spectators."

26 *AB v Bragg Communications Inc*, 2012 SCC 46 at para 11, [2012] 2 SCR 567 [*AB v Bragg*]; see also McLachlin, *supra* note 15 ("Openness signifies that the public and the press have free access to the courts of justice and are entitled to attend and observe any hearing. It signifies that court records and documents are available for public examination)."

27 *Edmonton Journal v Alberta (Attorney General)*, [1989] 2 SCR 1326 at paras 10–11, 64 DLR (4th) 577 [*Edmonton Journal*]. For an analysis of the open court principle and its origins, see Jacquelyn Burkell and Jane Bailey, "Revisiting Presumptive Accessibility: Reconceptualizing the Open Court Principle in an Era of Online Publication" (forthcoming). See also Piché, *supra* note 15.

28 *Canadian Charter of Rights and Freedoms, Part I of the Constitution Act, 1982,* being Schedule B to the Canada Act 1982 (UK), 1982, c. 11.

29 *Canadian Broadcasting Corp v New Brunswick (Attorney General); Re R. v Carson*, [1996] 3 SCR 480 at para 23, 182 NBR (2d) 81 [*CBC 1996*] .

30 *MacIntyre, supra* note 21.

31 Ibid. at 185. This passage is also quoted in *Edmonton Journal, supra* note 23.

32 *MacIntyre, supra* note 21 at 189. This passage is also quoted in *Edmonton Journal, supra* note 23.

33 See e.g., Eltis, *supra* note 15.

34 Daniel Morman and Sharon R Bock, "Electronic Access to Court Records", *NOV Fla B J* 78 (2004):10 at 13. The authors are quoting the *HeraldTribune. com* website.

35 *Canadian Broadcasting Corp v Canada (Attorney General)* 2011 SCC 2, [2011] 1 SCR 19 [*CBC 2001*] .

36 *CBC 1996, supra* note 29 at para 26.

37 *Edmonton Journal, supra* note 23.

38 *CBC 2001, supra* note 35.

39 *R v Canadian Broadcasting Corporation*, 2007 CanLII 21124 at para 50 (ONSC).

40 Ibid.

41 For more on this concept, see Burkell and Bailey, *supra* note 15; Piché, *supra* note 15 at 236–37; and Racicot, *supra* note 10 at 345. See also Arminda Bradford Bepko, "Public Availability or Practical Obscurity: The Debate over Public Access to Court Records on the Internet," *NYL Sch L Rev* 49 (2004) at 967; and Nancy S Marder, "From Practical Obscurity to Web Disclosure: A New Understanding of Public Information," *Syracuse L Rev* 59 (2008) at 441.

42 It should be noted, as one author demonstrated, that this is not necessarily a good thing. Although privacy advocates present practical obscurity as a positive thing, it should be pointed out that it also has the undesirable effect of limiting access to justice. See Racicot, *supra* note 10 at 350.

43 Eric Hartley, "Courts Confront Perils of Openness" (2012), online: *Hometown Annapolis* <*www.HometownAnnapolis.com*>.

44   See *Ontario (Finance) (Re)*, 1996 CanLII 7740 (ON IPC) [*Re Ontario Finance*]:
     "In Ontario, assessment information is publicly available by law. For
     years anyone has been able to go to the office of the clerk of a municipal-
     ity and view the assessment roll. However, the paper medium on which
     information was stored provided a built-in privacy protection. Although
     it was possible to go to a municipality and copy out the information
     contained on the paper rolls, using the appellant's situation as an
     example, in order to do so he would have to travel to 11 municipal offices
     and copy thousands of pages. The sheer enormity of this task made it
     unlikely that assessment information would be used other than for
     assessment-related purposes. Using words of the U.S. Supreme Court,
     I have described this as privacy protection based on 'practical obscu-
     rity'." See also Piché, *supra* note 15 at 237.
45   PIPEDA, *supra* note 8 at s 7.
46   *Privacy Act, supra* note 8.
47   See Amanda Conley et al., "Sustaining Privacy and Open Justice in the
     Transition to Online Court Records: A Multidisciplinary Inquiry,"
     Maryland Law Review 71 (2012) at 772; Woodrow Hartzog and Frederic
     Stutzman, "The Case for Online Obscurity," *California Law Review* 101:1
     (2012):1 at 21; Will Thomas Devries, "Protecting Privacy in the Digital
     Age," *Berkeley Tech L J* 18 (2003):283 at 301; Lewis A Kaplan, "Litigation,
     Privacy and the Electronic Age," *Yale Symp on L & Tech* 4 (2001):1 at 6;
     Caren Myers Morrison, "Privacy, Accountability, and the Cooperating
     Defendant: Towards a New Role for Internet Access to Court Records,"
     Vand L Rev 62 (2009) at 921; Peter A Winn, "Judicial Information
     Management in an Electronic Age: Old Standards, New Challenges,"
     Fed Cts L Rev 3 (2009) at 135; Peter A Winn, "Online Court Records:
     Balancing Judicial Accountability and Privacy in an Age of Electronic
     Information," *Wash. L. Rev* 79 (2004) at 307; Lynn E Sudbeck, "Placing
     Court Records Online: Balancing the Public and Private Interests," *The
     Justice System Journal* 27:3(2006) at 268; Bepko, supra note 41; Kristen M
     Blankley, "Are Public Records Too Public? Why Personally Identifying
     Information Should Be Removed from Both Online and Print Versions
     of Court Documents," *Ohio St L J* 65 (2004) at 413; John Losinger,
     "Electronic Access to Court Records: Shifting the Privacy Burden Away
     from Witnesses and Victims," *U Balt L Rev* 36 (2007) at 419; and David
     L Snyder, "Nonparty Remote Electronic Access to Plea Agreements in
     the Second Circuit," *Fordham Urb L J* 35 (2008) at 1263.
48   *Re Ontario Finance, supra* note 44. See also *Toronto (City) (Re)*, 2000 CanLII
     21004 (ON IPC). This same issue was later raised by the Canadian
     Judicial Council in its 2003 discussion paper on electronic access to
     court records: "Where court records are open to access by the public

but searching capacity is reduced by the need to identify files in court ledgers and file retrieval fees, 'practical obscurity' prevails. The theoretical openness is limited by logistical barriers. However, where electronic access exists, the definition of 'public' will likely expand" ((Judges Technology Advisory Committee, "Discussion Paper", *supra* note 19 at 36).

49 It should however be noted that such a document is currently being worked on by the Quebec Department of Justice for possible adoption in the coming months.

50 Judges Technology Advisory Committee, "Model Policy," *supra* note 12.

51 Section 31 of *PIPEDA* defines electronic documents as "data that is recorded or stored on any medium in or by a computer system or other similar device and that can be read or perceived by a person or a computer system or other similar device. It includes a display, printout or other output of that data."

52 In fact authors are still coming to the same conclusion some twenty years later. See e.g., Burkell and Bailey, *supra* note 15: "In the past, access to court documents required a visit to the specific court where the documents were held. Access was restricted to the opening hours of the court office, and those wishing to access the documents had to make those requests in person – thus fully anonymous access of those documents was not possible. All this changes with online documents, since these can be accessed at any time, using any computer with an Internet connection, typically anonymously and even invisibly. In other words, barriers or 'friction' in online court document access are greatly reduced if not eliminated, and as a result the personal information included in these documents is no longer protected by the 'practical obscurity' inherent in access to paper documents."

53 Judges Technology Advisory Committee, "Discussion Paper," *supra* note 19 at 36–37.

54 See Racicot, *supra* note 10.

55 See Kristin M Makar, "Taming Technology in the Context of the Public Access Doctrine: New Jersey's Amended Rule 1:38," *Seton Hall L Rev* 41 (2011):1071 at 1088.

56 For example, the CanLII website had to modify its terms of use to forbid these types of abusive uses of its databanks. See CanLII, "Terms," online: <http://www.canlii.org/en/info/terms.html>.

57 Which court records are according to the *Regulations Specifying Publicly Available Information*, SOR/2001-7, s 1(d).

58 PIPEDA, *supra* note 8 at Sched 1, s 4.3 ("The knowledge and consent of the individual are required for the collection, use, or disclosure of personal information, except where inappropriate").

59   *Regulations Specifying Publicly Available Information, supra* note 57 at s 1(d).

60   *Ibid.* See also Canadian Bar Association, "Submission on the Discussion Paper: Open Courts, Electronic Access to Court Records, and Privacy" (2004), online: <www.cba.org/cba/submissions/pdf/04-13-eng.pdf>.

61   *Mortgage administrator/broker should have confirmed consent prior to issuing letter of interest for mortgage financing in couple's name,* 2012 CanLII 96454 (PCC): "PIPEDA's regulations specify that publicly available personal information is that which appears in a record or document of a judicial or quasi-judicial body that is available to the public, *where the collection, use and disclosure of the personal information relate directly to the purpose for which the information appears in the record or document.*"

62   France Houle and Lorne Sussin, *Powers and Functions of the Ombudsman in the Personal Information Protection and Electronic Documents Act An Effectiveness Study* (Ottawa, Office of the Privacy Commissioner of Canada, 2010).

63   For example, the PACER system in the United States (http://www.pacer. gov/) allows just that. See Philip Leith and Maeve Mcdonagh, "New Technology and Researchers' Access to Court and Tribunal Information: the need for European analysis," *SCRIPTed* 6:1 (2009) at 33.

64   See Mark S Hayes, "The Impact of Privacy on Intellectual Property in Canada," *I P J* 20 (2006):67 at 83.

65   *Re Ontario Finance, supra* note 44.

66   Courtney Retter & Shaheen Shariff, "A Delicate Balance: Defining the Line between Open Civil Proceedings and the Protection of Children in the Online Digital Era," *Can J L & Tech* 10 (2012):231 at 238. See also Jennifer Stoddart, "Setting the "Bar" on Privacy Protection" (2008), online: *Office of the Privacy Commissioner of Canada* <https://www.priv. gc.ca/media/sp-d/2008/sp-d_080817_e.asp>.

67   CanLII, online: <www.canlii.org>.

68   *PIPEDA Report of Findings #2015-002,* online: *Office of the Privacy Commissioner of Canada* <https://www.priv.gc.ca/cf-dc/2015/2015_002_0605_e. asp>.

69   Globe 24h, online: <www.globe24h.com/>.

70   CanLII, "Privacy Policy", online: <www.canlii.org/en/info/privacy.html>.

71   See Globe24h, "Frequent Questions & Answers," online: <www. globe24h.com/faq.html>.

72   See *Thériault-Thibault v SOQUIJ,* 500-32-146975-158.

73   *Act Respecting the Société Québécoise d'Information Juridique,* CQLR c S-20.

74   As a matter of full disclosure, it should be mentioned that the author of this paper is the current vice-president of SOQUIJ's Board of Directors.

75   SOQUIJ, online: <soquij.qc.ca/>.

76   See *Wilson & Lafleur Inc c Société québécoise d'information juridique,* 2000 CanLII 8006 (QC CA).

77 *Thériault-Thibault c McGill Computer Store*, 2006 QCCQ 703 (CanLII).

78 See SOQUIJ, "Politique sur le caviardage" (2014), online: <soquij.qc.ca/documents/file/corpo_politiques/politique-sur-le-caviardage.pdf>.

79 Ibid.

80 See Luc Plamondon, Guy Lapalme and Frédéric Pelletier, "Anonymisation de décisions de justice," TALN 2004, Fès, 19–21 April 2004.

81 *Canada Evidence Act*, RSC 1985, c C-5, s 31.2.

82 For examples of what this data could be used for, see Eltis, *supra* note 15 at 301.

83 *CBC 1996, supra* note 29.

84 See Internet Live Stats, "Number of Internet Users," online: <www.internetlivestats.com/internet-users/>.

85 See Brian Nelson, "New Modem Will Speed up Internet Access" (1996) *CNN Interactive*, online: <www.cnn.com/TECH/9610/04/faster.internet/>.

86 See Internet Live Stats, *supra* note 84.

87 Ibid.

88 *MacIntyre, supra* note 21; and *Edmonton Journal, supra* note 23.

89 This has been decried by then privacy commissioner Jennifer Stoddart. See Kirk Makin, "Online Tribunal Evidence Leaves Citizens' Data open to Abuse," *The Globe and Mail*, August 20, 2008, A5. See also Eltis, *supra* note 15 at 292.

90 See Viktor Mayer-Schönberger and Kenneth Cukier, *Big Data: A Revolution That Will Transform How We Live, Work, and Think*, (Boston: Eamon Dolan/Houghton Mifflin Harcourt, 2013).

91 *MacIntyre, supra* note 21 at para 14. See also *AB v Bragg, supra* note 26 at para 13.

92 It should however be noted that such a study is to be conducted as part of the "Towards Cyberjustice" project led by the Cyberjustice Laboratory. See Cyberjustice Laboratory, "The Project," online: <www.cyberjustice.ca/en/the-project/>.

93 *Re Ontario Finance, supra* note 44.

94 Ibid.

95 *Toronto Star Newspaper Ltd v Ontario*, 2012 ONCJ 27 at para 41, as cited in *AB v Bragg, supra* note 26 at para 18.

96 *Google Spain SL, Google Inc v Agencia Española de Protección de Datos (AEPD), Mario Costeja González*, Case C-131/12.

97 Ibid. at para 94.

98 *Edmonton Journal, supra* note 23.

99 It should be noted, however, that the parallel drawn between eAccess to court records and the aforementioned right to be forgotten is not a perfect one since, unlike websites, court records have a regulated shelf life. See e.g., the Quebec *Archives Act*, CQLR c A-21.1, section 7.

100 By "officers of the court," we refer to "All persons who may practise as barristers, advocates, counsel, attorneys, solicitors or proctors in the Court," as per the *Supreme Court Act*, RSC 1985, c S-26, s24.

101 See Harry Woolf, *Access to Justice: Interim Report to the Lord Chancellor on the Civil Justice System in England and Wales* (London, Lord Chancellor's Department, 1995) as quoted by Master D E Short in many cases including *Simpson v Attorney General (Canada)*, 2011 ONSC 3642 at para 18 (CanLII); *1588143 Ontario Inc v Lantic Inc*, 2010 ONSC 1613 at para 36 (CanLII); *Bank of Montréal v Baysong Developments Inc*, 2011 ONSC 931 at para 41 (CanLII); *Green v Mirtech International Security Inc*, 2010 ONSC 1240 para 32 (CanLII); *Rohit v Nuri*, 2010 ONSC 17 at para 34 (CanLII); and *HMQ (Ontario) v Rothmans Inc*, 2011 ONSC 1083 (CanLII). This last case was however overturned since it was found that Master Short "erred by misapplying the "equality of arms" principle." See *Ontario v Rothmans Inc*, 2011 ONSC 2504 at para 105 (CanLII). For other applications of the "equality of arms principle," see e.g., *Homebrook v Seprotech Systems*, 2011 ONSC 3100 at para 7 (CanLII); and *IPEX Inc v AT Plastics Inc*, 2011 ONSC 4734 at para 55 (CanLII).

102 *Imperial Tobacco Canada Ltd v Québec (Procureur général)*, 2014 QCCS 842 (CanLII).

103 See D R Jones, "Protecting the Treasure: An Assessment of State Court Rules and Policies for Access to Online Civil Court Records," *Drake L Rev* 61:2 (2013):375 at 394.

104 Racicot, *supra* note 10 at 356.

105 Makar, *supra* note 55 at 1084.

106 Silverman, *supra* note 6 at 209.

107 *R v Canadian Broadcasting Corporation*, 2007 CanLII 21124 at para 82 (ON SC).

108 Ibid. at para 81.

109 Ibid. at para 50.

110 *R v Ranger*, [1998] OJ No 1654 (Ont Ct Justice Gen Div) (QL).

111 *An Act to Establish a Legal Framework for Information Technology*, CQLR c C-1.1, 12.

112 Ibid. at s 17.

113 *Edmonton Journal*, *supra* note 23.

114 Lawrence Lessig, *Code version 2.0* (New York, Basic Books, 2006).

115 Mark Stefik, *The Internet Edge: Social, Technical, and Legal Challenges for a Networked World* (Cambridge, MIT Press, 1999) at 14, as quoted in Lessig, *supra* note 114 at 6.

116 *An Act to Establish a Legal Framework for Information Technology*, *supra* note 111 at s 25.

117 Blanking is a process that consists of masking certain data when an individual does not have the proper security clearance to access said

data. As one author puts it: "For example, when a party or attorney authors a document for filing with a court, he or she could include markup for recognized categories of personal information that the public should be restricted from viewing. Once filed, this document would be stored on a justice information system capable of processing XML markup. Then, when a member of the public accesses this document at a courthouse computer terminal or over the Internet, generic text such as a series of Xs--possibly hyperlinked to a message that explains that personal information has been omitted--would be substituted for the tagged personal information. Moreover, when the same document was accessed by the judge or an attorney of record, the justice information system would be programmed to display the entire document, including the sensitive personal information. As this example makes clear, the justice information system would be programmed to respond to a hierarchy of user access privileges, providing to each user the information that he or she is authorized to view. Significantly, such a system would discriminate among users and not the methods by which they accessed the system. A particular user would be granted access to the same information, whether that user was accessing the system at the courthouse or over the Internet." See Silverman, *supra* note 6 at 211.

118 Lynn M LoPucki, "Court System Transparency," *Iowa L Rev* 94 (2009):481 at 528.

119 One such mean would be to make documents containing private data non-machine readable. See LoPucki, *supra* note 118 at 522.

120 Burkell and Bailey, *supra* note 15.

121 See Silverman, *supra* note 6 at 211 (we can "use XML tags to mark up sensitive personal information and control access to it programmatically); see also Conley et al., *supra* note 47.

122 *An Act to Establish a Legal Framework for Information Technology, supra* note 111.

123 Ibid. at s 24. As for paragraph 2 of section 69 of the Act, it simply states that: "69. [...] the Government may make regulations determining [...] (2) criteria for the use of extensive search functions in respect of personal information contained in technology-based documents that are made public for a specific purpose." The same principle was put forth in section 4.5 of Judges Technology Advisory Committee "Model Policy," *supra* note 12. This concept is analog to the "Right to be forgotten" recently recognised by the Court of Justice of the European Union in *Google Spain SL, Google Inc.* v *Agencia Española de Protección de Datos (AEPD), Mario Costeja González*: "the data subject may oppose the indexing by a search engine of personal data relating to him where their dissemination through the search engine is prejudicial to him and his fundamental rights to the protection of those data and to privacy

— which encompass the 'right to be forgotten' — override the legitimate interests of the operator of the search engine and the general interest in freedom of information."

124 Judges Technology Advisory Committee, "Discussion Paper", *supra* note 19 at 35.

125 *CBC 1996, supra* note 29 at para 26.

126 This seems to be the approach that was adopted in Florida. See Morman and Bock, *supra* note 34 at 16. For an example of the rules that could be adopted under Canadian law, see Racicot, *supra* note 10. Although the author promotes a case-by-case analysis, something that we believe to be impractical in the current context, the criteria he proposes offer an interesting starting point.

127 See Nicolas Vermeys and Karim Benyekhlef, "Reinventing Rituals – How to Develop Technological Solutions to Courtroom Conundrums" (forthcoming).

128 *Code of Civil Procedure*, CQLR c C-25.01.

129 See *Waldman v Thomson Reuters Corporation*, 2012 ONSC 1138 (CanLII). Leave for appeal denied (*Waldman v Thomson Reuters Corporation*, 2012 ONSC 3436 [CanLII]); although a settlement agreement was reached was reached in this case, rendering the point moot. See *Waldman v Thomson Reuters Canada Limited*, 2014 ONSC 1288 (CanLII); *Waldman v Thomson Reuters Canada Limited*, 2015 ONCA 53 (CanLII); *Waldman v Thomson Reuters Canada Limited*, 2015 ONSC 3843 (CanLII); and *Waldman v Thomson Reuters Canada Limited*, 2016 ONSC 2622 (CanLII).

130 See Kathryn Yardley, "Online Tribunal Evidence Leaves Citizens' Data Open to Abuse" (2 November 2008), online: *IP Osgoode* <www.iposgoode. ca/2008/11/yardley-kathryn-online-tribunal-evidence-leaves-citizens-data-open-to-abuse/#sthash.03QqlqUZ.dpuf>.

131 *Copyright Act*, RSC 1985, c C-42.

132 Andy Radhakant, "Robust Interpretation of Court Document Copyright," *The Lawyers Weekly* 34:18 (2014) at 15.

133 *Vallance v Gourlay-Vallance*, 2002 ABQB 822, 325 AR 296.

134 Jennifer Lee, "Dirty Laundry, Online for All to See," *New York Times*, September 5, 2002.

135 Karen Eltis, *Courts, Litigants and the Digital Age – Law, Ethics and Practice* (Toronto, Irwin Law, 2012) at 54 as cited in Piché, *supra* note 15 at 247.

136 2015 California Rules of Court, online: <www.courts.ca.gov/cms/rules/index.cfm?title=two&linkid=rule2_504>.

137 *CCH Canadian Ltd v Law Society of Upper Canada*, 2004 SCC 13 at para 51, [2004] 1 SCR 339 [*CCH Canadian Ltd*, SCC].

138 See *CCH Canadian Ltd v Law Society of Upper Canada*, 2002 FCA 187 at para 128, [2002] 4 FCR 213: "'Research' is not qualified in the Act, therefore, research for a commercial purpose, including legal research carried

out for profit by entities such as law firms, is not automatically excluded from this exemption. Research for the purpose of advising clients, giving opinions, arguing cases, preparing briefs and factums is nonetheless research. Of course, if a copy is made for non-private or commercial research purposes, such a fact may affect the fairness of the dealing." This paragraph was cited with approval in *CCH Canadian Ltd*, SCC at para 51.

139 *CBC 1996, supra* note 29 at para 26.

140 *Edmonton Journal, supra* note 23.

141 *Waldman* v *Thomson Reuters Corporation*, 2012 ONSC 1138. Leave for appeal dismissed (*Waldman* v *Thomson Reuters Corporation*, 2012 ONSC 3436).

142 *Waldman* v *Thomson Reuters Corporation*, 2012 ONSC 1138, par 2.

143 See *Waldman* v *Thomson Reuters Canada Limited*, 2014 ONSC 1288; *Waldman* v *Thomson Reuters Canada Limited*, 2015 ONCA 53; *Waldman* v *Thomson Reuters Canada Limited*, 2015 ONSC 3843; and *Waldman* v *Thomson Reuters Canada Limited*, 2016 ONSC 2622 (CanLII).

144 See Langdon Winner, *The Whale and the Reactor* (Chicago: University of Chicago Press, 1986).

145 This fear is shared by other legal scholars. See e.g., Eltis, *supra* note 15 at 316: "While the decision to publish details of a tort plaintiff's sexually contracted disease may have—at first glance—appeared to constitute a victory for access and transparency, it stands to reason that so doing may dissuade similarly situated plaintiffs from availing themselves of the justice process (for fear of having intimate details exposed not only in dusty court files but online, easily googled by potential employers, landlords, even suitors, and so forth). Indeed, the ultimate result would be to deter access to the courts, thereby frustrating the goal of access in its broadest and most immediate sense."

146 See Karim Benyekhlef and Fabien Gélinas, "Online Dispute Resolution," *Lex Electronica* 10:2 (2005) at 49, online: <www.lex-electronica.org/articles/v10-2/Benyekhlef_Gelinas.pdf>.

147 See Vermeys and Benyekhlef, *supra* note 127.

148 *Sale of Provincial Government Computer Tapes Containing Personal Information*, Re, 2006 CanLII 13536 at para 58 (BC IPC).

149 See *An Act to Establish a Legal Framework for Information Technology, supra* note 111 at s 25; see also PIPEDA, *supra* note 8 at Sched 1, s 4.7.3.

PART II

COURTROOM INTERACTIONS AND SELF-EMPOWERMENT

Troubling the Technological Imperative: Views on Responsible Implementation of Court Technologies

Jacquelyn Burkell

Technology is often presented as a panacea for the ills that trouble the justice system: the solution that will reduce costs, decrease delays, increase efficiency, and generally improve access to justice. In many cases we hold an untroubled relationship to this claim, comfortable in the dual assumption that technological advances are inevitable and will necessarily result in improvements to the justice system.[1] Courts, and the legal system in general, are exhorted to "catch up" to current technologies; technologically advanced judges are portrayed as "dragging" the court system into the digital age.

The four chapters in this section of the book examine courtroom interactions and self-empowerment. Individually, and as a whole, they probe the reality and consequences of implementing technologies in the court system, discussing in the process a wide range of court technologies, including online court information systems, e-filing, videoconferencing, and technologies for evidence presentation and review. On the whole, the authors of these chapters are hopeful if not unreservedly enthusiastic about court technologies. More importantly, each of these chapters echoes the same message: if technologies are to be implemented in the court system so as to improve that system and access to justice within it, we must proceed with care and deliberation. We cannot assume that there is a necessary or a necessarily positive relationship between court technologies and access to justice:[2] instead, we should proceed with cautious rather than unbridled optimism to ensure that technologies are implemented in such a way as to achieve the positive outcomes that we envision.

Donald Horowitz opens the section with an account of the development of Access to Justice Technology Principles within the Washington court system. He recounts his experience as chair of the committee that developed these principles, noting that the committee, and indeed the Access to Justice Board that created the committee, recognized the need to prepare for, constructively channel, and constructively use court technologies in order to ensure that those technologies enhanced access to justice and did not, in their implementation, do damage to the commitment to an "accessible, equitable, efficient and effective justice system." In his analysis, Justice Horowitz focuses on the importance of engaging a broad range of stakeholders in the development of system principles. In particular, he notes that while "buy-in" from the judiciary is critical for effective implementation of principles, consultation with a broad range of stakeholders, including those the system is designed to serve, is also crucial for a credible and legitimate process. The principles, developed by the Communications and Technology Committee of the Access to Justice Board established by the Washington Supreme Court, were adopted by the Washington State Supreme Court in 2004. These principles outline issues that must be considered in order to ensure that justice system technologies serve to enhance access to justice. Hence the principles serve as a blueprint for implementation of technologies in the court system.

In the next chapter, Sherry MacLennan provides us with a detailed analysis of the implementation, in British Columbia, of one important justice system technology: online legal information. She notes that the Legal Services Society of British Columbia introduced online self-help guides in direct response to a reduction in family law coverage available to low-income clients. Early on, the online court system "focused on court based self-help to replace the representation services lost due to coverage restrictions." At the same time, it was recognized that "technology supported by people" was "more empowering" for clients, and the online information system was supplemented by access to "live" assistance through helplines and consultation services. In addition, intermediaries were trained on the use of the system in order to assist clients with information access and use, and the information system was accessible to and used by counsel both to provide information to their clients and to stay up to date on family law matters. MacLennan provides us with insight, based on experience, on the complexity of even apparently "simple" systems, discussing the importance of content, accessibility, and design (including "gamification" of system and content, and guided pathways as a design principle) in ensuring that the online information system is useful and used. She also emphasizes the importance of collaboration, networking, evaluation, and integration with existing systems in the development and implementation of online information systems. Her contribution emphasizes the points that new technologies must interact with existing systems and processes, and care in design and implementation must be taken to ensure that new technologies optimally enhance the justice system.

Amy Salyzyn focuses on "Courtroom Technology Competence" in her contribution. She proposes this competence as an ethical duty of lawyers and provides strong arguments to support her claim that lawyers have an *ethical duty* to develop and maintain appropriate competence with respect to court technologies. Salyzyn's perspective is an interesting one, not entertained in the other chapters presented here: she takes court technologies as a "given" and, rather than exploring their implementation or development, discusses the attendant responsibilities incumbent upon those who, on behalf of their clients, must use at least some of these technologies in the courtroom. At the same time, her contribution rests on a realization shared by the other contributors to this section: court technologies are complex, and their implementation will not have unreservedly positive effects on courts and court processes. In particular, she notes that litigators have a responsibility to understand the technologies used in the courtroom in order both to identify potential malfeasance by others, and to optimally use those same technologies themselves in order to represent their clients. Having made the case that competence is an ethical responsibility, she explores potential regulatory avenues, including the use of surveys/audits to examine current state of lawyer competence in these areas, the inclusion of technical competence in professional codes of conduct, and the development and implementation of professional-education initiatives designed to improve technical competence among practicing lawyers. Although Salyzyn does not directly address judicial competence in courtroom technologies in her submission, the same arguments apply to this group. Ultimately, Salyzyn's chapter emphasizes the fact that courtroom technologies will alter the system and process of justice, and actors in the justice system have a responsibility to understand both the technologies and their impact.

The final chapter in this section focuses on one specific technology—tablets—and examines the implications of that technology for one specific aspect of the judicial process—jury deliberation. In "Tablets in the Jury Room: Enhancing Performance while Undermining Fairness?," Tait and Rossner take an empirical approach to the question of whether the use of tablets influences the process and outcome of jury review of evidence during deliberation. Their preliminary results—and note that this is only the first phase of a larger project examining the role of tablets in the jury room—raise the possibility that jury deliberation and indeed verdicts could be influenced by the use of tablets. Specifically, their results suggest that jurors using tablets engage in more vigorous debate than do jurors reviewing paper evidence, and are less likely to shift their initial opinion on the verdict as a result of group deliberation. Moreover, in these results, jurors using tablets are more likely to find the defendant "guilty" and they assign a higher likelihood of guilt to defendants. Taken together, these results suggest that the use of tablets for evidence review by juries does indeed alter the nature and outcome of jury deliberation, potentially increasing conflict or providing opportunity for open debate, and possibly increasing the influence of evidence on the jury decision. This latter point is particularly relevant since typically the *prosecution*, rather than the defense, presents the bulk of the evidence, the role of the defense being to respond to the presented evidence in order to create reasonable doubt. Thus, Tait and Rossner's results suggest that the implementation of technologies coupled with long-established court practices could have unexpected, and potentially detrimental, effects on the fairness of the justice system.

Technological change is as inevitable in the justice system as it is in other aspects of society, and there is every reason to embrace the changes with enthusiasm. Technology can, and undoubtedly will, enhance access to justice—*if we carefully and responsibly steward the process*. We should not implement technological change on the unexamined premise that the effects will be as anticipated and unreservedly positive, but instead proceed with impact and outcome in view. Each of the authors in this section emphasizes this responsibility, and their collective message should be taken to heart by those implementing technological change in the justice system.

Notes

1   See Jane Bailey, Jacquelyn Burkell and Graham Reynolds, "Access to Justice for All: Towards an 'Expansive Vision' of Justice and Technology," *Windsor Yearbook of Access to Justice* 31:2 (2013) at 181.
2   Ibid.

CHAPTER V

ATJ Technology Principles: Access to and Delivery of Justice

Donald J Horowitz

On March 31, 1968, five days before he was assassinated, Reverend Martin Luther King Jr. spoke to the future. Now more than forty-eight years later, we must at last heed his words:

> There can be no gainsaying of the fact that a great revolution is taking place in the world today . . . that is, a technological revolution, with the impact of automation and cybernation . . . Now, whenever anything new comes into history it brings with it new challenges and new opportunities. . . . [T]he geographical oneness of this age has come into being to a large extent through modern man's scientific ingenuity. Modern man through his scientific genius has been able to dwarf distance and place time in chains . . . Through our scientific and technological genius, we have made of this world a neighborhood and yet we have not had the ethical commitment to make of it a brotherhood. But somehow, and in some way, we have got to do this.[1]

Article 1, Section 32 of the Washington State Constitution, adopted in 1889 states: "*Fundamental Principles.* A frequent recurrence to fundamental principles is essential to the security of individual right and the perpetuity of free government."[2]

In this chapter, I will explore practical aspects of the meaning of Dr. King's words and Article 1 of the Constitution and summarize what happened when we, in Washington State, made a major effort to live up to them. This necessarily brief exploration shall nevertheless cover not only the past and present; it will also include my thoughts and suggestions about the future.

Washington State's Access to Justice (ATJ) Board

In April 1994, the Washington State Supreme Court stated that "Washington State's justice system is founded on the fundamental principle that the justice system is accessible to all persons," and recognized that such access is an essential component of a keystone of our democratic system—equal justice for all.[3] By Court Order of April 18, 1994 the Court created an ATJ Board, the first such entity in the United States.[4] In the Order, the ATJ Board was given the mission to facilitate, enhance, and safeguard that access. The Board was initially a temporary body, subject to renewal. The Board thereafter did effective work, and in November 2000 the Supreme Court reauthorized the ATJ Board to continue indefinitely, charging it with responsibility to assure high quality access for all persons in Washington State who suffer disparate access barriers to the justice system. In this Order, the Court also gave the ATJ Board the specific task, among others, to "develop and implement new programs and innovative measures designed to expand access to justice in Washington State."[5]

In the late 1990s, the Access to Justice Board and those who worked with it began to recognize the rapid growth of new communication and information technologies, that these technologies would have broad and deep effects on our society generally, and that the justice system would not be exempt. What these effects might be, what it could mean to the justice system, and what, if anything, should be done was not even close to being understood. But the importance of these changes was clear, and as a result the ATJ Board created a Communications and Technology (Comtech) Committee to try to figure this out and to make recommendations. The process began in the spring of 2000.

The first thing that became clear was that technological innovations and changes and their application to and adoption into the various core systems in the broader society, and in the justice system particularly, were still in their early stages. In the justice system, to use words familiar in Seattle, this was still a "drizzle" and so far only a few mild waves had been felt. At the same time, the Committee also recognized that a "monsoon" was on the way. Technological transformation was building in all areas and would inevitably and significantly impact and permeate the justice system and access to and use of the justice system by all. Major effects and consequences would be experienced by the public, by those who worked in or were related to the system, and by the decision-makers in the system. The committee concluded that in the absence of careful deliberation, planning, preparation, and action, the ongoing monsoon and the enormous changes it engendered could indeed lead to a tsunami. If, however, this great energy of change was prepared for, and constructively channeled and used, the public and the justice system would not only avoid significant damage but could use that energy to create and enable substantial benefits for all persons to a more accessible, equitable, efficient, and effective justice system.

Over a period of time the committee came to believe, and the ATJ Board agreed, that recent and ongoing developments in information, communication, and associated technologies including the internet, and the current and future use of such technologies posed both significant challenges and significant opportunities for full and equal access to the justice system. Two possible outcomes were contemplated. First, if we just let it happen, the technology would reflect, continue, perpetuate, and with its accompanying digital divide, increase and add to the historical obstacles and barriers to the poor, ethnic and racial minorities, persons with disabilities, the elderly, others easily taken advantage of or abused—indeed all who are disadvantaged or vulnerable, all who have not experienced equal and meaningful justice in accessibility, process, or outcome. Second, if the justice system was proactive, this great energy and potential transformation could be prepared for and used to ensure that the barriers—old and new—to accessing the justice system are eliminated, minimized, or avoided, and that pathways to the justice system and to justice itself are created or maximized.

The committee determined that, with respect to technology, if the justice system created, adopted, and lived by authoritative principles and standards that reflected its constitutional principles and stated values, and applied these principles to all who worked in or were involved with the justice system, to all who made decisions, to all who served the public—and to the public itself—then we could and would use technology to find and create various means to deliver on our fundamental national and state promises of equal justice for all, and do so in practical ways with concrete effects in people's daily lives.

Based on the Comtech Committee's recommendation, the ATJ Board made the following statement:

> The ATJ Board has come to believe that recent and ongoing developments in information, communication and associated technologies, including the internet, and the current and future use of such technologies pose significant challenges to full and equal access to the justice system. Technology can provide increased pathways for access to justice, but it can also create significant barriers. The ATJ Board is dedicated to ensuring that barriers to accessing the justice system are avoided, eliminated or minimized, and that pathways to the justice system are created or maximized.[6]

Development of Washington's ATJ Technology Principles

The ATJ Board created an Access to Justice Technology Bill of Rights ("ATJ-TBoR") Committee, to accomplish the following:

1. Develop and implement an Access to Justice Technology Bill of Rights ("ATJ-TBoR") premised on relevant principles contained in the United States and Washington State Constitutions, the mission and underlying principles and declarations generating the creation and operation of the Access to Justice Board, the principles contained in the Hallmarks of an Effective Statewide Civil Legal Services Delivery System adopted by the Access to Justice Board in 1995, and subsequent and effectuating documents and declarations.
2. Identify the strategies, means, and methods to ensure that the rights and principles contained in the Technology Bill of Rights are adopted, become publicly known and accepted, and have concrete, practical and effective consequences in the daily lives of all people in the State of Washington.[7]

During the three-year process which followed, the name of the product the committee had been assigned to develop and implement was changed from ATJ-TBoR to "Access to Justice Technology Principles" (ATJ Tech Principles), often referred to as "the Tech Principles" or "the Principles."[8] The change was made because: (a) it's a more accurate description; (b) it applied more broadly to all involved or potentially involved with the justice system, rather than a specific group or groups; and (c) the use of "Principles" carries far less pre-assumptions and potential legal baggage than "Bill of Rights." I will hereafter use language reflecting the Principles version.

The stated and adopted goals of the ATJ Technology Principles Committee were to:

1. Take optimal advantage of the unique opportunity provided by the confluence of time, place, resources, values and will at this moment in history so as to increase both access to the justice system and the quality and equality of justice delivered to all persons and groups within our scope of service and influence.

2. Develop, declare, adopt and implement a living body of just principles which in an ongoing way permeate and influence the justice system in the State of Washington and the lives and conduct of all persons or groups involved with or affected by the justice system. To the extent appropriate and acceptable to other states, jurisdictions and sectors throughout the United States and abroad, provide a model that may constructively be used or adapted.

3. Accomplish the foregoing in a manner that is thoughtful, balanced and connected to the realities of life, with implementation that is practical, guides consequences, and takes into account those who provide the services in the system and the end user. In the course of so doing, listen to, inform and build a broad-based constituency, develop a public and political will and a collaborative momentum deeply committed to creating and maintaining access to and quality equal justice in the daily lives of all persons.

4. For the quality, credibility and legitimacy of our process and the products we develop, it is essential that our process reaches out, receives, listens to and in fact uses information, viewpoints and suggestions from people and groups representing a broad array of backgrounds, experiences, perspectives and expertise, never neglecting to

include those the system is meant to serve—its consumers and end users. Inclusiveness is essential.[9]

I was asked to chair the Committee and the process. I was honored to be asked, but my acceptance was subject to certain conditions which I was authorized to seek. I understood how important this process and its outcome could be, but it had to be a quality outcome that was realistic and usable, and that would have credibility and legitimacy as to both the process and the product, not only with those in the justice system, but with a vast variety of stakeholders and affected people, groups, and communities throughout the state. The process had to include and involve a great many people from many disciplines and backgrounds—and had to take the time to do it right. It also had to have the assurance that our product would be seriously considered for adoption by those who could make it authoritative and effective, and, if adopted, that a serious effort would be made to implement the product in relevant, doable, and practical ways.

Securing Judicial Commitment

I arranged an appointment with Chief Justice Gerry Alexander of our State Supreme Court, a thoughtful person who himself believed in and lived the values of fairness for all people. I told him what the Committee was assigned to do by the ATJ Board, and why and how this had come about, and described the effort and process we were planning to undertake. I said I was meeting with him to request two guarantees—quickly adding that I would not be asking him for a guarantee that the Supreme Court would accept or adopt our product. However, I explained that I did want his assurance that when we submitted our product it would get serious consideration from the Supreme Court, which everyone knew had full authority to accept, reject, or modify all or part of the product. All I was asking for was serious consideration, no commitment as to what the Court's action would be. After some questions and conversation, he agreed. I then told him that in the event the court did accept or was willing to adopt the product— whether in its original form or in a modified form—we wanted his assurance that the Court would help us see to it that the document would not end up being pretty words on a library shelf and no more. If there was acceptance or adoption by the Court, we wanted assurance that the Court would support the development of an implementation strategy plan—to find ways and means to transform the ideas and words of the Principles into reality, practically and concretely—both in the justice system and in the lives of people served, affected by and involved in the justice system. We wanted support in transforming words approved by the Supreme Court into a reality sought by the Court. We wanted support in transforming a special project to an integral part of the justice system. The Chief Justice agreed.

Developing an Inclusive Process

The new ATJ Technology Principles Committee of the Washington State ATJ Board held a major organizing meeting attended by well over a hundred people in May 2001 at Seattle University Law School. After attracting many volunteers from various backgrounds, experiences, and disciplines who were willing to commit time and energy, the Committee and the initiative began its formal work in September 2001. First, the group developed a vision of what the effort was about, and then developed a structure and a process to achieve practical and concrete goals and objectives.

The committee members learned very early that we had to avoid being lazy in our thinking. At first we used words about serving all "citizens." Then we remembered that, of course, a person did not have to be a citizen to be subject to or to use the justice system. Perhaps you were vacationing, or visiting a friend, or doing business, or on an athletic team. We then thought about changing the word to Washington "resident," but that was at least as bad, and would not only exclude visitors and the homeless, but also exclude all people from another state who did not reside in Washington State. What became clear was the obvious—that any person who was subject to the law and legal system of our state, no matter who or where from, was entitled to the same justice as anyone else. Thus our operative word became "person." We learned an early lesson: "Justice for all" means "justice for *all*." Our words to focus on then became "equal," "accessible," and "quality."

The adopted Mission Statement of this new initiative was "to create a body of enforceable fundamental principles to ensure that current and future technology both increases opportunities and eliminates barriers to access to and effective utilization of the justice system, thereby improving the quality of justice for all persons in Washington State."[10]

This was the first such public policy initiative in the country. It quickly became apparent that this initiative was not focused solely on solving problems that affected only the justice system, but at its core was addressing fundamental issues of social justice and equity in a full-life, broad sense. What we learned as we moved from thought to action, from idea to reality, is that this initiative was by no means only about the justice system, as essential as that is, and even though that happened to be where we began and were first focused. Nor is the justice system only about lawyers, judges, court clerks, and such. The justice system is, in fact, the fulcrum by which other rights and obligations are made operative and effective. Thus, this initiative was in fact about quality of life, because at its core it was about access to all the basic opportunities and services that every human being needs and should have: justice, health care, housing, basic subsistence, economic opportunity, and the like. It was about fair access, but also meaningful access, relevant access, usable access, affordable access, access in the community, and wherever else access needs to be. It was about the use of technology, but also about the use of any other tools that can help provide or enhance meaningful access to essential opportunities and services. Our effort would only be pretty words if we did not focus on providing practical and concrete results in the daily lives of the people we hoped to serve. And it was not just about Washington, although that was our primary responsibility and where we began. It was about the quality of life of every person. *It was ultimately about fundamental values and delivering on those values.*

The method was to be a proactive rather than reactive engagement in a multidisciplinary, deliberative, inclusive, consumer-respectful, and responsive process with a careful and balanced approach to the emerging issues, opportunities, and problems brought about by technologies, especially new technologies, including the subject of new or drastically changing concepts, issues, discoveries, speeds, conditions, opportunities, and problems.

Many people and groups assumed—as had very often happened in what appeared to be similar situations in the past—that our method of creating the ATJ Technology Principles would be that a selected group of lawyers and judges would get together over a period of weeks, or at most a few months, and come up with the written product. We did not do that, and I assure you that the product our very different process ultimately produced was quite different from what only lawyers and judges would have produced.

For the legitimacy, credibility, and quality of both the process itself and its products, from the very beginning we understood it was essential that the process enabled, received, listened to, considered, and used information, viewpoints, and suggestions from people and groups representing a broad array of backgrounds, experiences, perspectives, and expertise, never neglecting to include those the system is meant to serve—its broad range of consumers and end users. From the first day, the project engaged in outreach and inclusion, an intrinsic part of the process to the very last day. Beginning with this vision, ATJ Tech leadership set out to include in its committees, and work with, a range of people, organizations, and efforts that were dealing with technology's impact on vulnerable populations as well as society in general. From the beginning, the initiative closely partnered with members and representatives of low-income people and communities, persons with disabilities, racial and ethnic minorities, Native American organizations, libraries and librarians, representatives of community centers, seniors, organizations working to bring basic (telephone, cable, and other) communication capabilities to all, a range of social-service agencies, and members and representatives of other traditionally underserved and vulnerable populations and communities, as well as government agencies, courts, judges, court administrators and clerks, lawyers, law schools, technologists, information and technology schools, the private sector, academics, and more.

To ensure that all those involved or interested in the project received authentic and practical information and perspectives, along with its many other efforts, our Outreach Committee conducted focus groups and interviews with a number of different underserved and diverse groups, including homeless, welfare recipients, persons formerly or currently held in the correctional system, immigrants, farm workers, victims of domestic violence, and judges. The knowledge gained from the focus groups, the then-recent 2003 Statewide Legal Needs Study, and other direct information sources, significantly informed other project committees in their work, and was central in informing the content of the ATJ Tech Principles themselves and their accompanying comments. That knowledge and information has and will continue to inform other documents, effectuating mechanisms and processes which enabled the ATJ Tech Principles project to meet its essential task of assuring the credibility, quality, relevance, and realistic effectiveness of the process and its products. We worked with agencies that serve people such as those who were in the focus groups because we understood that as the project planned and then engaged in the process of converting the Access to Justice Technology Principles into real and daily practice, it needed collaborators, allies and supporters; indeed, all groups working on these issues need each other. These collaborations strengthen the likelihood that the combined insights and influence will actually change for the better the way technology is planned, designed, developed, and deployed, not only in the justice system but also in other core social institutions. The results for the vulnerable and disadvantaged in our communities—and thus for all of us—can only be positive.

Beginning in 2002, the Committee created a total of 12 successive drafts of the ATJ Tech Principles. Every draft was sent to all persons and groups involved or interested, every one of whom was invited to comment and make suggestions, as well as assured that every comment and suggestion would be read and considered. The number of drafts we created and sent out testifies to the seriousness with which we treated such comments and suggestions.

In October 2004, the Committee submitted the ATJ Tech Principles produced through this inclusive process. Ultimately, on December 3, 2004, the Washington State Supreme Court, by Court Order, adopted the Principles submitted in full.[11] There were no dissents.

The full Supreme Court Order is found in Document A in the appendix to this chapter (see page 183). Document B, also in the appendix, is the actual Principles as adopted. However, to give the reader necessary context for the body of this chapter between here and Document A, the first two paragraphs of the Supreme Court Order are also set forth here:

> WHEREAS, the Washington judicial system is founded upon the fundamental principle that the judicial system is accessible to all persons; and
> WHEREAS, responding to the unmet legal needs of low and moderate income people and others who suffer disparate access barriers or are otherwise vulnerable, and the need for leadership and effective coordination of civil equal justice efforts in Washington State, the Supreme Court established an Access to Justice Board as a permanent body charged with responsibility to assure high quality access for vulnerable and low and moderate income persons and others who suffer disparate access barriers to the civil justice system. The Supreme Court further

ordered that, among other responsibilities, the Access to Justice
Board shall work to promote, develop and implement policy
initiatives which enhance the availability of resources for essential civil equal justice activities, develop and implement new
programs and innovative measures designed to expand access
to justice in Washington State, and promote the responsiveness
of the civil justice system to the needs of those who suffer disparate treatment or disproportionate access barriers...[12]

Shortly after the Supreme Court Order adopting the ATJ Technology
Principles was entered, our committee ensured that both the Order
and the Principles were translated and printed in the six most commonly used second languages in Washington State at that time:
Spanish, Vietnamese, Chinese, Japanese, Russian, and Arabic. We
then contacted persons and organizations in those communities, made
the Order and Principles available in both English and the appropriate
language, and advised how additional copies could be obtained.

Developing a Strategy for Implementation

Another year of work by a highly knowledgeable multi-disciplinary
group culminated in the ATJ Technology Principles Implementation
Strategy Plan. That Plan was accepted and a Report sent to the
Supreme Court and distributed throughout the justice and associated
systems. Chief Justice Gerry Alexander had fully kept his word of a
few years earlier, as did the Supreme Court itself. The time had now
come to end the project and institutionalize its product and its intent
throughout the justice system, to make it an essential thread in the
inherent fabric of the justice system.

In the interim between the beginning and end of this project,
the ATJ Board created a major standing committee, the Access to
Justice Technology Committee, to be its principal advisor, planner,
initiator, working body, liaison, and, with ATJ Board permission, its
acting body in dealing with technology and the justice system. A
principal part of this Committee's job was to assure that the ATJ
Technology Principles and the Committee were no longer thought
of or treated simply as projects, but instead were institutionalized
as ongoing integral and necessary parts of the Washington State
justice system. Thus, the ATJ Technology Committee was to be con-
sulted, or a Committee representative was to be made part of justice

system planning and action, when the development or use of technology was or might be relevant and considered, or when technology was not or had not been considered, but should have been. The Committee was also authorized, when and as appropriate, to present and participate with other relevant public and private persons and bodies.

In April 2010, the Supreme Court reconfirmed the ATJ Board's permanent place as an essential organ in the body of the Washington State justice system. In its 2010 Order, the Court stated:

The Access to Justice Board shall work to:

- Establish, coordinate and oversee a statewide, integrated, non-duplicative, civil legal services system that is responsive to the needs of the poor, vulnerable and moderate means individuals; . . . .
- Serve as an effective clearinghouse and mechanism for communication and information dissemination;
- Promote, develop, and implement policy initiatives and criteria which enhance the availability of resources for essential civil equal justice activities;
- Develop and implement new programs and innovative measures designed to expand access to justice in Washington State;
- Promote jurisprudential understanding of the law relating to the fundamental right of individuals to secure meaningful access to the civil justice system...[13]

Almost Twelve Years Later: Reflections on the Accomplishments of the Principles, and What Next

More than a decade has gone by since the Principles were adopted, and much has been accomplished as a result of the Principles and the state of mind, attitudes, and habits they engendered. Many accomplishments are apparent, while some of the most significant accomplishments are not highly visible but are nevertheless intrinsically important. Space does not allow a listing of all or even most of the accomplishments. Instead, I will focus on a few examples.

A very important consequence of the Principles is the ongoing and increasing involvement of the ATJ Board and its representatives and stakeholders in bar association and court processes, standards, consideration, and action relative to the extremely important area of court rules at all levels, their content, initiation, modification, adoption, or deletion. This includes initiation of ATJ Board, ATJ Committee, and ATJ stakeholder involvement relative to such rules, which has resulted in presence, consideration, increased knowledge and awareness, common efforts, and, recently, an ATJ representative appointed to full membership on the Washington State Bar Association Rules Committee. In addition, the ATJ Board recently created its own ATJ Board Rules Committee, much of it engendered by needed changes in discovery rules as they may pertain to technology and electronically stored information, and including the fact that such rules (indeed all rules) must be understandable and usable not only by trained lawyers but by so-called "pro se" (the status variously referred to as either unrepresented or self-represented) litigants.

Relative to this very important area of court rules, the ATJ Technology Principles enterprise is at last no longer thought of as a special and often annoying project but rather as an intrinsic and ongoing part of the justice and related systems, mostly a partner, not an antagonist. Some examples—and there are more—have included meaningful participation relative to rules on electronic filing and electronic service, the certification of persons who qualify to have court fees waived, the production for discovery purposes of electronically stored information, the protection of privacy in domestic cases and in abuse cases, the providing of accommodations to people with disabilities, and more.

While it is not the first time the ATJ Technology Principles have been referenced in court decisions and opinions, the case of *Gendler v Batiste*[14] is particularly instructive. In this case the Washington Supreme Court discussed and clearly relied on the ATJ Principles in the context of a public disclosure request case. In its opinion, the Court stated:

> This reasoning is consistent with *our Washington State Access to Justice Technology Principles* (hereinafter ATJ), http:// www.courts. wa/gov/court_rules/. *These principles apply to all courts of law and serve as a guide for all other actors in our state justice system.* ATJ, scope. The ATJ preamble declares, "The use of technologies in the Washington State justice system must protect and advance the fundamental right of equal access to justice. There is a particular need to avoid creating or increasing barriers to access." ATJ, pmbl. "`Technology'" includes "all mechanisms and means used

> *for the production, storage, retrieval, aggregation, transmission, communication, dissemination,* interpretation, presentation, or application of information." *ATJ, scope. "[A]ccess to justice" means the meaningful opportunity to acquire information necessary to assert a claim or defense. ATJ, pmbl.* WSP [Washington State Patrol] cannot shield otherwise disclosable accident reports under the guise of § 409 by depositing them in a forbidden DOT electronic database. *Permitting this would fly in the face of our well grounded principle that technology should enhance access to information that is necessary for justice, not create barriers.*[15] (Emphasis added)

This Supreme Court opinion and its specific language is an important message to all in or related to the justice system: That message—in my words—is: "Pay attention and act in accordance with the ATJ Principles." The case and the message have had and will continue to have important consequences for thinking about how to handle future kinds of public disclosure cases in a principled and equitable manner, and in all other areas where the ATJ Technology Principles apply.

The ATJ Principles have also been infused into the very mechanisms by which Washington courts and related agencies do business with the private sector through contract language that binds all parties to adhere to the Principles. For example, standard contract language in dealings with the Office of Civil Legal Aid states:

> ACCESS TO JUSTICE TECHNOLOGY PRINCIPLES – As a judicial branch agency, the Office of Civil Legal Aid is governed by Washington Supreme Court Order No. 25700-B- (December 3, 2004) (Adoption of Access to Justice Technology Principles). The Access to Justice Technology Principles were developed by the Access to Justice Board to assure that technology enhances rather than diminishes access to the justice system and justice system-related support services, and that it furthers the ability of people to achieve just results in their cases. Contractor agrees to adopt and biennially update a technology plan that incorporates the ATJ Technology Principles and to revise its Technology Principles Organizational Checklist biennially as may be necessary.[16]

A voluntary association named JusticeNet was initiated by the ATJ Tech Committee and community for the purpose of developing cooperation and support on a variety of matters involving technology.

JusticeNet allows for the harvesting of new approaches as well as opportunities for member organizations to do their jobs and meet their goals better and for more people. JusticeNet is comprised of more than 65 member organizations from courts, to policing and prosecutorial agencies, Native American tribes, universities, and library and information system organizations.[17]

In 2009 the first major work by JusticeNet enabled Washington State to receive a federal grant from the Department of Commerce, supported by the Department of Justice, in excess of $4 million. The grant enabled research on and the provision of technology infrastructure in key but often hard to reach places, and the use of various types of community agencies (such as schools, community centers, libraries, parks, and more) to provide information and assistance in multiple essential subject areas—including law and justice, health, education, employment, and more. The work to fully implement this knowledge is continuing.

The ATJ Principles also enabled a variety of other important access to justice initiatives, including:

- Development of Best Practices in Providing Access to Court Information in Electronic Form—supported by the American Bar Association with funding from the Public Welfare Foundation.[18]
- Support and advocacy of the expansion of broadband so as to enable access to information from homes and other readily available places—this to provide and increase digital equity. The ATJ Technology Principles Committee was asked to and did participate in the City of Seattle's Digital Equity Action Committee. The ATJ Technology Principles were used as an important resource. The same is true relative to Seattle's development of privacy policies with respect to information provided to and by the city concerning private individuals and groups.[19]
- Implementation of technology used to effectively connect qualified interpreters who are physically unavailable, or who reside or are otherwise in one part of the state, with courts and administrative tribunals in other parts of the state.[20]
- In partnership with the University of Washington Information School, enabling evaluation of justice system and other relevant websites as to accessibility, understandability, usability,

and more. On request thereafter the Information School participated in re-designing and otherwise improving accessibility, understandability, and usability in many such websites, including the Washington State Bar Association, the King County Bar Association, the Supreme Court's Minority and Justice Commission, and a number of legal aid organizations.[21]

- Launch of an interdisciplinary technological policy center, the Tech Policy Lab, by the University of Washington Law School, Information School, and Computer Science and Engineering School.[22]

- Participating in creating, distributing, making available online, and subsequently updating brochures to all courts in the state on how best to provide services to persons with disabilities, including the use of technology, using when needed assistive technology as well. The same was thereafter done relative to all administrative tribunals in the state, which service far more people than do the courts.[23]

- Providing comments relative to the consideration of various rules by relevant government agencies, including the Federal Communications Commission, the U.S. Department of Justice, the U.S. Department of Commerce, the U.S. Copyright agency, and many Washington State agencies of all three branches of our state government. The Committee and its members are now increasingly solicited for our comments. For example, an ATJ Tech Committee member (later its Chair) offered comments, along with other organizations, with respect to the potential negative effects of certain software on people with dyslexia. Ultimately, the proposed action was canceled.[24]

- Acting as an advisor for a number of states, counties, cities or agencies that have adapted, adopted or are otherwise using some of the ATJ Technology Principles and/or their progeny. It appears more of this may be on the way. We have recently participated with Canada in 2014 and India in 2015.[25]

The ATJ Technology Principles and Board have accomplished many more positive and helpful outcomes. Perhaps the most important accomplishment to date is that after initial avoidance and resistance, unwillingness to be "bothered," or to change old ways of doing things, our persistence and perseverance, along with the support of many others, increasingly places the Principles and the values they embody closer to or in the mainstream every day. The ATJ Tech Principles can no longer be ignored or avoided, and if there is resistance to a suggestion or proposed action, that resistance had better have substance and merit. No longer a "special" or temporary project, the Principles are at last close to being institutionalized and are being recognized as an inclusion document, an equality document, and an effectiveness document, rather than only a technology document.

That having been said, we cannot allow ourselves to fall into the trap of ignoring, avoiding, or resisting the truth—in this case a truth that is present and there to see but apparently difficult to visualize and internalize—and to undertake changing. Notwithstanding all the efforts of a great many people, organizations, and governments, despite the new and terrific tools and technologies we now have and will have, including the ATJ Principles, access to equal and quality justice is no closer for low-income and other vulnerable persons, families, and groups. Clearly, what we have been doing so far is not the whole answer, nor do we have the whole answer, but the road to get us there does exist and is increasingly visible.

The Continuing Challenge of the Inaccessibility of Justice

Unfortunately, in many instances, vulnerable persons are either not better off or are even worse off in terms of meaningful access to justice today than they were ten years ago. For example, in 2003, the Supreme Court of Washington's Task Force on Civil Equal Justice Funding published the first-ever report on the civil-legal needs of low-income and vulnerable Washingtonians. That report presented striking findings about the percentage of low-income households that experienced important civil-legal problems, the types of problems they experienced, differences in the prevalence and subject matter of legal problems experienced by different demographic subgroups, the percentage of households that sought legal help, where people went for legal help, and the impact of legal assistance in resolving their legal problems.[26]

In 2014, the Washington State Supreme Court established a committee to oversee a comprehensive and rigorous update of the 2003 Civil Legal Needs Study. The committee was to oversee a comprehensive research effort grounded in the core areas of the 2003 study's focus, augmented to understand new and emerging legal problems.

The Civil Legal Needs Study Update Report was concluded in June 2015 and published a few months later. The findings were that there was no change from the 2003 findings that more than 70% of low-income households had a civil-legal-need problem within the prior 12-month period, and that more than three-quarters of those either did not seek or were unable to obtain legal help with respect to those problems.[27] Also consistent with the findings of the 2003 study, large percentages of low-income people did not get help either because they did not understand that the problems they faced had a legal dimension or because legal help was not available. There was no change from 2003 to 2014 in the percentage of those people who were able to get legal help and who obtained some resolution of their problem—61% in both studies. There was also no change in the confidence or lack thereof exhibited by low-income people who had a legal problem—58% had a negative view of the justice system.[28] What was different in the 2014 study from the 2003 results was not better; it was worse. The per capita incidence of civil-legal problems grew from 3.3 per household per year in 2003 to 9.3 per household per year in 2014.[29]

Given these sobering results, I would hate to think of what the situation would be without all the commitment, work, and money, both state and federal, that have gone into trying to address these problems in the eleven years between 2003 and 2014. And this state of affairs is not unique to Washington.[30] For that reason, a number of organizations, including the American Bar Association, have been working hard to identify the road forward, a road that will actually get us to a better place.[31]

While I recognize that both the past and current initiatives are well intentioned and may in fact assist some people in the short term, I believe that meaningfully addressing the widespread inaccessibility of justice requires broader, more open, more systemic knowledge and action. The process for change requires recognition that the American justice system is well over 200 years old and was designed even earlier at a very different time with very different service goals, very different resources and tools, and a very different infrastructure than is needed now. For example, our system of 200-plus years ago was intended and designed to serve white male property owners, and the infrastructure which was designed and built accordingly reflected that—and fundamentally still does. We know that our present mission, intentions, and goals are very different from what they were in that time. Today, the justice system in the United States is intended to serve *all people*; it states this intention and is presumably committed to it. However, despite this expressed intention, the design of our justice system and its centuries-old infrastructure and operations have not changed, certainly not meaningfully changed. Rather, they have become essentially unworkable, indeed irrelevant, as to being accessible, usable, and actually delivering justice, especially equal justice, to and for all people, not just white male property owners. We have never yet thoroughly and carefully thought through and addressed the obsolete infrastructure of our justice/legal system, and the systemic redesign and changes that are required and must be made real in order to provide meaningful access to and delivery of quality justice to all, especially equal justice—including both process and outcome. This is what must be done, what has not been done or even begun, and what we must begin to do right now. To my knowledge this entire matter remains unaddressed and certainly will not be addressed by any recent or current well-intentioned efforts (although some current recommendations might perhaps become a part of systemic change).

For these reasons, while short-term modifications may be necessary, meaningful long-term accessibility and delivery of equal justice will require systemic changes in the American justice/legal system and its infrastructure and, I strongly suggest, those of other countries and governments. Whatever the outcome, it is necessary to do this, and certainly better than not making a serious effort. And this is the right time! We now have tools available that we have never had before, technological, information, communication and mobility tools that can serve, empower and enable the justice system, those who work in it, those who are subject to the system and are or potentially will be served by the justice system. We now have the ability to develop, find, share, communicate, present, enable, and empower information, knowledge, and services no matter the location and the people who should receive, understand, use, and benefit from it. And those capabilities are increasing.

I don't know what the ultimate answers will be, nor could I. Rather than my presumptuously and unwisely trying to prescribe what form the ultimate changes should take, I suggest here a process for moving with the spirit and toward the goals set forth in Dr. King's 1968 speech. Approximately fifty people from various parts of the United States and from different backgrounds and disciplines should be convened to participate in a several-day brainstorming session in the relatively near future. The participants should include not only judges, lawyers, legal academics, and workers at various levels in the justice system, but also appropriate information and communication technologists and experts, behavioral and political scientists, sociologists, stakeholders, and just plain thinkers.

Rather than my trying to ordain ultimate conclusions and recommendations, I suggest that this first stage strive to reach the following limited but highly important objectives: (1) agree on core values and considerations that will drive a longer-term substantive effort to fully address and propose solutions of the systemic and associated problems; (2) recommend how to structure, conduct, and strategize a longer-term and full substantive process and effort to gather or otherwise obtain information in whatever form and by whatever means, consider the same, report on what was done, what methods were used, the consideration and thinking, the findings, conclusions, and recommendations; (3) recommend how many people, and from what disciplines and backgrounds, should be in the second group involved in this longer-term, fully substantive effort, and to the desired extent, recommend specific persons of multidisciplinary backgrounds; and (4) recommend an approximate time frame for the total effort and report. In order to succeed, this effort must be convened by a highly respected, credible, bridging entity capable of engaging highly skilled and thoughtful persons from a broad array of disciplines with the personal backgrounds and experience to carefully, impartially, and fairly address a most significant and fundamental problem of values and daily life that has affected, and one way or another continues to affect, every person in the United States, and who will do their best to develop a fair and workable solution for all. I truly believe we can build a new infrastructure that is in fact efficient, economical, and effective, that will enable the justice system, and all of us, to live its values and keep its promises.

In this respect, we, in the State of Washington, know that we are not immune. As a parallel important beginning effort, we have recently begun the process of objectively evaluating the now eleven-year-old Access to Justice Technology Principles, and determining what changes, if any, should be made to improve both the Principles and their application—the Idea and the Reality.

Most of us have long been aware of the truism "Eternal Vigilance is the Price of Liberty."[32] I have learned and had confirmed many times the additional truism that "Eternal Vigilance is the Price of Justice."

Appendix

DOCUMENT A

THE SUPREME COURT OF WASHINGTON

IN THE MATTER OF THE ACCESS TO JUSTICE)   **O R D E R**

TECHNOLOGY PRINCIPLES   ) NO. 25700-B-449

_____   )

WHEREAS, the Washington judicial system is founded upon the fundamental principle that the judicial system is accessible to all persons; and

WHEREAS, responding to the unmet legal needs of low and moderate income people and others who suffer disparate access barriers or are otherwise vulnerable, and the need for leadership and effective coordination of civil equal justice efforts in Washington State, the Supreme Court established an Access to Justice Board as a permanent body charged with responsibility to assure high quality access for vulnerable and low and moderate income persons and others who suffer disparate access barriers to the civil justice system. The Supreme Court further ordered that, among other responsibilities, the Access to Justice Board shall work to promote, develop and implement policy initiatives which enhance the availability of resources for essential civil equal justice activities, develop and implement new programs and innovative measures designed to expand access to justice in Washington State, and promote the responsiveness of the civil justice system to the needs of those who suffer disparate treatment or disproportionate access barriers; and

WHEREAS, in working to fulfill those responsibilities, the Access to Justice Board recognized that developments in information and communication technologies, including the internet, pose significant challenges to full and equal access to the justice system, that technology can provide increased pathways for quality access, but it can also perpetuate and exacerbate existing barriers and create significant new barriers. The Board determined it must plan and act proactively to take maximum advantage of the opportunity to destroy or minimize such barriers and to create more effective and efficient means of access to the justice system and increase the quantity and quality of justice provided to all persons in Washington State; and

WHEREAS, in 2001 the Access to Justice Board empowered and charged a Board committee to engage in a broad-based and inclusive initiative to create a body of authoritative fundamental principles and proposed action based thereon to ensure that current and future technology both increases opportunities and eliminates barriers to access to and effective utilization of the justice system, thereby improving the quality of justice for all persons in Washington State; and

WHEREAS, over a three-year period the Board and committee fulfilled the responsibility of broad and inclusive involvement and the development of "The Access to Justice Technology Principles", with accompanying comments and proposed action based thereon; and The Access to Justice Technology Principles have been endorsed by the Board for Judicial Administration, the Judicial Information System Committee, the Board of Trustees of the Superior Court Judges' Association, the Board of Trustees of the District and Municipal Court Judges' Association, the Board of Governors of the Washington State Bar Association, the Minority and Justice Commission, the Gender and Justice Commission, the Attorney General, and the Council on Public Legal Education; and

WHEREAS, a statewide Judicial Information System to serve the courts of the State of Washington was created by the Supreme Court in 1976 to be operated by the Administrative Office of the Courts pursuant to court rule, and charged with addressing issues of dissemination of data, equipment, communication with other systems, security, and operational priorities; and

WHEREAS, consistent with the intent of this Order, pursuant to RCW 2.68.050 the courts of this state, through the Judicial Information System, shall, in pertinent part, promote and facilitate electronic access of judicial information and services to the public at little or no cost and by use of technologies capable of being used by persons without extensive technological ability and wherever possible by persons with disabilities, and;

WHEREAS, the application of the Access to Justice Technology Principles to guide the use of technology in the Washington State justice system is desirable and appropriate; and

WHEREAS, the wide dissemination of the Access to Justice Technology Principles will promote their use and consequent access to justice for all persons;

Now, therefore, it is hereby

ORDERED:

(a)   The Access to Justice Technology Principles appended to this Order state the values, standards and intent to guide the use of technology in the Washington State court system and by all other persons, agencies, and bodies under the authority of this Court. These Principles should be considered with other governing law and court rules in deciding the appropriate use of technology in the administration of the courts and the cases that come before such courts, and should be so considered in deciding the appropriate use of technology by all other persons, agencies and bodies under the authority of this Court.

(b)   The Access to Justice Technology Principles and this Order shall be published expeditiously with the Washington Court Rules and on the Washington State Bar Association website, and on the courts website as maintained by the Administrative Office of the Courts.

The following introductory language should immediately precede the Access to Justice Technology Principles in all such publications and sites:

> These Access to Justice Technology Principles were developed by the Access to Justice Board to assure that technology enhances rather than diminishes access to and the quality of justice for all persons in Washington State. Comments of the Access to Justice Board committee drafters accompanying the Principles make clear the intent that the Principles are to be used so as to be practical and effective for both the workers in and users of the justice system, that the Principles do not create or constitute the basis for new causes of action or create unfunded mandates. These Principles have been endorsed by the Board for Judicial Administration, the Judicial Information System Committee, the Board of Trustees of the Superior Court Judges' Association, the Board of Trustees of the District and Municipal Court Judges' Association, the Board of Governors of the Washington State Bar Association, the Minority and Justice Commission, the Gender and Justice Commission, the Attorney General, and the Council on Public Legal Education.

(c)   The Administrative Office of the Courts in conjunction with the Access to Justice Board and the Judicial Information System Committee shall report annually to the Supreme Court on the use of the Access to Justice Technology Principles in the Washington State court system and by all other persons, agencies, and bodies under the authority of this Court.

DATED at Olympia, Washington this 3rd day of December 2004.

	Alexander, C.J
Johnson, J	Bridge, J
Madsen, J	Chambers, J
	Owens, J
Ireland, J	Fairhurst, J

DOCUMENT B

The following are the Access to Justice Technology Principles as adopted by the Supreme Court, and the Comments to those Principles included by the Supreme Court.

Washington State Access to Justice Technology Principles

Adopted by the Washington State Supreme Court
December 3, 2004

An Initiative of the Washington State Access to Justice Board

Preamble

The use of technologies in the Washington State justice system must protect and advance the fundamental right of equal access to justice. There is a particular need to avoid creating or increasing barriers to access and to reduce or remove existing barriers for those who are or may be excluded or underserved, including those not represented by counsel.

This statement presumes a broad definition of access to justice, which includes the meaningful opportunity, directly or through other persons: (1) to assert a claim or defense and to create, enforce, modify, or discharge a legal obligation in any forum; (2) to acquire the procedural or other information necessary (a) to assert a claim or defense, or (b) to create, enforce, modify, or discharge an obligation in any forum, or (c) to otherwise improve the likelihood of a just result; (3) to participate in the conduct of proceedings as witness or juror; and (4) to acquire information about the activities of courts or other dispute resolution bodies. Further, access to justice requires a just process, which includes, among other things, timeliness and affordability. A just process also has "transparency," which means that the system allows the public to see not just the outside but through to the inside of the justice system, its rules and standards, procedures and processes, and its other operational characteristics and patterns so as to evaluate all aspects of its operations, particularly its fairness, effectiveness, and efficiency.

Therefore, these Access to Justice Technology Principles state the governing values and principles which shall guide the use of technology in the Washington State justice system.

Comment to "Preamble"
Access to justice is a fundamental right in Washington State, and the State Supreme Court has recognized and endeavored to protect that right in its establishment of the Access to Justice Board. From an understanding that technology can affect access to justice, these Access to Justice Technology Principles are intended to provide general statements of broad applicability and a foundation for resolving specific issues as they arise. The various parts of this document should be read as a whole.

A broad definition of the terms used herein is necessary to ensure that our underlying constitutional and common law values are fully protected. The terms used in this document should be understood and interpreted in that light.

These Principles do not mandate new expenditures, create new causes of action, or repeal or modify any rule. Rather, they require that justice system decision makers consider access to justice, take certain steps whenever technology that may affect access to justice is planned or implemented, avoid reducing access, and, whenever possible, use technology to enhance access to justice.

Scope

The Access to Justice Technology Principles apply to all courts of law, all clerks of court and court administrators, and to all other persons or parts of the Washington justice system under the rule-making authority of the Court. They should also serve as a guide for all other actors in the Washington justice system.

"Other actors in the Washington justice system" means all governmental and non-governmental bodies engaged in formal dispute resolution or rulemaking and all persons and entities who may represent, assist, or provide information to persons who come before such bodies.

"Technology" includes all electronic means of communication and transmission and all mechanisms and means used for the production, storage, retrieval, aggregation, transmission, communication, dissemination, interpretation, presentation, or application of information.

Comment to "Scope"

This language is intended to make clear that the Access to Justice Technology Principles are mandatory only for those persons or bodies within the scope of the State Supreme Court's rulemaking authority. It is, however, hoped and urged that these Principles and their values will be applied and used widely throughout the entire justice system.

It is also intended that the Access to Justice Technology Principles shall continue to apply fully in the event all or any portion of the performance, implementation, or accomplishment of a duty, obligation, responsibility, enterprise, or task is delegated, contracted, assigned, or transferred to another entity or person, public or private, to whom the Principles may not otherwise apply.

The definition of the word "technology" is meant to be inclusive rather than exclusive.

Requirement of Access to Justice

Access to a just result requires access to the justice system. Use of technology in the justice system should serve to promote equal access to justice and to promote the opportunity for equal participation in the justice system for all. Introduction of technology or changes in the use of technology must not reduce access or participation and, whenever possible, shall advance such access and participation.

Comment to "Requirement of Access to Justice"

This Principle combines promotion of access to justice through technology with a recognition of the "first, do no harm" precept. The intent is to promote the use of technology to advance access whenever possible, to maintain a focus on the feasible while protecting against derogation of access, and to encourage progress, innovation, and experimentation.

Technology and Just Results

The overriding objective of the justice system is a just result achieved through a just process by impartial and well-informed decision makers. The justice system shall use and advance technology to achieve that objective and shall reject, minimize, or modify any use that reduces the likelihood of achieving that objective.

Comment to "Technology and Just Results"

The reference to a "just process" reaffirms that a just process is integral to a just result. The reference to "well-informed decision makers" is to emphasize the potential role of technology in gathering, organizing, and presenting information in order that the decision maker receives the optimal amount and quality of information so that the possibility of a just result is maximized.

Openness and Privacy

The justice system has the dual responsibility of being open to the public and protecting personal privacy. Its technology should be designed and used to meet both responsibilities.

Technology use may create or magnify conflict between values of openness and personal privacy. In such circumstances, decision makers must engage in a careful balancing process, considering both values and their underlying purposes, and should maximize beneficial effects while minimizing detrimental effects.

Comment to "Openness and Privacy"

This Principle underlines that the values of openness and privacy are not necessarily in conflict, particularly when technology is designed and used in a way that is crafted to best protect and, whenever possible, enhance each value. However, when a conflict is unavoidable, it is essential to consider the technology's effects on both privacy and openness. The Principle requires that decision makers engage in a balancing process which carefully considers both values and their underlying rationales and objectives, weighs the technology's potential effects, and proceed with use when they determine that the beneficial effects outweigh the detrimental effects.

The Principle applies both to the content of the justice system and its operations, as well as the requirements for accountability and transparency. These requirements may mean different things depending on whether technology use involves internal court operations or involves access to and use of the justice system by members of the public.

Assuring a Neutral Forum

The existence of a neutral, accessible, and transparent forum for dispute resolution is fundamental to the Washington State justice system. Developments in technology may generate alternative dispute resolution systems that do not have these characteristics, but which, nevertheless, attract users who seek the advantages of available technology. Participants and actors in the Washington State justice system shall use all appropriate means to ensure the existence of neutral, accessible, and transparent forums which are compatible with new technologies and to discourage and reduce the demand for the use of forums which do not meet the basic requirements of neutrality, accessibility, and transparency.

Comment to "Assuring a Neutral Forum"

Technologically generated alternative dispute resolution (including online dispute resolution) is a rapidly growing field that raises many issues for the justice system. This Principle underlines the importance of applying the basic values and requirements of the justice system and all the Access to Justice Technology Principles to that area, while clarifying that there is no change to governing law.

This Principle is not intended in any way to discourage the accessibility and use of mediation, in which the confidentiality of the proceeding and statements and discussions may assist the parties in reaching a settlement; provided that the parties maintain access to a neutral and transparent forum in the event a settlement is not reached.

Maximizing Public Awareness and Use

Access to justice requires that the public have available understandable information about the justice system, its resources, and means of access. The justice system should promote ongoing public knowledge and understanding of the tools afforded by technology to access justice by developing and disseminating information and materials as broadly as possible in forms and by means that can reach the largest possible number and variety of people.

Comment to "Maximizing Public Awareness and Use"
While assuring public awareness and understanding of relevant access to justice technologies is an affirmative general duty of all governmental branches, this Principle expressly recognizes that the primary responsibility lies with the justice system itself. As stated in the Comment to the Preamble, none of these Access to Justice Technology Principles, including this one, mandates new expenditures or creates new causes of action. At the same time, however, planners and decision makers must demonstrate sensitivity to the needs, capacities, and where appropriate, limitations of prospective users of the justice system.

Communicating the tools of access to the public should be done by whatever means is effective. For example, information about kiosks where domestic violence protection forms can be filled out and filed electronically could be described on radio or television public service announcements. Another example might be providing information on handouts or posters at libraries or community centers. Information could also be posted on a website of the Council for Public Legal Education or of a local or statewide legal aid program, using an audible web reader for persons with visual or literacy limitations. The means may be as many and varied as people's imaginations and the characteristics of the broad population to be reached.

Best Practices

To ensure implementation of the Access to Justice Technology Principles, those governed by these principles shall utilize "best practices" procedures or standards. Other actors in the justice system are encouraged to utilize or be guided by such best practices procedures or standards.

The best practices shall guide the use of technology so as to protect and enhance access to justice and promote equality of access and fairness. Best practices shall also provide for an effective, regular means of evaluation of the use of technology in light of all the values and objectives of these Principles.

Comment to "Best Practices"

This Principle is intended to provide guidance to ensure that the broad values and approaches articulated elsewhere in these Access to Justice Technology Principles are implemented to the fullest extent possible in the daily reality of the justice system and the people served by the justice system. The intent is that high quality practical tools and resources be available for consideration, use, evaluation, and improvement of technologies in all parts of the justice system. This Principle and these Access to Justice Technology Principles as a whole are intended to encourage progress, innovation, and experimentation with the objective of increasing meaningful access to quality justice for all. With these goals in mind, the development and adoption of statewide models for best practices is strongly encouraged.

Notes

1   Martin Luther King Jr, "Remaining Awake Through a Great Revolution" (Address delivered at the National Cathedral, Washington, DC, 31 March 1968), online: <mlk-kpp01.stanford.edu/index.php/encyclopedia/documentsentry/doc_remaining_awake_through_a_great_revolution/>.

2   Wash Constitution Article I, § 32.

3   Order establishing Access to Justice Board for an Initial Evaluation Period of Two Years, No 25700-B- at 1, online: <www.wsba.org/~/media/Files/Legal%20Community/Committees_Boards_Panels/ATJ%20Board/Order%20Establishing%20Access%20to%20Justice%20Board%201994.ashx>.

4   Ibid.; many states have since followed this example. They may be called Boards or Commissions or such, but they have essentially similar duties.

5   Ibid.

6   Donald J Horowitz, "Technology, Values, and the Justice System: The Evolution of the Access to Justice Technology Bill of Rights," *79 Wash L Rev* 79 (2004):77.

7   Ibid. at 78.

8   See Document B.

9   Ibid. at 81.

10 Washington State Minority and Justice Commission, Minutes of Commission Meeting (3 October 2003), online: <www.courts.wa.gov/ programs_orgs/index.cfm?fa=programs_orgs.showMjcMinutes&theMi nutesFolder=01_Commission%20Meeting%20Minutes&minutes Name=20031003.htm>.

11 See Document A.

12 Ibid.; In the Matter of the Reauthorizing of the Access to Justice Board, No 25700-B-449 at 1, online: <http://www.wsba.org/~/media/Files/ Legal%20Community/Committees_Boards_Panels/ATJ%20Board/ Washington%20State%20Access%20to%20Justice%20Technology%20 Principles%20-%20Supreme%20Court%20Order%202004.ashx>.

13 In the Matter of the Reauthorizing of the Access to Justice Board, No 25700-B-524 at 1, online: <www.wsba.org/~/media/Files/Legal%20 Community/Committees_Boards_Panels/ATJ%20Board/ATJ%20 Board%20Order%202012%2003%2008.ashx> (reauthorizing the Board again in 2012).

14 *Gendler v Batiste,* 174 Wn (2d) 244 (2012) [*Gendler*].

15 Ibid. at 22–23.

16 ATJ Web, "Implementation," online: <old.atjweb.org/implementation/>.

17 Included among these are: Washington State Office of Public Defense; Washington State Office of Civil Legal Aid; Washington State Office of the Attorney General; Washington State Bar Association; Washington Defender Association; University of Washington Information School; Kalispel Tribe of Indians; Tulalip Tribe; Chehalis Tribe; numerous Dispute Resolution Centers and statewide, regional, and local civil legal-aid programs: Washington Courts, "State of the Judiciary Address," press release, January 13, 2011, online: <https://www.courts. wa.gov/newsinfo/?fa=newsinfo.pressdetail&newsid=1791>.

18 Washington Access to Justice Board, "Best Practices: Providing Access to Court Information in Electronic Form," online: <www.wsba.org/~/ media/Files/Legal%20Community/Committees_Boards_Panels/ATJ%20 Board/Providing%20Access%20to%20Court%20Information%20in%20 Electronic%20Form%20Best%20Practices%20%20Best%20Practices%20 Final.ashx>.

19 City of Seattle, "Digital Equity Action Committee Members," *seattle.gov,* online: <www.seattle.gov/community-technology/for-everyone/digital- equity-initiative/digital-equity-action-committee>.

20 Washington Courts, *2013-2015 Access to Justice Technology Principles Report to the Supreme Court* (30 November 2015) at 6, online: <www.wsba.org/~/media/Files/Legal%20Community/Committees_Boards_Panels/ATJ%20Board/Committee%20Files/Technology/ATJ-TechnologyPrinciplesReport2013-2015.ashx>.

21 *Access to Justice Board Annual Report* (February 2010) at 15, online: <www.wsba.org/~/media/Files/Legal%20Community/Committees_Boards_Panels/ATJ%20Board/Access%20to%20Justice%20Board%20Annual%20Report%202010.ashx>.

22 University of Washington, *Tech Policy Lab*, online: <techpolicylab.org/>.

23 Washington Courts, "Court Program Accessibility (ADA and Washington State Information)," online: <https://www.courts.wa.gov/committee/?fa=committee.display&item_id=1157&committee_id=143>.

24 US Copyright Office, "Facilitating Access for the Blind or Other Persons with Disabilities: Notice of Inquiry and Request for Comments," online: <www.copyright.gov/docs/sccr/>; Brian Rowe, "Comments," online: <http://www.copyright.gov/docs/sccr/comments/2009/rowe.pdf>.

25 Both Canada and India are involved in projects to integrate technology into their justice systems. Jane Bailey, "Digitization Of Court Processes In Canada" (working paper no. 2, Laboratory of Cyberjustice, Montreal, QC, 2012). Justice R.C. Lahoti, "Key Note Address," (address, International Conference on ADR, Conciliation, Mediation and Case Management, New Delhi, India, May 3–4, 2003).

26 Task Force on Civil Equal Justice Funding, *The Washington State Civil Legal Needs Study*, (September 2003), online: <https://www.courts.wa.gov/newsinfo/content/taskforce/CivilLegalNeeds.pdf>.

27 Civil Legal Needs Study Update Committee, *Civil Legal Needs Study Update* (October 2015) at 3, online: <http://ocla.wa.gov/wp-content/uploads/2015/10/CivilLegalNeedsStudy_October2015_V21_Final10_14_15.pdf> [*Civil Legal Needs Study Update*].

28 Ibid. at 17.

29 Ibid. at 5.

30 See Alan W Houseman, *Civil Legal Aid in the United States: An Update for 2013* (Center for Law and Social Policy, November 2013), online: <www.clasp.org/resources-and-publications/publication-1/CIVIL-LEGAL-AID-IN-THE-UNITED-STATES-3.pdf>; Task Force to Expand Access to Civil Legal Services in New York, *Report to the Chief Judge of the State of New York* (November 2010), online: <https://www.nycourts.gov/accesstojusticecommission/PDF/CLS-TaskForceREPORT.pdf>.

31 Rebecca L Sandefur, *Accessing Justice in the Contemporary USA: Findings from the Community Needs and Services Study* (Urbana, IL: American Bar Foundation, 2014), online: <www.americanbarfoundation.org/uploads/cms/documents/sandefur_accessing_justice_in_the_contemporary_usa._aug._2014.pdf>.

32 This truism developed over time and is not directly attributable to anyone. It is often mistakenly attributed to either Irish lawyer/politician John Philpot Curran or to Thomas Jefferson. It is most likely derived from Curran's speech in 1790, in which he said that "The condition upon which God hath given liberty to man is eternal vigilance; which condition if he break, servitude is at once the consequence of his crime and the punishment of his guilt." See Suzy Platt, ed., *Respectfully Quoted* (Washington, D.C.: Library of Congress, 1993), 200.

CHAPTER VI

Empowerment, Technology, and Family Law

Sherry MacLennan

Can ordinary people be empowered by the use of new technolo-gies and online services to deal with problems that are as com-plex and layered with emotion as family law issues typically are? In British Columbia, at the Legal Services Society,[1] we have provided free, web-based self-help services since 2002 and know that done right, online self-help is empowering for many. We also know that technology supported by people is even more empowering, and that for some, online self-help is not a viable option. However, as technol-ogy evolves, the opportunity arises to bring the best advances to the public and not only make existing tools easier to use, but to increase the pool of potential users by providing services that are more acces-sible. By providing online services to the many that want them and are empowered by them, service providers can focus on enhancing in-person services where they are needed most.

The Legal Services Society (LSS) is British Columbia's legal-aid provider and is unusual in having a mandate which includes the provision of public legal-education and information (PLEI) services.[2] Traditional legal aid services focus on representation for low income people with an array of criminal and civil problems. Until 2002, in addition to PLEI, LSS was typical in this regard and covered poverty-related civil matters as well as a wide range of family law problems, from simple divorce to custody to property division. As the province entered a period of austerity in 2002, the LSS was required to significantly reduce the number of people that could be legally aided, eliminating civil cases and curtailing family coverage. With few exceptions since then, family coverage has only been available in cases where violence exists or where there is an imminent risk of a child being permanently removed from the province.[3]

As a result of reduced family coverage, LSS significantly shifted its family PLEI program. From primarily informing people about their rights and listing resources for assistance through print publications, the LSS introduced a new website which featured self-help guides—Family Law in BC (www.familylaw.lss.bc.ca). On this site, information is presented to help users choose the correct self-help guide, which then walks them step-by-step through the paperwork and court processes necessary to have their issue adjudicated. Users are always informed of free public and private mediation options, but in the early years, the site focused on court-based self-help to replace the representation services lost due to coverage restrictions. The web-based information, self-help guides, and court forms could stand alone, but were supplemented with new services including family duty counsel and advice lawyers, and a telephone hotline where users could get legal advice. In addition, LSS provided widespread community education so that intermediaries in social service agencies could become familiar with the site, thus enabling them to help their clients experiencing family problems to access both the site and the new support services. LSS was able to undertake many of these initiatives to enhance access to justice in times of austerity as a result of the generous support of the BC Law Foundation[4] and Notary Foundation of BC.[5] LSS is the beneficiary of significant grants that enabled the launch of our family site and continued improvements to our web-based programs.

Some community intermediaries receive specialized advocacy training. In BC, these "advocates" are not lawyers but people from a variety of backgrounds who work as staff in social service agencies. They receive training to help people with specific legal problems, usually related to poverty issues, welfare, and other social service benefits. BC's advocates are funded by the Law Foundation and are a significant part of the justice ecosystem.[6] Many individuals who would never seek out counsel for fear of dealing with lawyers or of paying legal fees will enter the office of a trusted community agency. When we started the Family Law in BC Website (FLWS), these intermediaries were seen as the primary audience for the site. At that time, they were perceived as being more likely than the general public, and certainly more than the traditional legal aid clientele, to have access to computers and the internet, and to have the skills and abilities to use these new tools. Since then, we have seen the digital divide diminish and the audience expand well beyond the initial, intermediary target.

While the divide has diminished, it has not disappeared. Barriers continue to exist. Impoverished people may not have access to a computer or internet at home; if they live in small or remote communities, they may not even have access through public-access computers in libraries.[7] Some of the small Aboriginal communities which dot the province do not yet have internet access. In such communities, technology is not the tool that is turned to first or at all. Depending on age, education, and experience, even if there is access to a computer, a lack of digital literacy may prevent a user from taking advantage of it. Even in a sophisticated user, it is known that emotional state, as well as health issues as diverse as depression, cancer treatments, and diabetes, can affect a user's ability to assimilate and process information. Reading online is a different experience from reading print, and care must be taken in delivering services online in such a way as to consider the user interfaces and experience. Many intermediaries want to give their clients something to take away with them, or to review together when there is no online access. Print remains essential[8] and LSS fulfilled orders for more than 250,000 print publications in 2013.

So with these barriers why pursue online services for low-income people? There are several important reasons. The web offers incomparable advantages for providing services 24/7—accessible whenever and wherever needed.[9] Web services cover large geographic regions such as BC, at low cost. Low-income people access and use the internet in BC, and with increasing frequency by means of a mobile device. LSS has seen exponential increases in the visits to its sites from mobile devices and in clients providing mobile contact numbers over the last five years. As a result, LSS introduced a mobile website to ensure that information is available, and our newest website, Aboriginal Legal Aid in BC (aboriginal.legalaid.bc.ca) is fully mobile compatible.

The legal problems of low-income people, such as marriage breakdown, cut across socio-economic status. Increasingly, and regardless of economic background, people want to manage their own legal problems and are reluctant to engage counsel to do so for them, finding legal fees to be poor value for their money or having run out of money before a solution is obtained.[10] Legal-needs research suggests that people with legal problems want to be saved—and they want problem-solving processes that are easy to use and cheap. They want reasonably quick solutions and authoritative information that will assist them with processes that are transparent and lead to fair outcomes. People are looking for help and they want to get on with their lives.[11] They are looking to Google and the web for these results. Visits to the FLWS, described as "the Grand Central Station" for family law in BC, showed steady increases annually until 2013–14, when visits doubled to 65,648 visits per month. We attribute the increase in usage to two things: firstly, a modest advertising campaign ($10,000) in conjunction with the introduction of new family legislation in BC; and secondly, focused improvements to the website. One might assume that such increases are the natural result of being a unique source of online family law information in BC, but this is not the case. BC has a robust PLEI environment with multiple sources of family PLEI online, delivered by a range of providers, from public agencies to private lawyers.[12]

The strategies for successful online service delivery focus on content, accessibility, collaboration, networks, and evaluation.[13] We believe that these are essential to empowering the end user, even in complex and emotionally laden situations such as family law.

Content Is King

Legal content must be accurate, up to date, and trusted. Users need to trust the agency providing the content to keep it updated at all times and to alert them to changes in the law or process. We have achieved our reputation for reliable, accurate information through retention of a specialist family-law lawyer, strong relationships with government staff who can apprise us of changes in policy and the law, and dedicated staff who review multiple resources to keep up to date. Staff quickly respond to changes and post updates as required. RSS feeds alert subscribers to changes on the site and maintain a "What's New" section for reference.

Accessibility

A good site must address physical accessibility issues, such as adjustable font sizes, but accessibility refers to much more than that.

Accessibility is a factor at every stage, from the instant a user lands on the site and decides whether to stick around, to whether the site engages their interest and motivates them to continue to move forward with their issue. If the site discourages and overwhelms users because of legalistic vocabulary, densely packed text, or poor navigability, it is not accessible.

In 2012, the LSS Accessibility Initiative included a review of our online services.[14] While we were satisfied that we were meeting our content goals, we wanted to expand our reach. Our goal was to attract an audience beyond the traditional intermediary and sophisticated user in order to reach an audience more reflective of typical internet users. To the greatest extent possible, we wanted to include the least sophisticated users and provide a product that increased engagement of the original audiences at the same time. We wanted to extend our reach in order to serve the majority of people, who now expect to be able to use the web themselves for results and not be dependent on visiting an intermediary office for assistance. Self-help tools were expanded to include a live chat service. Users can now engage with volunteer law students who answer their questions (generally through pre-scripted answers) and direct them to relevant information. Such functional integration means the information provided is not only easy to understand, but also easy to find. This is a challenge when the content has expanded, as it has with the FLWS: the resource includes over 1,400 pages, and it continues to grow.

Additional support, such as LiveChat, empowers those who might otherwise be daunted by the site. Literacy levels across the general population in Canada are shockingly low, and BC is no exception: 40% of BC adults struggle with the skills necessary to do such everyday activities as read a newspaper, fill out a work application form, or read a map.[15] While care has been taken to use plain language principles, our Accessibility Initiative saw us work not only with an IT consultant to recommend improvements to navigation and the user design/interface experience, but also with the province's literacy association, Decoda Literacy Solutions, and an Aboriginal consultant, Sa'hetxw, for advice on engaging Aboriginal audiences online.

As observed by British academic and commentator Roger Smith, user expectations of a non-profit-run information site are high and shaped by what they see on other sites, usually commercial and sophisticated.[16] There is a matter of seconds during which a user will assess a not-for-profit information site as credible and relevant, and those judgments are shaped by their experience with other online resources.

Collaborate

LSS values collaboration, and in site development collaborates with experts, agencies that provide PLEI, front-line family law services, and the public with legal problems themselves. Gathering the perspectives of many individuals who work on the site or assist others with it is invaluable in ensuring that online resources meet the user's needs. We receive advice on navigation improvement and common user mistakes, which enables us to correct the site in order to meet these needs. An advisory committee and broader community consultations support content development and provide practical feedback. Working with members of the public in user testing and listening labs have allowed us to design new court forms, and an interactive do-your-own separation agreement met with immediate success.

Network

LSS uses its own networks of offices, the network of Law Foundation funded advocates and other community intermediaries, all of whom attend public legal education workshops to create a user base for the website. LSS has also engaged members of the private bar who saw the value in referring clients to the site for unbundled services, and identified the site as an education tool to allow paying clients to appreciate the work necessary to move a case through a litigation process. The site became a convenient resource for the bar and inter-mediaries to stay up-to-date on family law and to access court forms and procedural advice. Search engine optimization is important but does not replace the human network. It is human encouragement that can empower those who are unsure and give them the confidence to use the online tools, just knowing there is someone to ask and turn to if advice is needed. Our family duty counsel, advice lawyers, telephone advice, and chat service all form part of a support network for site users, introducing them to the site and assisting with its use. The legal-aid offices, local agents, and community partners forming the LSS network collaborate across 69 communities and have staff trained to assist end users with the site.

Evaluate

Evaluation is an important component of our site development. User surveys provide regular feedback, as do participants in community consultations. Questions about the use of LSS sites are included in longitudinal studies concerning family law services and in client-satisfaction surveys, as well as when we survey our service providers, from the telephone advice lawyers on the Family LawLine to the private bar. This information, when compiled with occasional reviews, such as our Accessibility Initiative and Divorce Guides reviews, enable us to be proactive in implementing changes to better meet the needs of our users.

The emerging trends in online service delivery further advance the strategies employed by successful sites, sometimes in unexpected ways. Research is being consumed by service providers who want to provide online tools that empower end users to solve their legal problems. Here is what we observe in terms of emerging trends in the digital delivery of legal services.

Escalation of Global Information Sharing

For many years, legal aid providers and public legal education providers have shared practical information and best practices in service delivery across provincial boundaries, networking regularly at national conferences. Where funding permits, Canadians also look to the south to learn from the American experience, through conferences such as the American Equal Justice Conference[17] and Technology Initiative Grants Conference.[18] Groups such as the International Legal Aid Group[19] bring a more global perspective on service delivery and contribute to the identification of best practices on the application of technology in legal aid and PLEI contexts.

Gamification

Gamification in the context of legal services generally refers to two things: firstly, the use of games in order to educate people, and secondly, the use of gaming design principles to motive site users to complete tasks online.[20] Some games being introduced in the US include simulations, text-based walk-throughs, and quizzes, all designed to teach civics, legal procedures, and basic law-practice skills to citizens and law students. Specific examples include Margaret Hagan's LawDojo apps, Citizen U-content quizzes and iCivics.[21] In BC, the Justice Education Society's Changeville[22] is an interactive game aimed at children whose parents are separating.

Guided Pathways

Guided pathways use an interactive question-and-answer approach to lead users to resources that can help solve their specific problems, providing bite-sized pieces of information along the way. Information is specific to the questions asked and answered, and does not over-whelm. An interesting convergence of thinking around this approach commenced in late 2013, which has led to a number of Canadian initiatives in 2014, including the LSS MyLawBC project.

In late November 2013, Roger Smith and Alan Paterson released a review of online legal information delivery which included sites from Canada, the USA, New Zealand, Australia, and Europe.[23] The guided-pathway approach was heralded as a particularly effective way of delivering the information a user wants and needs, in an engaging and dynamic manner, as opposed to traditional PLEI online, which tended to replicate printed fact sheets and was not taking advantage of the potential for interactivity offered by the web. The report particularly noted the Dutch Legal Aid site, Rechtwijzer, as a most effective and dynamic way to assist users.[24]

Then, in December 2013, the Legal Services Corporation (USA) released its Report of The Summit on the Use of Technology to Expand Access to Justice.[25] One of its key recommendations was to pilot more effective delivery of online legal information through guided-pathways approaches.

The value of a user-focused approach which actively guides the user online is evident when one reads the research done in the UK. Catrina Denvir has been doing research into how bright young people find information online.[26] She studied high-school and law-school students who were presented with an everyday legal problem to resolve. Her results were disheartening—the young people often had difficulty recognizing relevant sites and appropriate jurisdictions, and often needed strong hints as to the correct sites to use.[27] There was a tendency to use whatever came up first on Google, without analysis or review. One can see how an online service that leads users, based on their answers to questions, to reliable and relevant tools and information would empower them to confidently and capably address their issue.

The guided-pathway approach addresses another issue that is commonly referenced in literature about online PLEI. Users describe feeling overwhelmed by the number of resources available on the internet.[28] Even if the resources are narrowed to reliable information relevant to the appropriate jurisdiction, users ask themselves: Which one of these is right for me? Is one better? Which is the most up to date? With online PLEI, anyone can put up information and modify it to meet the needs of a particular audience or for a particular purpose, or because they have their own stylistic perspective to share. While an abundance of online resources is a wonderful asset, like a fully stocked library, the feedback from many is that they do not want to browse the shelves endlessly or do deep research. They don't have the time and want to solve their problem and get on with their lives. They want information that they can clearly count on, and not get endlessly looped to other resources. Guided pathways have the potential to meet these needs and respond to these common concerns.

Much of this research inspired the recently launched LSS MyLawBC project.[29] LSS worked with the HiiL group, the experts behind the Rechtwijzer, to develop a site that features guided pathways at its heart. In BC, the focus is on family law, family violence, wills, estates and life planning, and foreclosure. The BC government developed guided pathways to support its new online Civil Resolution Tribunal, which is also now live.[30] Other Canadian jurisdictions are currently planning guided-pathway projects.[31] This is a clear trend.

Emotional Design

One of the very interesting features of the Dutch Rechtwijzer site[32] for separating families was how it addressed the emotional context in which people were coming to the site and asked reflective questions to assist the user to move to a place where the possibility of negotiating a settlement is seen as a positive outcome. Design principles which encourage a feeling of human connection online and create a sense of journey have the potential to closely align with the guided-pathway approach. Emotional design[33] has significant potential to empower users and encourage completion of tasks needed to solve legal problems.

Integration of PLEI and Services

The evolution of traditional PLEI to service provision began with do-it-yourself guides. The introduction of online, interactive questions-and-answers-based guided pathways expanded service provision to diagnosis, triage, and referral. In the past, and typically today, options are presented to the user, who is then left alone without further guidance to make choices about next steps or which resources to utilize. Similarly, until very recently, there has been no effort to marry online PLEI with online dispute resolution (ODR) services, which have developed independently on a stand-alone basis.

Online tools to assist in negotiating agreements which enable parties to communicate with each other asynchronously and to engage the assistance of an online mediator have developed in recent years.[34] This is happening publicly and privately in BC, although both have remained relatively under the radar with respect to public awareness. In BC, the provincial government piloted such approaches in two of its agencies, the BC Property Assessment Appeals Board[35] and Consumer Protection BC.[36] The government has developed an enhanced version of these services in its Civil Resolution Tribunal project.[37] An ODR platform for small-claims court[38] was piloted in BC by the Justice Education Society, a PLEI provider. Privately developed online services seem relatively costly for potential customers and are not altogether user friendly, perhaps explaining why they have not caught on yet. Or the explanation may be that it takes more time for a cultural shift to happen, for the public to trust these services.

MyLawBC[39] includes an online negotiation platform for family matters to assist in the creation of a separation agreement. The FLWS do-your-own separation agreement has rapidly become the second-most popular self-help tool on the site, after do-your-own divorce. We plan to evaluate how people will choose to use these resources and how effective they are.

The Dutch have become global leaders in the integration of PLEI with online service delivery since they introduced the newest version of Rechtwijzer[40] in the fall of 2015. It links family PLEI through guided pathways to a full suite of ODR services. These consist of negotiation features, as well as the possibility of retaining online mediators or arbitrators to create a full separation agreement and obtaining follow up with a legal review of the separation agreement produced, including feedback for both parties. Services also cover an aftercare component so that users can follow up with each other should issues come up or circumstances change after the initial agreement is reached.

Conclusion

It is clear that we are in a time of rapid change in how and what services are delivered online. The sharing of information and research on a global basis is permitting emerging best practices to be adapted to meet local needs. Not-for-profit service providers and their funders welcome the research and are keen to have emerging best practices implemented, tested, and further refined. Current developments are exciting, as they are action oriented and have the goal of empowering people to solve their problems and get on with their lives in the way that they want, in a fair and timely manner.

Notes

1   The BC Legal Services Society is a non-profit organization in British Columbia Canada that provides legal information, advice and representation services to people with low incomes: BC Legal Services Society, About Us, online: <http://www.lss.bc.ca/about/index.php>.
2   For more information about BC Legal Services Society's online self-help information, visit www.lss.bc.ca.
3   For a timeline of cuts to BC legal aid, see Povnet, "A timeline of cuts to BC legal aid" (25 January 2010), online: <http://www.povnet.org/node/3629>.
4   For more information about the BC Law Foundation, visit<http://www.lawfoundationbc.org>.
5   For more information about the Notary Foundation of BC, visit: <http://www.notaryfoundationofbc.ca/resources/showContent.rails?resourceItemId=608>.
6   Kathryn E. Thomson, "Trusted Intermediaries, Technology & Legal Advocates in BC," Winkler Institute for Dispute Resolution, Justice Innovation Blog (27 January 2015), online: <http://winklerinstitute.ca/trusted-intermediaries-technology-legal-advocates-b-c/>.
7   For further discussion of the nature and dimensions of the digital divide in Canada, see Misty Harris, "Digital Divide Persists in Canada, both in Access an Internet fluency," *Financial Post*, March 21, 2013, online: <http://business.financialpost.com/2013/03/21/digital-divide-persists-in-canada-both-in-access-and-internet-fluency/?__lsa=d6a5-944d>; Michael Geist, "Canada's digital divide likely to widen," *The Toronto Star*, April 5, 2013, online: <http://www.thestar.com/business/tech_news/2013/04/05/canadas_digital_divide_likely_to_widen_geist.html>; Peter Nowak "Digital Divide: the High Costs of Arctic Broadband," *The Globe and Mail*, November 11, 2012, online: Globe and Mail <http://www.theglobeandmail.com>.

8   Karen Cohl and George Thomson, "Connecting Across Language and Distance: Linguistic and Rural Access to Legal Information and Services" (Toronto: Law Foundation of Ontario, 2008) at 62, online <http://www.lawfoundation.on.ca/wp-content/uploads/The-Connecting-Report.pdf>.

9   Ibid. at 39.

10   For more information on self-represented litigants, see Julie Macfarlane, "The National Self-Represented Litigants Project: Identifying and Meeting the Needs of Self-Represented Ligitations," Final Report (May 2013), online: <http://www.lsuc.on.ca/uploadedFiles/For_the_Public/About_the_Law_Society/ConvocationDecisions/2014/Self-represented_project.pdf>.

11   For further discussion of unmet legal needs, see Rebecca Sandefur, "White Paper: What We Know and Need to Know About the Unmet Legal Needs of the Public," *SC L Rev* 67 (2016) at 443; Hazel Genn and Sarah Beinart, *Paths to Justice: What people Do and Think about Going to Law* (Oxford, UK: Hart Publishing, 1999).

12   For more information about legal information providers in BC, visit: <http://www.legalaid.bc.ca/legal_aid/legalInformation.php>.

13   For further discussion of best practices for online providers of legal information, see American Bar Association, "Best Practice Guidelines for Legal Information Website Providers" (10 February 2003), online: <http://www.americanbar.org/groups/law_practice/committees/elawyering-best-practices.html>; Victorian Legal Assistance Forum, "Best practice guidelines for the development and maintenance of online community legal information in Victoria" (December 2013), online: <http://www.vlaf.org.au/cb_pages/files/VLAF%20online%20guidelines%20-%20Final%20draft.pdf>.

14   BC Legal Services Society, *Public Legal Education and Information Resources Accessibility Initiative* (June 2012), online: <http://www.lss.bc.ca/assets/aboutUs/reports/PLEI/pleiResourcesAIReport.pdf>.

15   Literacy BC, "Literacy in British Columbia," online: <http://communityliteracy.ca/wp-content/uploads/2011/06/Literacy-in-British-Columbia.pdf>.

16   Private Client Adviser, "New online court must take 'post-Amazon world' into consideration" (10 March 2016), online: <http://www.privateclientadviser.co.uk/news/legal-practice/new-online-court-must-take-post-amazon-world-consideration>.

17   The American Bar Association and National Legal Aid & Defender Association sponsor the Equal Justice Conference, which was held in Illinois in 2016: American Bar Association, General Information, online: <https://www.americanbar.org/groups/probono_public_service/ejc/general.html>.

18 For more information about the Technology Initiative Grants conference, visit: <http://www.lsc.gov/meetings-and-events/tig-conference>.

19 For more information about the International Legal Aid Group, visit: <http://ilagnet.org>.

20 Stephanie Kimbro, "Gamification vs Games for Legal Services" (18 May 2013), online: <http://virtuallawpractice.org/2817/gamification-vs-games-why-the-difference-matters-for-legal-services/>.

21 Ibid.

22 To access the game, visit: <www.changeville.ca>.

23 Roger Smith and Alan Paterson, "Face to Face Legal Services and Their Alternatives: Global Lessons from the Digital Revolution" (2013), online: <https://www.strath.ac.uk/media/faculties/hass/law/cpls/Face_to_Face.pdf>.

24 Ibid. at 59.

25 Legal Services Corporation, *Report of the Summit on the Use of Technology to Expand Access to Justice*, online: Legal Services Corporation <www.lsc.gov/sites/default/files/LSC_Tech%20Summit%20Report_2013.pdf>.

26 Catrina Denvir, *What is the Net Worth?: Young People, Civil Justice and the Internet* (PhD Thesis, University College London, 2014) [unpublished], online: <http://discovery.ucl.ac.uk/1437397/1/PhDThesis-CDenvir.pdf>.

27 Ibid. at 124.

28 PLE Learning Exchange Ontario, "How to help your clients," online: <http://www.plelearningexchange.ca/toolbox/helping-your-clients-find-reliable-legal-information/>.

29 <http://www.mylawbc.com>.

30 <https://www.civilresolutionbc.ca>.

31 Nate Russell, "Of Family Law Flowcharts and Guided Pathways" *Slaw* (15 December 2015), online: <http://www.slaw.ca/2015/12/15/of-family-law-flowcharts-and-guided-pathways/>.

32 <http://rechtwijzer.nl>.

33 For further discussion of "emotional design," see: Don Norman, *Emotional Design: Why We Love (or Hate) Everyday Things* (New York: Perseus Books, 2004).

34 Colin Rule, "New Mediator Capabilities in Online Dispute Resolution" (December 2000), online: <http://www.mediate.com/articles/rule.cfm>.

35 <http://www.assessmentappeal.bc.ca>.

36 <https://www.consumerprotectionbc.ca>.

37 <https://www.civilresolutionbc.ca>.

38 <http://www.smallclaimsbc.ca>.

39 <http://www.mylawbc.com>.

40 <http://rechtwijzer.nl>.

CHAPTER VII

The Case for Courtroom Technology Competence as an Ethical Duty for Litigators

Amy Salyzyn

Introduction

Courtroom technology has become a common feature of many litigators' practices. To be sure, the available technological tools vary greatly among courtrooms, ranging from relatively simple devices like audio-recording equipment or video screens on which evidence can be displayed to fully outfitted "e-courtrooms" that feature cutting-edge technology to assist in all aspects of trial proceedings. Notwithstanding this variability, there is now a strong case that lawyers need to understand and use an increasing number of technologies in order to effectively represent their clients in court.

This chapter considers whether the emerging ubiquity of courtroom technology translates into an *ethical duty* for litigators to have appropriate competence in relation to courtroom technology.[1] The position ultimately taken here is that courtroom technology competence is properly understood as an ethical obligation for litigators and should be of concern to lawyer regulators.[2] However, it is also argued that this ethical obligation should not be primarily addressed under the conventional rules-based system whereby lawyers' behaviour is reactively evaluated against minimum standards within a "quasi-criminal" lawyer disciplinary regime.[3] Instead, and for reasons discussed further below, it is argued that lawyer regulators ought to adopt policy approaches that focus on facilitating and encouraging best practices when it comes to lawyers' competence in courtroom technology.

This chapter unfolds in four parts. It starts off by making the case that lawyers need to understand and use an increasing number of technologies in order to effectively represent their clients in court (see Lawyer Competence in Courtroom Technology and Effective Client Representation below). Then, it sets out why appropriate competence in courtroom technology is properly seen as an ethical obligation for litigators and, therefore, falls within the mandate of lawyer regulators (see Technological Competence as an Ethical Duty, see page 220). The third part argues that lawyer regulators need to act more aggressively to monitor and ensure lawyer courtroom-technology competence given the absence of evidence that lawyers possess adequate competence in this area (see Why Lawyer Regulators Should Care about Courtroom-Technology Competence, see page 222). Finally, the chapter concludes by exploring policy options for lawyer regulators that could allow them to become more involved in facilitating increased lawyer competence in courtroom technology (see What Might Lawyer Regulators Do?, see page 224).

Lawyer Competence in Courtroom Technology and Effective Client Representation

This part outlines three interrelated reasons why it is appropriate to treat lawyer courtroom technology competence as an important aspect of effective client representation in contemporary litigation practices: (1) although courtroom technology is not uniformly used across courtroom settings, its presence has significantly increased in recent decades; (2) as a result, in a growing number of cases, lawyers must be able to appropriately use courtroom technology in order to optimally advance their clients' interests; and (3) additionally, understanding courtroom technology and its associated risks is sometimes necessary for lawyers to adequately protect their clients from technological misfeasance by others.

What Is "Courtroom Technology"?

Before proceeding with the analysis, it is necessary to first define how the phrase "courtroom technology" is being used in this chapter. The term "courtroom technology" has been defined in a variety of different ways by those who study the phenomenon.[4] Given that the particular technologies in use can easily change over time and from one setting to another, there are a number of advantages to using a more functional or categorical definition rather than attempting to enumerate all of the specific technological tools that courtrooms are currently using. For example, Fredric Lederer has observed, "modern trial courtroom technology can be roughly divided into information (evidence) presentation, remote appearances, court record, 'counsel communications,' (for example, internet access from counsel table), assistive technology (including interpretation), jury deliberations, and appellate matters."[5] This chapter borrows from Lederer's definition with a focus on technology used with respect to (1) information presentation, (2) remote appearances, (3) court record, and (4) jury deliberations (including jury use of social media). In addition, the chapter includes a fifth category: (5) information collection (including conducting online legal research).

The Increased Presence of Courtroom Technology

Anecdotally, there is widespread recognition of a significant increase in the presence of courtroom technologies in North America over the past several decades. To start with Canadian examples, the description for a 2010 continuing legal education program organized by the Canadian Bar Association on the topic of "Technology in the Courtroom" states that "[f]rom digital still cameras to electronic document displays to laptops equipped with presentation software, new technologies are making headway in Canadian courtrooms, and firm size need not be a limitation as software and services proliferate."[6] Similarly, the home page of the Canadian Centre for Court Technology, a not-for-profit corporation with a mandate to promote the use of technological solutions to modernize court services, observes that "[t]echnology is increasingly used in court processes, both in civil and criminal cases."[7] Similar observations can be found in relation to American courts. For example, in 2010, Lederer observed that "[c]ourtroom technology now is a fundamental aspect of trial practice for many lawyers…[and that] an ever increasing number of courtrooms are being equipped with at least the ability to electronically display evidentiary and other images to judge and jury."[8] A law review article written a year earlier similarly notes, "[t] echnology has infiltrated the lawyer's practice in nearly every area… [including] courtroom presentation and trial practice."[9]

Supporting these types of descriptive statements are several empirical studies. For example, the results of a 2014 survey of 12,500 private attorneys conducted by the American Bar Association (ABA) suggest that there is significant use of courtroom technologies in the United States. Among other things, the survey reports that 27.6% of surveyed lawyers who practice in a courtroom used a laptop with presentation software to present evidence and that 24.9% of those who used laptops in the courtroom used them to conduct online research (additionally, 23.3% and 21.7% indicated, respectively, that they used smartphones and tablets to conduct online research in the courtroom).[10] A 2003 Federal Judicial Center Survey on Technology also found widespread use of court technology.[11] For example, of the 90 district courts that responded to this survey,

> Ninety-four percent ha[d] access to an evidence camera and 66% to a digital projector and projection screen; 93% to wiring to connect laptop computers; 57% to monitors built into the jury box; 77% to monitors outside the jury box; 89% to a monitor at the bench; 88% to a monitor at the witness stand; 88% to monitors at counsel table or lectern; 77% to monitors or screens targeted at the audience; 80% to a color video printer; 91% to annotation equipment; 95% to a sound reinforcement system; 92% to a telephone or infrared interpreting system; 92% to a kill switch and control system; 81% to an integrated lectern; 93% to audio-conferencing equipment; 85% to videoconferencing equipment; 81% to real-time software for use by court reporter; 74% to a real-time transcript viewer annotation system; and 66% to digital audio recording.[12]

In Canada, a 2012 comprehensive report on the Digitization of Court Processes in Canada, authored by Jane Bailey, notes that "[d]ocument storage, viewing, manipulation and e-exhibit systems are available in a number of courts (e.g., Alberta, BC, Ontario, Nova Scotia), as are video display screens, and network connections for counsel."[13] In addition, the report observed that both audio-conferencing and video-conferencing are available "in courts across Canada for a wide variety of purposes."[14] Another 2012 report, authored by the Action Committee on Access to Justice In Civil and Family Matters, observed "teleconferencing and videoconferencing is generally available throughout Canada (by phone, video, Skype, etc.)."[15]

Although courtroom technologies of all types are not available in all courtrooms,[16] these anecdotal and statistical reports confirm a significant presence of various kinds of technology in courtrooms across North America.

Courtroom Technology and the Optimal Advancement of Client Interests

As a growing number of courtroom technologies come to be used, it will become increasingly difficult for lawyers who are hostile to, or unfamiliar with, such technologies to refuse to use them (or use them poorly) and still be able to claim that they are providing optimal client representation.[17]

Indeed, in certain circumstances, opting out may no longer be an option—there are a number of situations in which use of courtroom technology by lawers is mandatory.[18] A prosecutor, for example, may have little choice but to conduct a bail review hearing using videoconferencing equipment if that happens to be the practice in the jurisdiction in which she practices.[19] On the civil side, lawyers participating in complex commercial cases may find themselves subject to court orders requiring them to conduct an "e-trial," which calls for all evidence to be filed and presented electronically.[20] In both of these examples, it is not open to the lawyers involved to opt-out of using technology—in order to represent their client, they must "play ball," so to speak.

Even in situations where the use of courtroom technology is permissive rather than mandatory,[21] there may be reasons why using such technology is necessary for effective and efficient client representation. One such reason is cost. With respect to evidence presentation technology, for example, Lederer reports in a 2003 article: "Based on anecdotal evidence, our usual assumption is that evidence presentation technology saves a minimum of 1/4 to 1/3 of the otherwise traditional amount of time necessary to present a case. Courtroom 21 experimentation suggests a minimum time savings of about 10% even in a short one hour case, with only a few documents."[22]

By way of another example, one might imagine a civil trial in which a party could save several thousand dollars by having its overseas expert testify using videoconferencing rather than travel to attend the local court in person.[23] To the extent that a lawyer declines to present evidence electronically or to arrange for witness testimony via videoconferencing due to personal discomfort or unfamiliarity with the technology (as opposed to, for example, good-faith concerns about whether using such technology is in his or her client's best interests),[24] the client will end up paying more for legal representation than if he or she had retained a lawyer who was comfortable and familiar with the relevant technology and therefore willing to use it.

Beyond cost, issues relating to access and quality of service can also arise where lawyers refrain from using courtroom technologies or fail to use such technologies appropriately. For example, as Jane Bailey, Jacquelyn Burkell, and Graham Reynolds observe, videoconferencing can operate as a tool to "improve equity with respect to access to court proceedings" by, for example, "provid[ing] timely access to court proceedings for those living in remote communities otherwise served by relatively infrequently convened circuit courts" or "provid[ing] improved access to interpreters for members of linguistic minority groups, as well as low cost access to legal services and lawyers, which may be especially important for those living in or incarcerated in remote locations."[25] Given these phenomena, lawyers who refuse to use videoconferencing technology or who are unable to use it effectively may be undercutting meaningful access to the courts for some of the most vulnerable members of the public.

A connection can also be drawn between quality of service and the use of online legal research technologies. If an unexpected legal issue comes up during a courtroom hearing, the lawyer who is using a laptop or other mobile device to conduct online legal research in the courtroom is surely at an advantage over the lawyer who is unable to conduct contemporaneous research because he or she does not use such devices or does not know how to use them to carry out research. Likewise, the client of a lawyer who can receive and review real-time court transcripts, where available, also enjoys an advantage over the client whose lawyer does not have this ability.

Furthermore, there is reason to believe that lawyers who use technology to present evidence—like, for example, electronic whiteboards, digital projectors, or individual monitors for trial participants[26]—may enjoy a strategic advantage in certain circumstances. Although now somewhat dated, a 1998 study by the Judicial Conference Committee on Automation and Technology reported that 87% of the judges responding to the survey thought that video evidence presentation technologies helped them to understand the witness better, 81% thought it helped them understand testimony better, 72% thought it improved their abilities to question witnesses, and 83% found the technologies helped them to manage the proceeding.[27] Jurors were also surveyed, most of them reporting that they "believed that they were able to remain more focused on testimony and evidence" when evidence-presentation technologies were employed.[28]

The above study is limited in that it only measured subjective impressions. There are, however, empirical studies on the effects of visual technology on juror decision-making that suggest that such technologies can help jurors better understand and be persuaded by information presented by lawyers. For example, a 2012 article reporting the results of two controlled experimental studies on the effects of lawyers' use of PowerPoint presentations on liability judgments indicates, among other things, that "using PowerPoint enabled attorneys on either side of the case to persuade by helping decision makers to understand trial information better....[and that] [w]hen a lawyer used PowerPoint, participants thought better of his performance."[29] To be sure, as the authors of this article and other scholars have cautioned, the precise ways in which judges and jurors interact with electronically presented evidence is complex and the subject of ongoing empirical study.[30] However, this chapter proceeds on the basis of an uncontroversial premise in light of the studies to date: at least in certain circumstances, using technology to visually present evidence can lead to better comprehension and retention and can be more persuasive than evidence presented without the aid of such visuals.[31] The lawyer who refuses to use electronic methods of presentation or who cannot use these methods competently can, therefore, be said to be putting his or her client at a disadvantage.

Identifying and Responding to Technological Misfeasance by Others

In addition to the affirmative reasons in favour of using courtroom technology to ensure effective and efficient client representation, there is also a negative case for technological competence: in certain circumstances, understanding courtroom technology and its associated risks may be necessary to adequately identify and respond to technological misfeasance by others.

One major area in which misfeasance arises relates to social media. In an extensive study, Marilyn Krawitz observes that the inappropriate use of social media by jurors has emerged as a significant problem that courts now have to contend with.[32] As Krawitz notes, inappropriate juror use of social media can impact the fair trial rights of the accused in a criminal case in a number of ways. For example, she argues that social media "can affect a juror's conscious or subconscious mind" and potentially introduce jurors to information (not presented in court) that may be inaccurate or wrong.[33] A lawyer who does not have a basic understanding of how social media works is compromised in detecting juror misuse of social media. Moreover, in cases where a juror is caught misusing social media, the court has a variety of remedies available, ranging from simply questioning the juror to removing the juror or declaring a mistrial.[34] The lawyer who does not understand social media—for example, what it means to post something on Twitter or Facebook—will have a difficult time identifying and advocating for a remedy that best protects his or her client's interests in view of such juror misconduct.

Another area where misuse of technology can arise relates to evidence presentation. In the United States, for example, there has been significant coverage of prosecutorial misuse of PowerPoint presentations and computer animations. It has been reported that "[a]t least 10 times in the last two years, US courts have reversed a criminal conviction because prosecutors violated the rules of fair argument with PowerPoint."[35] There are additional examples of American courts finding prosecutorial use of computer animation to be misleading[36] The South Carolina Supreme Court in *Clark v. Cantrell* observed: "[A] computer animation can mislead a jury just as easily as it can educate them. An animation is only as good as the underlying testimony, physical data, and engineering assumptions that drive its images. The computer maxim "garbage in, garbage out" applies to computer animations."[37]

Although in some cases misuse of evidence presentation technology is obvious—take, for example, cases where the prosecution displayed a bloody butcher knife on a five-foot-by-five-foot screen or depicted the defendant as the devil[38]—the prejudicial effect in other cases can be subtler. As Neal Feigenson and Christina Spiesel observe in their comprehensive study of how visual and multimedia digital technologies are transforming the practice of law:

> Possibly the most fundamental concern about the new media displays is that they expand the role of implicit processes in legal argument and judgment and thereby increase the likelihood that factors other than the law and the evidence will improperly influence verdicts....[V]isual and especially multimedia displays make it easier for advocates to communicate arguably inappropriate messages without saying them explicitly.[39]

In light of this concern, and other potential risks with using evidence presentation technology, Feigenson and Spiesel argue that lawyers can "help to educate jurors about the possible meanings of visual displays, but they themselves need to be sufficiently educated about the uses and effects of digital visuals and multimedia."[40] In order to adequately detect and respond to misuse of evidence presentation technologies, lawyers must have some familiarity with these technologies and their attendant risks.

Issues of misfeasance may also arise in relation to e-discovery. Indeed, four years ago, Dan Willoughby, Rose Jones and Gregory Antine concluded, "e-discovery sanctions are at an all-time high."[41] In many, if not most, cases, problematic conduct in e-discovery relates to conduct that takes place prior to a court hearing.[42] However, e-discovery issues can also relate to conduct that takes place after a court hearing is underway. For example, in *United States v Johnson*,[43] charges of conspiracy to commit securities fraud, securities fraud, and witness tampering were brought against the defendant in relation to his activities with an internet company that he had founded and directed as chief executive officer.[44] The defendant's first trial "ended abruptly" when his counsel withdrew from the record after realizing that the client had provided them with a falsified email to use as an exhibit in cross-examining a government witness.[45] A mistrial was declared and, in the context of a subsequent retrial, the defendant was convicted of attempting to obstruct an official proceeding.[46]

A lawyer who does not have the requisite competence in relation to e-discovery is at a disadvantage when representing a client. In order to adequately protect a client's interest, a lawyer must be able to identify e-discovery misfeasance. Moreover, once misfeasance is uncovered, an adequate understanding of e-discovery is necessary in order for a lawyer to effectively make arguments as to appropriate sanctions. As Willoughby, Jones, and Antine point out in their survey of case law on e-discovery violations, courts have ordered a wide variety of sanctions for e-discovery violations ranging from dismissing claims, adverse jury instructions, and monetary awards for more serious violations to "evidence preclusion, witness preclusion, disallowance of certain defenses, reduced burden of proof, removal of jury challenges, limiting closing statements, supplemental discovery, and additional access to computer systems" for less serious violations[47] The authors also note that "more creative courts have imposed non-traditional sanctions, such as payments to bar associations to fund educational programs, participation in court-created ethics programs, referrals to the state bar, payments to the clerk of court, and barring the sanctioned party from taking additional depositions prior to compliance with the court's discovery."[48] The client who is the victim of e-discovery misfeasance needs a lawyer with sufficient understanding of e-discovery such that he or she can effectively argue for appropriate sanctions before the court.

Technological Competence as an Ethical Duty

The analysis above makes the case that lawyer courtroom technology competence is an important aspect of effective client representation in contemporary litigation practices. In short, it was argued that the use of courtroom technology is increasing and that litigators must be able to use and understand this technology in order to optimally advance their clients' cases and protect their clients from the technological misfeasance of others. Building on this practical context, this part makes the case that courtroom technology competence can be properly understood as an *ethical duty* of lawyers.

To be sure, the issue of lawyer competence in courtroom technology may be conceptualized from a variety of perspectives. The need for competence in this area can, for example, be seen as a private duty that lawyers owe to their clients.[49] One might also conceive of lawyer competence in courtroom technology as a public duty that lawyers owe to the courts in which they appear.[50] Alternatively, competence in courtroom technologies could be viewed as an essential professional skill that law schools ought to teach, along with legal research and writing, for example.[51] The focus of this chapter, however, is whether lawyer competence in courtroom technology is an *ethical duty* that falls under the jurisdiction of lawyer regulators.

It is also recognized that the issue of the appropriate use of courtroom technology engages important issues, beyond the question of lawyer competence, such as ensuring adequate funding of courts and proper judicial education. There is also the worrisome issue of how the use of courtroom technology may impact access to justice. To take a simple example, if a technology such as a computer animation can lead to a more persuasive presentation of one's case, the client who is able to afford such animation is in a better position than a client who cannot.[52] These are important matters that warrant further consideration. For the purposes of the analysis here, however, the focus is on the discrete issue of lawyer technological competence and the role of lawyer regulators in ensuring this competence.

So, returning to the focus of this chapter: what might justify the recognition of an ethical duty to have courtroom technology competence? The idea that there is an ethical duty for lawyers to be competent, as a general matter, is already well reflected in lawyer professional codes of conduct. The American Bar Association (ABA) *Model Rules of Professional Conduct* state, for example, in their first substantive rule that "A lawyer shall provide competent representation to a client. Competent representation requires the legal knowledge, skill, thoroughness and preparation reasonably necessary for the representation."[53]

The Federation of Law Societies of Canada *Model Code of Professional Conduct* similarly declares that "A lawyer must perform all legal services undertaken on a client's behalf to the standard of a competent lawyer" and defines a "competent lawyer" as "a lawyer who has and applies relevant knowledge, skills and attributes in a manner appropriate to each matter undertaken on behalf of a client and the nature and terms of the lawyer's engagement."[54]

In recent years, several commentators have argued that this generalized ethical duty to be competent includes a duty to be competent in using technology.[55] The ABA has gone even further and, in 2012, amended the Commentary to its rule on competence to refer explicitly to technology. Comment 8 to Rule 1.1 on Competence now reads as follows:

> To maintain the requisite knowledge and skill, a lawyer should keep abreast of changes in the law and its practice, *including the benefits and risks associated with relevant technology*, engage in continuing study and education and comply with all continuing legal education requirements to which the lawyer is subject.[56] (Emphasis added)

A number of states have adopted the above commentary regarding a lawyer's obligation to "keep abreast of changes in the law and its practice, including the benefits and risks associated with relevant technology," bringing it into effect in those jurisdictions.[57]

Although a few commentators have posited the existence of an ethical duty for lawyers to have competence specifically in relation to courtroom technology,[58] the existence of such a duty remains a relatively novel proposition in the area of legal ethics and, thus, is worthy of some extended analysis. The premise that a lawyer's ethical duty of competence includes competencies in using and understanding courtroom technology is well supported when one looks at current professional rules. The 2012 amendment to the ABA *Model Code of Professional Conduct* underscores this fact, but even in jurisdictions that do not specifically mention technology in their professional conduct rules, a reasonable reading of general provisions on competence strongly suggests that this ethical duty exists. As noted above, a client may be seriously disadvantaged in a court case if his or her lawyer declines to use helpful technological tools due to incompetence or is unable to detect technological malfeasance as a result of a lack of knowledge or understanding of relevant technologies. As the use of court technology is fast becoming "the norm"[59] rather than the exception, competence in using these technologies can be reasonably seen as falling within the language of general competence rules, namely, "relevant knowledge, skills and attributes" or "skill[s]... reasonably necessary for the representation."[60]

Why Lawyer Regulators Should Care about Courtroom Technology Competence

The beginning of this chapter makes the case that litigators, as a general rule, need competence with respect to courtroom technology to effectively represent their clients, and that this competence can properly be seen as an ethical duty of litigators. This argument, however, does not necessarily lead to the conclusion that law societies should be more actively involved in this area. An additional piece of the puzzle needs to be explored: do today's lawyers have sufficient technological competence? If the relevant skill set already exists among lawyers, then there would be little reason for lawyer regulators to devote their limited resources to becoming involved in the issue. This part argues lawyer regulators need to act more aggressively to monitor and ensure lawyer courtroom technology competence given the absence of evidence that lawyers generally possess adequate competence in this area.

A quick review of commentary online and in legal trade journals suggests a general consensus that lawyers, as a professional class, do not possess the requisite level of competence when it comes to using technology. An internet search of the terms "lawyer" and "Luddite," for example, yields close to 50,000 results,[61] including articles or blog posts with the titles: "Luddite Lawyers are Ethical Violations Waiting to Happen,"[62] "Don't be that Luddite Lawyer,"[63] "Can Lawyers Be Luddites?,"[64] and "Helping Law Firm Luddites Cross the Digital Divide."[65] One study that has received considerable attention is a "technology competence audit" conducted by Casey Flaherty.[66] In his former capacity as corporate counsel for Kia Motors Inc., Flaherty prepared and conducted an audit on the technology skills possessed by outside counsel retained by Kia. Among other things, the audit involved simple tasks like formatting a motion in Microsoft Word and creating an arbitration exhibit index in Excel.[67] The performance of outside counsel was not impressive. In Flaherty's words, "As far as I am concerned, all the firms failed—some more spectacularly than others."[68]

With respect to technology in the courtroom, there are a number of reported examples of lawyer incompetence. In his article "A Picture is Worth 999 Words: The Importance and Effectiveness of Courtroom Visual Presentations," Daniel W. Dugan details an incident during a 2007 breach-of-contract trial in California in which a lawyer caused a commotion in the courtroom when he repeatedly asked a witness to read a portion of a document to a jury that was being projected onto the lawyer's pants rather than the projection screen. This situation eventually caused one juror to become frustrated and intervene, asking, "Have you ever heard of PowerPoint?"[69] More recently, in 2013, a video of a prosecutor appearing to ineptly question a witness about her social media accounts in a high-profile murder trial went viral.[70]

The above examples, of course, only reflect the experiences of two lawyers who appear to lack adequate understanding of courtroom technology. A broader snapshot of how the profession is faring can be found in the 2014 ABA Litigation Technology Survey Report. Only 27.4% of the lawyers who responded to the survey and who practiced in a courtroom reported that they had received training in courtroom technology.[71] A variety of reasons were given by the remaining 72.6% as to why they did not receive training. For example, 32.6% of these lawyers indicated that they did not receive training because "courtrooms utilized do not have technology capabilities."[72] However, 32% indicated that "training is not available," giving rise to concerns that lawyers are not being given adequate opportunities to develop competence with relevant technology.[73] Even more troubling are the 5.7% who responded that they did not receive training because they were "not comfortable with technology."[74]

We do not have a comprehensive account of the exact type and level of skills that North American lawyers possess with respect to courtroom technology. The partial information that exists, based on both anecdotal accounts and empirical studies, suggests that there may be a problem with respect to current level of lawyer courtroom technology competence that demands attention from lawyer regulators. Indeed, the very fact that there is uncertainty about the level of competence in this area is itself a reason for lawyer regulators to become involved—rather than reactively waiting for lawyers to incompetently represent clients and the resultant complaints, regulators should be acting positively to ensure that the public is protected.

What Might Lawyer Regulators Do?

If competence in using courtroom technologies is an ethical obligation for litigators and should attract greater attention from lawyer regulators, how should lawyer regulators respond? This part evaluates three potential regulatory options: conducting surveys and/or audits; changing the rules of professional conduct for lawyers; and engaging in proactive educational initiatives such as developing best practices and facilitating mentoring opportunities.

Surveys and/or Audits to Develop a Clearer Sense of Current State of Competence

As a preliminary matter, the fact that we do not yet have a clear picture of lawyer competence when it comes to courtroom technology should make it a priority for regulators to devote resources to studying current levels of competence. One way to do this is to develop surveys similar to the ABA 2014 Legal Technology Survey Report that ask various questions of practicing lawyers, but focus more on assessing competence in relation to courtroom technology rather than on general use of technology (the latter being the primary focus of the ABA survey).

A limitation of a survey approach is, of course, that it would rely on the subjective self-assessment of lawyers as to their level of competence. As a result, a survey approach is likely to be skewed. There would seem, for example, to be a real risk that surveyed lawyers would over-estimate their abilities given that "[p]sychological studies of human decision-making processes in a wide variety of contexts have revealed that overconfidence is a ubiquitous phenomenon."[75]

Notwithstanding this limitation, a well-designed survey is likely to provide us with more (if not perfect) information about lawyer courtroom technology competence. Moreover, there is some promise that the simple fact of having lawyers participate in a survey of this type will yield positive results. An Australian study of lawyers who had participated in a self-assessment of various management practices found that having lawyers engage in self-reflection can, in and of itself, lead to improved ethical outcomes.[76]

A more aggressive approach to assessing lawyer courtroom technology competence could involve lawyer regulators conducting audits similar to the audit described above that Casey Flaherty used to assess the technology skills possessed by outside counsel. The advantage of this approach is that it would provide a more objective measure of actual skills than self-assessments. Moreover, there is precedent for this type of measure. A number of Canadian law societies, for example, conduct proactive practice-review programs whereby the practices of certain groups of lawyers (including new solo practitioners and new calls) are assessed on a variety of criteria.[77] Using these programs as templates, an audit could be developed to evaluate the courtroom technology competence of litigators. One challenge, of course, in developing such an audit would be to choose which skills to assess; as noted above, although the presence of courtroom technology is increasing as a general matter, its use varies across courtrooms. There is unlikely to be one set of technologies with respect to which lawyers in a certain jurisdiction can be assessed. Another major challenge is that lawyers—who, as a professional class, have been found to have "an especially strong desire for autonomy"[78]—are likely to be resistant to attempts to add another layer of external oversight and involvement concerning how they conduct their practices. For this reason, an audit may not be politically appealing to lawyer regulators—which are, of course, ultimately governed by lawyers given the profession's self-regulating status in North America.

Changing the Rules

Aside from surveys and audits, lawyer regulators may want to consider the possibility of adding a rule to professional codes of conduct that specifically mentions courtroom technology competence. A precedent exists with the ABA's 2012 addition of general technological competence in commentary to its *Model Rules of Professional Conduct*, above. Although the ABA amendment does not appear to have to date resulted in any specific disciplinary proceedings, it has attracted significant attention and inspired numerous articles and blog posts emphasizing the need for American lawyers to improve their technological competence.[79] In other words, it has increased the profile of technological competence as an ethical issue. As a possible starting point for discussion of a rule that specifically mentions courtroom technology competence, lawyer regulators could look to the following language suggested by Michelle Quigley in a 2010 article:

> Maintaining the requisite knowledge and skill necessary for competent representation includes a duty to keep abreast of technological advances that significantly affect the practice of law. For example, in certain circumstances, lawyers may have an ethical obligation to use courtroom technology in advocating for their clients and to be competent in the use of technology when doing so.[80]

Ultimately, however, beyond the signaling value of a rule mentioning courtroom technology competence, there are a number of reasons why a rule change would have only limited regulatory value.

As a number of legal ethics scholars have noted, conventional code and complaints-based disciplinary systems tend to deal with lawyer behavior in a very narrow manner by focusing on whether individuals are complying with minimum standards, and only reacting after problems have occurred in the first place.[81] Indeed, there are a number of reasons why the issue of courtroom technology competence may be particularly difficult to address through minimum standards. First, as noted above, different jurisdictions are likely to have different technologies available to lawyers, making it challenging to identify a single set of baseline skills that all litigators need.

Second, even if courtroom technologies were uniformly available across Canada, the identification of a set of baseline skills is likely to be frustrated by the reality that different types of courtroom practice will require different skills. It is also not possible to straightforwardly classify the use of courtroom technology as a good in all circumstances. For example, in the case of video-conferencing, although the use of technology can lead to potentially greater access, it is also important to note, as Jane Bailey, Jacquelyn Burkell, and Graham Reynolds have, that

It is difficult, if not impossible, to predict the effect of videoconferencing on court processes and outcomes, and indeed any effect is likely to be multifaceted. In the courtroom context, scholars have raised concerns about the use of videoconferencing, noting that it could have a negative impact on the perception of the witness by the court, the representation received by a defendant, the outcome of the court proceeding, or the experience of the justice system by a defendant.[82]

In the case of videoconferencing, then, there may be complicated and potentially subtle reasons why a lawyer might opt to use or not use this technology in a given scenario. This reality means that a rule stipulating, for example, that videoconferencing has to be used in every case in which it is available could be potentially detrimental to client interests.

Third, to the extent that lawyer regulators attempt to circumvent these types of problems by relying on general terms like "relevant," "appropriate," or "ordinary" to describe minimum competence standards, there are additional complications. As I have noted previously, "[w]hile tethering competence to 'relevant', 'appropriate' or 'ordinary' practice might make sense when it comes to well-worn techniques or behaviours within a professional community, it doesn't easily extend to technological competence where the average level of knowledge and skill among lawyers is variable."[83]

Fourth, in a number of cases, it may be unfair to assess lawyers against minimum standards given that lawyers may be reliant on court infrastructure and court staff in order to use technology effectively.[84]

Finally, assessing lawyers against minimum standards may give rise to unfairness in cases where the use of a courtroom technology has financial costs that a client is unwilling or unable to bear. To reiterate an example discussed above, although it might be true in a particular case that a computer animation will lead to a more persuasive presentation of a client's case, not every client will be willing or able to pay between $5,000 and $150,000 for an appropriate animation to be prepared by experts.[85] Where the client is not willing or able to pay for a particular technology, it would be unfair to hold the lawyer accountable for failing to use that technology.

Pro-active Educational Measures

The reactive nature of disciplinary rules is also a major limitation to the involvement of lawyer regulators in ensuring lawyer technological competence. As noted above, rather than waiting for a complaint that a lawyer violated an ethical rule and then evaluating whether that lawyer should be sanctioned, it would be better for regulators to try to avoid the problem in the first place.[86] Instead of reacting to complaints, a more productive policy choice might be for lawyer regulators to pursue proactive educational measures to assist litigators in using best practices when it comes to courtroom technologies. Best practices are also advantageous in that they can be tailored to different practice contexts and can be revised as the technological, legal, and social context evolves.

A number of possible methods could be used to advance lawyer education on courtroom technology. One option would be for lawyer regulators to provide lawyers with guidelines, ethics opinions, or practice standards that detail best practices when it comes to using courtroom technology. To their credit, a number of law societies and bar organizations have already begun to provide these types of resources to assist lawyers in increasing their technological competence.[87] In large part, however, these resources tend to deal with practice management issues outside the courtroom, for example, how to keep law firm computer systems secure and how to avoid unintentionally disclosing confidential client information when using electronic communications.[88]

In addition to guidelines, ethics opinions, or practice standards, lawyer regulators may consider developing or facilitating mentorship programs or roundtables on the topic of court technology. The Law Society of New South Wales, for example, established a Technology-based Skills Exchange Pilot Program that seeks to connect "experienced practitioners" with "tech-savvy practitioners" to facilitate "imparting knowledge about technology in practice and sharing of tips about the online and social media channels and their utilisation in a professional environment."[89] Another model of information sharing and skills exchange can be found in the Richard K. Herrmann Technology American Inn of Court, which in 2009 was "established for the purpose of bringing together judges, lawyers and law students to study the impact of technology on business and the effect of technology on the practice of law and in particular electronic discovery."[90] When it comes to roundtable discussions regarding court technology specifically (as opposed to technology generally), lawyer regulators might consider partnering with courts in order to ensure that all relevant stakeholders are at the table. For example, the Delaware Supreme Court Commission on Law and Technology, established in 2013, has "broad representation including judges from a variety of Delaware courts as well as lawyers in private practice from various sized law firms, the Department of Justice, in-house corporate counsel and information technology officers."[91]

To the extent that following best practices or engaging in mentorship programs are voluntary, lawyer regulators will want to consider putting in place incentives to encourage lawyers to proactively seek out ways to improve their competence in courtroom technology. Potential methods could include marketing incentives—for example, allowing lawyers to be accredited specialists in court technology—or financial incentives in the form of reduced licensing fees for lawyers who demonstrate a certain level of technological competence.[92] Another possibility might be to require litigators to complete a minimum number of hours each year of continuing professional development courses on court technology and/or certify on an annual basis their continuing competence in the area of court technology. Mandatory continuing legal education is already in place in many Canadian and American jurisdictions. The concept of certifying competence on an annual basis is more unique, although this model has recently been adopted by the Solicitors Regulation Authority in England and Wales.[93]

Conclusion

In order to properly represent their clients, litigators need to understand and effectively use courtroom technology. Not only can technology be important to presenting a client's case in a time-sensitive and cost-efficient manner, it can also impact how effective a lawyer is in presenting a client's case and convincing a judge and/or jury on its merits. Understanding technology is also important in order to identify and respond to potential technological misfeasance by others in the course of litigation. Given these realities, courtroom technology competence may be understood as part of a lawyer's overall ethical duty to represent clients effectively.

Notwithstanding the fact that lawyer courtroom technology competence may be properly viewed as an ethical duty, it is not an issue that has attracted much attention from lawyer regulators to date. It ought to. There is nothing to indicate that litigators currently possess the necessary competence in this area; indeed, there is reason to believe that they do not.

As a preliminary matter, lawyer regulators should improve their understanding of the current level of technological competence held by lawyers who practice in courtrooms through surveys and/ or audits. In terms of enforcing a duty to have competence in relation to courtroom technology, this chapter argues that regulators should be cautious about pursuing a rule-based disciplinary approach. Not only is this approach limited insofar as it involves reacting to problems once they occur, it is also an awkward fit when it comes to courtroom technological competence given the diversity of courtroom practice and the complications in the contexts in which courtroom technology is deployed, for example, different courtroom infrastructures and varying client willingness and capacity to use technology in a given case. As such, more proactive educational approaches should be pursued, including providing guidance as to best practices or pursuing mentorship programs.

Notes

1   Although the term "ethical" can carry a normative connotation, its use in this chapter is descriptive and intended to signal that the issue of courtroom technology competence is a proper subject for lawyer regulators to take interest in. The use of the term "ethical duty" as opposed to, for example, the term "professional duty" is also consistent with the general discourse on lawyer competence.

2   This chapter focuses on North American lawyers. Accordingly, the term "lawyer regulators" refers to provincial and territorial law societies in Canada and state bar and court authorities in the United States that have professional disciplinary authority over lawyers within their jurisdictions. Even though the focus is on North American lawyers, the analysis presented here will likely resonate in other jurisdictions where there is also an increased use of technology in courtrooms.

3   There is a large set of literature that has generally identified and analyzed limitations with the conventional rules based system. See sources at footnote 81 for further discussion. In using the term "quasi-criminal" to describe the conventional approach, I borrow from Ted Schneyer, "The Case for Proactive Management-Based Regulation," *Hofstra L Rev* 42 (2013) at 233.

4   See, e.g., Paul J De Muniz, "Oregon Courts Today and Tomorrow,"
      Willamette L Rev 50 (2014):291 at 313 (citing Martin Gruen, "The World of
      Courtroom Technology" (2003), online: Center for Legal & Court
      Technology <www.legaltechcenter.net/download/whitepapers/The%20
      World%20Of%20Courtroom%20Technology.pdf >, for the proposition that
      courtroom technology includes evidence presentation systems, assistive
      technology for individuals with disabilities, real-time foreign-language
      interpretation, teleconferencing, and videoconferencing); Fredric I Lederer,
      "Wired: What We've Learned About Courtroom Technology," *Criminal
      Justice* 24 (2010) at 18 (discussing courtroom technology as including, *inter
      alia*, "technology-based evidence presentation, remote testimony, multi-
      media court records, and assistive technology"); Fredric Lederer,
      "Courtroom Technology: A Status Report," in *Electronic Judicial Resource
      Management*, ed. Kamlesh N Agarwala and Murli D Tiwari, (Delhi:
      Macmillan, 2005) at 183 (dividing modern trial courtroom technology into
      information (evidence) presentation, remote appearances, court record,
      "counsel communication," (e.g., internet access from counsel table), assis-
      tive technology (including interpretation), jury deliberations, and appel-
      late matters); and Martin Gruen, "The World of Courtroom Technology"
      (2003) online: Center for Legal & Court Technology <www.legaltechcen-
      ter.net/download/whitepapers/The%20World%20Of%20Courtroom%20
      Technology.pdf> (defining "courtroom technology" as including the
      following basic categories: Communications; Remote-appearance systems
      (video-conferencing); Evidence presentation; Court record; Courtroom
      data; Control systems; and Infrastructure).
5   Lederer, "Courtroom Technology: A Status Report," *supra* note 4.
6   Nils Jensen, "Technology in the Courtroom" (23 February 2010), online:
      The Canadian Bar Association < www.cbapd.org/details_en.aspx?id=NA_
      ONFEB210>.
7   Canadian Centre for Court Technology, online: Canadian Centre for
      Court Technology <wiki.modern-courts.ca>.
8   Lederer, "Wired: What We've Learned About Courtroom Technology,"
      supra note 4 at 19.
9   Nelson P Miller and Derek S Witte, "Helping Law Firm Luddites Cross
      the Digital Divide – Arguments for Mastering Law Practice Technology,"
      S Methodist University L Rev 12 (2009):113 at 114.
10   American Bar Association, "2014 Legal Technology Survey Report:
      Litigation and Courtroom Technology" (2014), Vol. 3 at III-42, III-21, and
      III-23 [*ABA Report*].
11   Elizabeth C Wiggins, Meghan A Dunn and George Cort, "Federal
      Judicial Center Survey on Courtroom Technology" (December 2003),
      online: The Federal Judicial Center <www.fjc.gov/public/pdf.nsf/lookup/
      CTtech03.pdf/$file/CTtech03.pdf>.

12   Ibid. at 2.

13   Jane Bailey, "Digitization of Court Processes in Canada" (23 October 2012), online: Cyberjustice Laboratory <www.cyberjustice.ca/wordpress/wp-content/uploads/webuploads/WP002_CanadaDigitizationOfCourtProcesses20121023.pdf>.

14   Ibid.

15   Action Committee on Access to Justice in Civil and Family Matters, *Report of the Court Processes Simplification Working Group* (May 2012) at 7.

16   See, e.g., Jane Bailey, Jacquelyn Burkell and Graham Reynolds, "Access to Justice for *All:* Towards an 'Expansive Vision' of Justice and Technology," *Windsor Y B Access Just* 31(2013):181 at 202 (confirming that "at the current time [videoconferencing] technology is not universally available in courtrooms across Canada, and not all prisons have the facilities for remote appearances by incarcerated defendants").

17   Lawyer discomfort and misuse of technology is a frequent topic of commentary. See, e.g., Miller and Witte, *supra* note 9, at 117 (stating "[a]lthough many attorneys cling to their foam-core exhibits and paper tablets, it seems problematic for an attorney to argue about his small exhibit, which he holds several feet from the jury, when it could easily be coded, digitized, and then displayed on the blank plasma-screen television screens in the jury box and around the courtroom").

18   The insight that "[c]ourts that supply technology may be classified as permissive or mandatory" is taken from Lederer, "Courtroom Technology: A Status Report," *supra* note 4.

19   For discussion of use of video-conferencing in bail proceedings, see, e.g., Molly Treadway Johnson and Elizabeth Wiggins, "Videoconferencing in Criminal Proceedings: Legal and Empirical Issues for Direction and Research," *Law & Pol'y* 28 (2006) at 211 (observing at 211 that "[s]tate and federal courts are increasingly using videoconferencing to hold proceedings"); Lindsay Porter and Donna Calverley, "Trends in the use of remand in Canada" (2011), online: Statistics Canada <www.statcan.gc.ca/pub/85-002-x/2011001/article/11440-eng.htm> (commenting that "some courts now use video conferencing for routine hearings in order to expedite bail hearings and to reduce the costs associated with transporting accused persons to and from court houses"); Erich Schellhamer, "A Technology Opportunity for Court Modernization: Remote Appearances" (January 2013), online: Canadian Centre for Court Technology <wiki.modern-courts.ca/images/1/1b/A_Technology_Opportunity_for_Court_Modernization_-_Remote_Appearances.pdf>; and Anne Bowen Poulin, "Criminal Justice and Videoconferencing Technology: The Remote Defendant," *Tul L Rev* 78 (2004) at 1089.

20   For a case where this has happened, see, e.g., *Bank of Montreal v Faibish*, 2014 ONSC 2178 (CanLII).

21 As noted above, the insight that "[c]ourts that supply technology may be classified as permissive or mandatory" is taken from Lederer "Courtroom Technology: A Status Report," *supra* note 4.

22 Lederer, "Courtroom Technology: A Status Report" *supra* note 4, footnote 11. For discussion of cost efficiencies resulting from using court technologies, see, also, Sheryl Jackson, "Court-provided Trial Technology: Efficiency and Fairness for Criminal Trials," *C L World Rev* 39 (2010) at 236 (stating, "[t]here is now a substantial body of evidence elsewhere to support the view that the use of trial technology can generate very substantial overall costs savings, particularly flowing from a shortening of the time involved at trial and in trial preparation") and Andrew E Taslitz, "Digital Juries Versus Digital Lawyers," *ABA Criminal J* 19 (2004) (observing that "[d]igital systems help the lawyer to fuse the organizational clarity of the library culture with the speed and creativity of hyperlinked culture and, studies have shown, thereby dramatically to shorten the length of trials").

23 See, e.g., *Wright v Wasilewski* (2001), 52 OR (3d) 410 (CanLII) (ONSC) wherein the plaintiff successfully brought a motion to have the evidence of 20 American witnesses received through video-conferencing instead of incurring approximately $20,000 in order to have the witnesses brought to Ontario to testify.

24 In the case of video-conferencing, there may be, e.g., concerns about potential unintended effects of videoconferencing technology on credibility assessments. For further discussion, see, e.g., Amy Salyzyn, "A New Lens: Reframing the Conversation about the Use of Video Conferencing in Civil Trials in Ontario," *Osgoode Hall LJ* 50 (2012) at 429.

25 Bailey et al., *supra* note 16 at 201.

26 These particular technologies are among those cited as available in American courts in the *ABA Report, supra* note 10.

27 The Third Branch, "Courtroom Technology Draws Positive Response" (August 1998), online: United States Courts <www.uscourts.gov/news/TheThirdBranch/98-08-01/Courtroom_Technology_Draws_Positive_Response.aspx>.

28 Ibid.

29 Jaihyun Park and Neal Feigenson, "Effects of a Visual Technology on Mock Juror Decision Making," *Applied Cognitive Psychology* 27 (2013):235 at 244.

30 Ibid. at 243–245. See also discussion in Elizabeth Wiggins, "The Courtroom of the Future is Here: Introduction to Emerging Technologies in the Legal System," *Law & Pol'y* 28 (2006) at 182.

31 Michelle Quigley, "Courtroom Technology and Legal Ethics: Considerations for the ABA Commission on Ethics 20/20" (Spring 2010), online: Michigan State University College of Law <www.law.msu.edu/king/2009-2010/Quigley.pdf>.

32   Marilyn Krawitz, "Guilty as Tweeted: Jurors Using Social Media Inappropriately During the Trial Process" (2012), UWA Faculty of Law Research Paper (SSRN). For a recent example of a juror misusing social media, see: "Queens NY Juror Fined $1000 For Dishing on Facebook During Trial" *Jurors Behaving Badly* (4 November 2015), online: <jurorsbehavingbadly.blogspot.ca/>.

33   Ibid.

34   Ibid. at 10.

35   Ken Armstrong, "PowerPoint Justice: When prosecutors slide around the law," *The Marshall Project* (23 December 2014), online: <https://www.themarshallproject.org/2014/12/23/powerpoint-justice#.oAAmL3AZB>.

36   See, e.g., *Dunkle v Oklahoma,* 139 P (3d) 228 (Okla Ct Crim App 2006) (court finding that the prosecution's use of computerized animations was potentially misleading to the jury and that the record did not establish that the animations were fair and accurate representations of the evidence); see also *State v Stewart,* 643 NW (2d) 281 (Mo Sup Ct 2002) (court holding that a computer animation presented by the prosecution, which was heavily reliant on material based on conjecture, ought not to have been admitted).

37   *Clark v Cantrell,* 529 S.E.2d at 528 (South Carolina Sup Ct 2000) at 536 (approvingly quoting article in South Carolina Trial Lawyer Bulletin)

38   Armstrong, *supra* note 35.

39   Neal Feigenson and Christina Spiesel, *Law on Display* (New York, NYU Press: 2009) at 160.

40   Ibid. at 205.

41   Dan H Willoughby, Rose Hunter Jones and Gregory R Antine, "Sanctions for E-Discovery Violations by the Numbers," *Duke LJ* 60 (2010):789 at 790.

42   For example, one of the most well-known American e-discovery sanction cases, *Qualcomm Inc v Broadcom Corp,* 2008 US Dist Ct LEXIS 911 (SD Cal Dist CT 2008), involved a "failure to produce [a] massive number of critical documents at issue in [the] case" which, in the court's view, amounted to a "monumental and intentional discovery violation," warranting a monetary sanction of $8,568,633.24 against Qualcomm Inc.

43   *United States v Johnson,* 553 F Supp (2d) 582 (ED Va 2008) [*Johnson*].

44   Ibid. at 1.

45   Ibid. at 74.

46   Ibid. at 106.

47   Willoughby et al., *supra* note 41 at 804.

48   Ibid. at 804–805.

49   Under this framing, the lawyer lacking adequate competence could be the subject of a civil claim from a dissatisfied client. See, e.g., Jan L Jacobowitz and Danielle Singer, "The Social Media Frontier: Exploring a New Mandate for Competence in the Practice of Law," *U Miami L Rev*

68 (2014) at 445 (discussing potential liability in negligence for lawyers who fail to employ social media to obtain information relevant to a client's case).

50 This duty would relate to the inherent jurisdiction of courts to govern their own processes and sanction lawyers and parties who fail to abide by the applicable standards. See, e.g., Willoughby et al., *supra* note 41 (discussing wide range of judicial sanctions for e-discovery violations).

51 Indeed, a few law schools are already taking steps to train students in courtroom technologies and other relevant law practice technologies. See, e.g., the numerous student opportunities with William & Mary Law School's Center for Legal and Court Technology (William & Mary Law School, *Center for Legal and Court Technology*, online: William & Mary Law School <law.wm.edu/academics/intellectuallife/researchcenters/clct/>); the "Technology Enhanced Trial Advocacy" course at the Michigan State University College of Law, "An Innovative Curriculum online: <www.law.msu.edu/tpi/curriculum.html>; and Suffolk Law School's Institute on Legal Practice Technology and Innovation, online: <lawpracticetechnology.blogs.law.suffolk.edu>.

52 Although costs of such animation obviously vary from case to case, a sense of the potential costs can be found on the website of an American consulting firm. The estimates on this website include the following: between $5,000 and $15,000 for five minutes of a PowerPoint animation-style exhibit with average complexity; between $10,000 and $35,000 for ten minutes of animation built from drawings or schematics; and between $40,000 and $150,000 for a 15-minute 3-D animation of a complex subject (see Ken Lopez, "What Does Litigation Animation Cost?," online: <www.a2lc.com/blog/bid/68457/What-Does-Litigation-Animation-Cost-Includes-Animation-Examples>). For further discussion of fairness concerns, see, e.g., Fred Galves, "Where the Not-so-Wild Things Are: Computers in the Courtroom, the Federal Rules of Evidence, and the Need for Institutional Reform and More Judicial Acceptance," *Harv J of L & Tech* 13 (2000) at 165.

53 The American Bar Association, *Model Rules of Professional Conduct*, Chicago: ABA, 2013, Rule 1.1.

54 Federation of Law Societies of Canada, *Model Code of Professional Conduct*, Ottawa: FLSC, 2014, Rule 3.1-2 and Rule 3.1-1.

55 See, e.g., Andrew Perlman, "The Twenty-First Century Lawyer's Evolving Ethical Duty of Competence," *The Professional Lawyer* 22:4 (2014) at 24; Sam Glover, "You Already Have an Ethical Obligation to be Technologically Competent," *Lawyerist.com* (31 August 2015), online: <https://lawyerist.com/86726/already-ethical-obligation-technologically-competent/>; Karen Dyck, "A Duty to be Tech-Savvy?," *Slaw Online* (15 November 2015), online: Slaw.ca <www.slaw.ca/2015/11/11/a-duty-to-be-tech-savvy/>;

Amy Salyzyn, "Tackling Technology," *Slaw Online* (14 September 2014), online: Slaw.ca <www.slaw.ca/2014/09/30/tackling-technology/>.

56 *Model Rules of Professional Conduct, supra* note 52 at Rule 1.1, commentary 8 (emphasis added). This amendment was a result of the ABA Commission on Ethics 20/20, which was created in 2009 "to perform a thorough review of the ABA *Model Rules of Professional Conduct* and the U.S. system of lawyer regulation in the context of advances in technology and global legal practice developments" (American Bar Association, "ABA Commission on Ethics 20/20," online: <www.americanbar.org/groups/professional_responsibility/aba_commission_on_ethics_20_20.html>). For further discussion about the history of this commission, see, e.g., Laurel Terry, "Globalization and the ABA Commission on Ethics 20/20: Reflections on Missed Opportunities and the Road Not Taken," *Hofstra L Rev* 43 (2014) at 95.

57 A November 2015 blog post reports that 17 states have now adopted this Commentary (Robert Ambrogi, "Two More States Adopt Duty of Technology Competence," www.lawsitesblog.com, November 11, 2015; online: <www.lawsitesblog.com/2015/11/two-more-states-adopt-duty-of-technology-competence.html>.

58 See, e.g., Lederer, "Courtroom Technology: A Status Report," *supra* note 4; Michelle L. Quigley, "Courtroom Technology and Legal Ethics: Consideration for the ABA Commission on Ethics 20/20," *Professional Lawyer* 20 (2010) at 18.

59 Lederer, "Courtroom Technology: A Status Report" *supra* note 4.

60 Ibid. Indeed, even before the ABA rules were amended to specifically reference technology, Lederer argued that general provisions on lawyer competence should be viewed as "extend[ing] to competence in employing courtroom technology...[and thus, as] creat[ing] an affirmative duty on counsel to learn how to be at least an adequately competent high-tech trial lawyer, when attempting technology use."

61 Google search February 16, 2015, "Lawyer" and "Luddite."

62 Megan Zavieh, "Luddite Lawyers Are Ethical Violations Waiting To Happen" (2 December 2013), online: Lawyerist <https://lawyerist.com/71071/luddite-lawyers-ethical-violations-waiting-happen/>.

63 Bill Latham, "Don't be that Luddite Lawyer" (18 December 2013), online: The Hytech Lawyer <hytechlawyer.com/?p=2198>.

64 Jim Calloway, "Can Lawyers Be Luddites?" (18 December 2013), online: Law Practice Tips Blog <www.lawpracticetipsblog.com/2013/12/can-lawyers-be-luddites.html>.

65 Miller and Witte, *supra* note 9.

66 Casey Flaherty, "Could you pass this in-house counsel's tech test? If the answer is no, you may be losing business" (17 July 2013), online: American Bar Association <www.abajournal.com/legalrebels/article/could_you_pass_this_in-house_counsels_tech_test>.

67 Ibid.

68 Ibid.

69 Daniel W Dugan, "A Picture is Worth 999 Words: The Importance and Effectiveness of Courtroom Visual Presentations," *Reynolds Ct & Media L J* 1 (2011):503 at 503.

70 See discussion in Zavieh, *supra* note 61.

71 *ABA Report, supra* note 9 at III-50.

72 Ibid. at III-52.

73 Ibid.

74 Ibid.

75 Jane Goodman-Delahunty, Par Anders Granhag, Maria Hartwig and Elizabeth F. Loftus, "Insightful or Wishful: Lawyers' Ability to Predict Case Outcomes," *Psychology, Public Policy, and Law* 16:2 (2010):133 at 135.

76 Christine Parker, Tahlia Gordon, and Steve Mark, "Regulating Law Firms Ethics Management: An Empirical Assessment of an Innovation in Regulation of the Legal Profession in New South Wales," *Journal of Law in Society* 37:3 (2010):446 at 493.

77 These programs include Saskatchewan's Practice Review Program; see "Practice Review Program," online: Law Society of Saskatchewan <www.lawsociety.sk.ca/about-us/how-we- accomplish-our-purpose/committees/professional-standards/practice-review-program.aspx> (targeting "new sole practitioners," among other groups), and Ontario's "Practice Management Review" program (see "Practice Management Review," online: Law Society of Upper Canada <www.lsuc.on.ca/lawyer-practice-management- review/>) (targeting lawyers one to eight years from the call to the bar and in private practice). It should be noted that the Law Society of Upper Canada also conducts "Focused Practice Reviews" (targeting lawyers who have complaints history or have otherwise been flagged as requiring personal or professional assistance) and "Re-Entry Reviews" (targeting lawyers who are returning to private practice as sole practitioners, or in a firm of five or fewer lawyers, after an absence of 48 months over the past five years). See "Lawyer Practice Management Review, online: Law Society of Upper Canada <lsuc.on.ca/lawyer-practice-management-review/>.

78 Milton C Regan, "Nested Ethics: A Tale of Two Cultures," *Hofstra Law Review* 42 (2013):143 at 172, citing Larry Richard, "Herding Cats: The Lawyer Personality Revealed" Report to Legal Management, (August 2002), online: <www.managingpartnerforum.org/tasks/sites/mpf/assets/image/MPF%20-%20WEBSITE%20-%20ARTICLE%20-%20Herding%20Cats%20-%20Richards1.pdf>.

79 See, e.g., Matt Nelson, "New changes to Model Rules a wake-up call for technologically challenged lawyers" (13 March 2013), online: Inside Counsel <www.insidecounsel.com/2013/03/28/new-changes-to-model-rules-a-wake-up-call-for-tech>; Darla Jackson, "Lawyers Can't be

Luddites Anymore: Do Law Librarians Have a Role in Helping Lawyers Adjust to New Ethics Rules Involving Technology?," *Law Libr J* 105 (2013) at 395; G.M. Filisko, "Reality Bytes: New Rules Require You to Get with Tech Program—Like It or Not" (1 April 2013), online: American Bar Association Journal <www.abajournal.com/magazine/article/new_aba_rules_require_you_to_get_with_tech_programlike_it_or_not/>; Ed Poll, "Beware of Technological Incompetence" (30 July 2013), online: My Case <www.mycase.com/blog/2013/07/beware-of-technology-incompetence/>; Andrew Perlman, "Delaware Creates Legal Tech Commission" (17 July 2013), online: Legal Ethics Forum <www.legalethicsforum.com/blog/2013/07/delaware-creates-legal-tech-commission-.html>; and Megan Zavieh, "Luddite Lawyers Are Ethical Violations Waiting To Happen" (2 December 2013), online: Lawyerist <https://lawyerist.com/71071/luddite-lawyers-ethical-violations-waiting-happen/>.

80   Quigley, *supra* note 44 at 18.

81   For further discussion, see, e.g., Amy Salyzyn, "What if We Didn't Wait? Canadian Law Societies and the Promotion of Effective Ethical Infrastructure in Canadian Legal Practices," *Can Bar Rev* 92:3 (2015); Laurel Terry, "Trends in Global and Canadian Lawyer Regulation," *Sask L Rev* 76 (2013) at 145; Ted Schneyer, "The Case for Proactive Management-Based Regulation to Improve Professional Self-Regulation for US Lawyers *Hofstra L Rev* 42 (2013) at 233; "The Role of Ethics Audits in Improving Management Systems and Practices: An Empirical Examination of Management-Based Regulation of Law Firms," *St Mary's LJ on Legal Malpractice & Ethics* 4 (2014) at 112; Ted Schneyer, "On Further Reflection: How 'Professional Self-Regulation' Should Promote Compliance with Broad Ethical Duties of Law Firm Management," *Ariz L Rev* 53 (2011) at 577; John Briton and Scott McLean, "Incorporated Legal Practices: Dragging the Regulation of the Legal Profession into the Modern Era," *Legal Ethics* 11 (2008) at 241; Ted Schneyer, "Professional Discipline for Law Firms?," *Cornell L Rev* 77 (1991) at 1; Ted Schneyer, "A Tale of Four Systems: Reflections on How Law Influences the 'Ethical Infrastructure' of Law Firms," *S Tex L Rev* 39 (1998) at 245; Adam Dodek, "Regulating Law Firms in Canada," *Can Bar Rev* 90 (2011) at 383.

82   Bailey et al., *supra* note 16 at 202–03 (footnotes omitted).

83   Amy Salyzyn, "Technological Competence 101: Back to Basics?," Slaw Online (15 January 2015), online: Slaw.ca <www.slaw.ca/2015/01/29/technological-competence-101-back-to-basics/>.

84   See, e.g., the discussion in Fredric I Lederer, "Technology-Augmented Courtrooms: Progress Amid a Few Complications, or the Problematic Interrelationship Between Court and Counsel," *NYU Annual Survey of American Law* 60 (2004) at 675.

85   See *supra* note 51.

86   See, e.g., Fortney, "The Role of Ethics Audits" *supra* note 80 at 138. See also Amy Salyzyn, "What if We Didn't Wait? Promoting Ethical Infrastructure in Canadian Law Firms," *Slaw Online* (23 July 2013), online: Slaw.ca <www.slaw.ca>.

87   See, e.g., American Bar Association Legal Technology Resource Centre, online <www.americanbar.org/groups/departments_offices/legal_technology_resources.html>; Canadian Bar Association, *Practicing Ethically with Technology,* online <www.cba.org/CBA/activities/pdf/guidelines-eng.pdf>; and Law Society of Upper Canada, *Technology Practice Management Guideline,* online <www.lsuc.on.ca/with.aspx?id=2147491197>.

88   That said, there are two significant exceptions to this practice management orientation: regulatory resources dealing with (1) e-discovery and (2) social media. In 2014, the State Bar of California made waves when it released a draft ethics opinion for public comment that clarified that "attorney competence related to litigation generally requires, at a minimum, a basic understanding of, and facility with, issues relating to e-discovery" (The State Bar of California, "Proposed Formal Opinion Interim No. 11-0004" April 2014, online: <www.calbar.ca.gov/AboutUs/PublicComment/Archives/2014PublicComment/201404.aspx>). Numerous law societies and bar associations have now also offered guidance on the ethical use of social media, although such guidance generally focuses on lawyers' use of social media rather than appropriate use of social media in the courtroom (for a small sample set of existing guidance, see New York State Bar Association, Social Media Ethics Guidelines (18 March 2014), online: New York State Bar Association <www.nysba.org/Sections/Commercial_Federal_Litigation/Com_Fed_PDFs/Social_Media_Ethics_Guidelines.html>; Pennsylvania State Bar Association, Ethical Obligations for Attorneys when Using Social Media, online: Daniel J Siegel <www.danieljsiegel.com/Formal_2014-300.pdf >). One exception is the American Bar Association's formal opinion on "Lawyer Reviewing Jurors' Internet Presence," which stipulates, among other things, that "a lawyer may passively review a juror's public presence on the Internet, but may not communicate with a juror" and that "if a lawyer discovers criminal or fraudulent conduct by a juror related to the proceeding, the lawyer must take reasonable remedial measures including, if necessary, disclosure to the tribunal" (American Bar Association, Formal Opinion 466 "Lawyer Reviewing Jurors' Internet Presence," online <www.americanbar.org/content/dam/aba/administrative/professional_responsibility/formal_opinion_466_final_04_23_14.authcheckdam.pdf>.)

89   The Law Society of New South Wales, The Technology Mentoring Program, online: The Law Society of New South Wales <www.

lawsociety.com.au/ForSolictors/professionalsupport/supportingyou/ Mentoring/TechnologyMentoring/index.htm>. For further discussion, see also Amy Salyzyn, "Getting Ready: The Continuing Case for Technological Competence" (11 June 2014), online: Slaw <www.slaw. ca/2014/06/11/getting-ready-the-continuing-case-for-technological-competence/>.

90   The Richard K. Herrmann Technology American Inn of Court, History of the Richard K. Hermann Technology Inn of Court, online: American Inns of Court <home.innsofcourt.org/for-members/inns/the-richard-k-herrmann-technology-american-inn-of-court.aspx>.

91   Delaware State Courts, Delaware Supreme Court Commission on Law & Technology, online: Delaware State Courts <courts.delaware.gov/declt/>.

92   Susan Fortney discusses these types of incentives in the context of considering how to encourage lawyers to engage in proactive self-assessment of their ethical practices (see Fortney, *supra* note 80).

93   John Hyde, "Solicitors to require mandatory 'statement of competence,'" *The Law Society Gazette* (12 March 2015), online: The Law Society Gazette <www.lawgazette.co.uk/law/solicitors-to-require-mandatory-statement-of-competence/5047474.article>.

CHAPTER VIII

Tablets in the Jury Room: Enhancing Performance while Undermining Fairness?

David Tait and Meredith Rossner

Introduction

Conflict between principles of efficiency and fairness appears to characterize everything from taxation policy[1] to managing plea bargaining[2] and allocating water.[3] Giving iPads—or other computer tablets—to criminal juries raises similar concerns. The use of tablets could cause juror recall of evidence to improve or deliberation to accelerate. At the same time, some jurors may be disadvantaged, and undue weight might be placed on memorable pieces of evidence. Therefore, there may be a risk to a fair trial, and defendants who might otherwise be acquitted may be convicted.

This paper reports on the results of an experimental pre-test that examines the core issue of the risk to a fair trial using mock jurors and a written scenario, with 6-person juries deliberating for 15–30 minutes with visual evidence provided to them either on paper or tablets.

The study is funded by the Canadian Social Sciences and Humanities Research Council as part of the cyberjustice consortium based at the University of Montreal and headed by Karim Benyekhlef. The study has been developed by a team including David Tait (Western Sydney University), Christian Licoppe (Paris Tech), Meredith Rossner (London School of Economics) and Blake McKimmie (University of Queensland). The cyberjustice consortium brings together scholars from several countries with an interest in the impacts of emerging technologies on justice processes.

The aim of the tablets in the jury room project is to determine how use of tablets shapes the ways that juries think about and deliberate on evidence. This will be achieved by (1) documenting the current processes used to provide jurors with written and visual evidence; (2) examining the ways jurors and juries think about and deliberate on evidence using different technologies, with particular reference to the accuracy of recall, the comprehensiveness of issues reviewed, and interaction and collaboration among jurors; (3) measuring the impact of tablet use on fairness of the process and reliability of verdicts; and (4) developing protocols that optimize the quality and fairness of juror deliberation processes.

Background

In most common law jurisdictions, the right to be tried by a jury of one's peers is a fundamental right.[4] Fairness includes the right to a timely hearing before an impartial judge, with opportunity to confront one's accusers. Information given to jurors is carefully regulated to protect the rights of the accused and to ensure that jurors decide the case only on the basis of evidence tested in the courtroom. For instance, potential jurors with prior knowledge of a case may be excluded, and jurors may not conduct independent research using external sources.[5]

Traditionally, jurors had to base their decisions almost exclusively on oral evidence presented in an open court; this could include confessions, eyewitness testimony, and expert evidence. This was at times supplemented by physical evidence (e.g., the alleged murder weapon) or a representation (e.g., an X-ray), which was generally shown to the jury within the courtroom. If the jury had a subsequent query about evidence, they filed back into the courtroom and the judge read the transcript or presented the relevant item to them again. But criminal trials are becoming more complicated, and jurors can find it difficult to process the information and the evidence presented to them, with judicial reminders an inefficient way of assisting recall.[6] As trials become more complex, jurors may resort to stereotypes and decision-cues to evaluate the evidence and make a decision,[7] and may also fail to systematically consider all the issues.[8] These practices can erode the quality and fairness of juror deliberation processes.

To encourage more informed jury decisions, Australian judges— as well as judges in other common law countries—increasingly provide jurors with evidence to take with them into the jury room,[9] including interview transcripts, witness statements, photographs, and video footage. This may improve both individual and group decision-making processes. For individual jurors, technological aids can prompt juror memory, enhance comprehension, and increase engagement; for the jury as a whole, it may improve the thoroughness of the deliberation.[10] Providing each juror with his or her own copy of the evidence may encourage critical discussion and healthy debate among jurors—this in turn can challenge prejudices and lead to fairer outcomes.[11] Combining oral discussion with visual display could provide the jury with an efficient way of managing cognitive load.[12]

In general, mobile technologies may help to break down the so-called digital divide, bringing internet and information access to ordinary people through easy-to-use devices.[13] Tablets can improve learning outcomes for kindergarten pupils,[14] people with intellectual disabilities,[15] management students,[16] and even apes and dolphins.[17] Jurors are quintessential learners; they are chosen because they know nothing about the case and have no assumed knowledge of the science used in evidence. So tablets may improve their ability to follow the case. For "net generation" jurors who have spent on average 10,000 hours playing computer games and less than 5,000 hours reading books, screens will be more familiar than books.[18] In other settings, tablets may assist learners develop their imagination,[19] but the story jurors are asked to assess is that given to them by the prosecution. Their "learning" should not involve developing their own alternative narrative. Powerful or graphic imagery can influence verdicts, so readily accessed images and documents might exacerbate this problem.[20] Relative to the use of paper-based information and evidence, a tablet might also deflect the jurors' attention from the group project;[21] this in turn can undermine quality decision-making by the collective.[22]

On the other hand, providing jurors with a shared display that is linked to individual tablets might mitigate concerns about reduced juror interaction and allow the jury, as a collective, to become an "information processor" or a sense-making unit.[23] In this configuration, tablets are sites of action, enabling individual jurors to source relevant information, while the shared screen enables the collective to identify patterns and test claims.[24] This is not limited to high-tech solutions. There are various types of "multi-surface environments," including an interactive whiteboard managed by a single user or multiple users; interactive multi-user desktop screens (activated by fingers or smartphones); as well as plasma screens that serve as pinboards. Each of these may support different levels of accessibility and collaboration.[25] One issue that is particularly relevant to this research is the relative impact on collaboration of shared access to the common space or delegated control of this shared space to a single group member.[26] The particular configuration of technologies is likely to shape the ways jurors and juries think about and deliberate on evidence.

The jury environment is rather different from other contexts in which co-located participants collaborate: (1) jurors may not conduct independent research about the case; (2) jurors are under pressure to achieve consensus (or super-majority); (3) with 12 members, juries represent a large group, relative to the groups of 2 to 6 participants used in other research;[27] (4) jurors have no stake in the matter under investigation; (5) jurors are strangers to each other; and (6) the consequences of their decision for the lives of others can be substantial.

Methodology

The results reported here are from a pre-test of a larger field experiment investigating the impact of tablets on jurors in court. The pre-test reported here is designed to develop the script, develop observational methodology to analyze juror interactions, and provide initial estimates of likely effect sizes.

The study is made up of a sample of 106 mock jurors split into groups of four- to six-member juries. The sessions were held over a two-week period in March 2014. Jurors, undergraduate psychology students at the University of Queensland, read a five-page scenario (with six images included), taking about ten minutes. The scenario involved an accusation of an armed robbery of a bank, in which the identity of the accused was ambiguous based on evidence from a CCTV camera (he had a hat pulled down), and there was no evidence he was armed, but a link was established to the getaway car. The images were sourced from online newspaper accounts of an actual bank robbery in Sydney. The scenario was written to create some, but not too much, doubt and tested so that about 50% of the sample would return a guilty verdict. This was to encourage deliberation and it could also increase the influence of "peripheral" cues like the form in which evidence was produced on decision-making.

Groups were randomly assigned to one of two conditions for deliberation: with paper or tablet (an iPad), subject to the constraint that there were equal numbers of groups in each condition. Fifty-four of the jurors were in ten tablet groups, and fifty-two were in ten paper groups. Groups deliberated for 15–20 minutes, then completed a written survey.

Research participants completed a pre-deliberation verdict form to indicate their initial decision about guilt. Three responses were possible: guilty of armed robbery; guilty of robbery; not guilty. Post-deliberation measures included prior attitudes, reactions to evidence from prosecution and defence, reactions to the accused, reactions to the jury deliberation, and various measures of the culpability of the accused. Given the short scenario and brief deliberation time, one of the key items for the main study, comprehensiveness of memory, was not tested.

With respect to the post-deliberation verdict, jurors were asked to indicate the decision of their jury (guilty of armed robbery, guilty of robbery, or not guilty) rather than their individual view. Individual perspectives were obtained on the basis of an open-ended question that asked about the elements of the evidence that weighed in their decision, plus the likelihood of guilt and their confidence in their verdict. In most cases, their verdict choice was clear, apart from two cases where their answers were too vague; these cases were dropped from this part of the analysis. There were also two cases where the research participant indicated their post-deliberation verdict to be "Guilty of Armed Robbery," but in their detailed reasoning stated they found him guilty of robbery. In both cases the written argument was taken to be the respondents' correct verdict.

Analysis

There were significantly different individual verdicts based on the form of evidence used by the jury: jurors who used tablets were significantly more likely to convict than were jurors deliberating with paper. There are two ways of measuring this effect: by the juror verdict and by their estimate of likelihood of guilt.

Both sources of data showed the same pattern: jurors who used tablets for evidence review were more likely to convict and provided higher ratings for likelihood of guilt. One quarter (25%) of the jurors who used paper found the accused guilty after deliberation, compared to 56% of those using tablets (B=.43, SE=.21, df=1, Wald=4.4, p=.04). The conviction rate before deliberation was almost the same:

79% for the paper condition and 76% for the tablet condition. Likelihood of guilt was measured on a scale of 1 to 7. Jurors who used paper had an average score of 5.0 compared to jurors using tablets, who scored 5.85 (F=10.2, p=.002).

The same pattern holds when comparing *changes* in the scores for individuals. Jurors using paper *decreased* their likelihood of guilt score from their pre-deliberation to their post-deliberation survey (from 5.38 to 5.00), while jurors using tablets *increased* from 5.45 to 5.85 (F=9.2, p=.003).

A variety of other differences are consistent with the apparent enhanced perception of guilt that characterized those who deliberated using tablets. Those who used tablets found the prosecutor to be more credible than did those who used paper (4.9 vs. 4.2, F=9.6, p=.002), but did not display any differences in their evaluations of the defense lawyer. Given that the participants saw neither a prosecutor nor a defense lawyer, this difference probably just means that they agreed with the written statements about the case, described as the argument of the prosecutor. So perhaps this is just another way of characterizing perceived guilt. The tablet users in general also found the defendant to be more dangerous and violent (-.27 vs. .26, F=7.9, p=.006), and generally to be of bad character (-2.6 vs. 2.4, F=6.8, p=.01). The tablet users who considered him guilty after deliberation considered him *more* dangerous and violent than the paper users who considered him guilty (.54 vs. .08). Perhaps the vividness of the images somehow made him seem guiltier when tablets were used.

It should be noted that the difference between the groups was not in their initial views, which were almost identical. Instead, the difference between the groups emerged only in the results after deliberation, including the verdict (guilt down 54 percentage points for jurors using paper, but down only 20 points for those using tablets), and likelihood of guilt (down .38 for those using paper, up .48 for those using tablets). There was a small but non-significant difference between the groups in terms of satisfaction with the process of deliberation (5.6 for paper group, 5.3 for tablet group, F=1,3, p=.26). Jurors using tablets also reported slightly higher (but non significant) likelihood of "being pressured to agree" (2.6 vs. 2.2, F=1.6, p=.21); tablet jurors were also slightly more likely (non-significant difference) to indicate that they could "openly disagree" with other jurors (5.9 vs. 5.5, F=2.4, p=.12). There was a significantly higher level of conflict in the tablets groups, with the tablet jurors reporting more frequent incidents of "conflict about ideas" (3.2 vs. 2.8, F=3.3, p=0.07) and more "differences of opinion" (3.6 vs. 2.9, F=9.3, p=.003). So perhaps tablets gave jurors a chance to engage in a more vigorous democratic dialogue than is supported by more traditional forms of evidence.

So far the analysis has focused on individual jurors irrespective of the group within which they deliberated. Given the possible role of group dynamics on final outcomes, it is expected that the pre-deliberation disposition of the jury group would have an impact on the likelihood of individual members shifting their vote over the course of the deliberation. In particular, it would be expected that unanimous pro-guilt juries would move less than ones that are split, and that the more jurors voting not guilty to begin with, the more likely the group will move toward not-guilty verdicts. Six of the twenty juries were unanimous in finding the accused guilty before deliberation, while none of the juries were unanimous in finding him not guilty. This means that fourteen juries were split, six juries had one juror standing out against the tide of guilty verdicts, six had two jurors voting not guilty, while the remaining two had three jurors finding the accused not guilty.

For jurors in groups that used paper, but *not* tablets, during deliberation, there was a marked impact of having at least one *other* juror in the group who had voted not guilty before deliberation (27% guilty post-deliberation when at least one juror had made a pre-deliberation determination of not guilty vs. 48% on a jury with no juror voting not guilty before deliberation), and a similar pattern held for evaluations of likelihood of guilt (4.8 post-deliberation rating if at least *one* juror had voted not guilty before deliberation, compared to 5.2 if all jurors had voted guilty before deliberation). No such differences emerged for jurors in groups that used tablets (67% vs. 78% post-deliberation guilty verdicts, and 5.83 vs. 5.86 post-deliberation ratings for likelihood of guilt).

This suggests an interaction between experimental condition and number of other jurors voting not guilty. The jury verdict composition had an impact on the paper group and no discernible impact on the tablet group. Tablets perhaps immunize jurors from influence by others as they (arguably) put their heads down and concentrate on their own interpretation of the evidence. What will be important to see is whether sharing software remedies this anti-social tendency that the technology seems to encourage.

Discussion and Conclusion

Do tablets increase conflict, provide more space for open debate, or give undue weight to prosecution evidence? Such debates cannot be resolved with preliminary data from a test like this.[28]

The differences in post-deliberation verdicts and evaluations of likelihood of guilt reported here seem rather large and may reflect the nature of the experiment with written rather than oral testimony. A fuller study with a more representative sample and more realistic conditions with a live performance in a real court could produce somewhat different (probably more muted) differences between conditions.

Nonetheless, the study suggests a number of interesting hypotheses that can be explored more fully in a major study. The first hypothesis that emerges from these preliminary findings is that providing juries with evidence on tablets, which may be a more intensive or memorable medium, could undermine the fairness of the trial by increasing focus on and response to the prosecution evidence. This is particularly an issue because most of the evidence tends to come from the prosecution. Further, when the defense seeks only to counter the prosecution's case and does not provide equally graphic evidence of its own (which of course it is not required to do), it is at an additional disadvantage. The evidence used in this study was prosecution evidence; we have not tested the impact of tablets when defense evidence is also presented. Whether the colour of the images, the tactility of the medium, or the image on the screen adds extra veracity to the evidence also cannot be established from this preliminary study.

The second hypothesis is that having evidence on tablets may encourage a more vigorous debate, allowing minority voices to be heard and jurors more liberty to disagree. There is, however, another possibility that might also be considered: tablets may encourage greater compromise, in this case at the expense of the accused. This could be an issue where the defense is considering whether to allow alternative verdicts for juries.

The findings presented here are preliminary. The jurors in our study were students, who read a short scenario and engaged in a short deliberation. Future research with greater ecological validity and verisimilitude will produce more comprehensive findings.

Future research will also consider the use of sharing technology, allowing jurors to send images and notations to each other or to a shared screen. It is possible that such technology will influence the way the evidence is perceived as well as the quality of the deliberation. One thing is clear: if the results of this study were to hold for real-world trials, defendants (at least those who are not presenting any evidence of their own) should strongly prefer deliberation using paper evidence rather than evidence presented via tablet.

Notes

1   Robert P Inman and Daniel L Rubinfeld, "Designing Tax Policy in Federalist Economies: an Overview," *Journal of Public Economics* 60 (1996) at 307.

2   Stephen J Schulhofer, "Plea Bargaining as Disaster," *Yale Law Journal* 101 (1991) at 1979.

3   Michael R Moore, "Native American Water Rights: Efficiency and Fairness," *Natural Resources Journal* 29 (1989) at 763.

4   *Universal Declaration of Human Rights*, GA Res 217A (III), UNGAOR, 3rd Sess, Supp No 13, UN Doc A/810 (1948).

5   Daniel William Bell, "Juror Misconduct and the Internet," *Am J Crim L* 38 (2010) at 81.

6   Richard C Waites and David A Giles "Are Jurors Equipped to Decide the Outcome of Complex Cases," *Am J Trial Advoc* (2005) at 19.

7   Regina A Schuller, Deborah Terry and Blake McKimmie, "The Impact of Expert Testimony on Jurors' Decisions: Gender of the Expert and Testimony Complexity," *Journal of Applied Social Psychology* 35 (2005) at 1266.

8   Reid Hastie, David A Schkade and John W Payne, "A Study of Juror and Jury Judgments in Civil Cases," *Law and Human Behavior* 22:3 (1998) at 287.

9   New South Wales Law Reform Commission, *Report 136: Jury Directions in Criminal Trials* (Sydney, Australia: NSW Law Reform Commission, 2012).

10   Karen H Field, Mark A Zaffarano and Yihwa Irene Liou, "Bringing Technology to the Jury Deliberation Table," *The Justice System Journal* 18:3 (1996) at 317; Nancy S Marder, "Juries and Technology: Equipping Jurors for the Twenty-First Century," Brooklyn Law Review 66 (2001) at 1257.

11   Jasmine S Rijnbout and Blake M McKimmie, "Deviance in Organizational Group Decision-Making: The Role of Information Processing, Confidence, and Elaboration," *Group Processes & Intergroup Relations* 15 (2012) at 813.

12   Richard E Mayer and Roxana Moreno, "Nine Ways to Reduce Cognitive Load in Multimedia Learning," *Educational Psychologist* 38 (2003) at 43. The practice of giving evidence to the jury for use in deliberation is

generally not followed in civil-law countries where juries are used. The principle of orality tends to mean that the only evidence juries may consider is what they hear during the trial.

13   Jenna Burrell, "Evaluating Shared Access: Social Equality and the Circulation of Mobile Phones in Rural Uganda," *Journal of Computer Mediated Communication* 15 (2010) at 230.

14   Irina Verenikina and Lisa Kervin, "iPads, Digital Play and Preschoolers," *He Kupu* 2 (2011) at 4.

15   Debora M Kagohara et al., "Using iPods and iPads in Teaching Programs for Individuals with Developmental Disabilities: A Systematic Review," *Research in Developmental Disabilities* 34 (2013) at 147.

16   Joselina Cheng, "Flipping an MIS Class with Mobile Technology: An Examination of the Effects of the Use of iPads on Student Learning Outcomes and Satisfaction with Learning," *Journal of Research in Business Information Systems* 6:6 (2013) at 27.

17   Julian Smith, "Apps for Apes: Orang-utans want iPads for Christmas," *New Scientist* 212 (2011) at 69.

18   Kassandra Barnes, Raymond C Marateo and S Pixy Ferris, "Teaching and Learning with the Net Generation," *Innovate Article* 3:4 (2007) at 1.

19   Doug Reid and Nathaniel Ostashewski "iPads and Digital Storytelling: Successes and Challenges With Classroom Implementation," in *Proceedings of E-Learn: World Conference on E-Learning in Corporate, Government, Healthcare, and Higher Education 2011*, ed. Curtis Ho and Meng-Fen Grace Lin (Chesapeake, VA: Association for the Advancement of Computing in Education [AACE], 2011) at 1661.

20   Kevin S Douglas, David R Lyon and James R P Ogloff, "The Impact of Graphic Photographic Evidence on Mock Jurors' Decisions in a Murder Trial: Probative or Prejudicial?," *Law and Human Behavior* 21 (1997) at 485.

21   Helen Cole and Danaë Stanton, "Designing Mobile Technologies to Support Co-Present Collaboration," *Personal and Ubiquitous Computing* 7 (2003) at 365; Johan Eliasson et al., "Mobile Devices as Support Rather than Distraction for Mobile Learners: Evaluating Guidelines for Design," *International Journal of Mobile and Blended Learning* [IJMBL] 3 (2011) at 1.

22   J S Rijnbout, and B M McKimmie, "Deviance in group decision making: Group member centrality alleviates negative consequences for the group," *European Journal of Social Psychology* 42 (2012):915–923.

23   Verlin B Hinsz, R Scott Tindale and David A Vollrath, "The Emerging Conceptualization of Groups as Information Processors," *Psychological Bulletin* 121 (1997) at 43; Julian Seifert et al., "MobiSurf: Improving Co-Located Collaboration through Integrating Mobile Devices and Interactive Surfaces," in *Proceedings of the 2012 ACM International Conference on Interactive Tabletops and Surfaces*, ed. Orit Shaer et al. (New York, NY: Association of Somputing Machinery, 2012) at 51;

Katherine Vogt et al., "Co-located Collaborative Sensemaking on a Large High-Resolution Display with Multiple Input Devices" in *Proceedings of the 13th IFIP TC 13 National Conference: Human-Computer Interaction-INTERACT 2011, Part IV,* ed. Pedro Campos et al. (New York, NY: Springer, 2011) at 589.

24 Bertrand Schneider and Chia Shen, "Enhancing Tabletops: Multi-Surface Environments for Collaborative Learning," paper delivered at the *9th International Conference of the Learning Sciences (ICLS 2010)* [unpublished].

25 Stéphanie Buisine et al., "How Do Interactive Tabletop Systems Influence Collaboration?," *Comput Hum Behav* 28 (2012) at 49; Yvonne Rogers and Siân Lindley, "Collaborating Around Vertical and Horizontal Large Interactive Displays: Which Way is Best?," *Interacting with Computers* 16 (2004) at 1133.

26 D Stanton and H R Neale, "The Effects of Multiple Mice on Children's Talk and Interaction," *Journal of Computer Assisted Learning* 19 (2003) at 229.

27 Kathy Ryall et al., "Exploring the Effects of Group Size and Table Size on Interactions with Tabletop Shared-Display Groupware," in *Proceedings of the 2004 ACM Conference on Computer Supported Cooperative Work,* ed. Jim Herbsleb and Gary Olson (New York, NY: Association for Computing Machinery, 2004) at 284.

28 For a subsequent analysis using jurors drawn from a real jury pool, more realistic research materials and a larger sample, see Laura W McDonald, David Tait, Karen Gelb, Meredith Rossner, and Blake M. McKimmie. "Digital evidence in the jury room: The impact of mobile technology on the jury." *Current Issues Crim. Just.* 27 (2015) at 179.

PART III

TOWARD NEW
PROCEDURAL MODELS?

Continuity and Technological Change in Justice Delivery

Fabien Gélinas .

The speed at which technology has been changing the way we do things in many fields of human activity has been nothing short of astonishing. This great potential for change observed in technology once appeared to hold the promise of rejuvenating justice. To many of us, the adoption of new technology seemed the obvious course that would quickly generate new models and lead us to achieve cost- and time-effective justice delivery, the course, in other words, that would lead us to the Holy Grail of access to justice. This techno-utopian view was understandable at the time when computers first made their way into law firms and then into courtrooms. Programmes aimed at improving access to justice, such as small claims courts and legal aid, had already been implemented in many jurisdictions and deemed insufficient. The seemingly intractable problem of access to justice would finally find a solution in eAccess.

With hindsight, all agree that the practices, norms, and assumptions of justice delivery proved more resistant to change than had been anticipated. Without denying the enormous long-term potential of eAccess to justice, the chapters in this section take a step back from the techno-utopian view to reflect upon the extraordinarily complex web of values, norms, and practices that support our systems of justice. Change is difficult because law's function is in part to resist it, and because the values that underpin justice delivery are always in tension, and interwoven with norms and practices whose slow evolution is not always easy to grasp. These themes are addressed from the stand-points of sociology, political theory, and legal theory by Pierre Noreau, Daniel Weinstock, and Clément Camion, and taken up in two case studies by Katia Balbino de Carvalho Ferreira and Xandra Kramer, respectively on Brazil's and the European Union's e-justice initiatives. These illustrate both the potential and the challenges of top-down regulatory interventions in the complex web of values, norms, and practices found in large multi-jurisdictional entities.

Continuity and Incommensurability

One obvious reason for law's resistance to change is the legal profession's ingrained conservatism, which, as observed in several of the chapters in this section, is linked to the function of law as a "stabilizer" of social relations, and the pursuit of the core value of "predictability" through which it notably achieves this function. One of the ways in which law ensures predictability is by pursuing normative coherence. This means that no change to an element of the existing legal corpus can be made without a consideration of the corpus as a whole. Another way in which law nurtures predictability is by relying on procedure, or "secondary rules," to resolve disputes. If substantive agreement is not within reach, resolution under law can nevertheless be achieved through established and authoritative procedures, which in turn will generate normative clarifications that improve predictability for third parties. The resort to procedure also induces notions of due process that, in time, take on a fundamental importance, as is constitutionally recognized in many contexts. Those are fairly obvious reasons why the legal profession naturally balks at the prospect of change in general and why, in particular, the renewal of procedural models proves such a formidable task.

In his very significant contribution to this section of the book, Pierre Noreau, drawing on resources from the field of sociology, invites us to reflect upon the broader and deeper reasons for resistance to change in highly institutionalized settings. To this end, he proposes a highly textured model comprising three levels of social action that range from the symbolic to the instrumental: the abstract "referential" level of social values and world views; the middle level of norms; and the practical level of ways of actually engaging in social action. The model is not specific to change in legal relations but offers a useful reminder of the interrelation between the three levels and how they combine to erect tightly interwoven barriers to change. This reminder is very helpful in multiple ways and particularly in the identification and analysis of a mistake commonly made in attempts at introducing change, which consists in focusing on the normative level of action without paying attention to practices and the values in which norms are embedded. Deliberate attempts to introduce technology in legal processes without consideration of the values and practices of the legal profession are thus bound to fail. This conclusion has, of course, already been borne out by experience in many jurisdictions.

A further layer of difficulty and complexity in the introduction of change, which Daniel Weinstock usefully highlights in his contribution, is the fact that the values found at the referential, or symbolic, level are very often in tension rather than harmony. Therefore, even when taking account of the referential level, and when deliberately pursuing a value, such as equality, one can easily run afoul of another referential value and thus jeopardize a fragile equilibrium attained incrementally and not necessarily consciously through practices. As Weinstock concludes, any human institution must "try to balance a large number of values that are sometimes related in complicated ways" and "there is no algorithm to identify the right way to perform such balancing."

Weinstock's conclusion provides a good explanation for the historical insight, which Noreau points to, that important social change appears easier to achieve when brought "wholesale," that is, when a situation of crisis allows for the blanket rejection of social institutions and a purported replacement of the entire referential baggage, a major paradigm shift. As Noreau himself acknowledges, however, these "meta" crises, or revolutionary situations, are rare. And even when they do occur, the strong tendency of social actors has been to place new references within the frame provided by discarded references, and to follow well-established patterns of interaction where possible. The American Revolution provides a telling illustration of this phenomenon. The resulting constitution looks as though—and is often presented as if—it created a new order from whole cloth, when in reality, the bulk of legal relations and practices continued to be governed by the unwritten rules of the common law inherited from the old imperial regime. Change, even drastic change, must find some ground in existing, and ongoing, social practices, norms, and references.

Rule of Law, Private Harmony, and Efficiency

The paradigm shift that Noreau would welcome—if only the conditions were ripe for "revolutionary" change—would move, in his words, from "juridical truth and authority" to "party autonomy and a continuous adjustment of expectations and practices." As Clément Camion explains in his contribution, however, one should give serious consideration not only to what one might wish for, but also to what may be lost if the wish came true. The change in paradigm from "juridical truth and authority" to "party autonomy and a continuous adjustment of expectations and practices" outlined by Noreau appears to track very closely what the new Quebec *Code of Civil Procedure* aims to achieve: justice redefined as the ability to resolve one's disputes privately, at one's own cost, and without undue expectations or insistence as to the vindication of one's legal rights. This stance has been referred to, time and again, as the promotion of a culture of harmony. Although this may appear to many as the "conciliatory" way of the future, it bears mention that it has also been the way of the past. The fourth Qing emperor of China, Kangxi, is well-known for his application of Confucian principles of harmony to the question of civil justice. He recognized that there would be too much litigation if people were not afraid of the law courts and so made clear by way of edict his desire that "those who have recourse to the tribunals should be treated without any pity and in such a manner that they shall be disgusted with the law and tremble to appear before a magistrate."[1] In this manner, he continued, "good citizens who may have difficulties among themselves will settle them like brothers by referring to the arbitration of some old man or the mayor of the commune" and, as for "those who are troublesome, obstinate and quarrelsome, let them be ruined in the law courts."[2] The provisions of the new Quebec code seem at least compatible with this striking picture conjured up from the past. It is worth asking, however, what exactly is missing from the picture.

Clément Camion explains that what could go missing in a drastic move toward private justice is the contribution of the justice system, or the resolution of disputes, to the rule of law. To those who are not quite prepared to discard the rule of law as a "primitive" stage of social organization,[3] the loss matters a great deal. Camion points to the "positive externality" of public litigation: "during public adjudication, legal norms (both procedural and substantive) are articulated for future reference in the process of resolving disputes." Katia Balbino de Carvalho Ferreira, in her contribution to this section, likewise highlights the social importance of precedent and the promise of greater transparency in this respect offered by technology. When dispute resolution goes private, by contrast, "there is no 'public norm,' substantive or procedural, that is articulated and published for the benefit of third parties or society in general."[4] Perhaps more importantly, as Camion also explains, it is difficult to see how law's ability to meet "the fundamental human need to stabilize expectations" could survive if "juridical truth and authority" were to give way entirely to "party autonomy and a continuous adjustment of expectations and practices." No one takes issue with the immense difficulty attendant upon the project of providing a reliable and accessible enforcement of the legitimate *ex ante* expectations arising from laws and contracts; but no one, to my knowledge, has come up with a credible alternative to the rule of law as a basis for social organization. Thankfully, as Noreau acknowledges, the contextual conditions for the paradigm to shift away from rule-of-law references are unlikely to be met, and legislative attempts in that general direction are unlikely to have much impact, at least in the short term.

eAccess, Awareness, and Value Balancing

For Camion, information technology is an opportunity for bridging the knowledge gap that prevents both access to justice and a greater measure of dispute prevention. Instead of incessantly discussing efficiency in terms of costs, delays, and backlogs, and systematically ignoring the valuable contribution of litigation to the rule of law as well as the myriad other values fostered by a justice system, we should perhaps take more seriously the potential to bring about greater legal awareness and education. This potential has increased tremendously with information technology and certainly holds the promise of reducing the legal-knowledge gap that has plagued many access-to-justice initiatives.

In respect of the further uses of technology in legal proceedings, all are optimistic about the positive impact of their adoption, notably in the massive jurisdictional contexts of the European Union and Brazil, which are both addressed in this section. In her contribution, Katia Balbino de Carvalho Ferreira, with the benefit of her experience as a Brazilian federal judge, presents the integration of technology as an imperative, as well as an opportunity to expand the actual social reach of the justice system. Xandra Kramer, in her contribution, is also optimistic about the potential of technology to improve access to justice in the European space. She is mindful, however, of the risk, to the quality of both justice processes and results, inherent in the pursuit of efficiency. In his contribution, Weinstock also shows optimism but warns about the possible indirect consequences of every change in our practices, rightly insisting that the impact on the different values of the system should be borne in mind at every step. The contributions from the field, in Europe and Brazil, also provide a glimpse of the considerable difficulties of integrating technology in highly complex, multilevel judicial organizations and federal contexts.

Xandra E. Kramer's contribution, which provides a very useful high-level view of the main European initiatives regarding integration of technology and the cross-border difficulties they address, is particularly interesting in its consideration of procedural risk. Apart from the risk relating to the multiple languages used in the European Union, she looks at the tricky management of the relationship between geographically distant dispute resolution initiatives and the values of due process embedded in the European human rights instruments. Concerning the European small claims procedure, she explains that the hearing is in principle to be conducted in writing, and that an oral hearing is to be held only if it is considered "to be necessary or if a party so requests." This is a standard position seen in many contexts. The relevant regulation goes further, however, by stating that the party's request for an oral hearing can be refused if it is "obviously not necessary for the fair conduct of the proceedings." This is a noteworthy attempt at suggesting a "practicable" interpretation of the provisions guaranteeing the right to be heard. It is this kind of value-balancing exercise that is at the core of the socio-legal mediation needed to make technology work in the context of justice delivery.

There is consensus among the authors who contributed to this section about the importance of being alive to the complex web of values, norms, and practices that support our systems of justice. Change is difficult because law's function is in part to resist it, and because the values that underpin justice delivery are always in tension. These values are also intertwined with norms and practices that are constantly mediated and interpreted through human interactions, and which are therefore difficult to read. The chapters in this section give us a valuable framework for thinking, with the required sophistication, about legal change in general, and in particular about change brought by information technology to civil justice and its accessibility.

Notes

1   See Tahirih V Lee, *Contract, Guanxi, and Dispute Resolution in China* (London: Routledge, 1997) at 97; see also Jeffrey C Kinkley, *Chinese Justice, the Fiction: Law and Literature in Modern China* (Chicago: Stanford University Press, 2000) at 106.

2   Kinkley, *supra* note 1.

3   A Hong Kong barrister is famously reported to have told author Jerome A. Cohen, "The trouble with you Westerners, is that you've never got beyond that primitive stage you call the 'rule of law.' You're all preoccupied with the 'rule of law.' China has always known that law is not enough to govern a society" (Jerome A Cohen, *The Criminal Process in the People's Republic of China, 1949-63: An Introduction* [Boston: Harvard University Press, 1968] at 4). Note that the comment was made in the context of a discussion about the criminal justice system.

4   This point was famously made in Owen Fiss, "Against Settlement," *Yale L J* 93 (1983-84) at 1073.

CHAPTER IX

The Old...and the New? Elements for a General Theory of Institutional Change: The Case of Paperless Justice

Pierre Noreau

Demain ça s'dit ben. Aujourd'hui c'est du déjà dit
Hier, y'a pu rien à faire, Vaut mieux faire c'qu'on peut
'Vec c'qu'on peut faire[1]

The inevitable effects of the digital revolution have been heralded as being just around the corner in the field of law. Yet law is one of the only spheres that still resists the integration of new technologies even though these technologies have completely changed the landscape in a wide range of public service sectors: health care, education, and public transit, among many others.

We have to acknowledge that revolutions are rare. They are generally compelled by necessity, practical requirements, or whim. The reasons for such upheavals are enshrined afterward. They are drawn from this or that work that no one had read...or that everyone had criticized. Once these reasons become a reality, proponents, believing it is impossible to turn back (which is a cardinal virtue of rupture), claim to have "done the right thing" for the "right reason," forgetting that there exist three other possibilities in this matrix.

However, grand ideas struggle against existing habits, as there are never any ideas or standards more clear than those already to be found in custom.[2] This customary nature makes them all the more persuasive.

How can we explain that, on the institutional level, innovations take such a long time to go beyond prophecy? This question raises the broader issue of social change, a problem that has been the focus of a current of contemporary sociology. Through it runs a subtextual consideration of how to spur individuals, groups, and institutions to action. In the specific context of the use of new technologies in the field of law, such resistance to change has been especially clear. Twenty years ago, in Quebec, judges of the various courts still did not have access to personal computers. Even today, paper remains the primary vector for legal communication.

The problem posed by the computerization of legal services lies in the need for shared action that engages all stakeholders in the system in a specific initiative. For example, the simple service of documents accompanying the initiation or progression of legal action supposes that all of the entities concerned agree on that system of information exchange and the technology that makes it possible: digitalization of documents in a recognized format, use of a given mode or platform for transmitting and sharing files (a kind of digital court clerk), sharing of equivalent computer skills, and such. With respect to procedure, it is inevitable that there will be questions about the legal impact of new practices. However, all of the above shows mainly that any form of social innovation sooner or later requires a form of collective commitment.

This commitment is all the more necessary when it is a response to practical needs and unanimously censured problems, in particular with respect to waiting times and costs of the justice system. The advent of digital technology in the legal field takes place amid opposing institutional, financial, and strategic interests such that, on the practical level, the common good may conflict with the interests of various stakeholders.

Yet the problem of opposing interests is only one manifestation, among others, of a broader problem concerning the difficulties involved in reforming highly institutionalized fields, such as justice.[3] The radical transformation of large systems has always raised the problem of motivating stakeholders who are affected and constrained by such change. Lenin complained about the working class's inability to gain awareness of its collective interest and to take action to its own advantage.[4] Machiavelli identified the same difficulty in imposing any change at all on institutions: "the innovator has for enemies all those who have done well under the old conditions, and lukewarm defenders in those who may do well under the new."[5] Contemporary political sociology has studied individuals' intransigence with respect to collective reforms that would nonetheless improve their personal condition: "This logic is fortified at the individual level by the twofold observation that…his or her personal contribution will hardly affect the chances of obtaining the collective good and that the conduct adopted, in whatever direction, will probably go unnoticed."[6] It follows that no stakeholder involved feels a duty to take initiative without the support of exclusive incentives, in other words, specific advantages from which he or she could directly (and often personally) benefit.[7]

Analysis of how stakeholders think is an avenue of study often surveyed by theorists of change, and it remains one of the most fruitful approaches in contemporary sociology. However, the present text shall instead explore change from a more process-related perspective. What I mean by this is that I will study opposing effects, as well as reference points, norms, and mechanisms, that have the consequence of improving or limiting the chances that change will occur or that there will be evolution in ideas, structures, or social practices. While this does not make it possible to predict the way a society, institution, or simple organization may change, it provides a structure for the analysis of these processes. This text suggests elements of an inductive theory of institutional change. The introduction of technological innovations in legal activities will be used here as a laboratory. As illustrations, I will also use other examples from the recent history of the justice system or taken from everyday life. However, this is an ambitious project, and its goals will only be partly met. In the end, this paper offers only a general hypothesis (a model), the heuristic value of which remains to be shown. Thus, for now, aspects of the theory are evoked rather than demonstrated.

Innovations and the Scope of Social Change: Three Levels

Within any *field of social action*, changes involve both symbolic and instrumental dimensions.[8] The symbolic dimension refers to systems of ideas that are shared by members of the group, to reference ideologies, and to vectors of meaning: ritualized practices, allegories and emblems, beliefs and common knowledge, principles with ontological or self-referential authority, et cetera. The instrumental dimension refers, in contrast, to concrete or structural forms of action based on "practical reasons" that normally justify them: habits that are complementary and predictable, constant conjunction of cause and effect, shared common sense supporting a set of "naturalized," in other words self-evident, practices.

The stabilization of social relations depends largely on the constancy of these symbolic and instrumental references. Thus, practices and habits, and the symbolic meanings on which they are based, reinforce one another. Within a stable community, interpersonal relations essentially transit through these symbolic and instrumental conventions. Both are thus reified in society. They are generally relayed on the institutional level by a series of incentive-creating or imperative norms: rules and systems that control practices and principles that support them. These norms are the enshrinement within a society of a certain state of social relations, and they support established forms of socialization and their social meaning. For this reason, they can be obstacles to any practical or cultural innovation that could challenge them, and therefore, they play a conservative role.

On the analytical level, and to facilitate analysis, we can therefore identify three levels of action: referential (essentially symbolic), normative (institutional), and practical (organizational) relationships.[9] The referential level is the most heavily laden with meaning, while the organizational level is more concerned with the instrumental level and refers to relational and material imperatives directly related to actions. Between these two extremes, the normative (institutional) level refers to the structure of formal (and positive) norms that enshrine and bind, from a legal perspective, the form and meaning of social action within the group, community, or society studied. The normative level is consequently a conduit for and link between the symbolic and instrumental dimensions of action (Table 1).

Table 1: Level of Action of Instrumental and Symbolic Dimensions

	+ + Symbolic Dimensions	− − Instrumental Dimensions
Referential Normative Practical	↓	↑
	− − Symbolic Dimensions	+ + Instrumental Dimensions

Naturally, these three levels of action are related in complementary ways, and their mutual integration is the very condition for their stability within a given institution. This is a portrait of a highly institutionalized social field. At the same time, changes that can be experienced on any of these levels of action (no matter what the source) necessarily create dissonance with the other levels. The internal reworking of practices and meanings that such changes can require within the established community can then have many different outcomes depending on whether the changes are transposed in a positive way to the other levels of action, whether their expressions and (practical or symbolic) consequences are purely and simply rejected, or whether the changes are adapted in some way into the frameworks of practices, norms, and thought recognized by the members of the institution. In the latter case, innovations would be completely reinterpreted by stakeholders within already recognized, legitimized parameters. In any case, we can suppose that the more smoothly an innovation can integrate into established practical, normative, and symbolic categories, the more likely it is to easily penetrate the various levels of institutional action. This idea is the foundation for our general hypothesis. Two more specific hypotheses conclude this text.

Another variable in question concerns the cultural and social (referential), institutional (normative), and organizational (practical) *context* in which change can occur. It is likely that some contexts are more conducive than others to changes in practices, norms, and dominant ideas: political crises, chronic dissatisfaction regarding courts, severe dysfunctionality of an institution, or major incompatibility between the institution's norms, practices, or claimed purposes and its real operation. Such contextual conditions can challenge the equilibrium of systems that have become too "frozen," that have lost their reason for being, or whose historical legitimacy that can no longer be justified or is no longer seen as self-evident. Some theorists have pointed out the cycles that go along with social movements and that tend to explain the periodical predisposition of stakeholders in a system toward change.[10] Here, we will discuss the effects of context, but we will focus more on the interplay of opposing processes that limit, block, or permit change within stable institutions.

Our goal is to provide a framework for analysis of the conditions for stabilization and change within highly institutionalized fields of action. By proposing a distinction between the (self-)referential, normative, and practical dimensions of action, the typology used here highlights the different levels of action through which we can study the conditions that determine how an institution becomes stable or changes. Their purpose is therefore essentially analytic, given that these levels of action could be intellectualized or defined otherwise.

For the purpose of this analysis, properly speaking, there is no necessary distinction between innovations flowing from social or cultural change and those that could be born from changes in technology or techniques since, in the final analysis, technological changes are conditions for change that are ultimately social. Our intention is also to point out that such changes can be supported by cultural and therefore symbolic changes. Thus, we can assume that, no matter what form of technological change is envisaged, its chances of penetrating the field of practical action are not based purely on function but more broadly on normative and cultural issues, for the reasons of consistency and dissonance explained above. The proposed model is of general scope and can be used to identify salient points in any reform of practices, norms, and categories of action in highly institutionalized fields of action beyond the legal system. Backtracking, in order to provide further details about the preceding in the specific framework of the legal system, we will first study the (symbolic and instrumental) dimensions at stake in each level of action.

The Referential Level of Action

This is the level that is most heavily symbolically laden. Every field of social action is based on ideas, world views, ideologies, and values that, although broadly shared with other fields over the course of the same period, are embodied in ways specific to each individual institution.[11]

All major change in the systems of thought of a community of action is equivalent to a change in its social program. It is inevitable that such transformations, which are probably relatively unusual, modify the balance or meaning of the norms and practices of the institutions that such transformations penetrate. At the least, they make it difficult to maintain previous frames of reference. For example, in Quebec, the government's assumption of responsibility for education occurred at the same time as the religious framework of reference was wearing out, and the Church was consequently finding it difficult to maintain its grasp on public education. It was inevitable that this change in frame of reference would have consequences for the values, norms, and practices of educational institutions. This upheaval in social ideas would also have equivalent effects on higher education and, beyond the educational milieu, on healthcare institutions, social security systems, criteria for acknowledging established authority, and practices in all these areas of action at once. In short, paradigm shifts inevitably lead to major (and sometimes swift) changes in all related levels of action. We then witness change in the criteria that anchor "normality." However, these developments often occur in conjunction with the replacement of established social frameworks, such as in the example mentioned above, in which the Church was replaced by the state, and the clergy by the public service.

These upheavals can be of different scope, and affect some spheres of social activity rather than others. For example, in the area of scientific research, Thomas Kuhn provides a good explanation of how paradigm changes occur when the number of incompatibilities between hypotheses and facts becomes so great as to generate a crisis with respect to the trust that, until then, was placed in the explanatory capacity of previous theories. Thus, it seems that crisis plays a major role in the emergence of new theories. As Kuhn says,

> So long as the tools a paradigm supplies continue to prove capable of solving the problems it defines, science moves fastest and penetrates most deeply through confident employment of those tools. The reason is clear. As in manufacture so in science—retooling is an extravagance to be reserved for the occasion that demands it. The significance of crises is the indication they provide that an occasion for retooling has arrived.[12]

Indeed, these "shifts" frequently pave the way for deeper changes. There is rarely an intermediate state between conceptions of the world that are too different in terms of their foundations.[13] The established paradigm is then overthrown and gives way to alternative paradigms. This movement has consequences on all levels of institutional action.

The scope of these upheavals explains why they systematically clash with the power of inertia, if not the immobility of many components of the institution. At the very least, this situation explains why overturning terms and ideologies is so difficult to envisage. We can suppose that this difficulty rings even truer within older institutions. Indeed, the older the principle on which one claims such institutions are established, the more highly it is venerated. Within institutions where levels of action are very interlocked, any change in norms and practices, if not habits, is quickly treated as a challenge to superior principles that have been more or less enshrined. This difficulty arises especially in the legal system, which often likes to trace its origins back to the Roman Empire. Its foundations then become difficult to challenge, unless we are willing to admit that principles established 2,000 years ago have lost all relevance.

One of the difficulties that accompanies paradigm changes is related to the fact that ways of thinking (ideologies and systems of ideas) that support and give meaning to the action of an institution always have many components, each structured in relation to the others, so that it is difficult to challenge only one but not the whole. In law and justice, 500 years of political philosophy strengthen the meaning and central nature of these same principles, and this is not counting the work invested by the courts themselves in justifying their own actions. Changing the system of reference (the paradigm) thus amounts to trading one "sacred history" for another.

This is especially the case in law and justice. Paradoxically, the legitimacy of the institution is traditional (in the Weberian sense) and survives on the fringes of the forms of legal-rational legitimacy that it nonetheless guarantees. This is a fact to which attention is rarely drawn. Moreover, in the minds of the majority of citizens, law is above all valued for its normative dimension, in other words, for its moral meaning.[14] Ideals of justice people the collective imagination. Those who embody the judicial institution do not hesitate to reference them, with the help of *palais de justice* (the French term for courthouses, literally "palaces of justice") and officers "of justice." The legal institution is consistent with the prophecy of a world based on the legal equality of those subject to the law and on the impartiality of judges, whose function it is to "carry out justice."[15] It thus finds itself displaying a transcendent character. It has its priests and liturgical dress.[16] Sometimes we speak of *temples de la justice* ("temples of justice").[17] It has its own iconography: the gavel, tablets of the laws, and scales of justice held out by a blindfolded Themis...who also serves as enforcer, with sword in hand. To all of this is added a lexicon created out of Roman brocade and notions forged in the High Middle Ages, all of which ensures the mystification of the profane. In this institution, a religion is practiced whose constant rituals and antiquated formalism are periodically the subjects of television series.[18] The legitimacy of law thus flows from a form of staging. It carries meaning "in itself."

It is immediately apparent that we will think twice before shaking the columns of such a "temple." Such support from symbols and meanings explains why any innovation would be received with skepticism, if not suspicion, and this is often the case.

When it comes to computerizing justice activities (which is a reform that *a priori* involves very few normative aspects), players hold to these interlocking principles so as to cast doubt on the worth of practices that would nonetheless enable the institution to fulfil the practical requirements of its own mission. Consequently, no change to the system can be seriously envisaged. The introduction and conclusion of the text by Daniel Weinstock provide good illustrations of the neutralizing effects of this process:

> Let us therefore take it for granted that cyberjustice would entail major improvements in access to justice. Instead, I would like to look at the risks that could flow from over use of virtual tools in the legal context. I am beginning with the hypothesis that the *design* of any complex social institution has to take a multitude of values into account, values that are sometimes in tension. While use of virtual platforms may be an improvement in terms of access to justice, does it entail risks in relation to other values that are just as central for legal institutions, risks that could significantly reduce the improvements brought about by the introduction of new technologies?[19]

Any change in instituted practices raises, at all the other levels of action, deep questions about principles, the discussion of which can only cast doubt on the historical, philosophical, and ideological legitimacy of the innovations that one is attempting to inject.[20] From this perspective, a reform of legal and court practices runs the risk of never taking hold if it is not accompanied by ideological or normative justifications that could replace those that currently support the legitimacy of the system. The new *totalizing* discourse should ideally offer a completely new set of values and references able to reverse the direction and dispel the legitimacy of the previous paradigm, which has been based on procedural formalism and supposed symmetry of rights, third-party impartiality, rule of law, and the absolute positivity of standards of reference useful for managing disputes and regulating behaviour.

The principles and categories that could establish a new global discourse on justice are thus meaningless unless they impose a complete overturning of accepted reference points. The former discourse on justice would then vanish, leaving only an aftertaste of dust and broken promises. In its most radical form, and for the purposes of this exercise, such an upheaval would require, for example, establishing competition between opposing principles: autonomy rather than authority, or peacemaking rather than social order.[21] In the best of cases, the new paradigm has to build another world of reference points that render the established discourse obsolete (meaningless if not non-signifying). Thus, at the time of Galileo, one of the greatest difficulties that the theologians faced was to know whether the moon was a star, whether it was inhabited, and, if so, how the inhabitants could be descended from Adam and Eve.[22]

Many of these upheavals are based on the idea of social reappropriation of justice. Such reappropriation would directly benefit from the integration of digital technologies into justice: digital mediation platforms and diversification of digital means of dispute resolution, electronic court offices, accessible dockets, videoconferencing, access to clear, user-friendly legal standards by internet, email subpoenas and appearances, self-representation using digital technology, and so on. These are all practices that could reduce legal costs, naturally, but above all they make law something other than a monopoly in the hands of specialists. This re-establishes the meaning of law as a common good, if not as an everyday, public activity. However, all of this requires replacing one symbolic system (that of the truth of law and authority) with another: the autonomy of choice and constant adjustment of expectations and practices.

This form of upheaval in reference points is described in the text by Clément Camion,[23] who suggests that the notion of justice be made considerably broader. However, it is immediately clear what kind of a change in categories of reference such an exercise would require.

Because it presupposes reworking the very ideas that are the foundations of judicial activities, such an upheaval in the criteria underlying the justice system requires redefining what guarantees the legitimacy of the institution, and, by extension, that of its best-established and most ritualized practices. Thus, it does not suffice to replace one promise of justice with another.

In any case, such a shift in ideas inevitably opens up space for experimentation that can test other practices, other ideas, and other forms of authority, which are themselves based on criteria of legitimacy different from those that were, until then, taken as certain. A period of destabilization will follow, which soon creates nostalgia for the stability of the preceding period.

The question is whether such a complete upheaval in reference points is indispensable to the reform of public institutions (in this case, legal institutions), even though it would, at least in theory, facilitate the reform. In a frozen system, can we change something without having to change everything…at all levels of action? *A priori*, this necessity seems inevitable. Yet it is a point of view that we will temper below. For now, we have to accept that such a change in perspective can occur only in the *context* of almost total upheaval of established reference points and that it probably cannot occur unless there is redefinition of the very meaning of social life and the function of institutions. The upheaval would probably have effects in all areas of action (beginning with institutions), from our relationship with the environment to the relationship between men and women, parents and children, merchants and consumers, politicians and citizens, and so on.

Yet, such upheavals can occur only in revolutionary contexts or during social and political crises that are so deep that they require and justify a drastic change in collective and institutional living conditions.[24] In such cases, we speak of a *fluid political context*.[25]

Aside from such often unforeseeable (or at least unforeseen) contexts, established paradigms have every chance of enduring and of reinforcing established norms and practices. This said, aside from the fact that these revolutionary contexts are unusual, history teaches us that the objective conditions that accompany such major changes are rarely strictly ideological. For example, the French Revolution is probably easier to explain by the economic conditions of the period (the famous price of bread on July 14, 1789) than by the ideals promoted by the Enlightenment, even though those ideals gave direction to and provided a historical interpretation of the action. In any case, it is inevitable that such a movement toward de-institutionalization be followed by a strong movement toward re-institutionalization. Indeed, the enshrinement of a new "sacred history" and the stabilization of new standards (i.e., new norms) and new practices fulfil an ongoing need for establishing forms of socialization.[26] Table 2 provides a summary of these considerations.

Table 2: Change and Stability Factors for Collective Reference Points

Referential Level of Action	Change Factors	Stability Factors
Context	• Tensions and contradictions between social reference points and actual experiences • Upheaval in criteria for institutional legitimacy • Challenges of authority figures • Requirements favouring social reappropriation of justice	• Pacification and stability of social relations • Esteem for public institutions • Legitimacy of established social statuses and authority figures • Consistency between social and institutional systems of reference
Process	• Upheaval in collective priorities and the social program • Fluidity of ideas and social categories (What is justice?) • Existence of competing, known, structured paradigms • Legitimacy of conveyers of competing ideologies	• Preponderance of traditional forms of legitimacy • Inflexibility and complementarity of social categories and ideas • Symbolization and ritualization of community life • Consensus on values in public opinion and within elite groups

Finally, let us recall that if one thing can be learned from major historical changes, it is how robust established categories, practices, and reference points are. As I have already noted, in these matters "the dead seize the living." Sometimes after having been promoted in new terms, emergent principles are retranslated into the former terminology before they have had the chance to exist on their own. When this happens, what had been rejected returns. Perhaps this is the only way that social innovations can make a sustainable mark in the framework of highly institutionalized social fields such as justice. This will be the subject of the conclusion of the present text.

The Normative Level of Action

The ideas and systems of meaning that are the foundations for justice as understood in legal theory and political philosophy (meanings that partly determine social expectations) cannot be translated into material or relational terms except within a specific normative framework.

This refers to a set of more or less formalized norms that establish the frameworks for action in which the practical activities of stakeholders in a given field take place.[27] Immediate examples include constitutional, legislative, and regulatory provisions that establish the content of positive law. Legality becomes a marker for legitimacy and, by extension, at least on the institutional level, legality becomes the very criterion for legitimacy.

However, these frameworks themselves involve the projection of normativity, resulting from an extension of primary normativity and expressed in the form of objective constraints at all levels of action. For the justice system, this refers to the set of rules required to regulate relationships among stakeholders in the field. What is in question is thus not so much shared practices or habits but rather known references that those to whom the rules apply can use: the practical rules of the various courts of justice, norms drawn from case law and gradually acknowledged by the courts, the division of legal practice into different professional areas, the distribution of institutional and jurisdictional functions (in particular the balancing of interactions between judges and practitioners), the court schedule, performance indicators, codes of professional deontology, tables of legal fees (where applicable), and the breakdown of roles relating to the various functions of the justice system (security, court office personnel, bailiffs, prothonotaries, justices of the peace, judges, etc.).

In these cases, normativity acts as an obstacle to change, as we have already said. By fixing the legal categories of action, such obstacles stabilize, through time, the accepted, predictable forms taken by activities in the field. This *standardization* institutionalizes stakeholders' practices. Compliance is ensured through specific bodies, including tribunals and courts with specific jurisdictions; professional orders; management and discipline committees; and specialized institutions (e.g., detention centres and penitentiaries) with specific resources, whether public (linked to the state's governing functions) or private, especially within professional corporations (bar associations, chambers of judicial officers, etc.).

Once established, these norms (which include all of the reference points considered as constraining by stakeholders in the field, whether those reference points have been stated or not[28]) impose a framework for action situated halfway between symbolic foundations and concrete practices. Indeed, all institutionalized fields of action have specific borders corresponding to the characteristics of a legal "system" or "order," depending on the theory chosen.[29] In all cases, a specific regulatory space is established, designed to apply to equally specific stakeholders. This is especially the case of judicial activity. This said, healthcare and educational institutions work in the same way, and are also structured around specific, stable forms of normativity. By making forms of action objective, the translation into norms of these shared practices fixes reference points that are imperative for stakeholders in the field but also for social observers who are not part of the field. As such, this translation institutionalizes the reference points by fostering social legitimization of the action both inside and outside the field of action itself.

Every field of action is haunted by its own process of becoming frozen. This slide toward formalism is even more obvious in highly institutionalized fields of action. Since each system evolves through a series of sedimentary layers, the normative reference points of each system constantly become more complex. Complexification is part of the evolution of all stable fields of action and gives rise to four considerations.

The first lies in *the weight of previous norms* in relation to subsequent norms. All new norms (if they do not amend the old ones) have to be based on already established norms, even when the functionality of the older norms is becoming increasingly uncertain. On the level of its meaning, a norm's long history often gives it symbolic strength that confers pre-eminence. It is thus inevitable that, over a long period, norms that are introduced have to take into account the prior nature and thus precedence of already established norms. It follows that, even when they become obsolete, such ancient norms survive "in the hollows" of all the mechanisms in which their precedence has been taken into account. Prior normative choices thus impose themselves on later norms and over-determine the latter's content. By backtracking, we sometimes find that a norm's meaning is dependent on another that has disappeared.

The *second* consideration is related to the social and ideological conditions that inevitably preside over the establishment of a norm of any kind. If we take into account the fact that most norms are not designed to establish abstract principles but rather to solve practical problems, it is inescapable that rules defined within a system will be *marked by historical, cultural, financial, or organizational conditions existing at the time of their establishment.* It again follows that there is a form of hegemony of origins from which the system can no longer break away and which determines a general direction that is difficult to correct. Each norm retains the marks of the reasons that justified its definition. The difficulty comes from the fact that the legal shaping of the world is essentially a "conservative" activity. It always enshrines standards that were given precedence over others at a certain point in social history, by perpetuating them.[30] The tendency for stakeholders in a highly institutionalized field is therefore to give established norms intrinsic worth, since stability of action is generally considered a good in itself. This is the postulate that establishes the entire systemic analysis. The stability of a system is a condition for its own functionality and, at the same time enshrines its closure and, by extension, its confinement.[31] As initial significations—and original meanings—gradually wear away, and as practical justifications are lost to the mists of time, norms come to have no meaning other than the intrinsic value that we give to their stability. They thus become absorbed into their symbolic function alone. Paradoxically, their imagined worth far exceeds their use, and replacing them with another norm becomes all the more difficult. This tendency makes the replacement of long-established norms by other norms extremely unpredictable, even when the new norms are designed to solve very concrete problems encountered by stakeholders at the practical level of action. For example, in court, the principle of adversarial debate is still considered valid in itself, even though it is not always certain that it is conducive to discovering the truth. This question arises in particular with respect to expert witnesses.

Third, the *stratified normative* structure of highly institutionalized fields fosters constant complexification of their areas of action. The complexification generates problems entirely specific to stakeholders in the field and bodies responsible for regulating the field. For example, in justice, certain innovations are blocked by considerations that would surprise those less familiar with the subtleties of legal normativity. The Quebec bar association long opposed family mediation because it feared losing part of its monopoly over family law. Its arguments against such mediation included appealing to the deontological rule that a lawyer can represent only one party at a time. Developments have shown that this makes sense only in the context of disputes between spouses, which is precisely what family mediation is designed to prevent. Thus, the way the field evolves tends to entail that emergent problems are increasingly the fruits of the system's own complexity. The system has to deal with problems it creates for itself, so that new norms are designed above all to solve problems created by earlier norms. This is the simplest definition that can be given of what Teubner calls legal autopoiesis.[32] This inward-looking arrangement is clearly not conducive to the integration of other referential norms, in particular because they would require complete recalibration of the initial normativity. Since rules are interpreted in light of one another, it is inevitable that this inter-normative dynamic would make it even more difficult to integrate foreign standards into the system. We thereby avoid a form of normative reworking and, by extension, de-institutionalization of the field. Normativity's conservative function is thus confirmed.

Finally, although it establishes the "normal" forms of action, the statement of norms nonetheless constitutes, for stakeholders in the field, a space for discussion of the conditions for their practices and interactions. Despite the imperative scope of many institutionalized rules, the normative level of action provides a space for negotiation involving a number of components of the system. The negotiation space also circumscribes the acknowledged players in the field. Thus, normativity sets the scene for a form of institutional mediation between interests, the legitimacy of which is later recognized at the practical level of action. It establishes the conditions that guarantee the appropriation of the field by a set number of agents who mutually recognize one another. Hermeneutic analysis explains the interplay involving the interpretation of normativity in function of the necessities and characteristics of the action, so that the norms are often used as a framework for deliberation on the expectations of stakeholders in the field and the innovations that can be accepted.[33] It is thus inevitable that such normativity is consistent with the crystallized interests of such agents and enshrines their power relationships. It follows that normativity, notwithstanding the claim of stability that ensures its continuity, is often the product of ongoing renegotiation among stakeholders in the field. This shapes the "political dimension" of institutional normativity.

However, this latitude is not infinite, and therefore, the normative level of action remains fundamentally a moderating structure, and norms remain reproduction mechanisms. Thus, unless there is a major change in ideas or practices, this level of action's function is to resist any innovation that could challenge the consistency of what it circumscribes. This is particularly the case when the suggested innovations come from outside the field of action in question. There is a *limit of compatibility* beyond which the established norm resists change. The resistance can go so far as to marginalize or exclude certain innovations from the domain of legitimate practices. We can suppose that the more foreign the proposals are to stakeholders, the less likely they are to be integrated with ease. This is especially the case within fields of action with highly integrated, complementary components, as we see in judicial action. It follows that only practical necessity can foster a possible change (or re-interpretation of the content) of norms, especially if the necessity is supported by a change in social reference points or a compulsory change in practices, itself brought about by generalized change in social practices.[34]

With respect to integrating the advances offered by digital technology into legal activities, the same difficulties arise as those entailed by renegotiating the norms for the operation of the justice system as a whole. Technological changes do not have the normative neutrality that they are often ascribed, which is why we speak of "technical standards." As norms, they have to complement all of the normative standards recognized in the system. Consequently, introducing such norms gives rise to the same difficulties that accompany the addition or replacement of any legal norm. Even today, computerization of court files does not encounter many obstacles in the form of technical operating difficulties; rather, obstacles are due to the fact that computerization makes available sensitive information that used to be difficult to access. It thus violates a tacit rule in favour of a form of discretion regarding personal information contained in such files. The possibilities offered by technological advances thus have to be adjusted to the explicit or tacit norms that already govern justice activities.

As we have said, choosing a technical standard inevitably imposes a norm with universal scope on a broad set of stakeholders. We have shown above that normativity is also a space of ongoing negotiation in which the interests of those involved are at stake. The texts by Kramer as well as by Balbino de Carvalho Ferreira describe the difficulties that such negotiated choices suppose in large institutional groups, as is the case in the European Union and Brazil, where players from a number of jurisdictions clash as they are forced to come to agreements on the choice of technical norms and conditions for integrating them. Consequently, we have to take into account the fundamentally normative nature of the technology, whether the normativity is intrinsic to the standard chosen by the stakeholders in the system or associated with shifts in meaning that it imposes on various established legal norms. In all cases, this tension explains the special difficulty surrounding the integration of digital technologies into fields of action that are highly institutionalized and therefore subject to strong normative structures.

Again, the *effects of context* can favour or block a normative reform. This is in the case, in particular, when reinterpretation of a norm that was, until that time, well established requires that we recalibrate the meanings of many other norms. However, we can suppose that the resistance of peripheral norms can lead to *a minima* integration of new reference points, so as to reduce the need to perform complete normative rebalancing in the field. Thus, the latest reform of the Quebec *Code of Civil Procedure* (*Code*) in favour of more systematic recourse to "private dispute prevention and resolution" provides, in article 1, that "Parties must consider private prevention and resolution processes before referring their dispute to the courts." Naturally, it follows that such alternative dispute resolution does not interfere throughout legal proceedings, once they have been put in motion. Similarly, the *settlement conferences* that used to be integrated within the *Code* remain optional and are circumscribed by certain specific provisions. In consequence, all of these normative adjustments remain marginal in relation to the general conduct of proceedings and the system of normativity applicable within the field. Table 3 provides a reminder of some of the contextual and procedural conditions for normative change and stability.

This said, there is nothing to prevent such a normative upheaval from being favoured by a major adjustment of social practices and ideas (concerning the entire society in question as new generations become players) or an institutional crisis on a public scale—or that systematically blocks the norm-governed operation of the institution. The inventory of the many present dysfunctions of the judicial system tends however to show that even in the face of striking disorganization of all of a system's functionalities, the reference normativity continues to preserve forms of action and their formal legitimacy. Moreover, it manages to do so despite erosion of confidence in the courts, the tendency for individuals to self-represent, long waiting times inconsistent with the requirements of fairness (especially when the parties do not have equal resources), systematic monopolization of court time by commercial companies and public institutions, escalating use of expert testimony, failure to recover awards obtained through class action proceedings, lack of access to evidence in pending proceedings through dockets, lack of credible statistics on courts, the inability of most bar association members to earn a living from judicial activities, criticism concerning the way judges are appointed at the federal level, et cetera.

Table 3: Change and Stability Factors for Normative Reference Points

Normative Level of Action	Change Factors	Stability Factors
Context	• Development of a new criterion for normative legitimacy • Challenge to the normative effectiveness of a standard • Systematic contradictions among established norms • Dissatisfaction of a major stakeholder with respect to established norms • Change in power relations among stakeholders in the field	• Reduction of normativity to its symbolic dimension • Complete freezing of the field and reduction of its activity with respect to its own normativity (ritualization) • Continuity of the financial or cultural conditions that are the foundations for the established normativity • Stability of the players and the power relations internal to the field, and mutual neutralization of initiatives
Process	• Ongoing negotiation concerning the shared meaning of norms • Integration of a norm that is "compatible" with the others • Capacity of a new norm to change the balance of the normative whole • External imposition of another normativity	• Precedence of prior norms over new norms • Survival of established norms after they have become obsolete • Incapacity of new norms to impose themselves without requiring recalibration of established norms • Strong normative integration of the symbolic and practical dimensions of action

This shows the strength of law. Once articulated, the norm takes the place of the truth, or at least of abstract consensus on conditions for practice, despite all the evidence. Legal normativity thus often resists need, and it is inevitable that by becoming immured in this way, it places limits on the integration of many social and technical innovations into the everyday activities of the courts.

The Organizational and Practical Level of Action

There is a Chinese proverb that says one cannot look at the stars when there is a nail through one's shoe. This can be interpreted in many different ways, but the principle remains the same: practical contingencies can defeat any inspiration. Above all, the proverb reminds us that we cannot escape the tyranny of habits and of material, financial, and relational constraints on action—in short, the instrumental dimensions of action. They nail us to the ground. These are precisely the constraints that govern the practical (organizational) level of legal activity: model forms and legal documents, the nature of equipment and facilities, interactive computerized platforms (or their absence), methods of filing documents, the ergonomics of the location, et cetera. Here, we are speaking of the empirical aspects of legal activities and stakeholders' practical responses to logistical and normative constraints placed on their activity. The practical level of action acts as infrastructure for the referential level of action that provides its justification. We can also think of normative consensus that governs the way such constraints are taken into account. This is "materialization" of legal normativity.[35] Internalization of these norms and constraints by stakeholders is supported by a series of *practical reasons*, in other words, reasons that come to be seen as obvious and that justify existing forms of behaviour and conventions that are recognized in a field.[36] These are "forms of socialization" in the sense defined by the sociologist Georg Simmel,[37] and they are understood here as the standardized forms taken by interactions between players engaged in an ongoing relationship in a specific field of social activity. These forms of socialization determine the arrangement and conditions of sustainable exchange. They produce and guarantee a degree of stability of action, which makes behaviour predictable. Each social field thus establishes a space of mutual recognition and socialization: we can tell who belongs and who does not. This can be seen in the difference in treatment received by those who are represented in court and those who self-represent. The judge uses different titles (*Maître* or Counsellor, versus Mr. or Ms.), which distinguish those who belong to the system from those who do not.[38]

In the end, standardization of exchanges is conducive to making relations systematically routine. It ensures that expectations and initiatives become objective and framed in procedure. Naturally, there are disadvantages to such gradual stabilization of practices.

Simmel considers it to be a *tragedy of culture* that, in complex societies, individuals have a propensity to reduce their relations to formal conventions imposed upon them by the milieu. This limits the chances that these forms of socialization will be given new content. New forms of socialization that could favour ongoing changes in social life periodically appear in every field of action. Yet, if there is no constant tension between new and old forms of socialization, these same social relations risk turning gradually into habits. Established routine thus carries its own justification within itself. It confines practices to ritualization and does not aim to provide active functionality but rather formal necessity. Thus, it is only very recently that we have been able to eliminate the compulsory use of "legal-sized" paper in procedure, although this possibility may still be provided. The instrumental dimension of action is at once absorbed into its symbolic dimension: the permanence of paper.[39]

The immense savings that society draws from having many different forms of socialization (i.e., standardization of practices) flow from the possibility given to each individual to interact with a growing number of individuals in a depersonalized manner; in other words, without having to challenge one's own personality, feelings, or inner life. As we have already said, each milieu generates its own *forms of socialization*. This is the case in particular of the legal world, where what is at stake is not only integration of the rules imposed by the normative level of action but also the shaping of the attitudes, reflexes, and habits specific to the field of action where those practices are recognized. This explains why legal practitioners treat their entrance into the profession as a form of initiation. The internalization of these formalized reference points and "naturalized" reflexes accentuates the establishment of a "being-together" characteristic of each field of action. Here, the justice system is only one especially typical example of tendencies encountered in nearly every institution.[40] These tendencies often make specialized fields look esoteric to those who are excluded from them.[41] The very respect for forms and conventions ends up gaining value in itself. Moreover, the permanence of established forms gains the value of a "constant" in the social equation. This tendency can be seen everywhere. For example, although today the majority of men and women do not smoke, most of the shirts they wear continue to have a pocket which is the right size for a pack of cigarettes, and we are in consequence called upon to use it for something else, such as for carrying a pen, a cell phone, or business cards.[42]

The effects of this formalization (of this respect for form) are themselves strengthened by the complementarity and *automatic* nature of established practices. Replaying the same sequences of actions creates extraordinary savings in terms of thought and initiative. Once proceedings are launched, what follows can be read like a musical score. These tendencies have been seen in the criminal justice system but also in civil proceedings.[43]

At this level of action, habits and forms of socialization are directly associated with other imperatives of practice: division of labour, the structure and hierarchy of relationships in litigation firms (articling students, junior and senior associates, and partners), the financial structure of the office and the business model, the nature of relations between clients and professionals, and so on. Consequently, formalized practices and stakeholders' interests are associated with the same "organizational culture." However, this culture is anchored in a field of material constraints that strengthen one another. Thus, management of financial and human resources is intertwined with stakes concerning the implementation of social innovations. The difficulties in implementing settlement conferences can thus be explained partly by reluctance to have judges intervene very early in cases that "would in any case settle themselves long before they went to court." Implementation of this practice thus faced the obstacle of essentially financial imperatives introduced under the cover of "good administration of justice."

On the level of mutual adjustment of practices, the same problems arise in the justice system as at the referential and normative levels of action: adjustment and interlocking of reference points, practices, and habits. Practices, which are parts of series or refer to one another, structure a whole that is difficult to change. Judicial action is first and foremost built on stakeholders' mutual expectations, then on a system of action from which it becomes difficult to depart without voluntarily placing oneself out of the game. On the sociological level, shared practices are vectors for real social interactions. Thus, except in cases of marginal practices that can complement, without compromising, already accepted activities, consistency of action is inevitably required and protects the legal field from any radical innovation.

In short, a new practice is all the more likely to become effectively integrated within the repertoire of forms of established action if it can do so without causing any clashes. This brings to mind the way word processing has replaced typing and dictaphones have replaced stenography. They rapidly fit into the niche already established by practice. By contrast, a new practice may require complete retooling of ways of doing things. Such a practice can manage to impose itself only out of necessity, which makes it imperative that a large part of the repertoire of accepted practices can "theoretically" be modified. However, we know of very few cases likely to lead to such a change. For example, in courts of justice, despite the rapid development of televisual communication technologies in social spaces (Skype, videoconferencing, etc.), hearings are still conducted in the presence of the parties and witnesses.[44] In the context of a pilot project conducted in the judicial district of Longueuil, Quebec, the simple use of the telephone to notify the parties of the filing of an application initiating proceedings was considered a veritable innovation in case management. The year was 2010, and the project was able to advance only within the framework of a written protocol between the Court of Québec and the regional bar association. As we have said, the practical dimensions of action are identified by their material nature. Thus, the need to adapt spaces, schedules, budgets, human resources, and means of communication often slows innovation. Many innovations thus become "impossible to implement."[45]

Can we hope that a change at the normative level of action would be able to generate changes on the level of day-to-day practices? A study of the legal system is especially revealing in this respect. Justice is just one field of action that is not entirely in control of its normativity. Unlike certain self-regulated systems (e.g., small organizations, whether they are private or have a social purpose), some of the legal field's normativity is defined by the legislator. The series of amendments to the Quebec *Code of Civil Procedure* provides ample demonstration of the difficulty of imposing true changes regarding established legal practices "from the top," even when such change is set out in legislation. Indeed, the new provisions just recently adopted concerning abuse of procedure are still systematically evaded today. Judges and practitioners continue to refer to the body of case law and to prior concepts that the *Code of Civil Procedure* was very explicitly designed to replace: the notion of "colour of right," for example, still counts in such cases, despite the opposite presumption provided for in the *Code*.[46] Once again, the dead seizes the living. It is a syndrome along the lines of that experienced by people who have lost an arm or leg but still feel its presence and injury. As Machiavelli says, "while the laws of a city are altered to suit its circumstances, its institutions rarely or never change; whence it results that the introduction of new laws is of no avail, because the institutions, remaining unchanged, corrupt them."[47]

On the level of practical action, as on the normative level, formalism has often been a cemetery for social innovation. For example, regarding divorce, the constraints imposed on ex-spouses have never gone beyond the obligation to be informed that there are family-mediation services supported by the Minister of Justice. In order to evade this obligation, practitioners send their clients to attend an information session just before instituting the proceedings in question. Once a "pink passport" (in other words, the document showing that the client has indeed attended the session) has been obtained, the proceedings can go forward as usual since the legal obligations have been formally met. Likewise, it is probable that the provisions of the new *Code* concerning mediation and settlement will fail due to professional habits and reflexes characteristic of legal practice, despite strong calls for a *change in legal culture*.[48] A model clause added at the end of every demand letter will probably suffice to evade the application of measures favouring forms of private dispute prevention and resolution. Thus, the practices that we believed we could amend will be perpetuated.

However are some *contexts* more favourable than others to changes to deeply frozen or highly ritualized practices? In the most highly institutionalized fields, such as the public sphere and the legal system, the problem arises in the same terms as in a major company. As we have said a number of times, it is the interlocking of ideological references and systems of ideas, norms, and practices that makes it difficult to introduce new categories and practices. Sometimes the tensions that arise between the different levels of institutional action consolidate the *status quo* instead of fostering change. This is the case in particular when the consistency of a level of action is sufficient to resist changes that would seek to impose a different action. Thus, a return to square one is often a necessary condition for maintaining a degree of institutional peace (Table 4).

At the practical level of action, as we have said, all innovations are confronted with the tyranny of habit. We can once again suppose that these constraints cannot be avoided except when stakeholders' interests are directly related to the innovations that one is attempting to introduce. The advantages promised by innovations then establish a consensus based on practical, material, financial, or relational necessities. Once again, the most certain changes are based on necessity. In most organizations, no one is persuaded to change the accounting or computer system until its support service says it will no longer be providing updates. The change then occurs on the basis of a constraint that cannot be avoided.

Table 4: Change and Stability Factors for Practical Reference Points

Practical Level of Action	Change Factors	Stability Factors
Context	• Proven inefficiency of the legal system (delays, etc.) • Discrediting of archaic practices in justice system • Challenge of the personal and institutional costs of justice • Denunciation of difficulties inherent to the system: proceedings dropped, self-representation, etc.	• Effective access to civil and family justice at appropriate cost • Public expression of approval of judicial activities and judges' roles • High media visibility of cases consistent with public opinion • Positive outcomes of proceedings involving parties of disproportionate size
Process	• Integration of non-intrusive innovations • Response to specific shared (functional or financial) needs • Rebalancing of all practices in the field • Injection of specific resources for implementing the innovation	• Rejection of innovations threatening the balance of established practices • Functional distortion of innovating practices • Incorporation of innovating practices into the established judicial trajectory • Marginalization of innovations with respect to the usual organizational process

Other changes can occur if the advantages of the new practice are such that it would be irrational to do without it. However, even when stakeholders have a "common" interest in changing their practices, that interest has to meet the needs of each stakeholder in order to avoid mutual neutralization of those interests. In a zero-sum game, it is to each individual's advantage to avoid paying for a change that, initially, benefits other "players." However, such a change supposes that all the stakeholders in the field are in favour of it. As we noted above, new practices are more difficult to institute when "the innovator has for enemies all those who have done well under the old conditions." In such cases, any major stakeholder has the power to stop all the others from adopting the change. This situation has constantly slowed the rate of change in the justice system. The subdivision of functions (and balance of powers) among judges, practitioners, and the other organized stakeholders in the legal world (departments of justice, public security, court office personnel, courthouse administration) has often defeated ideas that could change power relations or simply the habits and interests of a given stakeholder. It follows that none of them feel they have the power to impose anything on the others. For example, community settings (NGOs) and initiatives regarding alternative and restorative justice (in criminal proceedings) have systematically remained on the margins of the justice system, whereas these "resources" have rapidly become recognized in the healthcare and social services systems.[49] Justice is a closed system.

However, we have to acknowledge that certain *contexts* are more favourable than others to the development, recognition, and integration of social and technological innovations. Over the course of the last 30 years, the creation of legal aid and the development of a special jurisdiction for small claims, the establishment of class action proceedings, and the recognition of family mediation have changed the landscape of justice from time to time, at least on the level of practices. However, we have to note that, in all cases, these innovations have been duplicates of practices and structures that have been experimented with elsewhere for decades. Moreover, all of these innovations have had the benefit of major financial investment in their establishment, so that they could be integrated without asking anything of existing stakeholders. These two conditions are characteristic of the instrumental dimensions that dominate the practical level of action. We also have to observe that, once integrated into the justice system, these innovations have taken already existing paths or have been developed at the margins of the system.

Nonetheless, some conditions are more conducive than others to experimenting with new practices. This is an issue we will discuss in the last part of this text. Thus, the redeployment of resources by the Quebec government—a context favourable to innovation in terms of reference points, norms, and practices—fostered a number of major changes in social activity in a very large number of fields. On this topic, Pierre Moscovici has spoken of contexts through which a norm of originality flows, more conducive to experimentation. Since such contexts are unusual, we have to identify the conditions for ongoing change within highly institutionalized systems, such as the legal system. Only by taking these avenues into account can we get around institutional obstacles of the kind often encountered in the justice system, in particular with respect to digital re-engineering of legal activities.

Innovation in Institutions: The Art of "Working With What We Have"

Once again, Machiavelli's words are germane:

> But since old institutions must either be reformed all at once, as soon as they are seen to be no longer expedient, or else gradually, as the imperfection of each is recognized, I say that each of these two courses is all but impossible.[50]

It does not follow that reform is impossible. Machiavelli's remark refers to two possible avenues for change: *total* or *partial*. We have already shown that *total* change makes sense only in contexts where reference points, norms, and practices are dissolved. Even in the relatively rare cases where change seems to have helped to advance history, we cannot avoid a reflexive return to old categories of reference. We have also already shown that the tyranny of instituted forms does not spare changes of much lesser scope. Thus, the conditions for the advent of these changes are probably much more important to the integration of new institutional practices than the simple fact that they are innovations. Fashionability is rarely sufficient unto itself.

The format of this text does not allow a systematic exploration of the various forms and strategies that could favour the spread of innovations and their integration into the repertoire of instituted practices. At most, we can simply mention a number of avenues that make such integration possible.

As a sub-hypothesis, in continuity with the preceding paragraphs, we can suppose that an innovation is all the more likely to occur in a highly institutionalized field if it begins by changing stakeholders' habits rather than their ideas or reference categories and norms. The latter changes would follow changes in practices rather than precede them. We would then be acting directly on the practical level of action; in other words, on the very level of organization where action becomes concrete and brings into play direct interactions among stakeholders in the field.

A second sub-hypothesis drawn from considerations discussed here also suggests that these innovations are all the more likely to take root if they mobilize the proponents of change and the stakeholders in the field in complementary ways. The next part of this text focuses mainly on these conditions. We will thus discuss two internal processes that favour the institutionalization of new social practices: the strategy of vectors and the strategies of absorption and retailoring. The former concerns the initiators of innovations and the latter, the receiving stakeholders.

The Strategy of Vectors of Change

Study of past reforms tends to show that the modernization of a highly institutionalized social milieu depends on the ability of proponents to present the innovation in forms that are already recognized in the system. This is the hypothesis of *vectors of change*.[51] This strategy can take different paths. Here we will explore a few. The principle is very simple: social and technological innovations are all the more likely to be included in the repertoire of recognized practices in justice if they take familiar forms of socialization.

Aside from the effects of context, of which we have already spoken, some factors are obviously likely to favour the institutional integration or absorption of a social or technological innovation. In all cases, such innovations have to be advocated by a certain number of stakeholders in the institution. Naturally, they can be inspired by initiatives that have appeared or were developed at the fringes of the system. Likewise, for reasons specific to the practical level of action, the cost of accessing and implementing such innovations has to be reduced to a minimum. This is especially true if the innovations take on known forms of action or temporarily duplicate those forms until they replace them.

There are many historical examples of these effects of form. In Paris, the plastic brooms used by streetcleaners look like the twig brooms used in the nineteenth century. The first automobiles were essentially horse carts with motors, and the first fridges were ice boxes in which the ice compartment had been replaced by a compressor.

Justice practices inspired by digital technology have a reasonable chance of taking hold only if they involve a simple transposition of established forms of socialization. For example, while electronic service of proceedings has a reasonable chance of rapidly becoming established as a new procedural standard, this is less the case for online dispute resolution platforms, which are much more likely to remain on the margins of the institution specifically because they directly challenge current legal practices. Similarly, the establishment of digital dockets and electronic registries will have more chance of crossing the threshold and becoming legal practices if they reproduce the categories and reference points imposed by the former paper methods: docket number in function of district and jurisdiction, cases filed according to parties' names, and so on. In contrast, use of new ergonomics or a different division of content (even though this would be possible using digital means) would be likely to slow down their implementation. Thus, the fact that computers were able to cross the border into office technology in less than a decade at the end of the twentieth century is partly because computer keyboards have the same key configuration as nineteenth-century typewriters. Yet the purpose of that configuration was mainly to limit the speed of typing and prevent the hammers from jamming when they were struck simultaneously. Still today, the iPhone uses the QWERTY keyboard in North America and the AZERTY keyboard in France, even though most users write their texts "with two thumbs" and do not know the origin of their keyboard.[52]

This strategy can take several different paths. The simplest is a series of "small lateral steps." For example, the establishment of an electronic registry (and filing of evidence using electronic means) is much easier to envision if most of the proceedings are already written in digital form and easy to file in PDF format. Filing them through an electronic registry would require only one more small lateral step. Likewise, the development of a publicly accessible digital docket, which would make all case materials available, is, in relation to electronic filing, only another small lateral step. In one of the texts included in this work, Kramer says that electronic sending of legal documents is all the easier to imagine if it requires only a shift from one mode of transmission to another.

Evidently, even at the most instrumentalized level of action, these changes always have symbolic dimensions. Maintaining lexical conventions is one of the constraints involved. In contrast, using categories inspired or suggested by the computer industry is probably the worst way to foster change. Re-using everyday lexical forms with which the stakeholders in the field identify is more consistent with the small-lateral-step strategy. The integration of computer technology into legal institutions then becomes only a variation on an activity, and the activity loses none of the meaning that it had in the framework of a given procedural sequence. Whether it is sent by email, fax, bailiff, or registered mail, a subpoena remains a subpoena.

In short, a new practice is more likely to be integrated within a judicial institution if it is already part of the personal habits of the stakeholders in the field. Widespread use of the communication platform offered by Skype has, in all likelihood, had more impact on the use of videoconferencing in court than all the pleas in favour of a digital revolution in justice. Here again, the small-lateral-step strategy seems best, and it is immediately apparent what role is played by the gradual succession of generations. Similarly, on the level of argumentation, the fact that administrative courts already generally use these communication technologies demonstrates their "transferability" within civil and criminal jurisdictions. Their institutional legitimacy is now virtually a given. Thus, justice simply imitates itself. In contrast, there is no worse discourse than that of *digital prophecy*, foretelling a complete reconfiguration of our categories of thought and action.[53] As we have said, the same applies to a new prophecy that would propose *in abstracto* a complete upheaval in the foundations of "judicial" justice. Future changes at least require, first, personal, daily appropriation.

This appropriation concerns not only the stakeholders in the justice system, but also non-stakeholder individuals who have to play a role within the system, as is the case of those who self-represent in court.[54] Regarding these individuals, it is not certain that we have to cite the "digital divide" and unequal level of "numeracy" as sources of unfair access to justice, at least in a society where 86% of households have internet access.[55] In contrast, 80% of Quebecers consider that they do not have access to the courts.[56] It is thus reasonable to suppose that internet platforms designed to assist individuals dealing with legal problems will probably facilitate such access. It is at least doubtful that these means of access would suddenly become the cause of additional unfairness, as Daniel Weinstock seems to suggest in this work. All things being equal, the illiteracy rate is probably a much greater barrier to access to justice than the unequal level of individuals' numeracy. In this vein, the diversity of habits and forms of communication offered by computerization is probably a solution to the problem posed by the large proportion of functionally illiterate people in our societies.[57]

Finally, coming back more specifically to traditional actors in the justice system, it is reasonable to consider that any change in practice will find better support within innovative environments than in the fringes among those most allergic to innovation. This notion of innovative environment, defined in a very broad way, encompasses many different things, depending on whether we are referring to technological, economic, or regional development. Some characteristics of these environments are, however, often noted: the proximity of actors associated with the innovation of practices; special relationships between those involved in practical operations and those doing basic and applied research (essentially academia); and development of new practical conditions for action in a controlled, consensual framework, which is generally a presupposition of experimental and pilot projects. Here also, integration of and experimentation with practices will be easiest when they are likely to draw upon the established skills of the new generation of legal experts (practitioners, judges, clerks, etc.).

Retailoring Strategies

Innovations suggested in a highly institutionalized field of action must not only be proposed in a pragmatic way but must also be relayed by players in the field. We are referring directly to the ability of these actors to "retailor" these innovations to their advantage. Here, we are returning to the concrete dimensions of the action as it can be envisaged, entirely enveloped in financial, material, and relational considerations.

Here again, the small-lateral-step strategy is most likely to facilitate deployment of an innovation. At least it makes the actions less costly and risky. By any standards, innovations are probably easier to integrate into a field of practice if every actor sees them as advantageous in terms of costs and benefits, whether on the level of profitability (more instrumental) or reputation (more symbolic). The notion of "retailoring" refers to integration of the categories and practices associated with innovations into actors' daily activities at the lowest cost possible.

This integration may be in response to the need to cover judicial practices with the trappings of modernity. The ongoing association of justice with archaic forms of procedure is probably more useful in films than in the contemporary reality of those who have to use the courts. The cost of photocopying briefs filed at the Court of Appeal or the Supreme Court alone is sufficient to persuade any client of the virtues of a USB key.[58] However, this is assuming that the lawyers acting as counsel do not base part of their revenue on the difference between the real cost of a photocopy and the fee charged to the client for making it. In any case, it is probable that, sooner or later, the legitimacy of justice will suffer from the nostalgic image in which it is clothed.[59] On another, very empirical scale, a change in practice will be all the more likely to be integrated into the field in a positive way if it meets (or, at least, does not interfere with meeting) the material, financial, and relational needs in question, and if it does not place the actors who subscribe to it at a disadvantage in relation to those who continue to resist the innovation. Indeed, the change has to provide the actor who uses the innovation with an empirical advantage until the innovation is "naturalized."

On the level of action, these practical innovations are all the more likely to become included in the repertoire of actions if they can be remodelled to fit into the framework of established practices. We can therefore speak of a form of colonization of innovation by instituted practices. For example, the pre-court mediation practices promoted by the provisions of the new Quebec *Code of Civil Procedure* are all the more likely to be integrated into the practical field if they can be used strategically by players (in particular to draw out or shorten the length of proceedings). In this sense, the concerns raised by Weinstock on the risk of a strategic takeover of new digital technologies do not take into account that such calculations are intrinsic parts of social activity and inevitable responses to the constraints imposed by each field of practice. Naturally, this can be turned into a question of applied ethics, but can it be avoided, and is it not the case that practitioners already "strategically" exploit the current malfunctions of the archaic justice system? Since retailoring these innovations is a condition for their acceptance into the repertoire of practices (and constraints) in the field, the strategic use that practitioners and judges are likely to make of them is a condition for their integration into the institution.

Finally, we cannot exclude the symbolic weight associated with judicial practices themselves, even though this is a dimension that is more incidental at the practical level of action, where we are now situated. However, we can wonder if retailoring a number of socially valued practices and transposing them on the level of judicial action is not the most efficient way to bring justice into the digital age. After all, the essential rites maintained by the Catholic Church have benefited from retailoring older practices, essentially of "pagan" inspiration. There is nothing to prevent judicial ritualization from doing the same. For example, the various courts of Quebec have just recently permitted the use of Twitter in court, in response to repeated requests by the media.[60] In short, we have to question judicial reception of the most ordinary digital social practices and, by extension, the conditions presiding over gradual renewal of the repertoire of judicial practices "from the bottom up," under the pressure of new technologies.

In a nutshell, any innovation has to find a clear part to play in the pre-established system of interests in the field of action into which it is meant to be integrated. Combined with a strategic approach to vectors of change, recourse to the interests of stakeholders in the field and to their ability to colonize the innovating practices is probably one of the conditions that makes the integration of innovations into the institution most certain. Therefore, identifying the normative and referential conditions for such integration is more likely to follow this move toward integration than to precede it. This is, at least, the hypothesis of change through social practices that the present text puts forth, even if it means that the conditions for a broader collective movement should also be explored, while avoiding the supposition that ideas always precede action, which is probably only the case over much longer periods than those we are studying here.

Conclusion: Change Through Transformation of Practices

Between change as an idea (at all levels of action at the same time) and the practice of change (the practical reduction of innovations) we find the conditions for reform of public institutions, or at least of highly institutionalized fields of action. In the context of previous work on healthcare reforms, we have shown that, regarding front-line services, the development of family medicine clinics preceded their promotion (based on the symbolism of relationships between doctors and patients) and translation into law. Thus, practices evolved before philosophical justifications and the normative frameworks that later provided support for them. Naturally, these movements occurred soon after one another, but this was thanks to the rapid reactions of political actors and government legal specialists. In fact, the parameters of this reform were first experimented with and adopted by actors in the field themselves (in other words, at the level of action) before becoming the subjects of change on the normative and symbolic, or referential levels of actions. Developed in response to practical needs, these innovations later benefitted from being invested with meaning. Similarly, the first theoretical work on the future of mediation and settlement practices also benefitted from broad practical experience with those innovations and from their empirical endorsement.[61]

We can thus speak of "bottom to top" change, if not of "induced" change. When all is said and done, even with regard to technological innovation, it is less the digital revolution that establishes the parameters of our collective life than the conditions of its resurgence in our society.

> *Demain ça s'dit ben. Aujourd'hui c'est du déjà dit*
> *Hier, y'a pu rien à faire, Vaut mieux faire c'qu'on peut*
> *'Vec c'qu'on peut faire*

> U.F.O., Plume et Cassonade

This paper was originally written in French. Thanks go to Mary Baker and to Emily Grant for the translation.

Notes

1 Lyrics from U.F.O., by Plume et Cassonade. "Tomorrow, it sounds good. Today, it's already been talked about. Yesterday, there's nothing we can do about it. It's best to do what we can with what we can do." [Our translation.]

2 These intuitions can already be found in the works of Portalis and Montesquieu. See Jean-Étienne-Marie Portalis, "Discours préliminaire sur le projet de Code civil," in *Écrits et discours juridiques et politiques,* (Presses universitaires d'Aix-Marseille, 1988), at 21–34 and Montesquieu, *The Spirit of the Laws,* Book 1, § 3.

3   Pascale Laborier, Pierre Noreau, Marc Rioux and Guy Rocher, *Les réformes en santé et en justice: le droit et la gouvernance* (Québec City: PUL, 2008), 286 pages.

4   Lenin, *What is to be Done?*, online: <https://www.marxists.org/archive/lenin/works/1901/witbd/index.htm>, at 347–530.

5   Machiavelli, *The Prince*, online: <https://www.gutenberg.org/files/1232/1232-h/1232-h.htm>.

6   Charles Tilly, "Individualisme, mobilisation et action collective," in *Sur l'individualisme*, eds. Pierre Birnbaum and Jean Leca (Paris: Presses de la Fondation nationale des sciences politiques, 1986), at 247. [Our translation.]

7   Mancus Olson, *The Logic of Collective Action* (Cambridge, MA: Harvard University Press, 1965), at 76–87.

8   This text has been inspired by general sociology. It borrows from many different sources. For example, I have used the notion of *field of action* relatively freely. Pierre Bourdieu employs a much more specific definition of this notion. From a closely related perspective, Norbert Élias uses instead the notion of *social configuration*. I am referring generally to a network made up of interactions linking social actors in a stable, complementary manner. The interactions determine a set of specific relationships that are empirically observable. In this text, this is especially related to consequences of institutionalization of social fields, in Berger and Luhmann's sense. Classical sociology has often used the notion of *institution* to designate stable sets of relationships and activities. This is a notion that is also used here. The concept of institution has often been associated with the idea of a structured society sure of its permanence. The same goes for the notion of *system*, which I also use as an equivalent. In the sense employed here, a system or institution (let us think of the justice system) is nothing more than a field of action that is especially well integrated. It can be said to be highly institutionalized. It follows that change is more difficult to institute within it than in new fields that are still developing. In such a field of action, institutionalization has been acquired. This does not mean that change is impossible. That is the subject of this article. Here, we approach such change based on an analysis of different *levels of action*. Similar theoretical approaches can be found in the work of Talcott Parsons and Alain Touraine, whose ideas have inspired me.

9   Although they are named differently here for the purposes of this article, these three levels correspond on the theoretical level to the three levels of institutionalization defined in an older text. They refer, respectively (and in a more dynamic way), to self-referential, instituting, and identity processes. See Pierre Noreau, "Comment la législation est-elle

possible? Objectivation et subjectivation du lien social," *McGill Law Journal* 47:1 (November 2001): 195–236. The main purpose of the terms used in the present text is to show the analytical utility of these three levels of analysis for studying conditions for stabilization and change in a field of action that is already highly institutionalized: the legal system. These texts are complementary, but their respective purposes should be kept in mind when reading them.

10 Albert O. Hirshman, *Bonheur privé, action publique* (Paris: Fayard, coll. Pluriel, 2013), 258 pages.

11 Thus, the certainty of a special relationship between humans and the gods, the existence of a certain order in the world, or that one has a predestined fate clearly guides the actions of members of a community in ways different from that of a community based on belief in non-determination of personal life and the collective promotion of the values of freedom and individual responsibility, as is generally the case in secularized societies. Different frameworks of reference thus determine equally different systems of justification. They have the potential to penetrate into all aspects of individual and collective action.

12 Thomas S. Kuhn, *The Structure of Scientific Revolutions*, 2d ed. (Chicago: University of Chicago Press, 1970), at 76.

13 As Alexis de Tocqueville reminds us in another context, between two inverse movements, for example, slavery and independence, "il n'y a point d'état intermédiaire qui soit durable" (no intermediate position can last). Alexis De Tocqueville, *De la démocratie en Amérique*, Volume 2 (Paris: Pagnerre, 1848), at 327–328.

14 Pierre Noreau and Pierre-Oliver Bonin, "Devenir juriste: étude sur la socialisation juridique des étudiants en droit" [forthcoming], 30 pages.

15 François Ost, *Dire le droit, faire justice*, (Brussels: Bruylant, coll. Penser le droit, 2012), 210 pages.

16 Antoine Garapon notes that in secularized societies, the judge has in a way replaced the priest: Antoine Garapon, *Bien juger* (Paris: Éditions Odile Jacob, 2001), at 224–225.

17 Association Française pour l'Histoire de la Justice, *La Justice en ses temples: Regards sur l'architecture judiciaire en France*, (Paris: Editions Errance; Poitiers: Éditions Brissaud, 1992), 328 pages.

18 In this book, Daniel Weinstock describes these more symbolic than real dimensions: "In a recent work and a series of articles, Linda Mulcahy put forward the hypothesis that people's feeling of respect for their legal institutions, and the related legitimacy and authority, is partly a function of their architecture. The architecture of courthouses (which are called 'Palais de Justice' in French, something that we should think about!) has always incorporated ideas about the important role of justice in society. At a certain time, according to Mulcahy, the goal was to

reflect the sacred nature of justice in the architecture and location of courts. […] Mulcahy has also expressed reservations about the use of virtual platforms in the context of court proceedings. […] court proceedings are socially important forms of ritual. The introduction of screens that in some cases replace embodied agents could make the proceedings seem less special by allowing people to testify elsewhere than in a highly ritualized space" (Chapter 10, p. 312 of this volume). Along the same lines, see: Louis Émond, "Le jugement entre droit et pédagogie," in *Les cadres théoriques et le droit*, ed. Georges Azzaria, (Cowansville, 2013), at 323–345.

19   Chapter 10, p. 305 of this volume.

20   We find equivalent procedures in literature on the introduction of alternative dispute resolution (ADR). See, for example, Richard Abel, "Conservative Conflict and the Reproduction of Capitalism: The Role of Informal Justice," *International Journal of the Sociology of Law* 9 (1981):245–267, and by the same author, "The Contradictions of Informal Justice," in *The Politics of Informal Justice*, Vol. 1, ed. Richard Abel (London, UK: Academic Press, Inc., 1982), at 267–320. The same goes for the principles of community justice. See Adam Crawford, *The Local Government of Crime: Appeals to Community and Partnerships*. (Oxford: Clarendon Press [Clarendon Studies in Criminology], 1999), 384 pages.

21   We can create many more oppositions, and thereby construct a conception of justice and law very different from the one that the Western world has inherited, by favouring authenticity over mystification, substance over formalism, equality over hierarchy, public service over the institution "in itself," prevention over remedy, support over command, functionality and rationality of solutions over their strict legality, consent over sanction or submission, citizen over "those subject to law," innovation over tradition, transparency of conventions over opacity of concepts and principles, continuity of human relationships over the triumphant rupture of the one who is found to be right, negotiated norms over the arbitrariness of a forgotten rule drawn from a great book of laws, etc.

22   Bertrand Russel, *Religion and Science* (London: Thornton Butterworth, 1935).

23   Chapter 11, pp. 317ff of this volume.

24   Examples of this are armed conflict, a worldwide economic crisis, or a climate or natural disaster. The interplay of generations may favour such shifts, as may public or political exploitation, or collective reaction to a situation that suddenly takes on emblematic or even historical meaning, as was the case in Tunisia during the Arab Spring.

25   Michel Dobry, *Sociologie des crises politiques: la dynamique des mobilisations multisectorielles*, 3rd edition (Paris: Presses des Sciences politiques), first published 1986, 432 pages.

26   Georg Simmel, "Disgression (sic) sur le problème: comment la société est-elle possible?," in *Georg Simmel: la sociologie et l'expérience du monde moderne*, ed. Patrick Watier, (Paris: Méridiens-Klincksieck, 1986), at 26. See also Joachin Israel, "Simmel et quelques problèmes fondamentaux de la connaissance," *Société* 37 (1991):237–240.

27   On the notion of framework of action, see Pierre Lascoumes and Évelyne Serverin, "Le droit comme activité sociale: pour une approche wébérienne des activités juridiques," *Droit et Société* 9:1 (1988):165–187.

28   They are thus considered "rules of the art."

29   On the notion of legal system, see: Michel Van de Kerkove and François Ost, *Le système juridique entre ordre et désordre* (Paris: P.U.F., 1998), 254 pages, and Guy Rocher, "Pour une sociologie des ordres juridiques," *Les Cahiers de droit* 29:1 (1988):91–120.

30   André-Jean Arnaud, "À la recherche d'un statut épistémologique propre," in *Le droit trahi par la sociologie*, ed. André-Jean Arnaud, (Paris: LGDJ [coll. Droit et Société], 1997), at 61–72. The most patent effects of this continuation can be seen above all in the cases of norms established to deal with temporary or context-dependent problems. For example, the provisions concerning civil union, which were adopted in 2002 to get around the problem of same-sex union (recognized in 2004) continue to apply today, and there are over 130 references to them in the *Civil Code of Québec*. All of this is a good illustration of the "continuity" of norms established on a succession of strata. In the same sense, in France, in many towns, household waste is recycled differently depending on whether it is glass (placed in containers at certain intersections) or other recyclable items (plastic, paper, metal), which are all gathered together. This differentiated (and probably more costly) procedure may seem surprising unless we take into account the fact that glass began to be recycled before the other items, and was for a time given precedence over them. Since the established rules and practices concerning glass were maintained, they still justify separate pick-up today, thereby confirming superposition of norms and the tendency of systems to continue temporary solutions even after more encompassing, efficient solutions have been found.

31   Günther Teubner, *Le droit un système autopoïétique* (Paris: PUF (coll. *Les voies du droit*), 1993), 196 pages, and Ost and de Kerkove, ibid.

32   Teubner, ibid. Likewise, regarding legislation understood as a vector of more all-encompassing normativity, most of the legislation that is now enacted by parliaments is designed essentially to amend existing legislation, in other words, to solve problems created by prior versions of laws, and this goes on until the general economics of the legislation in question is lost in the confusion of additions and norms, the purpose of which has been obscured.

33 On ongoing redefinition of the meaning of a norm, read the excellent article by Michelle Cumyn and Mélanie Samson, "La méthode juridique en quête d'identité," in *Les cadres théoriques et le droit*, ed. Georges Azzaria (Cowansville: Éditions Yvon Blais, 2013), at 57–92.

34 As an illustration, we can wonder whether electronic notification of legal proceedings might greatly reduce bailiffs' professional activities, which date back to antiquity. The debates concerning such virtual operations would draw from all levels of action (referential, normative, and practical) to require the maintenance of old, established notification methods.

35 Max Weber, *Le savant et le politique*, translated by Julien Freund, (Paris: Plon, collection « 10/18 », 1959), 183 pages.

36 These notions are borrowed from Pierre Bourdieu, *Raisons pratiques. Sur la théorie de l'action* (Paris: Le Seuil, 1994), 251 pages.

37 Simmel, ibid.

38 J. Macfarlane, *The National Self-Represented Litigants Project: Identifying and Meeting the Needs of Self-Represented Litigants: Final Report*, May 2013, 147 pages.

39 Similarly, exchanges with courts and judges outside of the strict jurisdictional function remained systematically by mail, even when email had long been the norm in other institutional settings. Now electronic communications have become more common within the legal institution, but exchanges nonetheless long involved both mail and digital means simultaneously.

40 Mary Douglas, *How Institutions Think* (Syracuse, N.Y.: Syracuse University Press, 1986).

41 Thus, receiving a court decision often generates different reactions depending on whether we look at public opinion or the assessment by members of the legal community. While criticism sometimes rains down from the side of opinion, legal practitioners are often full of admiration for the way an attorney presented evidence or the judge's skill in managing the case. Examples of this include the cases of Jian Ghomeshi, Guy Turcotte, and Andrée Ruffo.

42 Taking the clothing metaphor all the way, we can wonder what the purpose of neck ties and sleeve buttons is. Their functions are lost in the history of men's haberdashery.

43 Pierre Noreau, Jean Proulx, Serge Brochu, and Gilles Rondeau, "Innovation sociale en matière pénale: du clivage des professions à l'anarchie organisée," in *Le pénal en action. Le point de vue des acteurs*, eds. Guy Lemire, Pierre Noreau, and Claudine Langlois (P.U.L., 2004), at 131–153.

44 Here again, the world of justice does not escape the tyranny of habit, even when it would be advantageous to replace some habits by others, and we end up finding intrinsic virtues in practices that may no longer have the

functionality (or the necessary nature) that they used to have. For example, when analyzing use of videoconferencing in court, Daniel Weinstock supports the presence of the parties and witnesses in court because it facilitates assessment of their credibility and the proximity that it makes possible between the parties and the judge so that "both the guilty and the accusers, can recognize one another mutually as members of the same community." We might be tempted to note that this proximity is in contradiction with the principle that courts must deal with situations, not individuals, and that making such situations objective (rather than personalizing them) is intrinsically associated with the principle of legality. From this perspective, videoconferencing and use of negotiation platforms would, on the contrary, favour depersonalization of cases and make it possible to avoid the risk that, when assessing the facts and the law, the decision maker or third party might take subjective considerations into account. Nonetheless, the stumbling block encountered by these new technologies probably comes from the fact that they require that we replace a form of socialization, which is established, by another, which is not. All justifications are good if they support the status quo.

45   In a different but comparable context, the failure experienced by the inventors of so-called French Revolutionary Time (which was a form of decimal time proposed during the French Revolution, and would have divided the day into ten equal units) can be explained largely by the need to change not only the faces of all existing clocks and watches, but also part of the internal workings of the mechanisms. Online: <https://fr.wikipedia.org/wiki/Temps_décimal> (accessed on April 2, 2016).

46   See in particular this report on the implementation of the new norms concerning SLAPPs, online: <https://www.youtube.com/watch?v=ER6ocRIqwqw> (accessed on March 30, 2016).

47   Machiavelli, *Discourses on the First Decade of Titus Livius,* trans. Ninian Hill Thomson, Book 1, Chapter XVII.

48   Élisabeth Corté, Speech by the Honourable Élisabeth Corte, Chief Justice of the Court of Québec, September 4, 2014, "Cérémonie d'ouverture des tribunaux," 19 pages, online: <http://www.barreaudemontreal.qc.ca/loads/DocumentsActivites/JourneeduBarreau20140904/2014-all-JEC_Corte.pdf>.

49   In contrast, when they have been integrated, it has generally involved copying, as is the case with legal aid and community justice centres. In comparison, see the directory set up by the Ministère de la Santé et des Services sociaux, online: <http://www.msss.gouv.qc.ca/repertoires/dependances/> (accessed on April 1, 2016).

50   Machiavelli, *Discourses on the First Decade of Titus Livius,* trans. Ninian Hill Thomson, book 1, chapter XVII.

51   Concerning change in institutions, Machiavelli says: "Whoever takes upon him to reform the government of a city, must, if his measures are

to be well received and carried out with general approval, preserve at least the semblance of existing methods, so as not to appear to the people to have made any change in the old order of things; although, in truth, the new ordinances differ altogether from those which they replace. For when this is attended to, the mass of mankind accept what seems as what is; nay, are often touched more nearly by appearances than by realities." Machiavelli, *supra* note 50, chapter XXV.

52 For reasoned praise of "two-thumb" writing, see online: <http://www.slate.fr/story/114155/taper-ordinateur-deux-doigts-rapide> (accessed on April 9, 2016).

53 For an interesting example of this prophetic pompousness, online: <http://www.csc.com/fr/ds/71138/71285-révolution_numérique_7_tendances_qui_vont_changer_le_monde> (accessed on April 9, 2016).

54 Macfarlane, ibid.

55 On this, consult the findings of the studies by CÉFRIO, online: <http://www.cefrio.qc.ca/netendances/equipement-et-branchement-internet-des-foyers-quebecois-en-2015/la-grande-majorite-des-foyers-quebecois-sont-branches-a-internet/> (accessed on April 10, 2016).

56 This finding has remained constant ever since the first studies on the issue conducted in 1993 by the Centre de droit préventif du Québec.

57 Nonetheless, transposing judicial activities into digital form will not eliminate a number of inequities in the judicial system, in particular, concerning the opposition of *Repeater* and *One-shooter* knowledge and skills referred to in Kramer's text in this work.

58 For example, in the case between Claude Robinson and Cinar Corporation, the photocopy costs of the file submitted to the court amounted to $150,000. Online: <https://voir.ca/societe/2013/01/23/claude-robinson-claude-robinson-devant-la-cour-supreme-le-dernier-round/> (accessed on April 9, 2016).

59 It is useful to recall that individuals' level of trust in the justice system is rarely above 50%. In this sense, we can subscribe to Daniel Weinstock's remarks in the present work: "However, it is not sufficient for the justice system to produce equity, or at least that it not deepen inequalities. It also has to inspire trust among citizens." It at least seems that the present system does not manage to do this and that we have to try something else.

60 Similarly, the media visibility acquired in recent years by judges assigned to preside over certain commissions of inquiry (Gomery, Bastarache, Charbonneau), the work of which has been broadcast on television, probably explains the increase in public trust in the courts. It is likely that this will also favour an eventual reform of rules concerning cameras in court.

61 Pierre Noreau, *Droit préventif: le droit au-delà de la loi* (Montréal: Éditions juridiques Thémis, 2016), first published 1993, 165 pages.

CHAPTER X

Cyberjustice and Ethical Perspectives of Procedural Law

Daniel Weinstock

In Canada, as in other countries, there is an enormous problem of access to justice. Many courts are clogged, and people who have to rely on them for their cases to be heard are often required to wait for an unreasonably long time. Since access to justice is not entirely exempt from market forces, it is often prohibitively expensive for those who need it most. Like access to health care, which probably causes more ink to flow, access to justice is a major issue of distributive justice.[1]

One of the justifications for introducing virtual platforms into the administration of justice is the claim that it could help to alleviate this major distributive justice problem. "Cyberjustice" would shrink costs and waiting times related to justice proceedings by relieving congestion in the courts, reducing costs related to the need to pay various types of workers in the legal field, and so on.

In the present essay, I will not try to challenge these claims. Let us therefore take it for granted that cyberjustice would entail major improvements in access to justice. Instead, I would like to look at the risks that could flow from overuse of virtual tools in the legal context. I am starting from the hypothesis that the *design* of any complex social institution has to take a multitude of values into account, values that are sometimes in tension. While use of virtual platforms may be an improvement in terms of access to justice, does it entail risks in relation to other values that are just as central for legal institutions, risks that could significantly reduce the overall benefit brought about by the introduction of new technologies?

When we are assessing the emergence of such platforms, we have to avoid two extremes. On one hand, we have to avoid succumbing to the temptation to adopt institutional conservativism, which results in unfounded idealization of the procedures that we have at this time, and which sees any departure from present institutional forms as a sign of degeneration. On the other hand, we also have to avoid being tempted by technological determinism, which sees all technological advances as desirable. The more subtle question that we have to ask in relation to the emergence of information technologies and virtual platforms in justice processes is how to embody values that are always important in the administration of justice in a system that will give an even greater role to digital processes.

As a working hypothesis, I will assume that the changes that will be made to legal processes through the adoption of technological tools will be substantial, in other words, that such tools will replace traditional ways of administering law, rather than serve simply as instruments within procedures that are relatively similar to those with which we are already familiar. It may be that scenarios of this type will not be achievable in the near future. If this is the case, I hope that the following reflections will make it possible to find ways of achieving the values that will be in question here within procedures that have been dramatically reconfigured by new technologies.

The four normative considerations to which I will briefly refer in the following lines are equity, trust, respect, and what could be called epistemic confidence. I will briefly describe each of these values before drawing very preliminary conclusions about the way in which "cyberjustice" should be integrated into modern legal practices.

Equity

Equity is the value in the name of which cyberjustice proponents consider that the administration of justice should give a greater role to virtual processes. The best-off in our society can hire the best lawyers, and have the luxury of being able to expect that their cases will be heard. This suggests that, in these circumstances, law exacerbates rather than overcomes social inequalities.

It would thus be ironical if the introduction of tools and virtual processes into the administration of justice resulted in other costs from the point of view of equity. How could this be so? How could making proceedings less cumbersome, ensuring that certain types of functions are done by digital applications rather than by (paid) human beings do anything other than smooth out inequalities?

In order for the introduction of new technologies not to give rise to new inequalities, we have to ensure that we take measures to guarantee that the dividends are not distributed unequally. The introduction of information technologies into social institutions has not always improved equality. It is clear that when such technologies have been introduced in health care,[2] education,[3] and politics,[4] problems of inequality have arisen. These problems stem from the fact that in these areas, new technologies have been introduced without attacking "digital divide" problems present even in the most technologically advanced societies.

We can imagine two types of mechanisms through which the introduction of new technologies creates problems from the point of view of equity. The first is related simply to the fact that there is a digital divide. "Digital literacy," a term which has to be understood to include all competencies enabling individuals to use new information technologies and to feel at home in cybernetic worlds, was studied by Statistics Canada in 2011. According to the findings, digital literacy is unequally distributed across the population, and these are largely consistent with existing inequalities and vulnerabilities, for example, those related to levels of education.[5]

The second mechanism is related to the fact that in the context of a system of administration of justice based on an adversary logic, it is very likely that the introduction of any new technology into the system will give rise to strategic calculations. Any lawyer who takes seriously the responsibility to promote client interests will try to use any changes to case processing in ways that will benefit his or her client. It is difficult to predict precisely what form such strategic considerations will take in the case of new technologies, but it would be naïve to imagine that any change in the way justice is organized would not be the object of such strategic considerations.

In order to ensure that the improvements in terms of equity that will result from relieving congestion in the courts and the savings to be made through greater use of digital platforms are not accompanied by other inequities, it will be important to try to deal with the causes of potential unfairness when new technologies are introduced. How? First, we have to address the above-mentioned digital divide, which has already caused failures when new technologies have been introduced into other areas of public policy, such as those mentioned above. Cyber-literacy campaigns have to be conducted, and in so far as the divide is a function not only of unequal distribution of *knowledge* concerning how digital tools function but also of such technological *media*, we have to take action to ensure that people are not disadvantaged in material terms because they do not have access to the technological tools needed to enjoy all the benefits resulting from the virtual transformation of justice structures.

How can we ensure that the strategic use of new technologies will not give rise to new inequalities? In a context where the system of justice is based on arguments put forward by two adverse parties, there is not much that can be done to prevent strategic behaviour. The organization of systems based on contests between adversaries is based on the hypothesis that justice will emerge as "system effect" where two parties compete (within a framework of rules) to win their cases.

Strategic behaviour creates inequalities when adverse parties do not have comparable resources. What poses a problem is not so much strategic calculation but the fact that one party may be armed with powerful digital tools, while the other may have only an abacus.

We have seen above that proponents of cyberjustice may be hoping to serve the cause of equity in the field of justice by relieving congestion in the courts, thereby reducing both costly waiting times and also expenses related to the administration of justice. However, equality also depends on the adversaries in a legal case having comparable resources, no matter what other costs the introduction of new technologies may make it possible to avoid. It is difficult to see how, in itself, the arrival of new technologies would reduce access disparities in a society where access to justice still depends at least in part on market forces. On the contrary, as has been the case in other areas, there is reason to fear that if new technologies are introduced into a system in which there are still economic inequalities that make themselves apparent in individuals' capacities to pay for high-quality legal services, technologies will only exacerbate such inequalities.

The cause of equity in the field of administration of justice will thus be served by the introduction of new technologies to "virtualize" certain aspects of proceedings in so far as they are accompanied by measures that reduce the digital divide and the very unequal distribution of digital literacy among our fellow citizens. Further, these new technologies should not exacerbate the material inequalities already present in the administration of justice, making it likely that use of these new technologies will benefit those who already draw the greatest advantage from the legal system.

Trust

Naturally, equity is a fundamental value of the justice system, and any introduction of technologies tending to render certain aspects of the legal process virtual rather than embodied will have to ensure that the technologies do not reproduce social injustice and inequality.

However, it is not sufficient for the justice system to produce equity, or at least avoid deepening inequalities. It also has to inspire trust among citizens. A social system may very well be built around morally defensible values, but it will not succeed in making those values a reality in society unless people have enough trust in the system to take part in it rather than escape from it. A justice system that does not inspire people's trust is a system that they will not use to resolve their disputes unless they are forced to do so.

Of course, the justice and equity of a system are among the factors that help to inspire trust. Moreover, no one would want a system of justice that did not deserve to be trusted, in other words, one that did not provide justice to those who use it. However, trust is not related only to the effects produced by a social system, but to other types of factors as well.

Elsewhere I have defended the idea that it is difficult for complex systems to inspire trust. The reason is that trust is above all a dimension of interpersonal relations rather than relations that individuals have with impersonal entities such as complex institutions, the rules of operation of which are often impenetrable for common mortals.[6] Character dispositions and judgement abilities that we have acquired in order to decide to trust someone depend on our capacity to react in an appropriate manner to the messages that other people send us through their behaviour, non-verbal communication, and so on.

We have difficulty formulating judgments of trust or distrust in relation to complex institutions, but also in relation to human interactions mediated by technology. The arrival of the internet and the many technological platforms for engaging in commercial, as well as emotional, relationships has given rise to a great deal of thought on the conditions for establishing trust among individuals in a medium as new as the internet.[7]

Any user of a platform such as Airbnb or Uber knows that the success of these virtual commercial initiatives depends on the creation of simulated interpersonal relationships. The purpose of the information placed on these sites is of course to reassure sellers and buyers of the "objective" reliability of the person to whom they are preparing to rent an apartment. However, the sites also increase the number of mechanisms by which interpersonal relations are recreated, even among strangers who may never meet other than through the mediation of virtual tools.

The legal process probably does not inspire all of the trust that it should. That it instead gives rise to distrust is probably owing to the inequity that it too often seems to produce, and to the layers of bureaucracy that people come up against when they try to use it to assert their rights—and these are the very vices that we hope to deal with by introducing virtual elements into legal processes.

While some aspects of the legal process tend to produce distrust, others probably have the opposite effect, namely, that of rallying members of a community to legal institutions. The aspects of these procedures that tend to produce trust are probably those that give the parties involved the impression that they are dealing with members of their community and that they are being recognized, through their participation in these institutions, as members of the community. For example, in his writings on criminal law, the philosopher of law R. A. Duff insisted on the importance of aspects of ritual in criminal proceedings through which members of a community affirm one another as members of the same community. According to Duff, some aspects that may seem at the limit of theatricality help to humanize the judicial process of assigning criminal responsibility so that all concerned, both the guilty and the accusers, can recognize one another mutually as members of the same community.[8]

As in the case of equity, the introduction of technologies designed to eliminate a source of distrust must not introduce a new one. Like virtual platforms through which individuals transact, or set up blind dates, virtual platforms designed to replace certain aspects of embodied legal process by virtual equivalents will have to find a means of inspiring trust. If the hypothesis described here is plausible, designers will have to find ways of reintroducing the interpersonal dimension required so that individuals who use the platforms can make appropriate judgments with respect to trust. Here the point is not to defend the idea that the thing is impossible.

We have managed to do it in a number of virtual contexts. However, the institutional design we adopt in order to integrate virtual aspects into legal processes must not overlook considerations on how to produce trust.

Respect

One of the main issues that opposed two of the greatest philosophers of law of the twentieth century, H. L. A. Hart and Lon Fuller, concerned whether it was important for members of a complex modern society to have an "internal point of view" in relation to legal institutions. Hart considered that it was essential for the officers of such institutions—judges, lawyers, police officers—to be motivated by an attitude that was more than simply instrumental in relation to such institutions. In other words, it was important for them to adhere to the ideals and claims on which the legal system is based. Fuller, in contrast, lauded what he called "fidelity to law"; in other words, the loyalty that people feel to a system of law that treats them as subjects and agents.[9]

However, the debate between Fuller and Hart concerned the conditions that have to be met for us to be able to say that there is a system of laws. According to Hart, whether or not people have an "internal" attitude to law is not a necessary condition for the existence of such a system. However, he conceded that such an attitude was desirable.

It is desirable to have an internal attitude to law because without such attitude, the legal system cannot have *authority* in relation to those subject to it. For the purposes of the present argument, let us assume that a system of laws has authority if the rules that follow from it are seen by people as reasons to take action.[10] The fact of having authority means that a system has less need to count on coercion to obtain people's obedience. A system of justice that has authority in the sense defined here has to invest less in monitoring and punishing than a system that imposes itself on people through fear of detection and penalties.

Once again, it is not a question of wanting a legal system to have authority with respect to those subject to it without that authority being accompanied by the appropriate moral virtues. An unjust system that enjoys authority without meeting the appropriate moral conditions would not be desirable. Conversely, a legal system worthy of authority but unable to inspire a feeling of respect in people would not be desirable either.

As in the case of trust, it is not simply through the fact of embodying certain moral values, such as justice and equity, that a system can have authority. In order to prepare the transition toward a system of administration of justice that gives a greater role to virtual platforms, we have to study the aspects of the physical form of that system that could promote respect.

In a recent work and a series of articles,[11] Linda Mulcahy put forward the hypothesis that people's feeling of respect for their legal institutions, and the related legitimacy and authority they enjoy, are partly a function of their architecture. The architecture of courthouses (which are called *Palais de Justice* in French, something that we should think about!) has always incorporated ideas about the important role of justice in society. At a certain time, according to Mulcahy, the goal was to reflect the sacred nature of justice in the architecture and location of courts. Today, other values are embodied in the *design* of places of justice. The great bay windows of the Supreme Court of Germany were apparently chosen explicitly in order to give physical expression to the value of transparency that leaders wanted to breathe into the country and its primary institutions in the post-war period.

Mulcahy has also expressed reservations about the use of virtual platforms in the context of court proceedings. The possibility of testifying using technological means rather than in person could, in her view, have a negative impact on the perception that participants, as well as people in general, have of court proceedings as socially important forms of ritual. The introduction of screens that in some cases replace embodied agents could make the proceedings seem less special by allowing people to testify elsewhere than in a highly ritualized space.

Once again, this is not an attempt to exaggerate the degree to which the current administration of justice fully inspires people's respect or to claim that it would be impossible to create such an attitude of respect by introducing more virtual platforms within rituals of justice. The point is simply to ensure that, in the design of future institutional sites, heed will be paid to putting in place the conditions necessary to establishing the legitimacy of justice institutions—which may be difficult to engender in terms of people's internal point of view—in particular by taking into account the impact that disembodying justice could have on people's endorsement of it.

Epistemic Confidence

In this last section, I would like to look at another dimension of the justice process, in particular that of court proceedings. Not only do such procedures have to embody a certain number of moral values, but they also have to perform important epistemological functions. They have to make it possible for judges and juries to render fair verdicts based on epistemically defensible readings of the facts. Among other things, court proceedings have to be constructed in a way that increases the probability that the truth will come to light in virtue of the use of legal procedures.[12]

What are the aspects of the design of court proceedings that make them good epistemic tools? A major part of the answer to this question is related to the fundamental structure of the proceedings. In the case of a system based on opposition between two adverse parties, truth is expected to be an outcome of the system. The underlying hypothesis is that the two parties to a dispute both seek to reveal the facts most favourable to their cases, and that this will engender the truth as a kind of emergent property.

However, the capacity of legal proceedings to produce truth does not depend only on the main institutional pillars on which they have been built. This capacity also depends on details, which we do not take into account adequately except when we pay attention to the human dynamics that occur in justice processes and in court proceedings in particular. Speaking of the tendency that some theorists of criminal law have to reduce the theory of evidence to rules that define admissibility and inadmissibility, Paul Roberts writes that "orthodox conceptions of the Law of Evidence eschew any real interest in the dynamics of adjudication or the practical realities of fact-finding."[13] According to Roberts, the capacity of court proceedings to produce truth depends as much, for example, on the instructions the judge gives to the jury on how to understand evidence introduced in court as on the formal components that, in a way, constitute the architectural base of proceedings.

In *R v NS*, the Chief Justice of the Supreme Court of Canada refers to the "common law assumption that the accused, the judge and the jury should be able to see the witness as she testifies."[14] The justification for this assumption is largely epistemic: "Non-verbal communication can provide the cross-examiner with valuable insights that may uncover uncertainty or deception, and assist in *getting at the truth* (emphasis added)."[15] As we know, the Supreme Court's decision in this case was to not require in all circumstances that witnesses testify with their faces uncovered because in some situations the fact of not being able to observe the individual's expressions does not affect the ability of the cross-examiner or of the jury to assess the credibility of what he or she says. However, the Chief Justice also recognized that in some circumstances the non-verbal dimension and behaviour of a witness can have epistemic importance.

If virtual mediation were used, for example, to have distant witnesses testify or to introduce pieces of evidence by means other than testimony, there would be at least in principle a risk of losing certain epistemic advantages of traditional legal proceedings. As in the cases of equity, trust, and respect, I am not claiming that it would be impossible to compensate for the epistemic loss through other mechanisms that could be integrated into the use of virtual platforms. The point is rather to remind designers of these new technologies that it is important to include reflection on the epistemic dimension of justice proceedings and the challenges it imposes when we marginalize or reduce the role given to an individual's judgement of the credibility of another individual through in-person observation.

Conclusion

Every complex human institution has to try to balance a large number of values that are sometimes related in complicated ways. Whether the issue is an electoral system, market regulation authorities, or in the case that concerns us here, the design of justice proceedings, there is no algorithm for identifying *the* right way to perform such balancing.

The introduction of communications technologies and virtual tools intended to alleviate long delays in courts and reduce certain court costs could result in fabulous improvements in the access to justice, and therefore in the fairness of administration of justice systems. However, other values also have to be embodied by our justice systems. This short essay provides no answers. It simply points out that, in the way that we integrate new technologies, we have to take into account perverse effects in terms of equity and also ricochet effects on other values that could be produced by the introduction of such technologies into the administration of justice.

Notes

1   Deborah Rhode, *Access to Justice* (Oxford: Oxford University Press, 2005).

2   Mollyann Brodie et al., "Health Information, the Internet, and the Digital Divide," *Health Affairs* 19:6 (2000) at 255.

3   Gwen Solomon, Nancy Allen and Paul Resta, eds., *Toward Digital Equity: Bridging the Digital Divide in Education* (Toronto: Pearson, 2002).

4   Pippa Norris, *Digital Divide: Civic Engagement, Information Poverty, and the Internet Worldwide* (Cambridge: Cambridge University Press, 2001).

5   Statistics Canada, *Literacy for Life: Further Results from the Adult Literacy and Life Skills Survey* (Ottawa: Government of Canada, 2011), 141 at 141–60.

6   Daniel Weinstock, "Trust in Institutions," in *Reading Onora O'Neill*, ed. D Archard et al., (London: Routledge, 2013).

7   See in particular the work of Helen Nissenbaum, "Securing Trust Online: Wisdom or Oxymoron?," *Boston University Law Review* 81:3 (2001) at 635.

8   R A Duff, *Trials and Punishment* (Cambridge: Cambridge University Press, 1986).

9   H L A Hart, "Positivism and the Separation of Law and Morals," *Harvard Law Review* 71:4 (1958) at 593; Lon L Fuller, "Positivism and Fidelity to Law: A Reply to Professor Hart," *Harvard Law Review* 71:4 (1958) at 630.

10   Joseph Raz, *The Morality of Freedom* (Oxford: Oxford University Press, 1986).

11   Linda Mulcahy, "The Unbearable Lightness of Being? Shifts Toward the Virtual Trial," *The Journal of Law and Society* 35:4 (2008) at 464; Linda Mulcahy, *Legal Architecture* (London: Routledge, 2011).

12   Larry Laudan, *Truth, Error and Criminal Law* (Cambridge: Cambridge University Press, 2006); Susan Haack, *Evidence Matters* (Cambridge: Cambridge University Press, 2014).

13   Paul Roberts, "Groundwork for a Jurisprudence of Criminal Procedure," in *Philosophical Foundations of Criminal Law*, ed. R A Duff and Stuart P Green (Oxford: Oxford University Press, 2011) at 379.

14   *R v NS*, 2012 SCC 72 at para 23, [2012] 3 SCR 726.

15   Ibid. at para 24.

CHAPTER XI

Three Trade-Offs to Efficient Dispute Resolution

Clément Camion

Seeking efficiency first and foremost when designing dispute resolution processes carries the risk of producing unprincipled justice.

In this article, I explore actual and proposed measures promoting efficiency in civil dispute resolution. I argue that current, widespread focus on efficiency in judicial systems and civil justice reform endeavours worldwide may cripple other fundamental values of justice. We, decision-makers and academics, tend to define "efficiency" too narrowly. We also focus too much on efficiency, without sufficient consideration for other fundamental values of justice. For example, we intuitively embrace Alternative Dispute Resolution processes (ADR) such as mediation, or the notion that information technology implementation and eAccess to justice projects increase efficiency, without having consciously weighed the legitimate need for better, faster dispute resolution against the need for legal precedent. As a consequence, we risk confining the courts' jurisdiction to a narrow, if not trifling understanding of "public interest." This, in turn, may contribute to diminishing the legitimacy of the state and may undermine long-term social trust. In other words, the quest for efficiency in civil justice involves three trade-offs: (1) overlooking other fundamental values of justice besides efficiency; (2) systematizing resolution without precedent; and (3) ultimately narrowing the courts' jurisdiction to "public order" without sufficient consideration for what public interest means and should mean.

"Efficiency" Is Too Narrowly Defined to Mean Coping With Costs, Delays, and Backlogs

Let me start with an illustration of several decision-making processes inspired by the comic book and film series, *Batman*.

Batman's decision-making process is principled. He makes decisions with the goal of preventing harm to human lives through (what he deems to be) necessary force. His decision-making process is predicated on some sense of human dignity and the use of proportional means to protect the value of human lives.

Batman's nemesis, the Joker, also displays a principled decision-making process, albeit a perverted one. Led by a fundamental disregard for human life, the Joker seeks the most efficient way to achieve mass terror. In this respect, reducing human lives to mere means toward mass terror, through all types of deception, and more generally behaving erratically and unpredictably, can be construed as rational precisely because it is unforeseeable and thus efficient (toward achieving pure evil).

Both Batman and the Joker are involved in strategic thinking based on substantive values and thus, at times, both must delay decision-making. Two-Face's decision-making process, however, is purely procedural in nature. This villain goes about his affairs by reducing fundamental dilemmas to a binary choice, and resolving them by flipping a coin. By surrendering his fate to a coin flip (and at times, bending complex questions into a false dichotomy), he achieves extreme efficiency. In other words, pure efficiency in decision-making is achieved through a ritual where no value of justice intervenes. The authority of the coin is absolute. There is only gravitational force, and no consideration for the merits of the case.

The core of this paper will revolve around how we, as actors of the judicial system, policy-makers, and scholars of procedural law, define "efficiency" in the judicial context. I argue that we should broaden our understanding of what efficiency means in the judicial context in order to produce better policies and make better-informed reform decisions.

Why Do We Define "Efficiency" So Narrowly?

1. What Is Efficient Dispute Resolution?

Judicial efficiency may be defined as the ability of the judicial system to perform its function efficiently. An efficient judicial system produces the effects we expect it to produce using a proportionate, or rational, amount of resources, both public and private. This may seem trivial, but this simple definition raises difficult questions. What do we expect from the judicial system? What do we consider "efficient" in this context? How do we assess whether the required amount of resources is proportionate for private parties? What is the acceptable cost of justice on public resources?

2. "Productive Dispute Resolution"

In current streams of thought on civil justice and judicial reform, "managerial justice"—an approach to case management that favours increasing the power in the hands of judges and chief justices to better control proceedings—plays an important role in defining the judicial system's functions and its rationality. More and more, we have come to think of judicial systems as a set of actors and institutions dedicated to the "productive resolution of legal disputes," where "disputes" are defined as conflicts between two or more parties that survive negotiation, thus requiring a third-party neutral's intervention in order to be resolved. The third party may be a judge, or the law applied by a judge, but also an arbitrator, an *amiable compositeur*, a mediator, or even an online settlement service, such as a machine. Under this framework, the judicial system's output is, theoretically, the final resolution of legal disputes.[1] Overall, "efficient dispute resolution" thus reflects the notion that judicial processes must be geared toward productive dispute resolution. To that end, judicial processes should be focused and speedy, without undue burdens, and aimed at reaching a legally sound solution, using the least—or an appropriate or a proportionate—amount of time and resources, public and private.

This understanding of the judicial system is widespread, and its success is easy to understand; nobody likes waste. No one wants to achieve less with more, or even, less with the same resources. However, this definition proves problematic today for two reasons. First, "efficiency" has been narrowly construed to mean coping with costs, delays and backlogs.[2] Second, this narrow definition of "efficiency" has retained a lot of scholarly attention, to the detriment of other fundamental values of justice, mostly for lack of meaningful data.[3]

3. "Coping With Delays and Backlogs"

Many judicial systems worldwide are inefficient. Many reports document how judicial systems face serious challenges in terms of backlogs in the courts' case dockets, serious delays between the filing date and a court's final decision, and overwhelming costs for the parties as well as for the states, thus undermining access to justice for economic reasons. In addition, law is widely perceived as too complex, and lay persons often live with unresolved legal issues, for lack of information on what to do about them, and lack of education on how to detect the legal dimension of their everyday problems.

Although concern for judicial efficiency is not recent,[4] a distinct stream flowed from Lord Woolf's seminal 1996 reports in the United Kingdom;[5] followed by studies conducted by the Council of Europe's European Commission for the Efficiency of Judicial Systems (the CEPEJ);[6] closer to us in Canada, studies by the Canadian Forum on Civil Justice;[7] and more recently, the Honourable Justice Cromwell's report on access to justice[8]—to name just a few. These concerns arise in both common-law and civil-law jurisdictions. In all of these reports, and despite the broad societal issues undermining access to justice, solutions are presented in terms of "efficiency" gains, in reaction to challenges depicted in terms of docket backlog, delays, and costs, both public and private.

There are three types of measures available to cope with backlogs, delays, and costs: (i) procedural and managerial arrangements that save resources; (ii) substantive legal reforms that reduce the number of cases before the courts; and (iii) increasing the resources allotted to the court system.[9]

(i) Efficiency measures may consist, for example, in transferring cases from adjudication by a panel to adjudication by a single judge, or, where jury trials are available, by allowing majority verdicts as opposed to unanimous verdicts, thereby avoiding mistrials and thus doubling the need for resources. Sometimes called "managerial strategies," efficiency measures usually involve institutional or procedural changes. Although they may affect the parties' rights and obligations directly, for example when a default judgment is entered instead of a judgment on the merits, or, in criminal matters, when guilt may be pronounced on a majority verdict, such reforms generally leave substantive law untouched. Except for procedural rights, the rights and obligations of the parties remain the same.

However, a distinct type of efficiency measure consists in avoiding litigation altogether. This tendency has been described as the move to Alternative Dispute Resolution (ADR), or the "vanishing trial phenomenon."[10] If institutional design or procedural law adjustments are described as reformist, then ADR mechanisms may be (and often are) presented as revolutionary, because they consist in leaving aside the traditional procedural arrangements set out by states, and turning to private dispute resolution mechanisms. Although controversial not so long ago, such approaches to dispute resolution have gained considerable traction, so much that the default course of action has shifted, not only in practice but now also formally in statutory law, from formal public adjudication to private mechanisms.[11] With such efficiency measures, cases are dealt with by fewer judges, or by less stringent procedural rules, but with private resources instead of public ones, in a private setting instead of a public one.

(ii) Clearing the courts' dockets may also be achieved through substantive legal reform. Legal reforms often stem from the trivialization of certain acts or conduct in society, which used to require legal attention under the law, but no longer constitute socially meaningful "disputes" and are now considered a source of congestion in the courts rather than cases worthy of judicial attention. The existence of an overwhelmingly frequent pattern or a decrease in the moral stigmatization of certain acts or conduct—in other words, a mismatch between the law and consensual social practice—render trial-based adjudication meaningless or inconsequential, and thus wasteful of justices' time. The response consists in shifting the law's grasp regarding a specific type of dispute in order to move the dispute outside the traditional court system, ideally for better and faster resolution, or for no resolution at all. Such was the case when legislators shifted the law from fault-based to strict liability responsibility in work-related personal injury cases, leading to innovations in insurance policies,[12] or to no-fault compensation schemes in bodily injury road accident cases,[13] or from fault-based to no-fault divorce.[14] In such cases, legal reform really means streamlining dispute resolution by moving from a purely legal scheme to a quasi-judiciary, administrative, or even a privatized administrative scheme (public or private insurance compensation), or to a non-legal one (certain acts or types of conduct become legally irrelevant), thereby alleviating the workload on triers of facts. It is noteworthy that non-adjudicative alternatives have often been insurance-based solutions, where, from a systemic point of view, insurers play the role of mutualizing the costs and delays of litigation that lay persons cannot absorb on their own. Litigation between insurers may arise occasionally, but the stakes are generally high in intensity, with costs and delays being less of an issue than for injured persons who depend on compensation to go on with their lives. Substantive legal reform may also transform, intentionally or not, what was considered a "dispute" into a "non-dispute," in that case with no formal resolution at all. This usually happens when prior political or social motives or the legal basis for judicialization have become irrelevant, or even unconstitutional. Such is the case with the decriminalization of certain offenses, like recent reforms regarding simple possession of marijuana in certain states, or the decriminalization of abortion or homosexuality.[15]

(iii) Finally, increasing court resources, by appointing additional judges and adding to the courts' budget, is another type of measure used to reduce delays and backlogs—but not costs. It essentially comes down to admitting that all things considered, productivity cannot be increased; in that case, sustained efficiency requires more resources or less volume. Relying on resource increases is somewhat utopic in the context of systematically reduced public spending and states' ever-shrinking tax bases. As important and fascinating as this issue can be, possible solutions to balance state budgets lie outside the realm of the efficient administration of justice and far beyond the scope of this paper.

We Focus Too Much on Delays and Backlogs

What about costs? What about feelings of fairness and satisfaction? There is virtually no available data other than data on dockets, costs, and delays, and therefore no other metrics by which to assess, define, and ultimately address efficiency issues.

1. Lack of Data

If nobody hears the sound of a tree falling in the woods, can we safely say that no tree has fallen at all? Of course not. The fact that a phenomenon is not perceived does not entail that the phenomenon is not real. Lawyers, of all people, are familiar with the notion of wilful blindness; looking the other way is not a defense against knowing only a little bit, but enough, about an inconvenient truth.

The main reason why so many scholars and policy-makers focus on dockets and delays is that they are among the only reliable metrics available to assess the efficiency of adjudication. While other metrics are available, delays and dockets are the only points of performance that are being systematically measured, usually as part of the courts' management strategies. They are also easily comparable data. Where additional data is available, it is not necessarily usable or applicable, let alone comparable with other jurisdictions' data. Additional data may be too old and unreliable; moreover, it was often measured in another jurisdiction with very different procedural arrangements, making it cumbersome to use at best.

Enthusiasm for civil justice reforms in Canada seems to flow from the practitioners' subjective perceptions rather than sound data. The Honourable Supreme Court Justice Cromwell's report on access to justice in Canada, for example, refers to studies conducted in the United States and the United Kingdom when it comes to statistics about access to justice, not because such data is taken to be accurate, but because there is virtually no Canadian data available on the matter.[16] Foreign studies conducted in similar Anglo-American common law jurisdictions are the next best options available to understand our own judicial system.

I do not suggest that we are wrong when we say that there are clear issues preventing meaningful access to justice, that justice is too complex, too long, and too costly for too many people. However, given the statistical desert in which we currently evolve, systematically and routinely acquiring data, over the long run, and making sure that we train experts to both acquire and analyze it, is central to sound reform. One step toward building up our expertise consists in systematically including data collection and interpretation as part of funding applications for research and reform projects. Measuring impact is paramount to proposing sound rather than ideological policies. In the meantime, we should remain cautious not to restrict the way we define efficiency and the types of solutions we imagine for lack of broader data.

2. What Should We Measure, and How?

Although costs are in theory already quantified, measuring the costs of judicial dispute resolution is an exercise in night vision. It is confronted with many roadblocks to acquiring the data, which then proves complex to interpret. However, measuring costs, including a distinction between the public and private costs of litigation, would be a good starting point to further develop our knowledge and our expertise. But data collection should go further. The risk with focusing too much on efficiency measures, that is to say reducing costs, delays, and backlogs, is to fall into what I would call a "metonymy trap," where we conflate the container (productive dispute resolution processes) with the content (satisfying results from both individual and systemic standpoints). By focusing solely on currently available data, we run the risk of narrowing our statistical understanding of the judicial system to case dockets, costs, and delays, and of reducing productive dispute resolution to resolving the few problematic features that we are able to statistically assess today. This overlooks the human, multidimensional aspects of legal problems that the judicial system is supposed to help resolve. In other words, such a methodology comes down to fetishizing efficiency, keeping ourselves oblivious to the need for prevention, (e.g., through legal and financial education), and more importantly to the social roots of disputes, evidenced by the tendency of (physical persons') legal problems to come in clusters linked with health issues, poverty, and education shortcomings,[17] all calling for prevention and outreach rather than mere productive adjudication. Thankfully, such aspects are envisioned in the roadmap for change in access to justice.[18] Unfortunately, the roadmap for change is not sufficiently grounded in meaningful Canadian data.

There are also methodological implications. Because we are not acquiring enough meaningful data, we are progressively losing the expertise to analyze such data.

Fundamental Values of Justice Are Overlooked

What Is the Judicial System's Function—and What Should It Be?

Dispute resolution is at the heart of any judicial system. It is a fundamental building block with which we must work. However, the rule of law runs the risk of being left out of our definition of "judicial efficiency" if we only aim at dispute resolution. The judicial system's function is thus better defined as "productive dispute resolution *plus* the rule of law," or minimally, "dispute resolution *in accordance with* the rule of law," but maybe even "dispute resolution *actively promoting* the rule of law."

Some may think that the rule of law is a precondition for the very existence of a judicial system, thus also a precondition for such a system to be efficient. In other words, the rule of law would not be part of the equation and should not be considered when reflecting on judicial efficiency. However, such a view comes down to artificially classifying the costs of promoting the rule of law outside the judicial system, when, in practice, they are mostly absorbed by the judicial system and fall within ministry of justice or justice department budgets. Therefore, we should consider how productive dispute resolution and promoting the rule of law are intertwined.

1. Dispute Resolution…Plus the Rule of Law

The interrelation between dispute resolution and the rule of law can be described as follows: if the rule of law is an idea (and an ideal) and the judicial system's performance is the expression of that idea then, for all practical purposes, how the rule of law is perceived and criticized depends largely on how the judicial system performs (given that ideas can only be understood once they are expressed; otherwise they are doomed to remain in the realm of subjective thoughts).

There are fascinating philosophical debates about how we gain "access" to new ideas, for example on whether we are born with the idea, or at least a sense, of, say, justice. But for our purposes here, it is fair to say that the idea of the rule of law is not innate. We may have an instinctive, unsophisticated sense of fairness. But we know about the rule of law because we have been confronted with various expressions or interpretations of the idea, and hopefully we have seen that behaviours in the judicial system are in line with that idea, at least to an extent sufficient to render the idea of the rule of law credible and thus meaningful in practice. In that sense, the rule of law—any law, really—is a social construct. It is meaningful because it helps guide the practice of dispute resolution and because we attribute some credit to its practical validity.

Figure 1

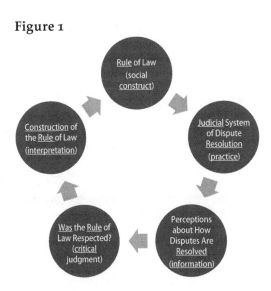

The rule of law is an idea held "intersubjectively," that is, a social construct. Maintaining the belief that the rule of law currently exists and *will continue* to exist in the future is crucial. You may lose a case once, but overall you agree to submit a case to the courts because you believe that they will be capable of delivering fair results in the future, regardless of whether or not one particular decision turns out to be in your favour.[19] This belief system is essentially an extension of the fundamental human need to stabilize expectations. In particular, adjudication is deemed to remain fair in the future, not because of wishful thinking but because it has been *rendered in an impersonal manner according to principles and values that will remain a constant*. This is more than merely respecting due process; it requires a fair process producing just decisions. What really matters is the notion that fair processes and just decisions are and will keep being delivered in the future. Defining what "fair processes and just results" means exactly is a tremendous task that we do not need to perform here. We only need to become familiar with the notion that an important issue of procedural reform is how do we send the signal now, in a specific instance of private dispute resolution, that the rule of law will continue to exist in the future?

Here is one possible answer.

2. Upholding Fundamental Values of Justice

During our research with Professor Gélinas, we summarized the ideals of civil procedure in a series of fundamental principles. We looked at civil procedure and procedural arrangements in civil- and common-law jurisdictions, hoping to identify *some* common ground, and we delved into the works of prominent scholars who emphasized the importance of simplifying the technicality of procedural arrangement to think about their underlying principles. In a way, we tried to sort out the necessary from the contingent in procedural justice. We also looked at the ALI/UNIDROIT Principles of Transnational Civil Procedure. To make a long story short, we then classified all the values we were able to identify on a gradient, ranging from values that are typically held by private actors to the more systemic and thus less easily incarnated ones that require "judicial offices" (as opposed to physical persons), courts, and faculties, that is to say, institutions.[20]

The following "tree of justice" summarizes our findings.

Figure 2

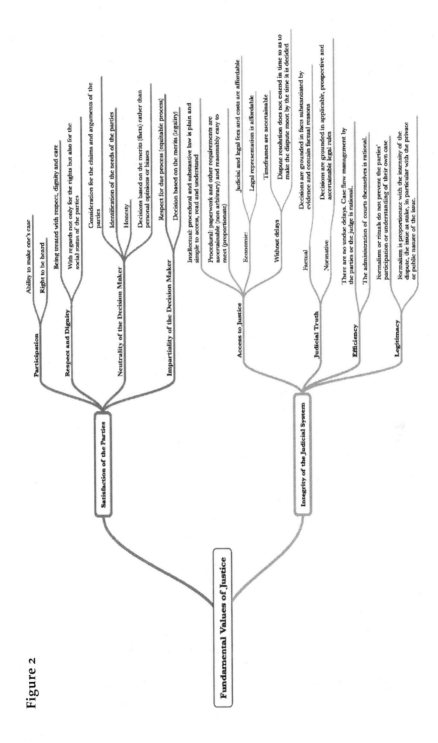

Fundamental Values of Justice

Satisfaction of the Parties

Participation
- Ability to make one's case
- Right to be heard

Respect and Dignity
- Being treated with respect, dignity and care
- With regards not only for the rights but also for the social status of the parties

Neutrality of the Decision Maker
- Consideration for the claims and arguments of the parties
- Identification of the needs of the parties
- Honesty
- Decisions based on the merits (facts) rather than personal opinions or biases

Impartiality of the Decision Maker
- Respect for due process (equitable process)
- Decision based on the merits (legality)

Integrity of the Judicial System

Access to Justice
- Intellectual: procedural and substantive law is plain and simple to access, read and understand
- Procedural: paperwork and other requirements are ascertainable (non arbitrary) and reasonably easy to meet (proportionate)
- Economic:
  - Judicial and legal fees and costs are affordable
  - Legal representation is affordable
- Without delays:
  - Timeframes are ascertainable
  - Dispute resolution does not extend in time so as to make the dispute moot by the time it is decided

Judicial Truth
- Factual: Decisions are grounded in facts substantiated by evidence and contain factual reasons
- Normative: Decisions are grounded in applicable, prospective and ascertainable legal rules

Efficiency
- There are no undue delays. Case flow management by the parties or the judge is rational.
- The administration of courts themselves is rational.

Legitimacy
- Formalism or rituals do not prevent the parties' participation or understanding of their own case
- Formalism is proportionate with the intensity of the dispute, the issue at stake, in particular with the private or public nature of the issue.

Where present, the principles identified in the tree of justice (Participation, Respect and Dignity, Neutrality, Impartiality, Access to Justice, Judicial Truth, Efficiency, Legitimacy) taken together reinforce the feeling that the process is fair, the solution is just, and ultimately, that it deserves to be respected. In other words, the bindingness of the solution is at stake (in fact, not in law).

Note that efficiency is only one in eight of the fundamental values identified. The need to put efficiency in perspective becomes immediately apparent when represented side by side with other incompressible values of justice.

The reason why people obey the law, or the terms of an agreement resolving their dispute, is not merely because there is a carrot, or a stick, or both, to incentivize them. Indeed, there is no carrot when losing a case, and law enforcement by police services would be untenable if it were to be systematically used. "Obedience" is much more complex and intricate.

In the aggregate, making sure that people feel that the process was fair, the decision just, and that fair processes and just decisions will keep on being delivered in the future is what makes people obey the law and self-enforce the rules. This does not mean that the possibility of sanctions (and ultimately police intervention) is irrelevant. But the difference between the possibility of police intervention and actual police intervention represents enormous economies of scale in law enforcement. Jeremy Bentham understood this very clearly when he designed the panopticon, and Michel Foucault, while illuminating and criticizing the adverse consequences of "surveillance," also identified how self-government has progressively been identified as the most efficient way of enforcing norms—much more so than physical punishment and sanctions that require enforcement.[21]

Restricting Public Courts' Jurisdiction to "Public Order"

Positive and Negative Externalities of ADR

1. Cheaper, Faster, and Closer to the Parties' Needs

What we commonly refer to as the "move to ADR" or the "vanishing trial" phenomenon affects the quality of dispute resolutions. By quality, I mean that we basically renounce what economists would call a "positive externality"; during public adjudication, legal norms (both procedural and substantive) are articulated for future reference in the process of resolving disputes. Among the benefits of ADR, we find faster and cheaper resolution of disputes. Proposed resolutions are often more flexible and thus closer to the parties' needs and interests rather than their positions. These positive internalities (benefits for the parties involved) are intrinsic to the resolution process. There are also positive externalities to ADR (benefits for the general public that are unintended by the parties and are not a relevant factor in deciding to choose ADR). For example, ADR produces the positive externality of clearing court dockets.

2. Privatizing the Expertise of Dispute Resolution

However, there are also negative externalities (losses for the general public) that have to do with the bindingness of a resolution. Court-based decisions are generally binding on third parties, usually not as individual decisions, but at least in the aggregate through the creation of jurisprudential streams and legal precedent. On the other hand, mostly because of standard confidentiality agreements, ADR does not produce legal precedent, that is to say, decisions that are at least potentially binding on third parties. The solution, and even more so the process, are very often confidential, meaning that there is no "public norm," substantive or procedural, that is articulated and published for the benefit of third parties or society in general. Privately developed norms are not kept on record, or even held by judges appointed by officials under public scrutiny. They are at best held in the expertise of a community of private arbitrators and mediators. The locus of knowledge, skills, and know-how, and ultimately power, progressively shifts outside of public officials' grip, into the private sector, and away from objective media (the office of a judge, printed or otherwise recorded materials, but also away from press coverage) into private expertise and oral transmission.

3. Favouring Short-Term Resolution Over Public Norms

ADR decisions are only binding, if at all, with respect to the parties themselves. Because they are closer to the parties' needs, especially where their bindingness is agreed upon after full knowledge of the implications for the parties, ADR decisions stand a very good chance of being self-enforced and are thus considered efficient, not only because of reduced costs and delays at the decision-making stage, but also at the execution stage. However, we may argue, so would a clear and well-known norm; it would be self-enforced through negotiation and would prevent disputes from arising in the first place.

Yet achieving legal clarity and sufficient legal education proves much more difficult than providing two parties with a forum to discuss their own specific case. It is costly and presupposes broad collective means of action; it also is inherently limited due to intrinsic vagueness in the law, and due to normative inflation, both in volume and technicality. The "beauty" of ADR is that it is predicated solely on the interest of the parties rather than on a well-shared collective understanding of the law that presupposes trust among peers and large-scale legal-education programs. In other words, private dispute resolution is more efficient because it is, by definition, personalized and customized. Ultimately, the tendency is to circumvent a costly intermediary—the law and the institutions that apply it—by substituting the back-and-forth movement from particular facts to general norms to particular solutions through "legal qualification" and "application of the law," for a simpler process moving directly from particular facts to particular solutions, provided that they respect the law. In essence, the move to ADR means that we are renouncing the benefits of the incremental refinement of legal norms through their confrontation with particular facts, for the sake of dealing with our issues more quickly and more cheaply. Short-term resolution outweighs long-term societal *vivre ensemble*.

Gauging the Need for Public Norms

Where should we draw the line between fast and cheap dispute resolution and the need to interpret the law? Should we let the "market" decide? Should we set a figure in dollar amount below which a case is deemed too low in intensity to be processed by public courts? Should we keep certain subject matters "public," that is to say "*inarbitrable*"? Which ones, and why?

1. "Public Order" As the Last Resort of State Legitimacy

Ultimately, the move to ADR comes down to renouncing abundant jurisprudence and bears the risk of confining the areas of public courts' legitimacy to certain issues that involve "public order."[22] For example, we may deem low-intensity consumer issues not to be of public concern and decide that ADR or ODR are more appropriate than small claims court to resolve those disputes. But it may turn out that a seemingly low-intensity consumer issue hides a systemic issue that is very much a concern for the general public. In a system where such issues are systematically expedited outside of courts, issues of concern to the general public may very well escape the grip of much-needed public adjudication.[23]

Without adequate metrics and sound data, there is no way of knowing in advance what is actually worthy of public courts' attention, nor how often such cases arise, nor with what social and societal ramifications. This fundamental uncertainty may well be the *raison d'être* of large court jurisdictions leading to complex, protracted public adjudication processes.

With the move to ADR, we seem to be shifting from a process-oriented judicial system that, in theory, is capable of dealing with any issue and may thus, at times, deal with unforeseeably important societal concerns, to a judicial system that will be prevented from hearing socially important cases because they do not sufficiently touch on public order.

This is of concern because the definition of "public order" is very political in nature. In short, political views on what public order should mean will end up defining the courts' jurisdiction.

Conclusion

We have identified several trade-offs to seeking judicial efficiency in dispute resolution:

1. "Efficiency" is too narrowly defined, having come to mean coping with costs, delays, and backlogs, a restriction which is understandable because we do not have sufficient meaningful data on other metrics. However understandable, this definition proves short-sighted and fetishist in the sense that it focuses so much on efficiency measures that it remains oblivious to the fact that legal problems tend to cluster with other health, poverty, and educational issues. Because we take "efficiency" to mean something too narrow, and because we focus too much on "efficiency" gains, we forget the wider social roots to legal disputes that need to be addressed.

2. Fundamental values of justice other than efficiency could be overlooked when designing or redesigning dispute resolution processes. Such values include Participation,

Respect and Dignity, Neutrality, Impartiality, Access to Justice, Judicial Truth, and Legitimacy. Taking them into account ensures that "fair processes leading to just results" are the norm and will remain the norm, which promotes a thicker version of the rule of law. In other words, even if focusing on "efficiency" meant a generally more productive dispute resolution system, "efficiency" alone would not be enough to sustain a rich and vibrant rule of law. Trying to compress other values of justice, in this respect, may undermine social trust in the long run.

3. Finally, seeking efficiency in dispute resolution also means, ultimately, restricting public courts' jurisdiction to "public order" cases, while leaving untouched the political question of what "public order" is and what it should be. This question is crucial because, ultimately, the definition of "public order" could be the last criterion by which to assess whether cases should be heard by public courts or forums, or whether they should be dealt with in private.

By way of conclusion, it is worth widening our understanding of the time frame of dispute resolution processes, in order to reflect briefly on the reason why disputes arise in the first place. As we have seen, the law and its application are, in a way, a costly intermediary in dispute resolution processes. In this respect, ADR processes intervene as more economical and less stringent alternatives. Although we do not question the need for an intermediary to intervene at some point when a dispute arises, we would like to stress the need for principled intervention in line with the fundamental values of justice identified in this article. This consideration seems highly important when considering technological innovations meant to foster eAccess to justice. How do electronic or online processes of justice fare when assessed with the framework represented by the tree of justice above? Do they fulfill all or most of the values of justice identified?

Finally, more upstream intervention may be the key to more efficiency. If legal education and prevention were taken seriously, lay persons would be better informed, more able to detect the legal dimensions of their issues, thus more precautious, more equipped to deal with the problems they encounter, more proactive and responsible, and more inclined to seek early advice; there would be more prevention, thus fewer disputes, and therefore less demand for dispute resolution in the first place. Such early, upstream intervention is demanding. It requires that legal norms be designed to be clear and efficient, and that they be communicated clearly and efficiently, even broadcast, online or in the traditional media. Beyond plain language, clear and efficient communication strategies are key to making legal information, rights, and obligations more transparent, and widely understood. Clear communication is an expertise worth considering when reflecting on efficient dispute resolution, including resolution online. It is especially relevant with regards to enhancing the legibility and usability of online services. It could also surprise many stakeholders, public and private alike, who will enjoy unsuspected efficiency gains.[24]

Notes

1   In practice, final resolution of a dispute may be undermined or perverted in several ways. To be perfectly productive, the final resolution of a dispute would ideally be self-executed by the parties themselves without further intervention. In this scenario, consensual resolution based on the needs of the parties proves particularly efficient. However, in a second-best-case scenario, the final resolution is binding on the parties, leaving only a possibility that things turn sour at the stage of executing the resolution. In this case, a very efficient decision-making process can be undermined by the uneasy or even impossible execution of the resolution, e.g., when a debtor is insolvent. In practice, the final resolution of a dispute may very well take the form of a default judgment or an interruption of the resolution process, clearing the court's dockets without much consideration for whether the final decision is in fact a resolution or a non-resolution. In such cases, a final but inadequate solution may boomerang back into the court system. Montreal's municipal court's docket, for example, is clogged with applications for judgment revocations, because the parties are informed of the proceedings against them at the time they receive notification of the judgment.

2   See Kim Taylor and Ksenia Svechnikova, *What Does it Cost to Access Justice in Canada? How Much is "Too Much"? And How Do We Know?: Literature Review* (Edmonton, AB: The Canadian Forum on Access to Justice, 2010); see also Action Committee on Access to Justice in Civil and Family Matters, *Access to Civil and Family Justice: A Roadmap for Change* (Ottawa: Action Committee on Access to Justice in Civil and Family Matters, 2013), online: <flsc.ca/wp-content/uploads/2014/10/ACCESSActionCommFinalReport2013.pdf> (recommending increased support for research in order to promote evidence-based policy-making).

For the United Kingdom's most recent domestic endeavour, see Lord Justice Rupert Jackson, *Review of Civil Litigation Costs: Final Report* (London: Ministry of Justice, 2009), with raw data on costs awards only.

3   See Fabien Gélinas and Clément Camion, "Efficiency and Values in the Constitution of Civil Procedure," *International Journal of Procedural Law* 4:2 (2014) at 206.

4   See, e.g., Roscoe Pound's speech at the ABA annual conference of 1906, Roscoe Pound, "The Causes of Popular Dissatisfaction with the Administration of Justice," *Annu. Rep. ABA* 29 (1906) at 395; see also, more recently but not recently, Thurman Arnold, "Due Process in Trials," 300 *Annals of the American Academy of Political and Social Science* (1955) at 123.

5   Harry Kenneth Woolf, *Access to Justice: Final Report to The Lord Chancellor on the Civil Justice System in England and Wales, Overview* (1996) at §1, online: <www.dca.gov.uk/civil/final/contents.htm>.

6   More information available at Council of Europe, online: <www.coe.int/cepej>.

7   The Canadian Forum on Civil Justice, *The Cost of Justice: Weighing the Costs of Fair and Effective Resolution to Legal Problems* (2012), online: <www.cfcj-fcjc.org/sites/defaut/files/docs/2012/CURA_background_doc.pdf>.

8   Action Committee on Access to Justice in Civil and Family Matters, *supra* note 2.

9   See generally Shimon Shetreet, "The Administration of Justice: Practical Problems, Value Conflicts and Changing Concepts," *University of British Columbia Law Review* 13 (1979) at 56.

10   The expression was coined by Galanter. See Marc Galanter, "The Vanishing Trial: An Examination of Trials and Related Matters in Federal and State Courts," *Journal of Empirical Legal Studies* 1 (2004):459 at 459, 460, 477, 483, 506, 514–17.

11   See Quebec's *Code of Civil Procedure*, CQLR c C-25.01, art. 1–7.

12   See, e.g., Geneviève Viney and Patrice Jourdain, *Traité de droit civil. Les obligations. La responsabilité, volume 2 (les conditions)* (dir. Jaques Ghestin) (Paris: LGDJ, 1982) at 18 (arguing that innovations in insurance policies made it possible to indemnify victims of "social risks" such as dangerous labour conditions (during the industrial revolution) by progressively abandoning the requirement to prove the employer's personal fault). See also, on the emergence of presumptions of fault and no-fault liability schemes in French civil law, Louis Josserand, *De la responsabilité du fait des choses inanimées* (Paris: A Rousseau, 1897).

13   This was achieved in Quebec through the *Automobile Insurance Act*, CQLR c A-25 and the *Fonds d'assurance automobile* (*An Act Respecting the Société de l'assurance automobile du Québec*, CQLR c S-11.011, art. 23.0.3). Several, but not all U.S. legislatures have enacted such schemes.

14 This was achieved in Canada with the modifications brought in 1985 to the *Divorce Act*, RSC 1985, c 3 (2nd Supp).

15 This was achieved in Canada with the *Criminal Law Amendment Act* of 1968–1969, RSC 1968–69, c 38.

16 Action Committee on Access to Justice in Civil and Family Matters, *supra* note 2 at 4 (particularly notes 29 and 31).

17 Ab Currie, "The Legal Problems of Everyday Life," in *Access to Justice (Sociology of Crime, Law and Deviance), Volume 12*, ed. Rebecca Sandefur, (Bingley, UK: Emerald Group Publishing, 2009) at 1; for the first Canadian study measuring the tendency of legal problems to cluster, see the Canadian Forum on Civil Justice, *Costs of Justice Project*, online: <www.cfcj-fcjc.org/a2jblog/everyday-legal-problems-and-the-cost-of-justice-in-canada>.

18 Action Committee on Access to Justice in Civil and Family Matters, *supra* note 2 at 11–14.

19 Tom R. Tyler, "Citizen Discontent with Legal Procedures: A Social Science Perspective on Civil Procedure Reform," *American Journal of Comparative Law* 45 (1997):871 at 894. See also, Tom R. Tyler, *Why People Obey the Law* (New Haven: Yale University Press, 1992), reedited in 2006 by Princeton University Press.

20 Gélinas and Camion, supra note 3; see also, Fabien Gélinas et al., *Foundations of Civil Justice: Toward a Value-Based Framework for Reform* (Berlin: Springer, 2015).

21 Michel Foucault, *Surveiller et punir* (Paris: Gallimard, 1975) (in particular the chapter on discipline at 159).

22 Even then, private arbitrators are not prevented from applying public-order rules.

23 On this particular subject, see Judith Resnik, "Diffusing Disputes: The Public in the Private of Arbitration, the Private in Courts, and the Erasure of Rights" 124 *Yale Law Journal* 2804 (2015).

24 In 1970, Citibank rewrote its loan agreement in plain language in an attempt to decrease the amount of litigation in link with this specific contract. Not only did it work, but the bank also gained market shares, training time for the employees was reduced by half, and the information given to clients was more accurate. More recently, Manitoba rewrote the Small Claims Court acts, forms, and brochures in plain language, with the effect of increasing the staff's productivity by 40%. See Joseph Kimble, "Writing for Dollars, Writing to Please," *Scribes Journal of Legal Writing* 6 (1996):1 at 8; see also Stéphanie Roy, "Rédiger des contrats clairs: une strategie d'affaires gagnante," in *Communication juridique et judiciaire de l'entreprise*, ed. Hugues Bouthinon-Dumas (Brussels: Larcier, 2015).

CHAPTER XII

The Electronic Process in the Brazilian Judicial System: Much More Than an Option; It Is a Solution

Katia Balbino de Carvalho Ferreira

Introduction

First, it is important to mention that I participated in this conference not only as a Brazilian federal judge who has experience with the development and use of cyberjustice, but also as a student in the master's program of the Université de Montréal, which provided me with an opportunity for cultural immersion and extensive research concerning the use of technology in courts as a means to enhance access to justice and to accelerate its delivery.

When I graduated from law school at the University of Brasília, in 1985, I first started working at the Faculty of Law, and a few years later (1987), I became a lawyer for the university. Arriving at work, I was given a traditional 1940-model Remington typewriter to write drafts of my opinions and petitions that would later be transferred by an assistant to better quality paper using an electric typewriter. Soon enough, aiming for celerity, I gained the right to use an XP computer and a matrix printer so that the files would not pile up on my desk for too long. The use of technology to enhance the development of legal activities has always been part of my beliefs for the future.

Everyone who is involved in making access to justice a reality for all individuals dreams of wide-open doors leading to timely and fair justice. And cyberjustice has been included as a possible path to achieve this goal.

Limited to the purpose of the conference and based on our experience in Brazil,[1] I want to share my conviction that there is no way to opt out of the technological revolution without the risk of paying a high price for being left out of the globalized world, since it has been a long time since humans could stay away from technology and still lead an integrated life.

Information and communication technology has revolutionized our lives, causing dependency on many different levels. Some examples include systems related to banking,[2] transportation, communications, health diagnosis and cure research, information, education, leisure, development of sports techniques, personal and commercial relations, and conflict resolution.

In the digital and globalized era, one cannot think of development or democratization of rights without considering the new configuration of social relations. For the judiciary, it is a challenging moment that invites us to review traditional formats and, with this transformation, improve access to and delivery of justice. Advancements should not be limited to procedural innovations, or else an important opportunity for integrating new concepts will be missed.[3]

The Brazilian minister of justice, Jose Cardozo, emphasized that computerizing the process of delivering justice is imperative to resolving many of the legal problems faced by the Brazilian judiciary. The implementation of electronic processes certainly confers more celerity, accessibility, and efficiency to the judicial system.[4]

Brazilian Justice in Numbers

Time and distance are new concepts in an internet-based society. Hence, if there are complaints about the tardiness of judicial decisions in a paper-based world, it is undeniable that the celerity which citizens could expect from the judiciary can be increased in an environment where research, communication, and decisions can be provided in shorter time frames, saving time and money.

In order to understand the use of cyberjustice in Brazil, it is important to take into consideration the structure of the judicial branch and the administrative autonomy of the courts. An autonomous and divided judicial system, with different specializations and levels, certainly faces some difficulties in developing solutions that will be uniform and meet the needs of all stakeholders.

The macro-organizational structure of the Brazilian judiciary system is established by article 92 of the Brazilian Constitution:

I – Supreme Federal Court
I-A – National Council of Justice
II – Superior Court of Justice
III – Federal Regional Courts and the Federal Judges
IV – Labour Courts and Judges
V – Electoral Courts and Judges
VI – Military Courts and Judges
VII – Courts and Judges of the states, of the Federal District and of the territories

Besides the Superior Court of Justice, there are three other superior courts: the Superior Labour Court (Article 111, I); the Superior Electoral Court (Article 118, I); and the Superior Military Court (Article 118, I). The federal justice system has five Federal Regional Courts (of appeals) responsible for all 26 states and a single federal district, and 27 federal judiciary sections.[5] The labour justice system has 24 Regional Labour Courts (of appeal), the electoral justice system has 27 Regional Electoral Courts (of appeal), and each of the 26 states of the federation and the Federal District has a Court of Justice.

The size of the Brazilian problem is reflected in the numbers. Since 2004, the Brazilian National Council of Justice has been presenting national statistics to inform the general public and identify challenges. Submitting this data to other institutions, to academic analyses, and to public evaluation is considered as a way to build shared solutions that may lead to the construction of a more fair society and favour the reduction of inequalities.

The Justice by the Numbers 2013/2014 revealed last week that in 2013, 95.14 million cases were being processed in Brazilian courts,[6] among which 70% corresponded to cases remaining from previous years (66.8 million) and 30% were new cases (28.6 million). It is important to mention that 16,429 judges were in charge of settling these disputes.

Systems Developed for Brazilian Courts

Every day, technology gains more ground in the courts. In Brazil, no judge can choose if she or he wants to adapt to new technologies.

Judges can decide their cases, but they cannot make the choice of having only paper-based procedures in their courts. Individual judges do not make these administrative decisions according to their own individual judicial priorities since they have to consider the administration of justice as a whole and the investments that are made to provide a better service to the public.

However, judges are appointed as members of committees and groups responsible for the development of tools and the implementation of new technologies in Brazilian courts in order to guarantee that systems are in line with the law and their way of working. Judges have a very active role in these processes, and besides deciding cases, they are frequently involved in the management of caseloads, searching for ways to decide the cases faster and better.

The electronic process can be a way to control the duration of the process in the courts and to organize the procedures necessary to prepare a case to be heard. The administration of the various stages of each and every file has to be afforded the reasonable time required for justice to be delivered.

Although my participation in this conference does not have the objective of comparing different systems implemented in Brazilian courts or giving exhaustive details about their development, I will provide some examples to illustrate the degree to which technology has modified the Brazilian judiciary.

Despite the fact that some people still face difficulties in integrating computers in their daily lives, computers undoubtedly not only replace typewriters, but also help us to manage time more efficiently.

In 1991, the Brazilian legislature included in rental law n. 8.245[7] the possibility of notifying the tenant by fax. Later on, in 1999, Brazilian federal law n. 9.800, known as the "Law of Facsimile," allowed for the electronic transmission of petitions to courts,[8] establishing conditions and limits for validity of the document and requiring the presentation of originals in court.

At the same time, for law professionals, it was made possible to follow the edition of laws, precedents from courts, and last but not least, the procedures in cases of interest. Initially, one of the major benefits of the use of technology in the judiciary was related to the automation of case information, providing the public with fast and transparent data about what happens in courts. In the late 1990s, many Brazilian tribunals implemented systems that would allow lawyers to obtain records about their cases without leaving their offices and before the judiciary official journal was released. Some systems even send automatic e-mails to the parties and lawyers associated with the case every time there is an update in the file history.[9]

In July 2001, Brazilian federal law n. 10.259, which created the federal small claims courts, provided a general regulation for the development of software to use in these new courts.[10] The absence of detailed rules led many courts to develop their own regulations and systems, adapted from the existing code of procedure. We had many different experiences implemented in different courts, from small-claims courts to the Supreme Court. And despite the effort of the National Council of Justice, based on Brazilian federal law n. 11.419 of December 2006, different parameters still coexist, because it is not an easy task to transfer the data stored in pre-existing systems that were developed in incompatible technological languages.

Supreme Federal Court (STF)

The Brazilian Supreme Court, with the goal of observing the provisions of Brazilian Federal Law 11.419/2006 and accelerating the delivery of justice, regulated cyberjustice by enacting Resolution 344/2007. The system named e-STF was officially launched on June 21, 2007 to process an extraordinary appeal.[11] Users needed to be previously registered in the STF, and petitions or documents could be sent electronically via the internet.[12]

In November 2007, Resolution STF n. 350 already regulated the use of digital certification for electronic petitions, but it was not mandatory for all users, and access to the system still required prior registration. However, the use of digital certification to send petitions and documents made it unnecessary to present originals in court.[13]

In October 2009, through Resolution STF n. 407, the mandatory use of digital certification for electronic petitions in the Supreme Court was established, although other alternatives remained available.[14] Since February 2010, eight types of actions can only be filed electronically, and by July 2010, the STF had more than 2,000 electronic files, which represented a small but important step toward computerization of the court.[15]

In October 2014, the Supreme Court already had more than half of its almost 50,000 cases processed completely in electronic files.

Superior Court of Justice (STJ)

The Superior Court of Justice was the first court with national jurisdiction to entirely eliminate paper-based files by developing a system
where all procedures are electronic. Speaking of numbers demon-
strating the intensive use of technology in the Superior Court of
Justice, between the months of January through March of 2009, more
than 236,000 cases were digitized, in addition to around 1,200 new
cases filed electronically every day.

Some highlights of the project "Justice in the Virtual Era" include:

- Faster justice—the distribution of lawsuits that would take
  at least seven days now takes a few seconds. The time spent
  in procedures to file an appeal to the STJ, which used to take
  six months, is now reduced to six days;
- Enhanced access—though the STJ is situated in Brasilia, the
  system allows lawyers from all over the country to send
  petitions, to search for information, and to be notified of
  judgments with no travel costs;
- Reduction of costs—in 2008, the STJ spent BRL$1.7 million on
  toner and ink cartridges for printers, more than BRL$600,000
  on paper, and almost BRL$7 million on postal services. These
  costs have significantly decreased with e-STJ;
- Environmental preservation—in the STJ, approximately
  300,000 cases are processed every year. In paper, this corresponds to more than 113 million pages, or between 26,000 and
  32,000 trees, 54 million litres of water, and 2.7 kWh of energy.
  Nature is certainly preserved thanks to electronic processes;
- Security—the use of digital certification to sign documents
  and access information guarantees the integrity of documents and protection of information; and
- Work environment—although some routines also have to be
  established in relation to the excessive use of computers, the
  storage of paper files used to be the cause of many diseases.
  Court personnel now achieve higher performance and have
  a better quality of life.[16]

The e-STJ is currently regulated by Resolution STJ n. 14, of June 28, 2013.

National Council of Justice (CNJ)

Although more than 25 different systems coexist in Brazilian courts, the National Council of Justice, created in 2004, undertook to bring federal and state courts, of different specializations, to the same digital standards, and it is trying to work on solutions that can be evenly implemented despite the diversity of infrastructures. In December 2013, through Resolution CNJ n. 185, Brazil undertook to adopt PJe as the only electronic process for all Brazilian courts by 2018.[17] In the meantime, all courts should have it installed in at least 10% of their units by December of this year. This system already has three versions: the first one was developed for the 5th Federal Region Court, the second for Labour Courts (PJe-JT), and the third, the national version, for all other courts.

The system has been in use since April 2010, and as of June 2014, more than 35,000 cases had been e-filed in 106 courts of the 5th Federal Region.[18]

Federal Court of the 1st Region (TRF1)

In the 1st Federal Region Courts there are four major electronic process systems, one for federal small claims (JEF virtual—developed in visual basic); another for tax courts (PJD-EF in ASP); another for civil courts (e-Jur in JAVA); and a pilot project of the PJe (also in JAVA) in civil courts of the Federal District judicial section. These complex systems do not intercommunicate, but the idea is to unify all components in the PJe platform, which also represents the substitution of pin codes for digital certificates.

Federal Court of the 4th Region (TRF4)

The TRF4 experiment is considered a success by all its users. The e-proc, originally created to meet the needs of federal small claims courts in 2003, was adapted to other types of cases. Today, almost three million electronic cases have already been filed within this consolidated system, which has recently inaugurated a special module for pre-conciliation online. It is expected that the investments made and the credibility of the software will guarantee its maintenance, despite the use of the PJe in other federal courts.[19] Interoperability may be the key to their coexistence.

Digital Certificate—A New Signature

Each day more courts are adopting systems that require the use of digital certificates. A digital certificate connects or correlates a person with a cryptographic key pair in order to guarantee the identification of the user, as well as the security and validity of electronic documents.

Through Provisional Measure 2200, of 28 June 2001,[20] the Brazilian government launched the Brazilian Public Key Infrastructure—PKI Brazil,[21] and adopted a legal model which observes the principles of authenticity, integrity, confidentiality, and legal validity for the certification of electronic documents, equipment, applications, and transactions. Authenticity ensures that the author is the person named in the certificate used in the signature. Integrity means that the document was not modified after its release. Confidentiality denies unauthorized people access to contents of messages or documents. Legal validity, associated with non-repudiation in crypto-technical parlance, establishes that the sender cannot refute authorship after signing once the information becomes verifiable by any third party and "with high assurance can be asserted to be genuine."[22]

The National Institute of Information Technology (ITI) is the Brazilian federal agency of the executive branch that supports the Brazilian Public Key Infrastructure—PKI Brazil, which is the first certificate authority of the chain—CA root. It also has the important goal of promoting digital inclusion[23] and, in a single-root architecture, accrediting, supervising, and auditing the other participants in the chain.

The ITI has accredited the AC-Jus—a first-level Certificate Authority for the Judiciary, created in December 2004.[24] Usually, the digital signatures produced by certificates mentioned above are legally equivalent to handwritten signatures, but the Cert-jus certificates include other particular characteristics such as the identification of public servants—their position, ID number, and where they work—which is a digital functional identity that ascribes responsibility for the production of the electronic document to a public agent.

The ITI announced that in 2011 and 2012 over two million digital certificates were issued per year in PKI-Brazil and each day new applications increase the use of this technology.[25]

The participation of the bar in the updating process of professionals is essential in helping lawyers overcome many obstacles they face in the use of new tools. For example, the bar of Rio de Janeiro, the second largest in Brazil, has been providing courses on digital certification and the electronic process. In addition, projects like the "Get Digital" caravan, which visited 60 subsections, was responsible for providing information to lawyers concerning the requirement of digital certification to access new technological judicial systems and to facilitate the acquisition of digital certificates, with an explanation of technical procedures.[26]

As President of the Technical Committee of CA-JUS in 2006/2007, I experienced the security procedures involving the expedition of digital certificates and the maintenance of the information in safe rooms with very strict access. However, given the growing demand, a considerable increase in the number of registration authorities, and the proliferation of applications that require these certificates, there is a risk of fraud during primary identification (presentation of physical documents) and this has to be taken seriously, in order to prevent the efficiency and reliability of the tool from being called into question.

The increased use of biometry to identify a user may be the next step to enhance trust in the ownership of the certificate, since it uses a key that cannot be borrowed or taken from a person, minimizing the possibility of error in the identification process.

Digital certification, despite the restrictions it still presents for some users, has been considered an essential instrument in providing validity to e-procedures and securing controlled access to files.

Conclusion

Nobody likes to spend a day in court. If justice is needed, something has already gone wrong. This can be even harder if individuals have to face overloaded courts, where time and costs are totally unpredictable. Despite the new challenges it can raise and in light of the results obtained to date, the use of technology in the courts can definitely be considered a mechanism to overcome large caseloads and to improve the reasonable duration of procedures.

If the whole world is communicating through the internet, it is no longer time to decide *if* technology will be used in courts, but rather *how* it is going to be used in order to guarantee efficiency and protection of rights.[27]

The electronic process, included in the list of services known as online dispute-resolution mechanisms, can help the judiciary resolve more quickly the disputes of the online and offline "community through the use of the tools of online technology and its 24-hours-per-day, 7-days-per-week, 365-days-per-year access."[28]

The new conflicts developed in a globalized society demand a new way of judging. We judges cannot produce individualized pieces of judicial art on a case-by-case basis with no consideration for precedent or potential impacts on other lawsuits and on the social, political, and cultural environments. The judiciary, as a social organizer, must do its part and the technological advancements in the courts may represent much more than a reduction of costs. They can speed up the rendering of decisions, guarantee and expand access to justice, and enhance democracy as a result of transparency of information and the participation of diverse social actors.[29]

We are certainly following a path where delivering justice without cyberjustice will no longer be an option. In addition, we must keep in mind that public justice, as well as public-health and educational systems, should be available to all citizens and efficiently provided by the state as a means to reducing inequalities in democratic societies.

Notes

1　Federal judge since November 1995, appointed President of the Permanent Commission to Standardize the Study of Information Technology Platform in Federal Courts by the Federal Council of Justice, and Chair of the Technical Commission of Judiciary Certifying Authority—AC-JUS—May 2006 / August 2007 (1104 Act PRESI TRF1 – 1193, 04/19/2006, 04/24/2006 and DJ CJF Ordinance no. 042, 04/24/2006); assigned by the Council of Federal Courts as member of the Committee of Procedures Systems and Records for the Federal Justice (Ordinance CJF n. 119 05/11/2011) and by the 1st Regional Federal Court as member of the Special Committee on Standard Procedures Records (Ordinance/ PRESI 600-298, from 05/11/2006 to 04/17/2008); of the Management Committee of e-JUS (Ordinance/PRESI 600-291, from 12/24/2007 to 04/17/2008); of the Committee for the Implementation of Tax Enforcement Virtual Procedures (PRESI 600-329 from 06/05/2006 to 04/17/2008); and of the Commission for the Creation of the Manual of Virtual Small-Claims System (Ordinance/PRESI 600-574 of 10/27/2005 to 04/17/2008); designated Head of Goals for the Judiciary for the years 2010, 2011, and

2012, for the 1st Regional Federal Court (Ordinance/PRESI/CENAG-282, 07/21/2010; Ordinance/PRESI/CENAG-165, 06/04/2011; and Ordinance/PRESI/CENAG-266, 07/20/2012), Coordinator of the Regional Committee of Procedures Records for 1st Regional Federal Court (Ordinance/PRESI/CENAG-199, 02/05/2011); and member of the Committee on Security of the Federal Courts (Ordinance CJF 09, 31/08/2011).

2   "Why do you think banks have become electronic?" The Honourable Justice Thomas Granger of the Superior Court of Justice, Ontario, asks matter-of-factly. "Banks have realized that you save money doing it. The government does the same thing." Luigi Benetton, "Guide to Courtroom Technology in Canada" *CBA Practice Link* (September 2009), online: <www.cba.org/cba/practicelink/ solosmall_technology/courts.aspx>

3   Rômulo Valentini, "A padronização de procedimentos no processo do trabalho e sua aplicabilidade no processo eletrônico – o constante aperfeiçoamento da prestação jurisdicional," *Revista do Tribunal Regional do Trabalho da 1ª Região* 23:52 (2012):133 at 136.

4   Jose Carlos De Araujo Almeida Filho, *Processo Eletrônico e Teoria Geral do Processo Eletrônico* (Rio de Janeiro: Ed Forense, 2008) at preface.

5   First instance for each state of the federation and the federal district.

6   Data are derived from all Brazilian Judiciary Courts, excluding the Supreme Federal Court. Information obtained by the National Council of Justice corresponds to numbers provided by the Superior Court of Justice, the Federal Regional Courts, the Labour Courts, the Electoral Courts, the Military Courts, and the courts of the states, of the Federal District, and of the territories.

7   Brazilian Federal Law n. 8.245/199, "art. 58. [...] V- desde que autorizado no contrato, a citação, intimação ou notificação far - se - á mediante correspondência com aviso de recebimento, ou, tratando - se de pessoa jurídica ou firma individual, também mediante telex ou fac-símile, ou, ainda, sendo necessário, pelas demais formas previstas no Código de Processo Civil." ["Art. 58. [...] V – once authorized in the contract, the summons, subpoena or notification shall be made by mail with note of receipt, or, in the case of legal entity or individual firm, also by telex or facsimile, or even, if necessary, by other provided forms in the Code of Civil Procedure."]

8   Brazilian Federal Law n. 9.800/1999, "art. 1º É permitida às partes a utilização de sistema de transmissão de dados e imagens tipo fac-símile ou outro similar, para a prática de atos processuais que dependam de petição escrita." ["Art. 1º The parties are allowed to use image and data transmission systems, images by facsimile or other similar, for the practice of procedural acts that rely on written petition."]

9   Alexandre Atheniense, "Advocacia e Informatica" (December 1996), *Jus navigandi*, online: <jus.com.br/artigos/1754/advocacia-e-informatica>.

10 Brazilian Federal Law n. 10.259/2001, "art 8 [...] § 2º Os tribunais poderão organizar serviço de intimação das partes e de recepção de petições por meio eletrônico; ...art. 24. O Centro de Estudos Judiciários do Conselho da Justiça Federal e as Escolas de Magistratura dos Tribunais Regionais Federais criarão programas de informática necessários para subsidiar a instrução das causas submetidas aos Juizados e promoverão cursos de aperfeiçoamento destinados aos seus magistrados e servidores." ["Art. 8. [...]§ 2º The courts may prepare a subpoena service of the parties using electronic communication; ... Art. 24. The Judicial Studies Centre of the Council of Federal Justice and the Judiciary Schools of the Federal Regional Courts will create computer programs necessary to support preparatory inquiries in cases submitted to the Courts and promote training for its judges and servers."]

11 "Recurso Extraordinário"—used to contest decisions that could have been provided without the correct observation of Constitutional provisions.

12 "Tramitação eletrônica de processos judiciais foi iniciada no STF em 2007," (2010) Supremo Tribunal Federal, online: <www.stf.jus.br/portal/ cms/ verNoticiaDetalhe.asp?idConteudo=156088&modo=cms>.

13 Ibid.

14 Paper-based petitions could be presented at the protocol section, sent by mail, by fax, or by email—the two latter ones had their validity conditioned to the presentation of the originals

15 The caseload in the Supreme Court in July 2010 corresponded to 90,164 cases. STF, *supra* note 12.

16 "Justiça na era virtual," Supremo Tribunal Federal, online: <www2.stf. jus.br/portalStfInternacional/cms/verConteudo.php?sigla=portal StfCooperacao_pt_br&idConteudo=190769&modo=cms> (information provided by the Supreme Court website).

17 Resolution CNJ n. 185/2013, "art. 34. As Presidências dos Tribunais devem constituir Comitê Gestor e adotar as providências necessárias à implantação do PJe, conforme plano e cronograma a serem previamente aprovados pela Presidência do CNJ, ouvido o Comitê Gestor Nacional [...] § 3º O cronograma deve relacionar os órgãos julgadores de 1º e 2º Graus em que o PJe será gradualmente implantado, a contar do ano de 2014, de modo a atingir 100% (cem por cento) nos anos de 2016, 2017 ou 2018, a depender do porte do Tribunal no relatório Justiça em Números (pequeno, médio ou grande porte, respectivamente)." ["Art. 34. The Presidencies of the courts should constitute a Management Committee and adopt the necessary measures of the implementation of PJe (electronic Judicial Procedure) according to a plan and schedule to be previously approved by the Presidency of the CNJ (National Council of Justice), after consultation with the National Management Committee

[...]§ 3º. The schedule should list the judging bodies of 1st and 2nd Degrees in which the PJe will be gradually deployed, from the year 2014, in order to achieve 100% (one hundred percent) in the years 2016, 2017 or 2018, depending on the size of the scale of the Court in the report Justice in Numbers (small, medium or large scale, respectively)."] Tarcisio Teixeira, *Curso de direito e processo eletrônico* (São Paulo: Editora Saraiva, 2014) at 436–37.

18 "Processo judicial eletrônico está implantado em 34 tribunais do país" (June 2014), *Consultor Jurídico*, online: <www.conjur.com.br/2014-jun-09/processo-judicial-eletronico-implantado-34-tribunais-pais>.

19 Jomar Martins, "Proposta do CNJ ameaça sistema criado pelo TRF-4" (December 2013), *Consultor Jurídico*, online: <www.conjur.com.br/2013-dez-12/proposta-cnj-ameaca-sistema-trf-juiz-assessor-presidencia>.

20 Re-edited as Provisional Measure 2200-02, 24 August 2001.

21 Infraestrutura de Chaves Públicas Brasileira (ICP Brasil).

22 Adrian McCullagh and William Caelli, "Non-repudiation in the digital environment," *Peer Reviewed Journal on the Internet* 5:8 (2000), online: <pear.accc.uic.edu/ojs/index.php/fm/article/view/778/687>.

23 Instituto Nacional de Tecnologia da Informação, online: <www.iti.gov.br/institucional/quem-somos>.

24 Resolution STJ/CJF nº 001, 20 December 2004, online: <www.acjus.jus.br/legislacao/resolucoes>.

25 *Revista Digital* v2 2012 at 7, online: <http://www.iti.gov.br/images/publicacoes/revista-digital/revista_digital_2_2012.pdf>.

26 Ibid. at 11–13.

27 Luiz Flávio Gomes, "Judiciário não pode resistir aos avanços da tecnologia" (October 2002), *Consultor Jurídico*, online: <www.conjur.com.br/2002-out-27/judiciario_nao_resistir_aos_avancos_tecnologicos>.

28 Lucille M. Ponte and Thomas D. Cavenagh, *Cyberjustice Online Dispute Resolution (ODR) for E-commerce* (Pearson: Prentice Hall, 2006).

29 Francisco Rossal De Araujo et al., "Avancos tecnologicos – Acesso ao Judiciario e outros temas," *COAD* 36 (2009) at 647.

* Thank you to Cristiano Therrien for translation from the Portuguese in notes 7, 8, 10, and 17.

CHAPTER XIII

Access to Justice and Technology: Transforming the Face of Cross-Border Civil Litigation and Adjudication in the EU

Xandra E Kramer

Introduction

The use of information and communication technology for the purpose of judicial proceedings is a topical issue in Europe. Some EU member states had already started many years ago to implement information and communications technology (ICT) applications within the courts and judicial proceedings.[1] This ranges from the basic digitalization of court administration to an advanced use of videoconferencing and the full online handling of procedures. Other member states are still in their relative infancy in implementing ICT within the judiciary. The overriding aim of these initiatives evidently is to achieve a better administration of justice.[2] Developments in the member states run parallel to and are in part influenced by those at the pan-European level.

In the European Union, e-justice has been on the agenda of the policy-maker for over a decade. The European Commission has invested in the setting up of legal atlases containing information for legal professionals and EU citizens and business; these currently are incorporated in the European e-Justice Portal.[3] The Commission has also been active in encouraging videoconferencing, the electronic transmission of documents, the connection of criminal records, and the setting up of databases and registers. In the first multi-annual European e-Justice Strategy (2008), the Commission stressed the need to create synergies of the initiatives at the European and national level.[4] The current Strategy on European e-Justice for 2014–2018 emphasizes the key role of the European e-Justice Portal, and outlines the objectives, modes, and measures of implementation.[5]

A leading pan-European project is e-Codex, which aims at improving cross-border access to justice for citizens and business and at enhancing the interoperability between legal authorities in the EU.[6] Its participants and partners currently include governments from over 20 European countries as well as a number of associations and research institutes.

The overriding aim of e-justice at the EU level is to improve access to justice, in particular for cross-border cases in civil and commercial matters, and, more recently, to enhance administration and collaboration in criminal matters. The focus of the present paper is on cross-border civil procedure. In recent years, several uniform civil procedures, notably the European order for payment and the European small claims procedure have been established. In these procedures, the use of ICT is encouraged, and has, to a certain extent, been operationalized. As part of a package to encourage alternative dispute resolution (ADR), a regulation on online dispute resolution (ODR) has been established recently. The implementation of e-justice at the European level has its limits, however, as it generally requires the cooperation of the member states, and creating legal and technical interoperability is challenging. At the same time, e-justice may pose challenges for procedural justice as a result of the often one-sided focus on efficiency of justice.

This paper discusses developments in e-justice in the EU, focusing on its implementation in cross-border civil litigation and adjudication. It questions the impact of e-justice on access to justice—as guaranteed by Article 6 of the European Convention on Human Rights and by Article 47 of the EU Charter on Fundamental Rights—its legal and practical limitations, and procedural challenges. As a full discussion of this topic would merit a monograph, and the literature on specific ICT applications and digital procedures is abundant, this paper can only offer a bird's-eye view from the perspective of European civil procedure. Section 2 discusses the EU policy and legislative framework of e-justice, while Section 3 focuses on the implementation of ICT in the European debt-collection procedures and the new ODR platform. In Section 4, the impact on access to justice as well as the limits and challenges of e-justice in the EU context is assessed, and Section 5 concludes the paper.

e-Justice in the EU: Policy Perspectives

Policy Framework and Initiatives

The activities of the European Union in the area of e-justice are linked to developments at the national level, where ICT plays an important role in public administration (eGovernment) and the administration of justice. A European framework for e-commerce was established in 2000,[7] and was followed by the initiation of EU activities on eGovernment.[8] As part of the Digital Agenda for Europe (one of the pillars of the Europe 2020 Strategy), the European Commission employs a diverse range of activities aiming at supporting a digital single market, enhancing interoperability, strengthening trust and security, investing in research and innovation, and securing ICT-enabled benefits for EU society.[9]

The advancement at the EU level depends to a large extent on the willingness and the advancement as regards ICT of the member states. In the present European e-Justice Strategy, voluntary participation is once again taken as the starting point, except for the EU legislative instruments that require the implementation of a specific project or ICT application.[10] European e-justice is based on decentralization and interoperability, and it covers projects with a European dimension in the area of civil, criminal, and administrative law.[11] As is also highlighted in this policy document, the main achievement has been the e-Justice portal, launched in 2010.[12] This website—"the one-stop shop" for European citizens and legal professionals—currently includes over 12,000 pages of content on EU and national law in all the official languages of the EU. It also has several interactive features, including dynamic electronic forms, a portal wizard to help choose among available European procedures, and language tools. Another noteworthy feature is the introduction of the European Case Law Identifier (ECLI), presenting a uniform format for case law for all member states' and EU courts.[13] In 2015, the Council adopted a recommendation to promote the use and sharing of best practices in cross-border videoconferencing in the member states, with a view to improving interoperability.[14]

Civil Justice and Facilitating Cross-Border Litigation

The focal point of e-justice in the field of civil law is the enhancing of access to justice in cross-border cases. This in part results from the specific competence of the European Union in "civil matters having cross-border implications," as laid down in Article 81 of the Treaty on the Functioning of the European Union (TFEU) concerning judicial cooperation in civil matters.[15] Despite a certain degree of harmonization, civil procedures differ greatly in the member states, and potential litigants having to enforce cross-border claims may still face legal and practical obstacles. These result, *inter alia*, from having to establish international jurisdiction, the need for cross-border service of documents, the taking of evidence, enforcement, diverging domestic procedures, and having to incur additional costs for local legal representation, the translation of documents, and travel expenses.

Traditional private international law instruments, and most significantly what is currently the Brussels I-bis Regulation, have introduced harmonized rules for international jurisdiction and the recognition and enforcement of judgements.[16] In the past 16 years, nearly 20 additional instruments have been established under the heading of judicial cooperation in civil matters, dealing with specific procedural law issues or the applicable law.[17] For procedural aspects, the regulations on the service of documents[18] and the taking of evidence[19] may be mentioned. More recently, three uniform European civil procedures have been established: the European order for payment procedure, the European small claims procedure, and the European account preservation order.[20] These procedures are intended to support effective recovery of debts in cross-border cases.

These legislative instruments on procedural law contain provisions that facilitate, encourage, and rely on the use of ICT. This operates at three different levels. First, through the European e-Justice Portal, electronic access is provided to the text of the instruments, to the standard forms (e.g., for filing a request for the service of a document or enforcement of a judgment in another member state), and to relevant national rules and information on implementation of EU law in the member states. In addition, electronic databases for case law and registers, including a European business register and an insolvency register, have been set up. Second, the instruments support electronic communication and communication by other technological means between judicial authorities, and between the parties and judicial or extra-judicial bodies. This includes the online submission of documents as well as videoconferencing for the purpose of evidence taking and oral hearings.[21] Third, and most far-reaching, is the full online conduct of European civil procedures. To date, the latter has only materialized in a few member states with regard to the European order for payment procedure.[22]

European Civil Procedure and the Use of ICT

Uniform Civil Procedures and Facilitating Technology

This section focuses on two European procedures introducing new models that enable the use of ICT in different stages of the process: namely, the European order for payment and small claims procedure.[23] In particular, the first one is designed to enable a full electronic handling of the procedure. The third European civil procedure—the European account preservation order—also fosters electronic communication, and relies on an online information system. This new procedure will not be discussed further, however, since it will only come into force in January 2017, and no practical information on its implementation and application is yet available.

1. European Order for Payment and Small Claims Procedure

The European order for payment procedure (applicable since December 12, 2008) and the European small claims procedure (applicable since January 1, 2009) were developed to make cross-border debt collection within the European Union more effective.[24] Although most member states already had specific procedures for these types of claims, the great divergence between domestic procedures and their limited application in cross-border cases justified the introduction of these first European civil procedures.[25] They are optionally available to the claimant in cross-border cases, in which at least one of the parties is domiciled or habitually resident in a member state other than that of the court or tribunal seized.[26]

The European order for payment procedure is a one-sided procedure for the collection of uncontested debts.[27] Upon the applicant's request, a European order for payment is to be issued by the seized competent court, ordinarily within 30 days.[28] If the debtor does not oppose the order within a prescribed period of 30 days after it has been served, the payment order must be declared enforceable, and can be enforced throughout the EU.[29] The European small claims procedure is an adversarial procedure that is currently available for claims with a value up to €2,000.[30] Following the adoption of a regulation amending the small claims procedure, this threshold will be raised to €5,000 in July 2017.[31]

The European regulations contain rules to simplify the procedure, and are conducted by means of standard forms, including a claim form, a correction form, an answer form (small claims), the

order for payment issue form, the opposition form (order for payment), and a form for enforcement. Along with a number of other
features that facilitate the use of ICT, this standardization makes
these procedures particularly suitable for digitalization.

The remainder of this section will focus on the legal framework
for ICT and its use in these procedures.[32] It should be noted that the
available information on the actual use of these procedures in the
member states is limited due to a lack of comprehensive empirical
data, in particular in relation to the European small claims procedure.
As is clear from a number of studies,[33] and from the Commission
report on the application of the European small claims procedure,
dating from November 2013, this procedure is seldom used in the
member states.[34] To extend the use of the procedure and to improve
its functioning, the European Commission put forward a proposal
to revise it.[35] At the end of 2015, the new regulation was adopted and
it will take effect on July 14, 2017.[36] The European order-for-payment
procedure is more successful, as is confirmed by the report of the
European Commission on the application of this procedure, published in October 2015.[37]

2. Access: Online Information, Dynamic Forms, and Submission
The use of both European procedures is facilitated by two key factors
within the EU e-justice program: information and relevant standard
forms are electronically accessible, and the regulations facilitate the
electronic submission of the forms through which communication
between the agents (primarily parties and courts) in these procedures
is conducted. Basic information on these European procedures is
available on the European judicial atlas for civil matters (currently
linked to the e-Justice portal), which has a separate section on each
procedure. Apart from providing general information and links to
the text of the regulations and the standard forms, the atlas provides
relevant information per member state (e.g., the courts having jurisdiction, accepted means of submission of documents, and language
requirements), which appears when one clicks on the competent
member state on a map.

The European e-Justice Portal has a section entitled "dynamic
forms," which includes a wizard that assists users in deciding
whether and which of the two European procedures can be used.[38]
It includes separate sections on the two procedures with a brief
explanation, a link to the practice guides that have been developed

for these procedures, and links to the standard forms of the European order for payment[39] and to the European small claims procedure.[40]

The standard forms are of essence for simplifying access to the European procedures and standardizing their application in the national court having jurisdiction.[41] Since legal representation is not compulsory in these European procedures,[42] they are developed as "do it yourself" procedures. Clicking, for instance, on application form A for the European order-for-payment procedure leads to a map of the EU. Selecting the country to which the applicant wants to send his or her form leads to brief information on how the form can be sent (by post, directly to the court, by fax, email, or another electronic means), and in which language(s) the application should be made. Short explanations guide the user in filling out the form. In addition, the European small claims regulation requires member states to provide practical assistance in completing the forms.[43] However, in practice this assistance is not always available, and it often has an ad hoc character.[44]

As far as possible, the standard forms use closed encoded fields that can be ticked. On completion, the form can be sent to the competent court or judicial body within the member state selected. A PDF can be generated, and the user is reminded as to which language(s) the selected member state accepts. The user can select a language, and the standard items in the form are translated into the chosen language. The open fields are not translated, in particular the description of the evidence, and, for the small claims procedure, a factual description of the basis of the claim as well as evidential documents to be enclosed. Since this information is crucial for the court to have an understanding of the case and the claim, the claimant should provide for a proper translation. Only a few member states accept forms in a language other than their official language(s).

As regards the submission of the application form (order for payment) or the claim form (small claims) and other documents, the regulations provide that this can be done in paper form (directly to the court or by post), or "by any other means of communication," including electronically, as far as available in the member state concerned.[45] The European order-for-payment regulation adds that if the application is submitted electronically, it has to be signed by an e-signature in accordance with the EU Electronic Signatures Directive.[46] The regulations, therefore, do not oblige member states to have the legal and technical possibility of receiving electronic applications. Currently, more than half of the member states enable an electronic submission of the application for a European order for payment, by e-mail, or through an electronic filing system.[47] Almost half of the member states allow for the electronic submission of the claim in the European small claims procedure.[48] It is to be expected that this number will gradually increase, since a number of member states are currently developing electronic communication systems.

3. Electronic Handling of the European Order for Payment

The European order-for-payment procedure is designed with a view to maximizing its efficiency and enabling electronic processing.[49] For instance, it is not required that evidence to support the claim be submitted along with the application form; the essence of this procedure is to establish that the claim is uncontested rather than to prove its existence.[50] To this end, the defendant is informed that the order is issued solely on the basis of the information provided by the claimant.[51] The defendant can oppose by filing a simple opposition form within 30 days, and in which case the procedure will continue as an adversarial procedure under the domestic rules of the competent member state.[52] The regulation specifically provides that the examination of the application may take the form of an automated procedure.[53] It is submitted that a fully automated processing without a human interface seems somewhat at odds with a prima facie examination of the merits to exclude clearly unfounded claims or inadmissible applications, as indicated by the regulation.[54] In addition, the regulation enables the electronic service of documents, in particular the order for payment.[55] According to the 2015 Commission report on the application of this regulation, the electronic service of documents under this regulation is not yet a reality.[56]

To operationalize a fully electronic procedure takes considerable time and requires a legal and technological infrastructure. A number of member states have concentrated the handling of this procedure in one specific court or authority, which may simplify the practical implementation of an electronic order for payment. In 2009, Austria and Germany implemented a successful pilot for the electronic handling of the procedure between these two countries.[57] This also serves as a model for other member states. In a brochure from the Austrian government, the functions are described as follows:

> The simple processing of applications by input of data form A and the computerised production of subsequent printed forms

and procedural steps; the essential details of the case are readily available in a "register" (table); all procedural steps are set out in order in a "register" (table); all further steps such as correspondence and notes are performed from the list of contents; autotext can be freely set and saved for all purposes; procedural forms and decisions can either be printed and distributed by mail or electronically transmitted via the ERV (Electronic Legal Communication).[58]

The European order for payment procedure was also the first test case to be piloted within the e-Codex project.[59] The nine member states that currently participate in this pilot enable the electronic exchange of documents (application form, correction form, order for payment form, and so on) either as sending state, receiving state, or both.[60] The electronic sending of the (application) forms, which from the perspective of the user is the biggest advancement, is possible either through the European e-Justice Portal or the national portals.

4. Use of Technology in the European Small Claims Procedure and Revision

The European small claims procedure is designed as a low-threshold procedure for the collection of small claims by both consumers and (small) businesses.[61] The electronic processing of the procedure is more complicated due to its adversarial nature, requiring more extensive information on the case, the submission of evidence, and a more intensive exchange of documents among the three actors (claimant, court, and defendant). Following the European order for payment procedure, the small claims procedure is currently piloted under the e-Codex project in six participating member states.[62] The aim is to facilitate the electronic submission of claims, as enabled by the regulation (see the section on "Access: Online Information, Dynamic Forms, and Submission," above), and, in general, the digital communication between the court and the parties.

To reduce the costs and time inherent to oral hearings in the cross-border context, the regulation prescribes that the European small claims procedure is in principle to be conducted in writing.[63] To secure the right to be heard, as embedded in Article 6 of the European Convention on Human Rights[64] and in Article 47 of the EU Charter of Fundamental Rights, the court, according to Article 5 of the regulation, is to "hold an oral hearing if it considers this to be necessary or if a party so requests." It may only refuse a party's request if an oral hearing is "obviously not necessary for the fair conduct of the proceedings." To decrease costs and to save the time and trouble resulting from parties having to appear in a foreign court, the regulation provides that the required oral hearing may be held through videoconferencing or other communication technology (e.g., Skype).[65] The same goes for the taking of evidence—the hearing of witnesses or experts.[66] This possibility is subject to the technical means available in the member states, the majority of which do have audio and video equipment available in all or some of their courts. Detailed data on the actual use are not available, however, but it seems that the use of videoconferencing within this procedure is very limited.[67]

The new regulation amending the small claims procedure which will take effect in July 2017, aims at making the procedure more attractive by, *inter alia*, extending the scope of the procedure[68] and increasing the use of ICT. A first amendment is that the postal service of documents, which is the primary prescribed method of service under this regulation, is extended to the electronic service of documents.[69] Whether it will be used depends upon the technical means and the admissibility under the law of the member state involved. The recitals of the new regulation also express that for all other written communications between parties, other persons involved in the proceedings, and the courts, "electronic means should be used as the preferred means to the extent possible, where such means are available and admissible."[70]

A second amendment is that member states are to ensure that the remote payment of court fees is possible. Member states should offer at least one of the following means of payment: (a) bank transfer; (b) credit- or debit-card payment; or (c) direct debit from the claimant's bank account.[71] This amendment is certainly to be welcomed, since in a number of member states only payment in cash, stamps, or by cheque is possible, or other practical obstacles exist that make payment problematic.[72]

A third amendment that was proposed by the European Commission involved imposing an obligation to use videoconferencing, teleconferencing, or other means of distance communication for the purpose of oral hearings and the taking of evidence, where the person to be heard was domiciled in another member state.[73] However, this met with resistance since it would force member states to have the necessary technical infrastructure in all the local courts having competence in this procedure. It would also interfere with the discretion of the judge to hold oral hearings in a way that was regarded most suitable. A new recital underlines in a less obligatory way that member states should promote the use of distance communication technology. It provides that arrangements should be made such that the competent courts are appropriately equipped in order to ensure the fairness of the proceedings and refers to the above-mentioned Council recommendation on cross-border video-conferencing.[74] Article 8 of the new regulation provides that oral hearings "shall be held by making use of any appropriate distance communication technology" as far as these are available and unless the use of such technology "is not appropriate for the fair conduct of the proceedings."

The New ODR Regulation: Creating an Online ADR Platform

Promoting the use of alternative methods of dispute resolution has been a focal point in EU civil justice. As yet it has met with only limited success, although in some member states well-functioning ADR mechanisms are in place.[75] A directive of 2008 regulates a number of issues regarding cross-border mediation,[76] and in 2013, two related instruments were adopted to more actively enhance the use of ADR in both in cross-border and domestic consumer disputes.[77] The first one, a directive on consumer ADR, provides the legal framework obliging member states to enable consumers and traders to submit their disputes to ADR.[78] It outlines the principles of ADR (including impartiality, transparency, effectiveness, fairness, and liberty), and provides rules on information to the consumer and on cooperation among ADR entities.

More important for the present paper is the second instrument, a regulation on consumer ODR that provides tools "facilitating the independent, impartial, transparent, effective, fast and fair out-of-court resolution of disputes."[79] It applies only to disputes arising out of online contracts.[80] The European Commission has developed an *ODR platform* (single point of entry) pursuant to this regulation that has been operational since February 2016.[81] This platform links to the national ADR entities that are authorized in accordance with the directive on consumer ADR. The main functions of the ODR platform are to provide an electronic complaint form; to inform the respondent; to identify the competent ADR entities and transmit the complaint to the agreed entity; to offer a free-of-charge electronic case management tool; to provide translations; to provide an electronic form to the ADR entity to submit information and the result of the ADR; to provide information; and to generate data.[82] Each member state has designated an ODR-contact point, hosting at least two advisers, who—particularly in cross-border cases—provide assistance in the use of the ODR platform.[83]

By means of this platform, consumers can, free of charge, submit their complaints online by filling out a standard form.[84] The completed complaint form will be processed and transmitted to the trader, informing the latter that parties have to agree on ADR and on the competent ADR entities. The trader should indicate within 10 days whether he or she is obliged to use a specific ADR entity (e.g., for a specific branch of business) or is willing to accept one of the identified ADR entities.[85] If parties agree to ADR and on the ADR entity, the complaint will be automatically transmitted to the ADR entity. If this entity agrees to deal with the dispute, it must finalize the dispute within 90 days, and will communicate the outcome through the platform.[86] It is not compulsory to conduct the ADR procedure itself through the platform, but in any case it cannot require the physical presence of the parties or their representatives.

It is to be hoped that the ODR platform will function well and that potential users will find their way to it in order to have an added value to the existing plethora of national ADR systems and—limited—ODR mechanisms, and to the traditional or partially online court procedures.

Enhancing Access to Justice and Procedural Challenges of ICT

Legal Framework and Potential of ICT for Access to Justice

Access to justice in Europe is guaranteed by Article 6 of the European Convention on Human Rights and by Article 47 of the EU Charter of Fundamental Rights. This not only requires *de lege* access to justice but also effective access to justice in fact.[87] In past years, the European institutions and many of the member states have made a substantial effort to create a legal framework and to invest in the technical infrastructure with the aim of enabling the use of ICT. These are important contributions to realizing access to justice since they make legal sources more accessible and enable the electronic submission of claims.

The European e-Justice Portal has been developed as a one-stop shop for justice in the EU. It provides extensive information on EU and national law as well as access to, *inter alia*, business and insolvency registers, and it includes several interactive features. Regulations in the area of European civil procedure provide the legal framework to serve documents, take evidence, exchange documents between legal authorities in the member states, submit claims, and conduct procedures using electronic and other technological means.[88] Within the cross-border context, the European order for payment procedure and the small claims procedure contribute to access to debt recovery by laying down a uniform procedure to be conducted by means of standard forms. The forms are designed to support the do-it-yourself character of these procedures, so that professional legal support is in principle not needed. These forms are electronically available in all official languages of the EU, and the e-Justice portal is equipped with a translation tool.[89] The e-Codex project and a number of small-scale private initiatives contribute to furthering the required technological infrastructure and interoperability for the purpose of European procedures.

The ODR regulation, operationalized by the ODR platform, adds yet another layer to dispute resolution in the EU.[90] It facilitates the online request for ADR, primarily by consumers, and the transmission to the respondent and eventually the ADR entity, as well as communication of the outcome. This process is aided by information on and the identification of competent ADR entities within the member states, by the translation of documents, and by online access to designated ODR contact points within the member states.

Limits of e-Justice in European Civil Procedure

The development of e-justice in the EU faces a number of limits and practical problems. A legal limitation is the dominantly voluntary nature of EU member states' participation. As the present European e-justice strategy also stresses, "Voluntary participation in European e-Justice projects is at the discretion of each individual Member State."[91] The exception is when a legislative instrument "includes a requirement to implement a specific project in the context of the European e-Justice system." As was discussed above, most provisions on information and communication technology in the European civil procedure instruments only enable the use of these means, and do not oblige member states to have them in place.[92] The fact that member states want to stay in control was once again made clear by the rejection of the proposal imposing the obligation to use videoconferencing or other distance means for the purpose of the oral hearing and the taking of evidence in the European small claims procedure.[93] For instance, the Dutch government was of the view that the use of videoconferencing could only be strongly encouraged by the regulation, and wanted to ensure that there was no interference with Dutch developments to introduce digitalization in court proceedings.[94] In some member states, for instance in France, several hundred local courts have jurisdiction for this procedure, and it would require structural investments to have the necessary equipment available in all these courts, or a reform of the national territorial jurisdiction system. Implementation of the ODR regulation is politically easier in that regard, since the European Commission is responsible for operation of the ODR platform and the costs incurred, and it requires little in the way of structural investments on the part of individual member states.

The technical and practical challenges facing the present e-justice framework in Europe are of considerable complexity and only a few can be highlighted here. Substantial efforts have been made in recent years to increase technical interoperability, as the European civil procedures only provide a common legal framework. At the grassroots level, this has to be made functional and applied by the member states, by their multiple courts and other judicial bodies, by legal practitioners, and by the end users. The member states have considerable legal procedural diversity and different levels of advancement in implementing ICT.

Particularly in the first years of the applicability of the European procedures, there were many technical and practical shortcomings in the use of the standard forms, including difficulties saving the form[95] and dysfunctional links to the forms used on websites of the member states.[96] Since then, most problems—though not all of them—have been resolved. As was mentioned above in the discussion on the reform of the European small claims procedure, parties face difficulties in paying court fees.[97] The same applies to the European order-for-payment procedure. Transparency is also an issue as regards what technical means are available in the different member states. Another problem with respect to the European e-Justice Portal is that information is not always up to date, especially as far as information on the member states is concerned, and that not all tools are user friendly.

Another practical issue in the EU context is that of language diversity. Multilingualism lies at the foundation of the EU's cultural diversity, and it is also crucial in the single digital market. There are currently 24 official languages in the EU, and all legal sources, relevant information, and regular updates to these, including those on the e-Justice portal, have to be available in all these languages. Apart from the translation and interpretation problems this poses, it makes cross-border litigation challenging. Despite calls for a more liberal approach, most member states only accept legal documents in their own official language(s). The European civil procedure regulations partly tackle the issue by limiting the need for translation, while the availability of the standard forms in all languages, along with the language tools on the e-Justice portal, greatly assist in overcoming language-related obstacles. However, the translation is limited to the form's closed fields; this, for instance, leaves the claimant responsible for the translation of the factual description and basis of the claim as well as of any attachments that require translation in the European small claims procedure.

To illustrate some of the issues, I conducted a brief experiment. I instructed a student assistant—who had no specific knowledge on the topic—to use the wizard on the dynamic forms section of the e-Justice portal, and to fill out the European small claims form.[98] My fictitious case was a claim for compensation under EU law due to a delayed flight, a typical European small claims case where a Dutch consumer had booked a flight from Brussels (Belgium) to New York with a French airline. It took the student considerable time and effort to locate the wizard on the portal in order to determine which European procedure applied, although the application itself was easy. I directed him to file the claim in France, but also asked whether he would be able to easily determine by himself which court(s) would have international jurisdiction. He reported the following issues. In the first section of the form regarding information on the claimant and respondent, there was a notification that in "some Member States" the inclusion of only the P.O. box number of the defendant was not sufficient, and that the document would not be served. Information was lacking with regard to which countries this concerned, and what the consumer was supposed to do if he only had a P.O. box number. Regarding the question as to the ground on which the court addressed was regarded as having international jurisdiction, on the basis of my directions the student understood he would have to tick the "domicile of the defendant" because this would lead to France. But without my directions, he would have ticked "domicile of the consumer" instead, which would lead to the Dutch courts. However, in this case the Dutch courts would not have jurisdiction pursuant to the Brussels I-bis Regulation and the case law.[99] The information provided for this item (including a link to the European Judicial Atlas) is not sufficient and transparent enough for an average consumer. In addition, the student considered the question difficult as to whether costs of the procedure and legal interest were claimed, as information on what costs could be claimed and when legal interest could be claimed was not readily available. One of the last steps was to select the competent court within the chosen member state. Based on the postal code of the airline in my fictitious case, two French courts were mentioned; however, it was not clear whether the form could in fact be sent to either of them. In the end, it was possible to generate a PDF, and it was indicated which languages were accepted by the selected member state; the language could be chosen from a dropdown menu (which included all languages, not only the ones allowed). The form including the questions and tick-box answers was translated, but the open fields remain in Dutch—and the user was not notified of this. After the PDF was created, it was not clear how the claim form could be sent; this was indicated only at the beginning when France was pre-selected, but this information was no longer displayed at the end.

Efficiency and Procedural Challenges

To conclude this section, certain procedural challenges to the ongoing development of e-justice in the EU will be addressed briefly. The main goal of introducing ICT in European civil procedure is to increase the efficiency of procedures. Although this is an important aspect of guaranteeing access to justice and a fair trial, and also considering that procedural delays are still a major problem in many member states, a one-sided focus on the overall efficiency of justice bears the risk that one could lose sight of the quality of individual justice. To state the obvious, fast and cheap procedures are not necessarily good ones.

The European debt-collection procedures and the digitalization of litigation and adjudication largely rely on active consumers and traders who are able to locate and apply the relevant information, and to pursue claims in principle without the help of legal professionals. Though the e-Justice portal and the standard forms are generally user-friendly, not all relevant information is easily traceable.

Information provided by member states is often limited, only accessible in the local language (since reference is made to applicable national provisions), and may be outdated. This may also result in an information asymmetry between consumers and small businesses on the one hand, and bigger companies on the other. Using the European procedures also requires an assessment of particular legal and more complex practical issues, including international jurisdiction, procedural costs, and interest. This may also explain why in fact the European small claims procedure is still seldom used, and why the European order for payment is often used by repeat players that are bigger professional parties.

A final point to be made is that standardization through the online forms makes procedures more rigid. The format of the European order for payment procedure leaves little room for an assessment beyond the limited information in the closed forms. From the Dutch perspective, it has been argued that this procedure offers less protection to debtors than domestic law.[100] The case law of the European Court of Justice shows that in some cases debtor protection beyond the strict context of the regulation is required.[101] The forms of the European small claims procedure leave limited room for a genuine adversarial procedure, and the lack of oral hearings limits the possibility of reaching the core of the dispute in more complex cases, or of establishing a settlement.[102] Videoconferencing may solve some of the issues, but the lack of a live human interface is sometimes regrettable and may impoverish proceedings.

Conclusion

This paper discussed developments in e-justice in the European Union, zooming in on uniform civil procedures for cross-border debt collection and the ODR regulation and platform. Specifically within the cross-border context, European debt-collection procedures aim to increase access to justice by introducing uniform and form-based procedures facilitated by technological means. The new ODR platform is expected to boost ADR in the EU as well as to facilitate the process by means of the online submission and handling of the request.

The new European legal framework and the technological advancements support access to justice and may trigger procedural innovation, though this often depends upon the voluntary compliance of the member states and the technical means available in them.

Challenges for e-justice in the EU include the reality of having to deal with 24 official languages, access to accurate information, and the user-friendliness of the systems. It is submitted that, in general, efforts to advance European electronic procedures and ODR are a valuable contribution to access to justice. However, great care should be taken to prevent the legal and factual complexity and individual procedural justice from becoming lost in translation for the sole purpose of efficiency.

Notes

1   For instance, Austria and Germany introduced an automated handling of their payment procedure (*Mahnverfahren*) from the 1980s, followed by the implementation of fully electronic procedures from the 1990s. In England, the Money Claim Online (MCOL) system was initiated in 1999. Some of the national procedures and experiences are reported in *The Circulation of Agency in E-Justice: Interoperability and Infrastructures for European Transborder Judicial Proceedings*, ed. Francesco Contini and Giovan Francesco Lanzara (New York: Springer, 2014) (in particular chapters 4–7).

2   Marco Velicogna, "Justice Systems and ICT: What Can Be Learned from Europe?," *Utrecht Law Review* (2007) at 129.

3   European e-Justice Portal, online: <https://e-justice.europa.eu>.

4   European Commission, *Towards a European e-Justice Strategy*, COM (2008), 329 final.

5   European Commission, *Strategy on European e-Justice (2014-2018)*, Official Journal 2013, C376/06, 21 December 2013, followed by European Council, *Multiannual European e-Justice Action Plan 2014-2018*, Official Journal 2014, C182/2, 14 June 2014.

6   See "e-codex: About the Project," e-Justice Communication via Online Data Exchange, online: <www.e-codex.eu/>. For an institutional and technical introduction, see Marco Velicogna, "Coming to Terms with Complexity Overload in Transborder e-Justice: The e-Codex Platform," in *The Circulation of Agency in E-Justice: Interoperability and Infrastructures for European Transborder Judicial Proceedings*, ed. Francesco Contini and Giovan Francesco Lanzara (New York: Springer, 2014) at 309.

7   Directive 2000/31/EC on electronic commerce, *Official Journal* 2000, L178/1.

8   See European Commission, *Towards interoperability for European public services*, COM (2010) 744 final.

9   See European Commission, "Digital Agenda for Europe," online: <https://ec.europa.eu/digital-agenda/en>.

10 European Commission, *Strategy on European e-Justice, supra* note 5.

11 Ibid. at 9.

12 Ibid. at 8.

13 Currently 11 member states have implemented ECLI (status as of 1 November 2015).

14 Council Recommendation, *Promoting the use of and sharing of best practices on cross-border videoconferencing in the area of justice in the Member States and at EU level*, Official Journal 2015, L C 250/1.

15 This provides that the EU needs to develop judicial cooperation in civil matters having cross-border implications, based on the principle of mutual recognition of judgements and of decisions in extrajudicial cases.

16 Regulation No 1215/2012 of the European Parliament and of the Council on jurisdiction and the recognition and enforcement of judgements in civil and commercial matters (recast), *Official Journal* 2012, L 351/1. This regulation was preceded by another one, which in turn relied on the Brussels Convention of 1968.

17 For an overview, see, *inter alia*, Xandra Kramer, *European Private International Law: The Way Forward, In-depth analysis European Parliament*, Research Report for the JURI Committee (Brussels: European Parliament, 2014), at 12–14, online: <papers.ssrn.com/sol3/papers.cfm?abstract_id=2502232>.

18 Regulation (EC) No 1393/2007 of the European Parliament and of the Council on the service in the member states of judicial and extrajudicial documents in civil or commercial matters (service of documents), and repealing Council Regulation (EC) No 1348/2000, *Official Journal* 2000, L 324/9.

19 Council Regulation (EC) No 1206/2001 of 28 May 2001 on co-operation between the courts of the member states in the taking of evidence in civil or commercial matters, *Official Journal* 2001, L 174/1.

20 Regulation (EC) No. 1896/2006 of the European Parliament and of the Council creating a European order for payment procedure, *Official Journal* 2006, L 399/1; Regulation (EC) No 861/2007 of the European Parliament and of the Council establishing a European Small Claims Procedure, *Official Journal* 2007, L 199/1; Regulation 664/2014 creating a European Account Preservation Order to facilitate cross-border debt recovery in civil and commercial matters, *Official Journal* 2014, L 189/59. The latter will be applicable as of 18 January 2017.

21 For the electronic filing of documents, see Article 7 European Order for Payment Regulation and Article 4 European Small Claims Regulation, and for videoconferencing, Articles 10 and 17 Evidence Regulation and Article 8 European Small Claims Regulation.

22 See section on "Legal Framework and Potential of ICT for Access to Justice."

23 See section on "The New ODR Regulation: Creating an Online ADR Platform."

24 They are applicable in 27 of the 28 EU member states. Due to Denmark's special position under the judicial cooperation section of the TFEU, these regulations are not applicable in Denmark.

25 See recitals 7–8 to the European Order for Payment Regulation and recital 7 of the European Small Claims Regulation and Article 1 of both regulations.

26 As defined in Article 3 European Order for Payment Regulation and the European Small Claims Regulation.

27 Article 2 European Order for Payment Regulation.

28 Article 12 European Order for Payment Regulation.

29 Articles 16, 18, 19, and 20 European Order for Payment Regulation.

30 Article 2 European Small Claims Regulation.

31 Regulation (EU) 2015/2421 of the European Parliament and of the Council of 16 December 2015 amending Regulation (EC) No 861/2007 establishing a European Small Claims Procedure and Regulation (EC) No 1896/2006 creating a European order for payment procedure, *Official Journal* 2015, L 341/1. The Commission proposal was to raise the threshold to €10,000, but this was not adopted.

32 On aspects of semantic interoperability in relation to these procedures, see Marta Poblet et al., "Building Semantic Interoperability for European Civil Proceedings Online," in *The Circulation of Agency in E-Justice: Interoperability and Infrastructures for European Transborder Judicial Proceedings*, ed. Francesco Contini and Giovan Francesco Lanzara (New York: Springer, 2014) at 287.

33 See, *inter alia*, a report by the European Consumer Centre, *ECC-Net Small Claims Procedure Report*, (September 2012), online: <http://ec.europa.eu/consumers/ecc/docs/small_claims_210992012_en.pdf>. For an empirical study conducted in the Netherlands, see Xandra Kramer and Elena Alina Ontanu, "The Functioning of the European Small Claims Procedure in the Netherlands: Normative and Empirical Reflections," *Nederlands Internationaal Privaatrecht* 3 (2013) at 319.

34 European Commission, *Report from the Commission to the European Parliament, the Council and the European Economic and Social Committee on the application of Regulation (EC) No 861/2007 of the European Parliament and of the Council establishing a European Small Claims Procedure*, COM(2013) 795 final, 19 November 2013, in particular at 2–3.

35 Proposal for a Regulation of the European Parliament and of the Council amending Council Regulation (EC) 861/2007 of 11 July 2007 establishing a European Small Claims Procedure and Council Regulation (EC) 1896/2006 of the European Parliament, COM(2013) 794 final.

36 Regulation (EU) 2015/2421, *supra* note 31.

37 European Commission, *Report from the Commission to the European Parliament, the Council and the European Economic and Social Committee on*

the application of Regulation (EC) 1896/2006 of the European Parliament and of the Council creating a European Order for Payment Procedure, COM(2015) 495 final, 13 October 2015 (in particular at 3–4 and the Annex).

38 European E-Justice Portal, "Dynamic Forms" (6 August 2016), online: <https://e-justice.europa.eu/content_dynamic_forms-155-en.do>.

39 European E-Justice Portal, "European Payment Order Forms" (6 August 2016), online: <https://e-justice.europa.eu/content_european_payment_order_forms-156-en.do>.

40 European E-Justice Portal, "Small Claims Forms" (6 August 2016), online: <https://e-justice.europa.eu/content_small_claims_forms-177-en.do>.

41 See also Marco Mellone, "Legal Interoperability in Europe: An Assessment of the European Payment Order and the European Small Claims Procedure," in *The Circulation of Agency in E-Justice: Interoperability and Infrastructures for European Transborder Judicial Proceedings,* ed. Francesco Contini and Giovan Francesco Lanzara (New York: Springer, 2014) at 245.

42 Article 24 European Order for Payment Regulation; Article 10 European Small Claims Regulation. This is regardless of the domestic rules on legal representation in the Member State addressed.

43 Article 11 European Small Claims Regulation provides that the Member States must ensure that the parties can receive practical assistance in filling in the forms.

44 See also European Commission report, European Small Claims Regulation, *supra* note 8 at 7.

45 See Article 7(5) European Order for Payment Regulation, "in paper form or by any other means of communication, including electronic, accepted by the Member State of origin and available to the court of origin;" Article 4(1) European Small Claims Regulation, "directly, by post or by any other means of communication, such as fax or e-mail, acceptable to the Member State in which the procedure is commenced."

46 Article 7(6) European Order for Payment Regulation, referring to Article 2(2) of Article 2(2) of Directive 1999/93/EC of the European Parliament and of the Council on a Community framework for electronic signatures *Official Journal* 2000, L 13/12.

47 Information provided on the European e-Justice Portal and the European Judicial Atlas (14 Member States as of 6 August 2016). See also European Commission report, European Order for Payment Regulation, *supra* note 37 at 6.

48 Based on information on the European e-Justice Portal and the European Judicial Atlas (13 Member States as of 6 August 2016). See also European Commission report, European Small Claims Regulation, *supra* note 34 at 4–5.

49 For a more in-depth analysis by the present author, see Xandra E Kramer, "Enhancing Enforcement in the European Union: The European Order for Payment Procedure and Its Implementation in the Member States, Particularly in Germany, the Netherlands, and England," in *Enforcement and Enforceability. Tradition and Reform*, ed. C H van Rhee and A Uzelac (Oxford: Intersentia, 2010) at 17.

50 Article 7(e) European Order for Payment Regulation.

51 Article 12(4) European Order for Payment Regulation.

52 Articles 16 and 17 European Order for Payment Regulation.

53 Article 8 European Order for Payment Regulation. Recital 16 of the preamble adds that the examination does not need to be carried out by a judge.

54 Recital 16 provides that the information in the application form, including the description of the evidence, "would allow the court to examine prima facie the merits of the claim and inter alia to exclude clearly unfounded claims or inadmissible applications," and Article 8 prescribes the examination to assess whether the claim appears to be founded.

55 Article 13(d) (service with acknowledgement of receipt) and Article 14(1) (f) (service without proof of receipt) European Order for Payment Regulation. However, direct service of an order by a court on a party in another Member State is not possible pursuant to the Service Regulation; see also the European Commission report, European Order for Payment Regulation,, *supra* note 37 at 8.

56 Ibid.

57 See European Public Sector Award, "Project for electronic Processing of the European Order for Payment Procedure" (13 March 2013), online: <www.epsa-projects.eu/index.php?title=Project_for_electronic_processing_of_the_European_order_for_payment_procedure>.

58 Republic of Austria, Federal Ministry of Justice, "The Use of IT within Austrian Justice" (29 January 2014), online: <https://www.justiz.gv.at/web2013/file/8ab4ac8322985dd501229ce3fb1900b4.de.0/itbrosch%C3%BCre-en.pdf>.

59 See e-Codex, "European Order for Payment," online: <www.e-codex.eu/pilots/european-order-for-payment.html>. In August 2015, a new pilot between Germany and Greece was initiated. For the implementation of the e-Codex pilot in Greece, see George Pangalos, Ioannis Salmatzidis, and Ioannis Pagkalos, "Using IT to Provide Easier Access to Cross-Border Legal Procedures for Citizens and Legal Professionals: Implementation of a European Payment Order E-CODEX pilot," *International Journal for Court Administration* 6:2 (2014) at 43.

60 See also European Commission report, *European Order for Payment Regulation, supra* note 37 at 6.

61 For an extensive analysis by the present author, see Xandra Kramer, "The European Small Claims Procedure: Striking the Balance between Simplicity and Fairness in European Litigation," *Zeitschrift für europäisches Privatrecht* 2 (2008) at 355.

62 See e-Codex, "Small Claims," online: <www.e-codex.eu/pilots/small-claims.html>.

63 Article 5 European Small Claims Regulation.

64 The European Court of Human Rights ruled that the right to an oral hearing is not absolute. See ECtHR 12 November 2002, no. 28394/95 (Dory v Sweden), online: <http://www.echr.coe.int/echr/>. The court ruled that in having regard to the demands of efficiency and economy, a court may abstain from an oral hearing if the case can be adequately resolved on the basis of the case file and the parties' written observations. See also Kramer, *supra* note 6 at 371.

65 Article 8 European Small Claims Regulation.

66 Article 9(1) European Small Claims Regulation.

67 European Commission, *Proposal amending the European Small Claims Regulation, supra* note 36 at explanatory memorandum.

68 See section on "Legal Framework and Potential Of ICT for Access to Justice" and note 31. The monetary ceiling will be raised to €5,000. The Commission's proposal to extend the definition of "cross-border cases" was not adopted.

69 To this end, Article 13 *amending* the European Small Claims Regulation (Regulation (EU) 2015/2421) provides that the claim form and the judgement are to be served by postal service or by electronic means, where such means are technically available and the party has accepted to be served by electronic means or is according to national law obliged to accept these.

70 Recital 8 *amended* European Small Claims Regulation.

71 Article 15a *amended* European Small Claims Regulation.

72 European Commission, *proposal amending the European small claims regulation, supra* note 36 at explanatory memorandum, 8. See also Gar Yein Ng, "Testing Transborder Civil Procedures in Practice: Findings from Simulation Experiments with the European Payment Order and the European Small Claims Procedure," in *The Circulation of Agency in E-Justice: Interoperability and Infrastructures for European Transborder Judicial Proceedings*, ed. Francesco Contini and Giovan Francesco Lanzara (New York: Springer, 2014), 265 at 274–75.

73 European Commission, *Proposal amending the European small claims regulation, supra* note 36 at explanatory memorandum, 7–8.

74 See section on "The New ODR Regulation: Creating an Online ADR Platform" and note 15.

75 For an extensive comparative study, see Christopher Hodges, Iris Benöhr and Naomi Creutzfeldt-Banda, eds., *Consumer ADR in Europe* (Oxford: Hart Publishing, 2012).

76 Directive 2008/52/EC of the European Parliament and of the Council on certain aspects of mediation in civil and commercial matters, *Official Journal* 2008, L 136/3.

77 Directive 2013/11/EU on alternative dispute resolution for consumer disputes and amending Regulation (EC) No 2006/2004 and Directive 2009/22/EC (Directive on consumer ADR), *Official Journal* 2013, L 165/63; Regulation (EU) No 524/2013 on online dispute resolution for consumer disputes and amending Regulation (EC) No 2006/2004 and Directive 2009/22/EC (Regulation on consumer ODR), *Official Journal* 2013, L 165/1. For an overview of these instruments, see Michael Bogdan, "The New EU Regulation on Online Resolution for Consumer Disputes," *Masaryk University Journal of Law and Technology* 9:1 (2015) at 155.

78 It applies to C2B disputes, and only where national law permits B2C disputes.

79 Article 1 Regulation on consumer ODR. For further details on this regulation, and in relation to other developments on ADR, see Pablo Cortés and Arno R Lodder, "Consumer Dispute Resolution Goes Online: Reflections on the Evolution of European Law for Out-of-Court Redress," *Maastricht Journal of European and Comparative Law* 21:1 (2014) at 14.

80 Article 4(1)(e) Regulation on consumer ODR.

81 See <https://webgate.ec.europa.eu/odr/>.

82 Article 5(4) Regulation on consumer ODR.

83 Article 7 Regulation on consumer ODR.

84 Article 8 Regulation on consumer ODR.

85 Article 9 Regulation on consumer ODR.

86 Article 10 Regulation on consumer ODR.

87 As already recognised in old case law of the European Court on Human Rights: *Golder v United Kingdom*, ECtHR (1975) Series A, No. 18, and *Airey v Ireland*, ECHR (1979) Series A, No. 32. See also Article 47(3) of the EU Charter where explicit reference to effective access to justice is made in the context of legal aid.

88 See in particular sections on "The New ODR Regulation: Creating an Online ADR Platform" and on "Legal Framework and Potential of ICT for Access to Justice."

89 See section on "Legal Framework and Potential of ICT for Access to Justice."

90 See section on "Limits of e-Justice in European Civil Procedure."

91 European Commission, *Strategy on European e-Justice, supra* note 5; see section on "Uniform civil procedures and facilitating technology."

92 See sections on "The New ODR Regulation: Creating an Online ADR Platform" and on "Enhancing Access to Justice and Procedural Challenges of ICT."

93 See section on "Legal Framework and Potential of ICT for Access to Justice."

94 Dutch Parliamentary Documents (*Tweede Kamer*), file 22 112, no. 1758.

95 See, e.g., on a simulation in Italy, Gar Yein Ng, *supra* note 72 at 270–71.

96 See, e.g., on experiences in the Netherlands, Kramer and Ontanu, *supra* note 33 at 21.

97 See section on "Legal Framework and Potential of ICT for Access to Justice."

98 The experiment was carried out on 5 November 2015 by a third-year bachelor student at Erasmus School of Law, who had not yet done a course on private international law or on international litigation.

99 CJEU 9 July 2009, Case C-204/2008, ECR 2009 I-6073 (*Rehder v Air Baltic Corporation*). Research on experiences in the Dutch courts also exposed difficulties in establishing jurisdiction in consumer cases; see Kramer and Ontanu, *supra* note 33 at 325. The jurisdiction rules on consumer cases are difficult, since particular cases, including the booking of a flight, are excluded from the consumer section in the Brussels I-bis regulation.

100 Xandra Kramer, "European Procedures on Debt Collection: Nothing or Noting? Experiences and Future Prospects," in *EU Civil Justice: Current Issues and Future Outlook*, ed. Burkhard Hess et al. (Oxford: Hart Publishing, 2016), 99 at 109–10 (with further references to research carried out by the present author for the Dutch Ministry of Security and Justice [report in Dutch]).

101 CJEU 14 June 2012, Case C-618/10, ECR (*Banco Español de Crédito*), ECLI:EU:C:2012:349; CJEU 4 September 2014, joined cases C-119/13 and C-120/13 (*Eco Cosmetics*), ECLI:EU:C:2014:2144.

102 See Kramer and Ontanu, *supra* note 33 at 325–26, 328 (relying on interviews conducted at Dutch courts).

eAccess to Justice – Brief Observations

Guy Canivet

Good morning,

I must first of all ask you to accept my apologies. Having agreed, many months ago, to participate in your conference on "eAccess to Justice," I am today prevented from doing so by the schedule of the Conseil Constitutionnel, or Constitutional Council.[1]

I am truly very sorry. Therefore, I have proposed that I deliver a brief presentation by way of an audiovisual recording.[2]

The manner in which I address you is not without relevance to the subject of your conference. It demonstrates, in any case, the advantages of this mode of communication, which you know well. It also reveals its limits. While an audiovisual communication avoids the time and cost of travel, which are not negligible for a trip between Paris and Montreal, it deprives me of the pleasure of meeting you in person and of reconnecting with friends, which is always a delight in Quebec; it thwarts my interest in hearing you speak and participating in your discussion. On balance, I have much to lose [through this mode of communication]; in addition to being deprived of the pleasure of reconnecting with you or of getting to know you, I would have learned a great deal from you, much more than what I have to share to you.

The setting of this recording, in the courtroom of the Constitutional Council—even though the quality may not be optimal—allows me to tell you that the French constitutional jurisdiction does not lag too far behind in terms of cyberjustice.

As you can see, it benefits from a courtroom with recording capability. In certain disputes, notably relating to elections, it holds hearings by videoconference, which is particularly useful given that the territory of the Republic includes many remote overseas communities. These hearings are recorded and can be viewed live on the internet; they are thus accessible to all citizens. All the procedures are paperless. Communication with lawyers is electronic. Applications are filed online, and the hearing of cases is online as well. Documents between the Council and the government, parliament, public administrations, and jurisdictions is carried out by electronic messages. Decisions, translated into many languages, are classified and made available to the public in a database accessible on the Council's website. If you consult it, you will note that this site is quite well-designed. For example, visitors to the site are able to consult the schedule of cases. We have access to all the legal and case-law databases of Légifrance, which is the service providing public access to the law in France, and we can consult all of the electronic legal publications available in France.

Our experience regarding e-access to law and to justice is certainly very standard. But it seems to me worthy of being shared. This leads me to a few brief reflections.

As your conference demonstrates, around the world, experiences of cyberjustice are numerous and varied; be it access to internet services of courts, tele-procedures, paperless records, remote consultation of records, access to case-law databases, online decision support, or even e-justice, all these technical advances not only call into question the access of individuals to courts but, much more than that, they radically change judicial methods, professional practices, the mode of making decisions, the public character of hearings, and finally the perception of justice by the public.

In many countries, these initiatives are developing at an accelerating pace. All this brings about enormous transformations in juridical institutions. However, these changes are more or less well-prepared and sometimes poorly mastered; this, it seems to me, requires analysis, which I propose to carry out in four stages.

The First Stage Is that of Sharing Experiences

This is one of the goals of your conference. The court systems of states have much to gain from studying and comparing electronic initiatives in place elsewhere, whether experimental or operational.

While I was serving on the Court of Cassation, where diverse information and communication systems were developed, I benefited greatly from visits to Singapore, Brazil, the United States, Canada, and elsewhere... Particularly special were the Cyberjustice Laboratory at the University of Montreal, which I have visited many times, and my deeply engaging dialogues with those overseeing it. The pooling of knowledge and shared experiences are central. It is thus necessary to create and foster spaces of sharing.

Second Stage: Standardization

All these initiatives modify the essential aspects of legal techniques in significant ways: access to court systems, modes of expression, the adversarial process, the rights of the defence, and the protection of litigants and of personal information.

They affect, in consequence, fundamental legal guarantees. The quality of justice rendered depends simultaneously on the technical reliability of systems and the ability of citizens to use them, their equal ability to gain access to these techniques, the training that is offered to them, their mastery of and familiarity with this new way of appearing before the courts.

All this poses problems of an ethical, technical, psychological, juridical, social nature... These must be taken into account when determining, on an international scale, the criteria that these modes of administering justice must respect. This supposes a standardization of practices, a sort of quality label for e-justice.

Therefore, within the Council of Europe, the European Commission for the Efficiency of Justice (CEPEJ) has the mission of further reflection on the potential of new technologies to improve the functioning of the justice system. It has published a report on "L'utilisation des technologies de l'information et de la communication (TIC) dans les systèmes judiciaires européens" (the use of information and communication technologies [ICT]) in European judicial systems), which undertakes a critical analysis of diverse European experiences and offers a variety of recommendations.

The Third Stage Is that of Evaluation

Cyberjustice is not an end in itself; it is not a question of surrendering without reserve to the allure of technology. These technical developments are only of interest if they result in better allocation of judicial resources, reduced costs for the state and the user, improved services for litigants, improved professional tools, increased security of decisions, and favour their enforcement and recognition.

Beforehand, the implementation of these initiatives must thus be preceded by a serious study of their impact, an evaluation in terms of cost and benefit that measures their effect on stakeholders. And afterward, when they are in place, these initiatives must be evaluated periodically in a neutral, independent, and rigorous manner, in order to correct and update them.

In this respect, the report of the CEPEJ that I have already cited identifies many imperfections in the programs implemented in the different European judicial systems: mediocre performance due to the poor design of systems; inappropriate strategies for innovation; numerous malfunctions; the absence of maintenance; poor public awareness; insufficient training of professionals; and, finally, the failure to update practices. Clearly, all these shortcomings must be analyzed in order to detect their causes and put in place the means to avoid them in the future. With a bit of methodical rigour in these matters, every failure carries with it the hope of a future success.

The Fourth Stage Is that of Anticipation ...

Anticipation based first on new technologies in order to imagine its possible applications in the judicial sphere. I will give but one example: What would be the effect of "big data" on case-law databases, decision support systems, the standardization of decisions relating to indemnities and pensions? Are we moving toward the use of artificial intelligence in judgments?

But it is also necessary to anticipate reforms of structure, organization, and practices that the introduction of these technical innovations will require. In France, the Institut des Hautes Études de la Justice has put in place a program for the study of the justice of the future. By way of example, a debate recently occurred regarding the construction of new courthouse in Paris. After long hesitations due to opposition by professionals, the decision was finally made, three years ago, to construct a new courthouse, since the historic location on the Île de la Cité had become totally inadequate. The project, significant in both scale and cost, was, it has been alleged, designed based on the current state of operations, without accounting for future developments—cybercourts, e-justice, and paperless records. Whether or not this is true I do not know, but it is this argument of insufficient adaption of structures and methods that opponents to the project used to call it into question.

In any case, whatever their effect, the modes of e-access are only instruments aiming to increase the efficiency of communications within justice systems, of communications toward the outside, and to rationalize "judicial production." They must leave intact the essential function and spirit of justice. These values must be protected. They require that we take a moment to reflect before yielding to the technological dynamic. But you already know this well!

Finally, the immense potential of digital technology obliges us to discern and preserve the essence of justice and perhaps to raise questions that have otherwise remained unexplored; for example, that which our Spanish colleagues call "the principle of presence," which requires in certain cases that the judges and the parties be physically present.

These are the few, very modest observations that I propose for your discussion on the preparation of the justice of the future, for which you have gathered today. I wish you much success in your work.

Notes

1   The Council's website defines the Council as follow: "The Constitutional Council was established by the by the Constitution of the Fifth Republic adopted on 4 October 1958. It is a court vested with various powers, including in particular the review of the constitutionality of legislation." Online: <http://www.conseil-constitutionnel.fr/conseil-constitutionnel/english/presentation/general-presentation/general-presentation.25739.html>.
2   This postscript is a transcript of Guy Canivet's recording. Thank you to Emily Grant for the translation of the original French.

Bibliography

Note: The following bibliography is a general bibliography of a selection of key books, chapters of books, articles, and reports relating to eAccess to justice and cyberjustice. It is not an exhaustive list of the references of this book. For such a list, the reader should refer to the endnotes of each chapter.

Anderson, Hon Paul H. *Future Trends in Public Access: Court Information, Privacy, and Technology*, Future Trends in State Courts 2011 (National Center for State Courts, 2011).

Antonov, Jaroslav Valerievich. "Legal Mechanisms of E-justice for Ensuring Independence and Impartiality of Arbitrators in Light of International Practice," in Alexander J Bělohlávek, Filip Černý & Naděžda Rozehnalová, eds., *Czech (& Central European) Yearbook of Arbitration 2014: Independence and impartiality of arbitrators*, jurisnet, llc ed (2014) 3.

Aresty, Jeffrey M. "Digital Identity and the Lawyer's Role in Furthering Trusted Online Communities" (2006) 38 *University of Toledo Law Review* 137.

Aubert, Benoit A, Gilbert Babin & Hamza Aqallal. "Providing an Architecture Framework for Cyberjustice" (2014) 3:4 *Laws* 721.

Baar, Carl et al. *Alternative Models of Court Administration* (Ottawa: Canadian Judicial Council, 2005).

Baboolal-Frank, Rashri. *Revolutionising the Civil Courts in South Africa Through Information Technology*, SSRN Scholarly Paper ID 2648638 (Rochester, NY: Social Science Research Network, 2015).

Bailey, Jane & Jacquelyn Burkell. "Implementing technology in the justice sector: A Canadian perspective" (2013) 11:2 *Canadian Journal of Law and Technology* 253.

Bailey, Jane, Jacquelyn Burkell & Graham Reynolds. "Access to Justice for All: Towards an 'Expansive Vision' of Justice and Technology" (2013) *Windsor Y B Access Just* 31:181.

Bailey, Jane. "Digitization of Court Processes in Canada" (23 October 2012), online: Cyberjustice Laboratory <www.cyberjustice.ca/wordpress/wp-content/uploads/webuploads/WP002_CanadaDigitizationOf CourtProcesses20121023.pdf>.

—— (guest ed.) "Technology, Social Media and Law" (2014) Special edition *Laws*.

Barral-Viñals, Immaculada. "Consumer Complaints, Access to Justice and e-Confidence: From ADR to ODR," in Marta Poblet et al., eds., *Courts and Mediation New Paths for Justice* (European Press Academic Publishing, 2011) 97.

——. "E-consumers and effective protection: the online dispute resolution system" in Mel Kenny & James Devenney, eds., *European Consumer Protection Theory and Practice* (Cambridge; New York: Cambridge University Press, 2012) 82.

Beaton, Vanessa, *Literature Review*, Working paper n°3, Laboratoire de Cyberjustice, 23 October 2012.

Bédard, Serge et al. *Gouvernance, audit et sécurité des TI* (Brossard, Québec: Publications CCH, 2008).

Benyekhlef, K, E Paquette-Belanger & A Porcin. "Vie privée et surveillance ambiante: le droit canadien en chantier" (2013) 65 *Droit et cultures* 191.

Benyekhlef, Karim & Ester Mitjans, eds. *Circulation internationale de l'information et sécurité* (Montréal: Thémis, 2013).

Benyekhlef, Karim & Fabien Gélinas. "L'expérience internationale des modalités de règlement des conflits liés au droit d'auteur dans l'environnement numérique" (2001) 35:4 Unesco - *Bulletin du droit d'auteur* 5.

——. "Online Dispute Resolution" (2005) 10:2 *Lex Electronica*, online: <http://www.lex-electronica.org/fr/anciens-numeros.html>.

Benyekhlef, Karim & Nicolas Vermeys. "Buenas practicas en Applicaciones de Ciberjusticia," in José Antonio Caballero, Carlos Gregorio de Gràcia & Linn Hammergren, eds., *Buenas practicas para la implementacion de soluciones tecnologicas en la administracion de justicia* (Buenos Aires: IIJusticia, 2011) 29.

——. "Le passage à la cyberjustice" (2011) *Droit Montréal* 12.

Benyekhlef, Karim & Pierre Trudel, eds. *État de droit et virtualité* (Montréal: Thémis, 2009).

Benyekhlef, Karim, Emmanuelle Amar & Valentin Callipel. "ICT-Driven Strategies for Reforming Access to Justice Mechanisms in Developing Countries," in *The World Bank Legal Review* (2015) 325.

Benyekhlef, Karim, Nicolas Vermeys & Cléa Iavarone-Turcotte. "Analyse comparative des principales caractéristiques des systèmes d'administration des tribunaux judiciaires," Rapport présenté au Conseil canadien de la magistrature, Rapport, 6 juillet 2011, Conseil canadien de la magistrature.

Benyekhlef, Karim. "L'administration publique en ligne au Canada : précisions terminologiques et état de la réflexion" (2004) 2:110 *Revue française d'administration publique* 267.

——. "La résolution en ligne des différends de consommation : un récit autour (et un exemple) du droit postmoderne," in Pierre-Claude Lafond, ed., *L'accès des consommateurs à la justice* (Cowansville: Yvon Blais, 2010) 89.

——. "Les systèmes intégrés d'information de justice au Canada et aux États-Unis," in Georges Chatillon, ed., *L'administration électronique au service des citoyens: actes du colloque, Paris, les 21 et 22 janvier 2002* (Bruxelles: Bruylant, 2003) 185.

Bernoider Edward & S Koch. "Aligning ICT and Legal Framework in Austria's e-Bureaucracy, from Mainframe to the Internet," in *ICT and Innovation in the Public Sector: European Studies in the Making of e-Government*, eds. Francesco Contini and Giovan Francesco Lanzara, (New York: Palgrave Macmillan, 2009).

Blankley, Kristen M. "Are Public Records Too Public? Why Personally Identifying Information Should Be Removed from Both Online and Print Versions of Court Documents" (2004) *Ohio St L J* 65 at 413.

Bouclin, Suzanne & Marie-Andrée Denis-Boileau. "La cyberjustice comme réponse aux besoins juridiques des personnes itinérantes: son potentiel et se embûches" (2013) 31:1 *Windsor Yearbook of Access to Justice* 25.

Braun, Sabine & Judith L Taylor, eds. *Videoconference and remote interpreting in criminal proceedings* (Cambridge, United Kingdom: Intersentia, 2012).

Burkell, Jacquelyn & Jane Bailey. "Revisiting Presumptive Accessibility: Reconceptualizing the Open Court Principle in an Era of Online Publication" (forthcoming).

Burkell, Jacquelyn & Lisa Di Valentino. Videoconferencing Literature Review Summary, Document de travail n°4, Laboratoire de Cyberjustice, 23 October 2012.

Cabral, James E et al. "Using Technology to Enhance Access to Justice" (2012) 26:1 *Harvard Journal of Law & Technology* 241.

Caprioli, Eric A. "Gestion des identités numériques: quel cadre juridique pour la confiance dans les communications électroniques internationales?" (2011) 45 *Revue du droit des technologies de l'information* 29.

Carter, Jane S. *Going Paperless in a Consolidated Limited Jurisdiction Court Feasible or Not?* (National Center for State Courts, 2014).

Chabot, Gérard. "La cyberjustice: réalité ou fiction ?" (2003) 2003:34 Recueil Dalloz 2322.

Conley, Amanda et al. "Sustaining Privacy and Open Justice in the Transition to Online Court Records: A Multidisciplinary Inquiry" (2012) *Maryland Law Review* 71 at 772

Contini, Francesco & Giovan Francesco Lanzara, eds. *The Circulation of Agency in E-Justice: Interoperability and Infrastructures for European Transborder Judicial Proceedings* (New York: Springer, 2014).

Contini, Francesco & Antonio Cordella. "Italian Justice System and ICT: Matches and Mismatches Between Technology and Organisation," in Agusti Cerrilo I Martinez And Pere Fabra I Abat, *E-Justice: Information and Communication Technologies in the Court System* (New York: Information Science Reference, 2009) at 117.

Cortés, Pablo. "A new regulatory framework for extra-judicial consumer redress: where we are and how to move forward: A new regulatory framework for extra-judicial consumer redress" (2015) 35:1 *Legal Studies* 114.

———. "Online Dispute Resolution for Consumers – Online Dispute Resolution Methods for Settling Business to Consumer Conflicts," in Mohamed S Abdel Wahab, Ethan Katsh & Daniel Rainey, eds., *Online Dispute Resolution: Theory and Practice A Treatise on Technology and Dispute Resolution* (The Hague: Eleven International Publishing, 2012) 151.

De Araujo Almeida Filho, Jose Carlos. *Processo Eletrônico e Teoria Geral do Processo Eletrônico* (Rio de Janeiro: Ed Forense, 2008).

Dellapenna, Joseph. "The Internet and Public International Law: Law in a Shrinking World: The Interaction of Science and Technology with International Law" (1999) 88 *Kentucky Law Journal* 809.

Demoulin, Marie. *Droit du commerce électronique et équivalents fonctionnels: Théorie critique*, Collection du Crids (Larcier, 2014).

Devanesan, Ruha & Jeffrey Aresty. "ODR and Justice – An Evaluation of Online Dispute Resolution's Interplay with Traditional Theories of Justice," in Mohamed S Abdel Wahab, Ethan Katsh & Daniel Rainey, eds., *Online Dispute Resolution: Theory and Practice A Treatise on Technology and Dispute Resolution* (The Hague: Eleven International Publishing, 2012) 263.

Devries, Will Thomas. "Protecting Privacy in the Digital Age" (2003) *Berkeley Tech L J* 18:283.

Ding, Ying. "Online dispute resolution for consumers in e-commerce: an example from the Taobao platform" (2014) 17:1 *Wuhan University International Law Review* 208.

Duan, Zhuozhen. "The rise of the internet and its impact on the openness of the justice system in mainland China: improvements and limitations" (2013) 1:1 *Journal of Open Access to Law*, online: <http://ojs.law.cornell.edu/index.php/joal/article/view/15>.

Dugan, Daniel W. "A Picture is Worth 999 Words: The Importance and Effectiveness of Courtroom Visual Presentations" (2011) *Reynolds Ct & Media L J* 1:503 at 503.

Dumoulin, Laurence & Christian Licoppe. "Deux sites pour un process. L'unité de lieu à l'épreuve de la visioconférence" in Lionel Miniato & Wanda Mastor, eds, *Les figures du procès au-delà des frontières* (Paris: Dalloz, 2014).

———. "La visioconférence dans la justice pénale : retour sur la fabrique d'une politique publique" (2011) 2 *Les cahiers de la Justice-Revue de l'ENM* 29.

———. *Les comparutions par visioconférence : la confrontation de deux mondes. Prison et tribunal. Synthèse du rapport final* (Institut des Sciences sociales du Politique et Télécoms Paris-Tech, 2013).

Ebner Noam. "ODR and Interpersonal Trust," in Mohamed S Abdel Wahab, Ethan Katsh & Daniel Rainey, eds., *Online Dispute Resolution: Theory and Practice A Treatise on Technology and Dispute Resolution* (The Hague: Eleven International Publishing, 2012) 215.

———. "E-Mediation" in Mohamed S Abdel Wahab, Ethan Katsh & Daniel Rainey, eds, *Online Dispute Resolution: Theory and Practice A Treatise on Technology and Dispute Resolution* (The Hague: Eleven International Publishing, 2012) 369.

Eltis, Karen. "The Judicial System in the Digital Age: Revisiting the Relationship between Privacy and Accessibility in the Cyber Context" (2011) 56:2 *McGill Law Journal* 289.

———. *Courts, Litigants and the Digital Age: Law, Ethics and Practice* (Ottawa: Irwin Law, 2012).

Espinosa, Philip G. "Paperless Court of Appeals Comes of Age" (2014) 15:1 *J App Prac & Process* 99.

Fabri, Marco. "Some European and Australian e-Justice services," Working paper n°1, 2012, online: <http://www.cyberjustice.ca/wordpress/wp-content/uploads/webuploads/WP001_EU_Australia_e-justice_IRSIG20121019.pdf>.

———. "The Italian Style of E-Justice in a Comparative Perspective", in Agusti Cerrilo i MARTINEZ and Pere Fabra i ABAT, *E-Justice: Information and Communication Technologies in the Court System*, New York: Information Science Reference, 2009, at 1.

Farrow, Trevor & Patrick Molinari. *The Courts and Beyond: The Architecture of Justice in Transition* (Montreal: Canadian Institute for the Administration of Justice, 2013).

———. "What is Access to Justice?" (2014) *Osgoode Hall Law Journal* 51:3 :957 at 964; see also Ab Currie, *The Legal Problems of Everyday Life: The Nature, Extent and Consequences of Justiciable Problems Experienced by Canadians* (Ottawa: Department of Justice Canada, 2007) at 55–56 and generally 55–67, 88.

Féral-Schuhl, Christiane. *Cyberdroit : le droit à l'épreuve de l'Internet* (Paris: Dalloz, 2010).

Field, Karen H., Mark A Zaffarano & Yihwa Irene Liou. "Bringing Technology to the Jury Deliberation Table" (1996) *The Justice System Journal* 18:3 at 317.

Flávio Gomes, Luiz. "Judiciário não pode resistir aos avanços da tecnologia" (October 2002), *Consultor Jurídico*, online: <www.conjur.com.br/2002-out-27/judiciario_nao_resistir_aos_avancos_tecnologicos>.

Foggo, Gavin, Suzanne Grosso, Brett Harrison & Jose Victor Rodriguez-Barrera. "Comparing E-Discovery in the United States, Canada, the United Kingdom, and Mexico," online: <http://www.mcmillan.ca/Files/BHarrison_ComparingE-Discoveryintheunitedstates.pdf>.

Fowlie, Frank. "Online Dispute Resolution and Ombudsmanship," in Mohamed S Abdel Wahab, Ethan Katsh & Daniel Rainey, eds., *Online Dispute Resolution: Theory and Practice A Treatise on Technology and Dispute Resolution* (The Hague: Eleven International Publishing, 2012) 325.

FRANCE-Conseil d'Etat. *Etude annuelle 2014 du Conseil d'Etat - Le numérique et les droits fondamentaux* (La Documentation française, 2014).

Francisco Rossal De Araujo et al. "Avancos tecnologicos – Acesso ao Judiciario e outros temas" (2009) *COAD* 36 at 647.

Garapon, Antoine. *La prudence et l'autorité : l'office du juge au XXIe siècle*, Rapport, Institut des Hautes études sur la justice, May 2013.

Gascón Inchausti, Fernando. "L'introduction des nouvelles technologies dans le procès civil espagnol" (2010) 2010:4 *Procédures* 35.

Gautrais, Vincent & Pierre Trudel. *Circulation des renseignements personnels et web 2.0* (Montréal: Thémis, 2010).

Gautrais, Vincent, Karim Benyekhlef & Pierre Trudel. "Les limites apprivoisées de l'arbitrage cybernétique : l'analyse de ces questions à travers l'exemple du Cybertribunal" (1999) 33:3 *Revue juridique Thémis* 537.

Gautrais, Vincent. *Neutralité technologique* (Montréal: Thémis, 2012).

——. *Preuve technologique* (Montréal: LexisNexis Canada, 2014).

——. "Les aspects relatifs à la sécurité," in Daniel Poulin et al., eds., *Guide juridique du commerçant électronique* (Montréal: Thémis, 2003) 129.

Gélinas Fabien et al. *Foundations of Civil Justice: Toward a Value-Based Framework for Reform* (Berlin: Springer, 2015).

Gélinas, Fabien et al. *Foundations of Civil Justice* (Cham: Springer International Publishing, 2015).

Gélinas, Fabien, Clément Camion & Karine Bates. "Forme et légitimité de la justice – Regard sur le rôle de l'architecture et des rituels judiciaires" (2014) 72:2 *Revue interdisciplinaire d'études juridiques* 37.

Gélinas, Fabien. "Interopérabilité et normalisation des systèmes de cyber-justice: Orientations" (2006) 10:3 *Lex Electronica*, online: <https://papyrus.bib.umontreal.ca/xmlui/handle/1866/2309>.

——. "Virtual Justice and the Rule of Law" in Karim Benyekhlef & Pierre Trudel, eds, *État de droit et virtualité* (Montréal: Thémis, 2009) 293.

——. "Interpreting the Model Law: Methodology and the Singapore Experience," in David Foxton and David Joseph, eds., *Singapore International Arbitration, Law and Practice*, (LexisNexis Canada, accepted, 2014) (with F. Bachand).

——. "Modelling Fundamental Legal Change: The Paradox of Context and the Context of Paradox" (2015) 28:1 *Canadian Journal of Law & Jurisprudence* 77.

Gillieron, Philippe. "From Face-to-Face to Screen-to-Screen: Real Hope or Tue Fallacy?" (2007-08) 23 *Ohio St. J. on Disp. Resol.* 301.

Goyal, Monica. "Access to Justice: Courts and Technology: A Twitterchat", (2013), online: *Slaw* <http://www.slaw.ca/2013/11/25/access-to-justice-courts-and-technology-a-twitterchat/>.

Gramatikov, Martin, ed. *Costs and quality of online dispute resolution: A handbook for measuring the costs and quality of ODR* (Antwerp; Portland, Or: Maklu Publishers, 2012).

Gras, Antonin & Bertrand Du Marais. "Vers un 'Cyberjuge administratif' ? La numérisation de la justice administrative en France," Working paper, n°13, 8 September 2015.

Gratton, Eloïse. *Practical guide to e-commerce and Internet law* (Markham, Ontario: LexisNexis, 2015).

Greenleaf, Graham, Andrew Mowbray & Philip Chung. "The Meaning of 'Free Access to Legal Information': A Twenty Year Evolution" (2013) 1:1 *Journal of Open Access to Law*, online: <http://ojs.law.cornell.edu/index.php/joal/article/view/11>.

Greenwood, J Michael & Gary Bockweg. "Insights to Building a Successful E-Filing Case Management Service: U.S. Federal Court Experience" (2012) 4:2 *International Journal for Court Administration* 2.

Gregory, John D. "Current practices of online dispute resolution: the Canadian experience" (2012) 36:4 *HUFS Law Review* 3.

Hagen, Gregory. "The Use of Electronic Signatures in Courts and Beyond : Some Questions," in Trevor Farrow & Patrick Molinari, eds., *The Courts and Beyond: The Architecture of Justice in Transition* (Montreal: Canadian Institute for the Administration of Justice, 2013).

Hattotuwa, Sanjana. "Mobiles and ODR: Why We Should Care" in Mohamed S Abdel Wahab, Ethan Katsh & Daniel Rainey, eds., *Online Dispute Resolution: theory and practice: a treatise on technology and dispute Resolution* (The Hague: Eleven International Publishing, 2012) 95.

Hofer, Inga. *The Rise of Courtroom Technology and its Effect on the Federal Rules of Evidence and the Federal Rules of Civil Procedure* (Student Scholarship, Michigan State University, 2007) [unpublished].

Hoogen, Ronald van den & Peter van Rotterdam. "True-to-Life requirements for using videoconferencing in legal procedings," in Sabine Braun & Judith L Taylor, eds., *Videoconference and remote interpreting in criminal proceedings* (Cambridge, United Kindom: Intersentia, 2012) 215.

Horowitz, Donald J. "Technology, Values, and the Justice System: The Evolution of the Access to Justice Technology Bill of Rights" (2004) 79 *Wash L Rev* 79:77.

Howes, David. "E-Legislation: Law-Making in the Digital Age" (2002) 47:1 *McGill Law Journal* 39.

Iavarone-Turcotte, Cléa. "Et s'il était possible d'obtenir justice en ligne?" (2012) 17:2 *Lex Electronica*, online: <http://hdl.handle.net/1866/9280>.

———. *La résolution en ligne des conflits de consommation à l'aune de l'accès à la justice* (Thémis, 2015).

Jackson, Brian et al. *Fostering Innovation in the U.S. Court System: Identifying High-Priority Technology and Other Needs for Improving Court Operations and Outcomes* (RAND Corporation, 2016).

Jackson, Darla. "Lawyers Can't be Luddites Anymore: Do Law Librarians Have a Role in Helping Lawyers Adjust to New Ethics Rules Involving Technology?" (2013) *Law Libr J* 105 at 395.

Jackson, Sheryl. "Court-provided Trial Technology: Efficiency and Fairness for Criminal Trials" (2010) *C L World Rev* 39 at 236.

Jacob, Marie-Claire, Adrien Salas & Guillaume C Branconnier. "Les méandres du cyberespace : la compétence des tribunaux québécois relativement aux contrats conclus en ligne" (2014) Août Repères, online: <http://www.lareferencev2.editionsyvonblais.com/maf/app/document?&src=rl&srguid=ioad60079000001491a98a8386c928d4d&docguid=mDDDB7DCB4CB64CDC8F2A189C516AEC02&hitguid=mDDDB7DCB4CB64CDC8F2A189C516AEC02&spos=1&epos=1&td=1&crumb-action=append&context=57&&showSnippets=true>.

Jensen, Nils. "Technology in the Courtroom" (23 February 2010), online: The Canadian Bar Association <www.cbapd.org/details_en.aspx?id=NA_ONFEB210>.

Jones, D R. "Protecting the Treasure: An Assessment of State Court Rules and Policies for Access to Online Civil Court Records," (2013) *Drake L Rev* 61:2 :375 at 394.

Kaminski, Dan. "Que font faire les technologies à la justice pénale ?" (2013) 37:3 *Déviance et Société* 255.

Kaplan, Lewis A. "Litigation, Privacy and the Electronic Age" (2001) *Yale Symp on L & Tech* 4:1.

Kastner, Philipp. "Cyberjustice in the Context of Transitional Justice," Working paper n°9, Laboratoire de Cyberjustice, November 2013.

Katsh, Ethan M & Janet Rifkin. *Online dispute resolution: resolving conflicts in cyberspace* (San Francisco: Jossey-Bass, 2001).

Katsh, Ethan. "ODR: A Look at History - A Few Thoughts About the Present and Some Speculation About the Future," in Mohamed S Abdel Wahab, Ethan Katsh & Daniel Rainey, eds., *Online Dispute Resolution: Theory And Practice: A Treatise On Technology And Dispute Resolution* (The Hague: Eleven International Publishing, 2012) 21.

Kaufmann-Kohler, Gabrielle & Thomas Schultz. *Online Dispute Resolution: Challenges for Contemporary Justice,* (Julian Lew ed., Kluwer Law Int'l 2004).

Kitoogo, Fredrick Edward & Constantine Bitwayiki. "e-Justice Implementation at a National Scale: The Ugandan Case" in Adolfo Villafiorita, Regis Saint-Paul & Alessandro Zorer, eds, *E-Infrastructures and E-Services on Developing Countries* (Springer Berlin Heidelberg, 2010) 40.

Koulu, Riikka. "Disintegration of the State Monopoly on Dispute Resolution: How Should We Perceive State Sovereignty in the ODR Era?" (2014) 2 *International Journal of Online Dispute Resolution*, online: <http://www.elevenjournals.com/tijdschrift/ijodr/2014/2/IODR_2352-5002_2014_001_002_002>.

———. "Three Quests for the Justification in the ODR Era: Sovereignty, Contract and Quality Standards" (2014) 19:1 *Lex Electronica* 43.

Kumar Bhardwaj, Raj. "The Indian Judicial System: Transition from Print to Digital" (2015) 13:3 *Legal Information Management* 203.

Larson, David Allen. "Access to Justice for Persons with Disabilities: An Emerging Strategy" (2014) 3:2 *Laws* 220.

Lederer, Fredric I. "Courtroom Technology: For Trial Lawyers, the Future is Now" (2004) 19:1 *Criminal Justice Magazine* 14.

———. "Technology-Augmented Courtrooms: Progress Amid a Few Complications, or the Problematic Interrelationship Between Court and Counsel" (2004) *NYU Annual Survey of American Law* 60 at 675.

———. "Wired, What We Have Learned About Courtroom Technology" Winter 2010 ABA Criminal Justice.

———. "Excerpts from: Basic Advocacy and Litigation in a Technological Age: Traditional and Innovative Trial Practice in a Changing World," 2005, online: <http://www.legaltechcenter.net/download/articles/Excerpts%20from%20Basic%20Advocacy%20and%20Litigation%20In%20a%20Technological%20Age.pdf>.

Lempert, Richard et al. *A Modern Approach to Evidence: Text, Problems, Transcripts and Cases*, 5th ed. (West Academic Publishing, 2014).

Licoppe, Christian & Laurence Dumoulin. "Proximité ou distance ? Autour du développement de la visioconférence dans la justice française," in Jacques Poumarède, ed., *Territoires et lieux de justice* (Paris: La Documentation, 2015).

Licoppe, Christian & Maud Vernier. "Interpreting, video communication and the sequential reshaping of institutional talk in the bilingual and distributed courtroom" (2013) 20:2 *International Journal of Speech Language and the Law*.

Licoppe, Christian, Maud Verdier & Laurence Dumoulin. "Courtroom Interaction as a Multimedia Event: The Work of Producing Relevant Videoconference Frames in French Pre-Trial Hearings" (2013) 23:1–2 *Electronic Journal of Communication*, online: <http://www.cios.org/www/ejc/v23n12toc.htm#licoppeetalfr>.

Licoppe, Christian. "Interpreting, video communication and the sequential reshaping of institutional talk in the bilingual and distributed courtroom" (2013) 20:2 *International Journal of Speech Language and the Law*.

———. "Two modes of referring to the case file in the courtroom. The use of indirect reported text and text-as-addressed speech in case summaries" (2014) 36 *Language and Communication* 83.

Lillo L, Ricardo. "El uso de nuevas tecnologías en el sistema judicial: experiencias y precauciones," in José Antonio Caballero, Carlos Gregorio de Gràcia & Linn Hammergren, eds., *Buenas practicas para la implementacion de soluciones tecnologicas en la administracion de justicia* (Buenos Aires: IIJusticia, 2011) 117.

Lloyd, Ian J. *Information Technology Law* (Oxford University Press, 2014).

Lodder, Arno R & John Zeleznikow. "Artificial Intelligence and Online Dispute Resolution," in Mohamed S Abdel Wahab, Ethan Katsh & Daniel Rainey, eds., *Online Dispute Resolution: Theory and Practice A Treatise on Technology and Dispute Resolution* (The Hague: Eleven International Publishing, 2012) 73.

———. *Enhanced Dispute Resolution Through the Use of Information Technology* (New York: Cambridge University Press, 2010).

Lord Justice Briggs. *Civil Courts Structure Review: Interim Report* (Judiciary of England and Wales, 2015).

Losinger, John. "Electronic Access to Court Records: Shifting the Privacy Burden Away from Witnesses and Victims" (2007) *U Balt L Rev* 36 at 419.

Lupo, Giampiero & Jane Bailey. "Designing and Implementing e-Justice Systems: Some Lessons Learned from EU and Canadian Examples" (2014) 3:2 *Laws* 353.

Lupo, Giampiero, in collaboration with Marco FABRI. "Evaluating e-Justice. The Design of an Assessment Framework for e-Justice Systems," *Towards Cyberjustice* project working paper, Cyberjustice Laboratory, University of Montréal, Montréal, QC, 2014.

Magnuson, Eric J & Samuel A Thumma. "Prospects and Problems Associated with Technological Change in Appellate Courts: Envisioning the Appeal of the Future Performance-Focused Technology" (2014) 15:1 *J App Prac & Process* 111.

Makar, Kristin M. "Taming Technology in the Context of the Public Access Doctrine: New Jersey's Amended Rule 1:38," (2011) *Seton Hall L Rev* 41:1071 at 1088.

Marder, Nancy S. "Juries and Technology: Equipping Jurors for the Twenty-First Century" (2001) *Brooklyn Law Review* 66 at 1257.

Marta Poblet, ed. *Mobile Technologies for Conflict Management : Online Dispute Resolution, Governance, Participation*. Law, Governance and Technology Series; 2 (Dordrecht: Springer Netherlands, 2011).

Martinez, Agusti Cerrillo I. "E-Justice in Spain," in Agusti Cerrilo I Martinez & Pere Fabra I Abat, *E-Justice: Information and Communication Technologies in the Court System* (New York: Information Science Reference, 2009) at 98.

Mason, Stephen. *Electronic signatures in law*, 3rd ed. (New York: Cambridge University Press, 2012).

McDonald, Laura W, David Tait, Karen Gelb, Meredith Rossner & Blake M McKimmie. "Digital evidence in the jury room: The impact of mobile technology on the jury" (2015) *Current Issues Crim. Just.* 27 at 179.

McKechnie, Dougal. "The Use of the Internet by Courts and the Judiciary: Findings from a Study Trip and Supplementary Research" (2003) 11:2 *International Journal of Law and Information Technology* 109.

Mensah Attoh, Koffi Sylvain. "L'Afrique et la cyberjustice" (2014) N° Spécial IDEF-ACTES DU 33ème CONGRES DE L'IDEF Revue de l'ERSUMA : Droit des affaires - Pratique Professionnelle 189.

Michal Medows, Ariella. "Legal and Policy Aspects of the Intersection Between Cloud Computing and the U.S. Healthcare Industry," (11 September 2015), online: *JOLT Digest* <http://jolt.law.harvard.edu/digest/bioethics/legal-and-policy-aspects-of-the-intersection-between-cloud-computing-and-the-u-s-healthcare-industry?utm_source=feedly&utm_medium=rss&utm_campaign=legal-and-policy-aspects-of-the-intersection-between-cloud-computing-and-the-u-s-healthcare-industry>.

Miller, Nelson P & Derek S Witte, "Helping Law Firm Luddites Cross the Digital Divide – Arguments for Mastering Law Practice Technology" (2009) *S Methodist University L Rev* 12:113.

Mizrahi, Sarit. *Cyberjustice: An Overview* (2016), Working paper, Cyberjustice Laboratory.

Mohamed S Abdel Wahab. "ODR and e-Abritation – Trends & Challenges," in Mohamed S Abdel Wahab, Ethan Katsh & Daniel Rainey, eds., *Online Dispute Resolution: Theory and Practice A Treatise on Technology and Dispute Resolution* (The Hague: Eleven International Publishing, 2012) 399.

Morek, Rafal. "Regulation of Online Dispute Resolution: Between Law and Technology" (2003) 77.

Moriarty, Laura J. *Criminal Justice Technology in the 21st Century* (Springfield: Charles C. Thomas, 2005).

Myers Morrison, Caren. "Privacy, Accountability, and the Cooperating Defendant: Towards a New Role for Internet Access to Court Records" (2009) *Vand L Rev* 62 at 921.

National Center for State Courts. *Best Practices in Court-Based Programs for the Self-Represented: Concepts, Attributes, Issues for Exploration, Examples, Contacts, and Resources* (2008).

Odima, D O. "E-justice: Define Steps by The Judiciary of Kenya" (2014) Scientific Conference Proceedings, online: <http://www.sciary.com/journal-scientific-scientificconferenc-article-254062>.

Odinge, Owenga & Emile Lambert. "Vers l'émergence d'une justice on-line" (2002) 7:2 *Lex Electronica* 1.

Onana Etoundi, Félix. "La cyber justice au service des opérateurs africains et arabes : état du contentieux civil africain" (2014) N° Spécial IDEF-ACTES DU 33ème CONGRES DE L'IDEF Revue de l'ERSUMA : Droit des affaires - Pratique Professionnelle 179.

Online Dispute Resolution Advisory Group. *Online Dispute Resolution for Low Value Civil Claims* (Civil Justice Council, 2015).

Ost, François & Michel Van de Kerchove. *De la pyramide au résau ? pour une théorie dialectique du droit* (Bruxelles: Publications des Facultés universitaires Saint-Louis, 2002).

Pangalos, George, Ioannis Salmatzidis & Ioannis Pagkalos. "Using IT to Provide Easier Access to Cross-Border Legal Procedures for Citizens and Legal Professionals - Implementation of a European Payment Order e-CODEX pilot" (2014) 6:2 *International Journal for Court Administration* 43.

Park Jaihyun & Neal Feigenson. "Effects of a Visual Technology on Mock Juror Decision Making" (2013) *Applied Cognitive Psychology* 27:235 at 244.

Parker, Christine, Tahlia Gordon & Steve Mark. "Regulating Law Firms Ethics Management: An Empirical Assessment of an Innovation in Regulation of the Legal Profession in New South Wales" (2010) *Journal of Law in Society* 37:3 :446 at 493.

Pattavina, April, ed. *Information Technology and the Criminal Justice System* (Thousand Oaks, Calif.: Sage Publications, 2005).

Pearlstein, Arthur, Bryan Hanson & Noam Ebner. "ODR in North America," in Mohamed S Abdel Wahab, Ethan Katsh & Daniel Rainey, eds., *Online Dispute Resolution: theory and practice: a treatise on technology and dispute Resolution* (The Hague: Eleven International Publishing, 2012) 443.

Peltz-Steele, Richard. "Electronic Court Record Access: Present Landscape, Neutral Principles, and the Looming Interloper of Contextual Privacy," in Charles N Davis & David Cuillier, eds., *Transparency 20: Digital Data and Privacy in a Wired World* (Peter Lang Publishing Inc, 2014) 67.

Perlman, Andrew. "The Twenty-First Century Lawyer's Evolving Ethical Duty of Competence" (2014) *The Professional Lawyer* 22:4 at 24.

Philippe, Mirèze. "ODR Redress System for Consumer Disputes - Clarifications, UNCITRAL Works & EU Regulation on ODR" (2014) 1:1 *Internal Journal of Online Dispute Resolution* 57.

Piché, Catherine. "Justice Wide Open: Transparency of the Judicial Process in Modern Technological Courtrooms," in Dominique Custos, ed., *Transparency, a governance principle, Proceedings of the XIIth Congress of the International Association of Legal Methodology* (Bruxelles: Bruylant, 2014) 223.

Poblet, Marta & Graham Ross. "ODR in Europe," in Mohamed S Abdel Wahab, Ethan Katsh & Daniel Rainey, eds., *Online Dispute Resolution: Theory And Practice: A Treatise On Technology And Dispute Resolution* (The Hague: Eleven International Publishing, 2012) 465.

Ponte Lucille M & Thomas D Cavenagh, *Cyberjustice Online Dispute Resolution (ODR) for E-commerce* (Pearson: Prentice Hall, 2006).

——. *Cyberjustice: Online Dispute Resolution (ODR) for E-Commerce* (Upper Saddle River, N.J.: Pearson/Prentice Hall, 2005).

Ponte, Lucille M. "Boosting Consumer Confidence in E-Business: Recommendations for Establishing Fair and Effective Dispute Resolution Programs for B2C Online Transactions," (2001-02) 12 *Alb. L.J. Sci. & Tech.* 441.

Potter, Sandra, Phil Farrelly & Derek Begg. "The E-Court Roadmap: Innovation and Integration An Australian Case Study," in Agusti Cerrilo I Martinez and Pere Fabra i Abat, *E-Justice: Information and Communication Technologies in the Court System* (New York: Information Science Reference, 2009) at 165.

Poulin, Anne Bowen. "Criminal Justice and Videoconferencing Technology: The Remote Defendant" (2004) *Tul L Rev* 78 at 1089.

Quigley, Michelle. "Courtroom Technology and Legal Ethics: Considerations for the ABA Commission on Ethics 20/20" (Spring 2010), online: Michigan State University College of Law <www.law.msu.edu/king/2009-2010/Quigley.pdf>.

Rabinovich-Einy, Orna & Ethan Katsh. "Digital Justice - Reshaping Boundaries in an Online Dispute Resolution Environment" (2014) 1:1 *Internal Journal of Online Dispute Resolution* 5.

——. "Lessons from Online Dispute Resolution for Dispute Systems Design," in Mohamed S Abdel Wahab, Ethan Katsh & Daniel Rainey, eds., *Online Dispute Resolution: Theory and Practice A Treatise on Technology and Dispute Resolution* (The Hague: Eleven International Publishing, 2012) 51.

——. "Lessons from Online Dispute Resolution for Dispute Systems Design," in Mohamed S Abdel Wahab, Ethan Katsh & Daniel Rainey, eds., *Online Dispute Resolution: Theory and Practice A Treatise on Technology and Dispute Resolution* (The Hague: Eleven International Publishing, 2012) 51.

——. "Technology and the Future of Dispute Systems Design" (2012) 17 *Harvard Negotiation Law Review* 151.

Rabinovich-Einy, Orna. "Technology's Impact: The Quest for a New Paradigm for Accountability in Mediation" (2006) 11 *Harvard Negotation Law Review* 253.

Rainey, Daniel & Ethan Katsh. "ODR and Government," in Mohamed S Abdel Wahab, Ethan Katsh & Daniel Rainey, eds., *Online Dispute Resolution: Theory And Practice: A Treatise On Technology And Dispute Resolution* (The Hague: Eleven International Publishing, 2012) 249.

Rainey, Daniel. "ODR and Culture," in Mohamed S Abdel Wahab, Ethan Katsh & Daniel Rainey, eds., *Online Dispute Resolution: Theory and Practice A Treatise on Technology and Dispute Resolution* (The Hague: Eleven International Publishing, 2012) 197.

———. "Third-Party Ethics in the Age of the Fourth Party" (2014) 1:1 *Internal Journal of Online Dispute Resolution* 37.

Regan, Milton C. "Nested Ethics: A Tale of Two Cultures" (2013) *Hofstra Law Review* 42:143 at 172.

Reiling, Dory. "Doing justice with information technology" (2006) 15:2 *Information & Communications Technology Law* 189.

Rhode, Deborah. *Access to Justice* (Oxford: Oxford University Press, 2005).

Roberge, Jean-François. "'Sense of Access to Justice' as a Framework for Civil Procedure Justice Reform: An Empirical Assessment of Judicial Settlement Conferences in Quebec (Canada)" (2016) 17 *Cardozo Journal of Conflict Resolution* 323.

———. *Le sentiment d'accès à la justice et la Conférence de règlement à l'amiable*, Rapport de recherche sur l'expérience des justiciables et avocats à la Cour supérieure du Québec et à la Cour du Québec (Faculté de droit, Université de Sherbrooke, 2014).

Rogers, Vikki. "Knitting the Security Blanket for New Market Opportunities – Establishing a Global Online Dispute Resolution System for Cross-Border Online Transactions for the Sale of Goods," in Mohamed S Abdel Wahab, Ethan Katsh & Daniel Rainey, eds., *Online Dispute Resolution: Theory and Practice A Treatise on Technology and Dispute Resolution* (The Hague: Eleven International Publishing, 2012) 107.

Rossner, Meredith, David Tait & Jane Goodman-Delahunty. "Students vs. Jurors: Responding to Enhanced Video Technology" (2014) 3:3 *Laws* 618.

Rowden, Emma et al. *Gateways to Justice: Design and Operational Guidelines for Remote Participation in Court Proceedings* (University of Western Sydney, 2013).

Rule, Colin & Harpreet Singh. "ODR and Online Reputation Systems – Maintaining Trust and Accuracy Through Effective Redress," in Mohamed S Abdel Wahab, Ethan Katsh & Daniel Rainey, eds., *Online Dispute Resolution: Theory And Practice: A Treatise On Technology And Dispute Resolution* (The Hague: Eleven International Publishing, 2012) 175.

Salyzyn, Amy. "A New Lens: Reframing the Conversation about the Use of Video Conferencing in Civil Trials in Ontario" (2012) *Osgoode Hall LJ* 50 at 429.

———. "Technological Competence 101: Back to Basics?" Slaw Online (15 January 2015), online: Slaw.ca <www.slaw.ca/2015/01/29/technological-competence-101-back-to-basics/>.

Saman, Wan Satirah Wan Mohd & Abrar Haider. "Electronic Court Records Management: A Case Study" (2012) *Journal of e-Government Studies and Best Practices* 1.

Scassa, Teresa et al. "Consumer Privacy and Radio Frequency Identification Technology" (2006) 37:2 *Ottawa Law Review,* 215.

Schellhamer, Erich. "A Technology Opportunity for Court Modernization: Remote Appearances" (January 2013), online: Canadian Centre for Court Technology <wiki.modern-courts.ca/images/1/1b/A_Technology_Opportunity_for_Court_Modernization_-_Remote_Appearances.pdf>.

Senécal, F & K Benyekhlef. "Groundwork for Assessing the Legal Risks of Cyberjustice" (2009) 7 *Canadian Journal of Law and Technology* 41.

Serbena, Cesar Antonio & Maurício Dalri Timm Do Valle. "An overview on the computerization and evaluation of the Brazilian judicial system," in Cesar Antonio Serbena, ed., *E-justice and governance: collected studies* (Curitiba: UFPR, 2015) 21.

Serbena, Cesar Antonio, ed. *E-justice and governance: collected studies* (Curitiba: UFPR, 2015).

Shaw, Thomas J. *Information Security and Privacy: A Practical Guide for Global Executives* (Chicago: American Bar Association, 2011).

Sherman, Jo. "Court Information Management Policy Framework to Accommodate the Digital Environment" (Discussion paper prepared for the Canadian Judicial Council, 2013), online: <www.cjc-ccm.gc.ca/cmslib/general/AJC/Policy%20Framework%20to%20Accommodate%20the%20Digital%20Environment%202013-03.pdf>; European Network of Councils for the Judiciary, "ENCJ Working Group: Judicial Ethics Report 2009-2010," online: <www.encj.eu>.

Sherwin, Richard K, Neal Feigenson & Christina Spiesel. "Law in the Digital Age: How Visual Communication Technologies Are Transforming the Practice, Theory, and Teaching of Law" (2006) 12:2 *Boston University Journal of Science & Technology Law* 227.

Silveira, Lucas, Raul Sidnei Wazlawick & Aires Jose Rover. "Assessing the Brazilian e-Justice Interoperability Model" (2015) 13:5 *Latin America Transactions, IEEE* (Revista IEEE America Latina) 1504.

Snyder, David L. "Nonparty Remote Electronic Access to Plea Agreements in the Second Circuit" (2008) *Fordham Urb L J* 35 at 1263.

Sourdin, Tania & Chinthaka Liyanage. "The Promise and Reality of Online Dispute Resolution in Australia," in Mohamed S Abdel Wahab, Ethan Katsh & Daniel Rainey, eds., *Online Dispute Resolution: Theory And Practice: A Treatise On Technology And Dispute Resolution* (The Hague: Eleven International Publishing, 2012) 483.

Sudbeck, Lynn E. "Placing Court Records Online: Balancing the Public and Private Interests" (2006) *The Justice System Journal* 27:3 at 268.

Szlak, Gabriela R. "Online Dispute Resolution in Latin America – Challenges and Opportunities," in Mohamed S Abdel Wahab, Ethan Katsh & Daniel Rainey, eds., *Online Dispute Resolution: Theory and Practice A Treatise on Technology and Dispute Resolution* (The Hague: Eleven International Publishing, 2012) 529.

Tait, David. "Judges and jukeboxes: sentencing information systems in the court room" (1998) 6:2 *International Journal of Law and Information Technology* 167.

——. "Popular sovereignty and the justice process: Towards a comparative methodology for observing courtroom rituals" (2001) 4:2 *Contemporary Justice Review* 201.

Taslitz, Andrew E. "Digital Juries Versus Digital Lawyers" (2004) *ABA Criminal J* 19.

Thibeault, Alexandre. "Initiatives de justice mobile," Working paper n°10, Laboratoire de Cyberjustice, 3 October 2013.

Thiessen, Ernest, Paul Miniato & Bruce Hiebert. "ODR and eNegotiation," in Mohamed S Abdel Wahab, Ethan Katsh & Daniel Rainey, eds., *Online Dispute Resolution: Theory and Practice A Treatise on Technology and Dispute Resolution* (The Hague: Eleven International Publishing, 2012) 341.

Tiaglo, O V. "Complete Electronic Justice: Pro et Contra" (2013) 2013:1 *Форум права* (Law Forum) 1051.

Treadway Johnson, Molly & Elizabeth Wiggins. "Videoconferencing in Criminal Proceedings: Legal and Empirical Issues for Direction and Research" (2006) *Law & Pol'y* 28 at 211.

Trudel, Pierre. "Vers une intégration du droit à la vie privée et des technologies de sécurité," in Karim Benyekhlef & Ester Mitjans, eds., *Circulation internationale de l'information et sécurité* (Montréal: Thémis, 2013) 199.

——. *Introduction à la Loi concernant le cadre juridique des technologies de l'information* (Cowansville, Qc: Éditions Yvon Blais, 2012).

Van den Herik, Jaap & Daniel Dimov. "Towards Crowdsourced Online Dispute Resolution" (2012) 7:2 *Journal of International Commercial Law and Technology* 99.

Velicogna, Marco. "Electronic Access to Justice: From Theory to Practice and Back" (2011) 1:61 *Droit et cultures*, online: <http://droitcultures.revues.org/2447>.

——. "ICT within the Court in the E-justice Era" (2014) 6 Effectius Newsletter, online: <http://effectius.com/yahoo_site_admin/assets/docs/Effectius_July_2010_Newsletter_Issue_6.20780135.pdf>.

——. "Justice Systems and ICT: What Can Be Learned from Europe?" (2007) *Utrecht Law Review* at 129.

Verdier, Maud, Laurence Dumoulin & Christian Licoppe. "Les usages de la visioconférence dans les audiences judiciaires en France : les enjeux d'un protocole de recherche basé sur l'enregistrement audiovisuel des pratiques" (2012) Numéro 25, Ethnographiques.org, online: <http://ethnographiques.org/2012/Verdier,Dumoulin,Licoppe>.

Vermeys Nicolas W. & Karim Benyekhlef. "Reinventing Rituals – How to Develop Technological Solutions to Courtroom Conundrums" (forthcoming).

———. "ODR and the Courts," in Mohamed S Abdel Wahab, Ethan Katsh & Daniel Rainey, eds., *Online Dispute Resolution: Theory And Practice: A Treatise On Technology And Dispute Resolution* (The Hague: Eleven International Publishing, 2012) 295.

———. "Premiers éléments d'une méthodologie de réformation des processus judiciaires par la technologie," in Daniel Le Métayer, ed., *Les technologies de l'information au service des droits : opportunités, défis, limites* (Bruxelles: Bruylant, 2010) 209.

Vermeys, Nicolas W & Patrick Gingras. "Chronique - Revue jurisprudentielle canadienne sur les technologies de l'information" (2014) Septembre 2014 Repères, online: <http://www.lareferencev2.editionsyvonblais.com/maf/app/document?&src=rl&srguid=ioad60079000001491aaob3ef e6d19e82&docguid=mA613BD8A63A94B26914C595AE56C4607&hitgu id=mA613BD8A63A94B26914C595AE56C4607&spos=1&epos=1&td=21 &crumb-action=append&context=68&&showSnippets=true>.

Vermeys, Nicolas W. *Droit codifié et nouvelles technologies : le Code civil* (Cowansville: Éditions Yvon Blais, 2015).

———. *Responsabilité civile et sécurité informationnelle* (Cowansville: Éditions Yvon Blais, 2010).

Vermeys, Nicolas, Julie M. Gauthier & Sarit Mizrahi, "Étude sur les incidences juridiques de l'utilisation de l'infonuagique," préparée pour le gouvernement du Québec, mars 2014.

Vermeys, Nicolas, Marie-Andrée Boutin-Clermont & Sarit Mizrahi. *Étude sur le chiffrement des données transmises ou hébergées dans le nuage* (Laboratoire de cyberjustice et Centre de recherche en droit public, 2015).

Vermeys, Nicolas. "Code source et sources codifiées : pour une cyberjustice québécoise ouverte et accessible" (2010) 14:3 *Lex Electronica*, online: <https://papyrus.bib.umontreal.ca/xmlui/handle/1866/9360>.

———. "La cyberjustice et l'espace OHADA: Des outils virtuels pour une avancée réelle" (2013) Numéro spécial JADA: *Journal africain du droit des affaires* 102.

———. "Le cadre juridique réservé aux bibliothèques numériques" (2013) 59:3 Documentation et bibliothèques 146.

Veronese de Castro, Alexandre Fontainha, Fernando & Roberto Fragale Filho. "Les usages des technologies de l'information et de la communication dans l'administration judiciaire au Brésil" (2011) 61 *Droit et Cultures* 55.

Vilalta, Aura Esther. "ODR and E-Commerce," in Mohamed S Abdel Wahab, Ethan Katsh & Daniel Rainey, eds., *Online Dispute Resolution: Theory and Practice A Treatise on Technology and Dispute Resolution* (The Hague: Eleven International Publishing, 2012) 125.

Vlis, Evert-Jan van der. "Videoconferencing in Criminal Proceedings," in Sabine Braun & Judith L Taylor, eds., *Videoconference and remote interpreting in criminal proceedings* (Cambridge, United Kingdom: Intersentia, 2012) 13.

Wahab, Mohamed S Abdel, Ethan Katsh & Daniel Rainey, eds. *Online Dispute Resolution: Theory And Practice: A Treatise On Technology And Dispute Resolution* (The Hague: Eleven International Publishing, 2012).

Wahab, Mohamed S Abdel. "Online Dispute Resolution for Africa," in Mohamed S Abdel Wahab, Ethan Katsh & Daniel Rainey, eds., *Online Dispute Resolution: Theory and Practice A Treatise on Technology and Dispute Resolution* (The Hague: Eleven International Publishing, 2012) 561.

Walker, J Douglas. *Intelligent Video Technologies Enhance Court Operations and Security*, Future Trends in State Courts 2006 (National Center for State Courts, 2006).

Wallace, Anne. "'Virtual justice in the bush': the use of court technology in remote and regional Australia" (2008) 19 *Journal of Law and Information Science* 1.

Whelan, David P. *Practice law in the cloud* (Aurora, Ontario: Canada Law Book, 2013).

Wiggins, Elizabeth. "The Courtroom of the Future is Here: Introduction to Emerging Technologies in the Legal System" (2006) *Law & Pol'y* 28 at 182.

Willoughby, Dan H, Rose Hunter Jones & Gregory R Antine. "Sanctions for E-Discovery Violations by the Numbers" (2010) *Duke LJ* 60:789 at 790.

Wing, Leah & Daniel Rainey. "Online Dispute Resolution and the Development of Theory," in Mohamed S Abdel Wahab, Ethan Katsh & Daniel Rainey, eds., *Online Dispute Resolution: Theory and Practice A Treatise on Technology and Dispute Resolution* (The Hague: Eleven International Publishing, 2012) 35.

Winn, Peter A. "Online Court Records: Balancing Judicial Accountability and Privacy in an Age of Electronic Information" (2004) *Wash. L. Rev* 79 at 307.

Winn, Peter A. "Judicial Information Management in an Electronic Age: Old Standards, New Challenges" (2009) *Fed Cts L Rev* 3 at 135.

Woolf, Harry Kenneth. *Access to Justice: Final Report to The Lord Chancellor on the Civil Justice System in England and Wales, Overview* (1996) at §1, online: <www.dca.gov.uk/civil/final/contents.htm>.

Xuclà, Jordi. *Access to justice and the Internet: potential and challenges*, Doc. 13918 (Committee on Legal Affairs and Human Rights - Council of Europe, 2015).

———. *Access to justice and the Internet: potential and challenges*, Doc. 13918 (Committee on Legal Affairs and Human Rights - Council of Europe, 2015).

Yun, Zhao et al. "Online Dispute Resolution In Asia," in Mohamed S Abdel Wahab, Ethan Katsh & Daniel Rainey, eds., *Online Dispute Resolution: Theory and Practice: A Treatise on Technology and Dispute Resolution* (The Hague: Eleven International Publishing, 2012) 511.

Zorza, Richard. *New Curriculum Helps Improve Access for the Self-Represented*, Future Trends in State Courts 2008 (National Center for State Courts, 2008).

Cases Cited

1588143 Ontario Inc v Lantic Inc, 2010 ONSC 1613 (CanLII).

AB v Bragg Communications Inc, 2012 SCC 46, [2012] 2 SCR 567.

Alberta (Attorney General of) v Krushell, 2003 ABQB 252, [2003] 7 WWR 174.

Attorney General of Nova Scotia v MacIntyre, [1982] 1 SCR 175, 132 DLR (3d) 385.

Bank of Montréal v Baysong Developments Inc, 2011 ONSC 931 (CanLII).

Bank of Montreal v Faibish, 2014 ONSC 2178 (CanLII).

Canadian Broadcasting Corp v Canada (Attorney General), 2011 SCC 2, [2011] 1 SCR 19.

Canadian Broadcasting Corp v New Brunswick (Attorney General), 2011 SCC 2, [2011] 1 SCR 19.

CCH Canadian Ltd v Law Society of Upper Canada, 2002 FCA 187, [2002] 4 FCR 213.

CCH Canadian Ltd v Law Society of Upper Canada, 2004 SCC 13, [2004] 1 SCR 339.

CJEU 14 June 2012, Case C-618/10, ECR (*Banco Español de Crédito*), ECLI:EU:C:2012:349.

CJEU 4 September 2014, joined cases C-119/13 and C-120/13 (*Eco Cosmetics*), ECLI:EU:C:2014:2144.

CJEU 9 July 2009, Case C-204/2008, ECR 2009 I-6073 (*Rehder v Air Baltic Corporation*).

Clark v Cantrell, 529 S.E.2d at 528 (South Carolina Sup Ct 2000).

Dunkle v Oklahoma, 139 P (3d) 228 (Okla Ct Crim App 2006).

Edmonton Journal v Alberta (Attorney General), [1989] 2 SCR 1326, 64 DLR (4th) 577.

European Court of Human Rights (ECtHR) 12 November 2002, no. 28394/95 (Dory v Sweden).

Ford v Quebec (Attorney General), [1988] 2 SCR 712, 54 DLR (4th) 577.

Gendler v Batiste, 174 Wn (2d) 244 (2012).

Golder v United Kingdom, ECtHR (1975) Series A, No. 18, and *Airey v Ireland*, ECHR (1979) Series A, No. 32.

Google Spain SL, Google Inc v Agencia Española de Protección de Datos (AEPD), Mario Costeja González, Case C-131/12.

Green v Mirtech International Security Inc, 2010 ONSC 1240 (CanLII).

HMQ (Ontario) v Rothmans Inc, 2011 ONSC 1083 (CanLII).

Homebrook v Seprotech Systems, 2011 ONSC 3100 (CanLII).

Hunter v Southam Inc, [1984] 2 SCR 145, 11 DLR (4th) 641.

Imperial Tobacco Canada Ltd v Québec (Procureur général), 2014 QCCS 842 (CanLII).

IPEX Inc v AT Plastics Inc, 2011 ONSC 4734 (CanLII).

Irwin Toy Ltd v Quebec (Attorney General), [1989] 1 SCR 927, 58 DLR (4th) 577.

Lac d'Amiante du Québec Ltée v 2858-0702 Québec Inc, 2001 SCC 51, [2001] 2 SCR 743.

Mortgage administrator/broker should have confirmed consent prior to issuing letter of interest for mortgage financing in couple's name, 2012 CanLII 96454 (PCC).

Ontario (Finance) (Re), 1996 CanLII 7740 (ON IPC).

Ontario (Public Safety and Security) v Criminal Lawyers' Association, 2010 SCC 23, [2010] 1 SCR 815.

PIPEDA Report of Findings #2015-002, online: *Office of the Privacy Commissioner of Canada* <https://www.priv.gc.ca/cf-dc/2015/2015_002_0605_e.asp>.

Qualcomm Inc v Broadcom Corp, 2008 US Dist Ct LEXIS 911 (SD Cal Dist CT 2008).

R v Canadian Broadcasting Corporation, 2007 CanLII 21124 (ON SC).

R v Ranger, [1998] OJ No 1654 (Ont Ct Justice Gen Div) (QL).

R v NS, 2012 SCC 72, [2012] 3 SCR 726.

Re R v Carson, [1996] 3 SCR 480, 182 NBR (2d) 81.

Rohit v Nuri, 2010 ONSC 17 (CanLII).

Sale of Provincial Government Computer Tapes Containing Personal Information, Re, 2006 CanLII 13536 (BC IPC).

Simpson v Attorney General (Canada), 2011 ONSC 3642 (CanLII).

Society of Composers, Authors and Music Publishers of Canada v Canadian Association of Internet Providers, 2004 SCC 45, [2004] 2 SCR 427.

State v Stewart, 643 NW (2d) 281 (Mo Sup Ct 2002).

Thériault-Thibault v McGill Computer Store, 2006 QCCQ 703 (CanLII).

Thériault-Thibault v SOQUIJ, 500-32-146975-158.

Toronto (City) (Re), 2000 CanLII 21004 (ON IPC).

Toronto Star Newspaper Ltd v Ontario, 2012 ONCJ 27.

United Food and Commercial Workers, Local 1518 (UFCW) v Kmart Canada Ltd, [1999] 2 SCR 1083.

United States v Johnson, 553 F Supp (2d) 582 (ED Va 2008).

Vallance v Gourlay-Vallance, 2002 ABQB 822, 325 AR 296.

Waldman v Thomson Reuters Canada Limited, 2014 ONSC 1288 (CanLII).

Waldman v Thomson Reuters Canada Limited, 2015 ONCA 53 (CanLII).
Waldman v Thomson Reuters Canada Limited, 2015 ONSC 3843 (CanLII).
Waldman v Thomson Reuters Canada Limited, 2016 ONSC 2622 (CanLII).
Waldman v Thomson Reuters Corporation, 2012 ONSC 1138 (CanLII).
Waldman v Thomson Reuters Corporation, 2012 ONSC 3436 (CanLII).
Wilson & Lafleur Inc c Société québécoise d'information juridique, 2000 CanLII 8006 (QC CA).
Wright v Wasilewski (2001), 52 OR (3d) 410 (CanLII) (ONSC).

Legislation Cited

Act Respecting the Société Québécoise d'Information Juridique, CQLR c S-20.
An Act respecting Access to Documents Held by Public Bodies and the Protection of Personal Information, CQLR c A-2.1.
An Act to Establish a Legal Framework for Information Technology, CQLR c C-1.1, 12.
Archives Act, CQLR c A-21.1
Automobile Insurance Act, CQLR c A-25.
Brazilian Federal Law n. 10.259/2001.
Brazilian Federal Law n. 8.245/199.
Brazilian Federal Law n. 9.800/1999.
Canada Evidence Act, RSC 1985, c C-5.
Canadian Charter of Rights and Freedoms, Part I of the Constitution Act, 1982, being Schedule B to the Canada Act 1982 (UK), 1982, c. 11.
Charter of Fundamental Rights of the European Union, Official Journal 2000/C 364/01.
Civil Code of Quebec, L.R.Q., c. C-1991.
Code of Civil Procedure, CQLR c C-25.01.
Copyright Act, RSC 1985, c C-42.
Criminal Law Amendment Act of 1968–1969, RSC 1968–69, c 38.
EU, Council Recommendation, *Promoting the use of and sharing of best practices on cross-border videoconferencing in the area of justice in the Member States and at EU level*, Official Journal 2015, L C 250/1.
EU, *Council Regulation (EC) No 1206/2001 of 28 May 2001 on co-operation between the courts of the Member States in the taking of evidence in civil or commercial matters*, Official Journal 2001, L 174/1.
EU, *Directive 2000/31/EC on electronic commerce*, Official Journal 2000, L178/1.
EU, *Directive 2008/52/EC of the European Parliament and of the Council on certain aspects of mediation in civil and commercial matters*, Official Journal 2008, L 136/3.
EU, *Directive 2013/11/EU on alternative dispute resolution for consumer disputes and amending Regulation (EC) No 2006/2004 and Directive 2009/22/EC (Directive on consumer ADR)*, Official Journal 2013, L 165/63.

EU, *Proposal for a Regulation of the European Parliament and of the Council amending Council Regulation (EC) 861/2007 of 11 July 2007 establishing a European Small Claims Procedure and Council Regulation (EC) 1896/2006 of the European Parliament*, COM(2013) 794 final.

EU, *Regulation (EC) No 1393/2007 of the European Parliament and of the Council on the service in the Member States of judicial and extrajudicial documents in civil or commercial matters (service of documents), and repealing Council Regulation (EC) No 1348/2000*, Official Journal 2000, L 324/9.

EU, *Regulation (EC) No 861/2007 of the European Parliament and of the Council establishing a European Small Claims Procedure*, Official Journal 2007, L 199/1.

EU, *Regulation (EC) No. 1896/2006 of the European Parliament and of the Council creating a European order for payment procedure*, Official Journal 2006, L 399/1.

EU, *Regulation 2015/2421 of the European Parliament and of the Council of 16 December 2015 amending Regulation (EC) No 861/2007 establishing a European Small Claims Procedure and Regulation (EC) No 1896/2006 creating a European order for payment procedure*, Official Journal 2015, L 341/1.

EU, *Regulation 664/2014 creating a European Account Preservation Order to facilitate cross-border debt recovery in civil and commercial matters, Official Journal 2014*, L 189/59.

EU, *Regulation No 1215/2012 of the European Parliament and of the Council on jurisdiction and the recognition and enforcement of judgements in civil and commercial matters (recast)*, Official Journal 2012, L 351/1.

EU, *Regulation No 524/2013 on online dispute resolution for consumer disputes and amending Regulation (EC) No 2006/2004 and Directive 2009/22/EC (Regulation on consumer ODR)*, Official Journal 2013, L 165/1.

Fonds d'assurance automobile (An Act Respecting the Société de l'assurance automobile du Québec), CQLR c S-11.011.

Freedom of Information and Protection of Privacy Act, RSA 2000, c F-25.

Personal Information Protection and Electronic Documents Act, SC 2000, c 5.

Privacy Act, RSC 1985, c P-21.

Regulations Specifying Publicly Available Information, SOR/2001-7.

Resolution CNJ (National Council of Justice), n. 185/2013.

Resolution STJ/CJF nº 001, 20 December 2004, online: <www.acjus.jus.br/legislacao/resolucoes>.

Supreme Court Act, RSC 1985, c S-26.

Wash Constitution Article I, § 32.

Contributors

Jane Bailey is a Full Professor in the Common Law Section (English) at the Faculty of Law, University of Ottawa, who teaches cyberfeminism, technoprudence, contracts, and civil procedure. She is the co-principal investigator with Dr. Valerie Steeves on "The eQuality Project," which is funded by a seven-year SSHRC Partnership Grant, and team leader of Working Group 1 on a seven-year MCRI project entitled "Rethinking Processual Law: Towards Cyberjustice." Her current research focuses on how "big data" and behavioural targeting shape the online environment in ways that set youth up for conflict, as well as the privacy and equality concerns arising from surveillance, and the relationship between technology and access to justice.

Katia Balbino de Carvalho Ferreira has been a Federal Judge in Brazil since November 1995. Her numerous appointments and assignments include: President of the Permanent Commission to standardize the Study of Information Technology Platform in Federal Courts by the Federal Council of Justice and Chair of the Technical Commission of Judiciary Certifying Authority (AC-JUS), May 2006 to August 2007; assigned by the Council of Federal Courts as member of the Committee of Procedures Systems and Records for the Federal Justice and by the 1st Regional Federal Court as member of the Special Committee on Standard Procedures Records from May 2006 to April 2008; member of the Management Committee of e-JUS from

December 2007 to April 2008; member of the Committee for the Implementation of Tax Enforcement Virtual Procedures from June 2006 to April 2008; and as a member of the Commission for the Creation of the Manual of Virtual Small Claims System from October 2005 to April 2008); Head of Goals for the Judiciary for the years 2010, 2011, and 2012, for the 1st Regional Federal Court; and member of the Committee on Security of the Federal Courts in August 2011.

Renaud Beauchard is a specialist in rule-of-law projects and African investment law. He has undertaken numerous African missions on behalf of the World Bank and the Millennium Challenge Corporation (MCC). His major projects include assistance to the MCC Access to Justice project's efforts to reform Benin's courts, regulatory offices, and procedural codes. Mr. Beauchard is a French national who is fluent in English.

In France, Mr. Beauchard formerly specialized in matters concerning admiralty, collisions, commercial law, employment law, insurance litigation, international trade, maritime pollution, and transportation. Mr. Beauchard has regularly served as counsel in international commercial litigation and arbitration, including such major tort and environmental disputes as the "Erika" and "Mont Blanc" cases.

From August 2009 to April 2011, Mr. Beauchard served as a consultant to the World Bank's Office of Evaluation and Suspension (OES). In this capacity, he assisted the evaluation and suspension officer in reviewing accusations leveled against allegedly fraudulent, corrupt, coercive, or obstructionist companies and individuals. Mr. Beauchard has also advised OES on comparative-law issues and sanctions policy.

Karim Benyekhlef has been a Professor in the Faculty of Law at the Université de Montréal since 1989. He has been seconded to the Centre de recherche en droit public (Public Law Research Centre) since 1990 and served as its Director from 2006 to 2014. He was also the Director of the Regroupement stratégique Droit, changements et gouvernance (Strategic Law, Change and Governance Group), which brings together some fifty researchers, from 2006 to 2014. At the same time, he was the Scientific Director of the Centre d'études et de recherches internationales de l'Université de Montréal (CÉRIUM—Université de Montréal International Research and Study Centre) from 2009 to 2012. He is now Director of the Cyberjustice

Laboratory, which he founded in 2010. He holds the Chaire de recherche en information juridique Lexum (Lexum Research Chair on Legal Information) and serves as a member of CÉRIUM's science and advisory committees.

Jacquelyn Burkell is Assistant Dean of Research and Associate Professor in the Faculty of Information and Media Studies at the University of Western Ontario. Dr. Burkell's research focuses on the empirical study of the interaction between people and technology, with a particular emphasis on the role of cognition in such interactions. Specific aspects of this research include the impact of presentation on information use and understanding, the design of human-computer interfaces, and the social impact of technology. With respect to this latter topic, she is interested in the impact of computer mediation on communication and the perception of self. Much of this work focuses on anonymity in online communication, examining how the pseudonymity offered by online communication is experienced by online communicators, and how this experience changes communication behaviour and interpretation. Dr. Burkell is also involved in research on the credibility of online information and information sources. Part of this work will focus on intelligent agents and virtual representatives as information sources, examining whether the credibility of these sources is assessed according to the same criteria used to establish the credibility of human information sources.

Clément Camion is a lawyer at the New York bar and a graduate of McGill University, Faculty of Law. He graduated magna cum laude in Political Science and Philosophy from the Université de Montréal. His research interests are centered on the construction and deconstruction of notions of sovereignty and the state, the divide between public and private entities, as well as constitutionalization processes in both historical and contemporary settings. He is also an advocate of plain language and clear communication in the legal field, and is pursuing several projects meant to foster access to justice, including through his work with the plain legal language and clear communication leader organization in Quebec, Éducaloi.

Guy Canivet is a member of the Conseil Constitutionnel de la République française. He was appointed on February 22, 2007, by the president of the National Assembly, and took the oath of office on March 5, 2007, before the president of the republic.

Fabien Gélinas teaches and conducts research in the areas of international-dispute resolution, contract law, and legal theory. Formerly General Counsel of the International Court of Arbitration of the International Chamber of Commerce, he is a member of the Quebec bar and acts as an arbitrator and as a consultant on dispute resolution and legal reform.

In April 2013, he was appointed a Norton Rose Faculty Scholar in Arbitration and Commercial Law for a two-year term. In November 2014, he was elected president of the Arbitration Committee of the Canadian Chamber of Commerce.

Donald Horowitz was a King County Superior Court Judge and Senior Assistant Attorney General for the State of Washington, serving as Chief Counsel for the Department of Social and Health Services. After retiring from his private law practice in 1991, he has served as a mediator and arbitrator while remaining involved in a broad range of community service projects.

Mr. Horowitz has authored legislation in a variety of areas, including the Mandatory Child Abuse Reporting Act; Crime Victim Compensation Act; Adoption Subsidy Act; the law allowing emergency medical care for children whose parent or guardian is unavailable; and the law requiring interpreters for persons with hearing disabilities in courts and other legal proceedings. He has been an instructor for the National Institute of Trial Advocacy and an Adjunct Professor of Civil Trial Practice and Consumer Protection at Seattle University School of Law. He has served as a mediator for the United States District Court for the Western District of Washington and a judge pro tem and arbitrator for King County Superior Court. In 2010, Mr. Horowitz was awarded the WSBA's highest honor, its Award of Merit.

Xandra Kramer is Professor of law at the Erasmus School of Law (Rotterdam, the Netherlands). She studied law at Leiden University (cum laude), specializing in private international law, civil procedure, comparative law, and philosophy (and where she was awarded the Leiden University thesis prize). She received the Ars Aequi prize (1996) for her first article, written as a student. She was an Assistant Professor at Leiden University and obtained her PhD on provisional measures and private international law in 2001. She worked as an associate professor at Erasmus School of Law and was appointed full professor in February 2011 (chair, European Civil Procedure).

Giampiero Lupo received his PhD in Political Science-Comparative and European Politics in 2010 at the University of Siena. He is a former researcher of the University of Bologna, working on deliberative democracy, quality of democracy, justice systems, and e-justice. He is a researcher at the IRSIG-CNR (Research Institute on Judicial Systems—National Research Council), of Italy, participating on a set of international projects such as "Building Interoperability for European Civil Proceedings Online," e-CODEX, and *Towards Cyberjustice*, and publishing the results of his research in peer-reviewed books and articles the results of his research. His main scientific interests are e-justice, quality of democracy, quality of justice systems, access to justice, and deliberative democracy.

Sherry McLennan joined the Legal Services Society of British Columbia as a staff lawyer in 2000, following a career in private practice in both BC and Saskatchewan. While at LSS, she has worked in a number of capacities that saw her implement the family duty counsel program and later manage intake, offices, and local agents. Since becoming director in 2009, Sherry has overseen the integration of information and referral services in the application process, and the expansion of public legal education and information services to include community partners and enhanced Aboriginal services. Sherry is the Chair of the BC Public Legal Education & Information Working Group and sits on the advisory committees of two national access to justice projects: the National Self-Represented Litigant Project and the Evolving Legal Services Project.

Pierre Noreau is Full Professor at the Centre de recherche en droit public de l'Université de Montréal, where he has been teaching and conducting research since 1998. He is trained in political science and law, and works particularly in the area of law and sociology. His empirical work deals notably with the judicial system, alternative dispute resolution, access to justice, the political mobilization of law, and ethnocultural diversity and law from the perspectives of legal pluralism and the institutionalization of social relations. His more recent work deals with family mediation, communal justice, the implementation of law by actors of the penal system, law, and cultural communities, and the conditions of interdisciplinary research in law. In addition to his training in law, Pierre Noreau holds a doctorate from the Paris Institute of Political Studies (Sciences Po).

Dr. Graham J. Reynolds teaches and researches in the areas of copyright law, intellectual-property law, property law, and intellectual property and human rights. Prior to joining the Allard School of Law in 2013, Graham was an Assistant Professor at the Schulich School of Law at Dalhousie University, where he was the Co-Editor in Chief of the *Canadian Journal of Law and Technology* and a member of Dalhousie University's Law and Technology Institute. The recipient of an award for excellence in teaching, Graham has completed graduate studies at the University of Oxford, where he studied on a Rhodes Scholarship, a Pierre Elliott Trudeau Scholarship, and a Social Sciences and Humanities Research Council of Canada Doctoral Award. He has also served as the judicial law clerk to the Honourable Chief Justice Lance Finch of the British Columbia Court of Appeal. Graham's doctoral work focused on the intersection of freedom of expression and copyright in Canada.

Meredith Rossner's research interests focus on the intersection of social interaction and judicial processes. This has led to a number of research projects on the emotional and ritual elements of the justice process, with a particular focus on the role of lay people. She has conducted research on the emotional dynamics of restorative-justice conferences, the dynamics and democratic potential of jury deliberation, and how design and technology impact justice proceedings.

Prior to joining the Faculty of Law at the University of Ottawa as an Assistant Professor, **Amy Salyzyn** received her LLM from Yale Law School and her JD from the University of Toronto Law School. Amy has also served as a judicial law clerk at the Court of Appeal for Ontario and has practiced at a Toronto litigation boutique. Her litigation practice included a wide variety of civil and commercial litigation matters including breach of contract, tort, professional negligence, securities litigation, and employment law, as well as administrative law matters. In fall 2011, she was a Visiting Researcher at Osgoode Hall Law School.

In addition to legal ethics, Amy's research focuses on gender and the law, law and technology, and civil-justice reform. In 2013, Amy was the Research Director for a project on ethical infrastructure in Canadian law firms that was undertaken by the Canadian Bar Association Ethics and Professional Responsibility Committee. She was also awarded the 2013-14 OBA Foundation Chief Justice of

Ontario Fellowship in Legal Ethics and Professionalism (Fellowship in Studies) to study the ethical implications of lawyers' pre-litigation demand letters.

David Tait is the Leader of the Justice Research Group. He is a scholar in criminology and sociology with a background in social statistics, guardianship and mental health, sentencing, jury research, and urban sociology. Prior to taking up his position at Western Sydney University, David was Associate Professor/Senior Lecturer at the Law School of the University of Canberra from January 2005 until May 2009.

Professor Tait is currently Co-ordinator of the Court of the Future Network. He has a special interest in justice processes, particularly how justice is performed and experienced in different cultural and national settings. This has led to research on juries, mental health and guardianship tribunals, restorative-justice conferences, court safety, and remote witness communications. In this he collaborates with a range of academic fields, including law, psychology, forensic science, architecture, media studies, and management. He is currently leading large cross-disciplinary teams in three ARC Linkage grants and one ARC Discovery grant.

Nicolas W. Vermeys, LLD (Université de Montréal), LLM (Université de Montréal), CISSP, is a professor at the Université de Montréal's Faculté de droit (Faculty of Law), a researcher at the Centre de recherche en droit public (Public Law Research Centre, or CRDP), the codirector of the maîtrise en commerce électronique (an e-commerce master's program offered by the Université de Montréal in collaboration with HEC Montréal) and the associate director of the Cyberjustice Laboratory. He also serves as a legal adviser for the law firm of Legault Joly Thiffault. Mr. Vermeys is a certified information system security professional (CISSP) as recognized by the International Information System Security Certification Consortium (or ISC), and is the author of numerous publications relating to the impact of technology on the law, including *Actes illicites sur Internet: Qui et comment poursuivre?* (Yvon Blais, 2011), *Responsabilité civile et sécurité informationnelle* (Yvon Blais, 2010), and *Virus informatiques: Responsables et responsabilité* (Thémis, 2006). He also sits as a member of the boards of SOQUIJ, Éducaloi, and the Canadian Center for Court

Technology, and serves as a member of the scientific panel of different law journals, including *Lex Electronica*, for which he served as
editor-in-chief from 2001 to 2003. Mr. Vermeys' research focuses on
legal issues pertaining to information security, developments in the
field of cyberjustice, and other questions relating to the impact of
technological innovations on the law. He is often invited to speak on
these topics by the media, and regularly gives lectures for judges,
lawyers, professional orders, and government organizations in
Canada and abroad.

Law, Technology and Media

Edited by Michael Geist

The *Law, Technology and Media* series explores emerging technology law issues with an emphasis on a Canadian perspective. It is the first University of Ottawa Press series to be fully published under an open access licence.

Previous titles in this collection